THE TRANSFORMATION OF MODERNITY

The Transformation of Modernity

Aspects of the past, present and future of an era

Edited by
MIKAEL CARLEHEDEN
Örebro University, Sweden

MICHAEL HVIID JACOBSEN
University of Aalborg, Denmark

LONDON AND NEW YORK

First published 2001 by Ashgate Publishing

Reissued 2018 by Routledge
2 Park Square, Milton Park, Abingdon, Oxon, OX14 4RN
711 Third Avenue, New York, NY 10017

Routledge is an imprint of the Taylor & Francis Group, an informa business

A Library of Congress record exists under LC control number: 2001093279

ISBN 13: 978-1-138-70323-0 (hbk)
ISBN 13: 978-1-138-63106-9 (pbk)
ISBN 13: 978-1-315-20328-7 (ebk)

List of Content

Acknowledgements

Throughout the genesis of this book many people have been involved and in one way or the other have contributed at various stages to its completion. We would like to extend our gratitude to the financial sponsors of the conference in which the initial versions of the chapters were presented: The Danish Social Science Research Council and The C. W. Obel Foundation. Moreover, we would like to thank the Department of Social Science and Organisation at the University of Aalborg and especially Helle Wæver for her support during both the conference and during the process of producing this volume. We would also like to thank our editor at Ashgate Publishers, Katherine Hodkinson, for assisting us in our effort to share the ideas of the conference with a wider public. Finally, thanks also to Steven Sampson for helpful comments and proofreading of the manuscripts and to Inger M. Kiis for constructing the layout of the book.

Örebro and Aalborg, September 2001

Mikael Carleheden and Michael Hviid Jacobsen

Introduction

MIKAEL CARLEHEDEN and MICHAEL HVIID JACOBSEN

Modernity

Most contemporary social scientists and social philosophers would generally agree with Anthony Giddens' claim that modernity 'refers to modes of social life or organisation which emerged in Europe from about the seventeenth century onwards and which subsequently became more or less worldwide in their influence' (Giddens, 1990, p.1). Modernity, Giddens continues, has now not only been extended throughout the globe, but is also intensively felt in the most intimate spheres of our personal lives: '(T)he intrinsic nature of modern institutions' (and we should perhaps add - of cultural beliefs and values) is, he goes on, of a different kind than 'the traditional social orders'. Furthermore, following the institutionalisation of the rule of modernity, social change continues to be more profound in scope and more rapid than in any other social epoch of our world history (Giddens, 1990, p.6). Modernity cannot rest. Many of us would probably agree with Giddens also on this point. Nor is his more substantive suggestion disputed that surveillance, capitalism, industrialism and military power should be regarded as the most typical social institutions of modernity (Giddens, 1990, p.55ff).[1] But this is how far we dare to go in proclaiming a general agreement in contemporary social theory concerning the concept of modernity. However, this volume deals with a much more controversial aspect of modernity. It is about the *transformation* of modernity.

Transformation

Let us make use of Piotr Sztompka's (1993) distinction between changes *in* a social system and changes *of* a social system. In the first case, Sztompka talks about 'reproduction', in the second about 'transformation'. This book asks whether we are currently experiencing a transformation *of* modernity. The question can also be formulated in the following way: Can we still today - as did the classical social theory of modernity - manage with a distinction, which basically only allows us to distinguish between the traditional and the modern? More and more studies of our times claim that this classic distinction cannot grasp the particularity of the present social situation. Some would argue that we need new concepts and theories which help us to go *beyond* modernity. Others, rather, talk about a transformation of social institutions and cultural beliefs and values *within* modernity, while a third party defends the classic distinction, claiming that it is sound enough to enable us to understand contemporary social life.[2] All three approaches are discussed in the present volume. Yet these contributions should not be understood as a simple continuation of the polemic between 'modernists' and 'postmodernists' which occurred in the 1980s and 1990s. Rather, it is a discussion of what we have learned from this debate in a social theoretical sense.

In this volume, the conception of a transformation of modernity is dealt with from different perspectives and on different levels. The contributions have been grouped into three general topics. The first section focuses on more general or abstract historical developments, the second on changes in the intimate spheres of social life, while the third deals with global and political issues. Furthermore, knowledge presupposes distinctions and contrasts. In our case, this means that we cannot understand the present without contrasting it with the past and the future. This is especially true when the subject matter is modernity. Modernity can be viewed as a special relation seen between past, present and future. The authors in this volume all use these distinctions to make sense (or non-sense) of the conception of a transformation of modernity. This is why we have given this anthology the subtitle *Aspects of the Past, Present and Future of an Era*.

The contributions are revised versions of some of the papers presented at the *Transformation of Modernity* conference held at Højgaarden, Denmark in autumn 1999. Participants included a wide range of international scholars from a variety of social scientific disciplines and from philosophy. The discussions during this conference were very stimulating and helped the contributors of this book to refine their arguments. Below we present the slightly revised preamble of the conference, which describes the thematic of the discussions that took place and the backdrop for the contributions in this book. We then present the key ideas of each contribution in condensed form.

The Transformation of Modernity: An Invitation to a Conference

For more than 30 years it has been argued that contemporary society is undergoing a fundamental transformation. The portrait of the modern society or modernity given by social philosophers and social scientists from Hobbes to Parsons is now no longer understood as descriptions of the final and highest stage in the social evolution of mankind. Modern society is not 'the end of history', but only yet another more or less contingent social and cultural formation on planet earth.

Modern society has often been described as the result of at least four interdependent 'revolutions': the scientific, the capitalistic, the industrial and the political. Contemporary social science and social philosophy do not claim, however, that we are in the midst of a social change of the same magnitude as the shift from medieval to modern society. We are not experiencing the end of modernity, but the transformation of the meaning and significance of the four revolutions that in the first round made modern society possible. This contemporary transformation has been conceptualised in many different ways: from early to late modernity, from modernity to postmodernity, from classic to new modernity, from simple to reflexive modernity, from first to second modernity, from high to another modernity. It is possible, however, to trace general traits, which reappear - in different versions - in most conceptualisations. We will mention some of these conceptualisations below.

The Disenchantment of Science and Technology

The social significance of the scientific revolution is often understood in terms of a general shift from a cosmological world-view to a mechanistic and rationalistic one. Nature became 'disenchanted', that is, it lost its spiritual essence and was reduced to material and instrument for the satisfaction of human needs. Modern people believe that they can master both nature and their own history with the help of science and technique. Such mastery presupposes rational control not only of outer nature, but also of social and inner human life. 'Instrumental reason' became, thus, not only one of the most important forces of production but also a crucial part of politics (social engineering) and led to a general reification of cultural life. In short, science and intellectuals took over the social role which religion and priests had in pre-modern societies (Bauman, 1987).

In this context, the transformation of modern society means that science and technology themselves are now undergoing a process of disenchantment. The more or less blind faith in science and instrumental reason declines. This disenchantment process is related to the historic experience of the social application of science. Science and technology have turned out to be not only forces of production, but also forces of destruction (Auschwitz, Hiroshima, Chernobyl, neurosedine, environmental pollution, clientisation of citizens, mad cow decease, normalisation of differences, etc.). The current debate about genetic technology is a good illustration of this tension within late modernity. The transformation of modern society in this sense has been conceptualised as the emergence of a 'risk society' (Beck, 1992). Disenchantment also derives from the fact that science and philosophy have become reflexive and have thus turned their methods upon themselves. This self-examination has led - at least among the social sciences and the humanities - to an ambivalent self-relativisation, a loss of confidence or a new humbleness before 'the other of reason'.

These two aspects of the disenchantment with science are connected in the practice of the new social movements, which are critical of the social applications of science. These movements usually have no difficulty in mobilising their own scientific expertise, a practice which contributes to the relativisation of scientific knowledge. The declining trust in science also entails a declining legitimacy of politics as social engineering. The reported shift from 'elite-directed' to 'elite-challenging' political practice (Inglehart, 1997) should be understood in this context.

The disenchantment with science can in turn be related to changes in value orientation in the Western societies, changes which point towards a 're-enchantment' of the world (Ritzer, 1999). The lost faith in science has created a utopian void. This void might help explain the increase in various post-materialistic values. Social scientists report a strange mixture of new and traditional forms of spirituality, values of belonging, esteem and self-realisation and aesthetic approaches towards the world and the self.

Globalisation of Economy and Politics

The most talked about aspect of the transformation of modernity is without doubt 'globalisation' (Giddens, 1990; Castells, 1996; Bauman, 1998; Beck, 2000). The modern society was born within the boundaries of nations. It was built in the framework of a national economy, a nation-state and - in most cases - a national culture. With the development of the new communication technologies, the significance of national borders is diminishing. According to some influential social scientists, we are already today living in a global 'network society' (Castells, 1996). Globalisation becomes a strong transformative force when capitalism uses the new global technologies to liberate itself from the control of the nation-state. Economic globalisation thus means that the capacity of the nation-bound welfare state is weakened, that is, the historic compromise between capital and labour is endangered. As a reaction to this liberation of capital from national politics, however, we have seen a massive growth of international and even transnational political institutions, a development which gives new substance to the idea of universal human rights and 'cosmopolitan democracy' (Held, 1995; Held and Archibugi, 1995). The absolute sovereignty of the nation-state has been called into question. Globalisation thus transforms the classic modern logic of both economy and politics.

Post-Industrialisation

According to many of the classic social scientists, the division of labour is the most significant trait of a modern society. Integration through differentiation in the domain of production was their answer to the question 'how is society possible'? Blue-collar work, in its classical industrial form, was one of the most important consequences of this process of differentiation. Just as the first conceptualisations of modern society, the first conceptualisations of the transformation of modern society were in the area of production. In the late 1960s, social scientists were declaring that we were shifting from industrial to post-industrial forms of production. Instead of manual work, the key terms for understanding contemporary forms of production were information, knowledge or service. Late modernity is the age of mass education. More horizontal and less differentiated organisations develop. The unskilled manual worker - an archetype of classic modernity - is disappearing. With the disappearance of the worker, the working class and working class culture is also losing its social significance. The underclass of late modernity is not composed of alienated workers, but marginalised unemployed.

The Post-Traditional Society

Modern society is a 'post-traditional' society. Cultural norms and values are not homogenous and given in a concrete sense. Modern norms are more abstract. One important example is the norm of individuality. It forces individuals to find or construct their own personal identities in a culture, characterised by a plurality of life forms. Modern individuals are typically equipped with a reflexive distance to values. This kind of pluralism and individualism was to some degree already present in early modernity. In this aspect, late modernity is only a more radicalised version, but the radicalisation has had some important transformative consequences.

In some crucial aspects, early modern society was not post-traditional. Some traditional norms were re-interpreted in a scientific language as 'natural'. The hierarchical relationship between men and women is an example of such a naturalised norm. In the case of sexuality, it has even been argued that modern norms were more regulative than pre-modern ones. Norms and values related to race and ethnicity are other obvious examples. Sexism, homophobia and Eurocentrism were not themes for classic social science and philosophy.

In late modernity, traditional modern norms about gender, sexuality and ethnicity are questioned. The struggle for equality and recognition in these domains is just as characteristic of late modernity as was the worker's struggle of early modernity. In the case of gender, the extended value and norm reflexivity has meant that one of the cornerstones of early modernity, that is, the normative institution of the nuclear family, is rapidly losing its social significance. Women can no longer be simply defined as secondary to men. Women take on more and more autonomy. Hence, the smallest unit of late modern society is not the family but the individual. In most western countries today, the majority of people no longer live in nuclear families. Late modern people are rather living in 'the very normal chaos of love' (Beck and Beck-Gernsheim, 1995). The denaturalisation of sex and sexuality has led to a 'transformation of intimacy' (Giddens, 1992).

Purposes and Themes of the Conference

The general purpose of the conference is to discuss the claim that modern society is in the process of being transformed in a fundamental sense and to achieve a better understanding of the social logic of this transformation. This general purpose involves two closely connected tasks. First, we have to discuss the validity, significance and consequences of the transformation of modernity as described above. Is it possible to talk about a disenchantment with science and technique? Are we experiencing a cultural shift from materialistic to post-materialistic values? How can we explain the 'new spirituality' in Western countries? What are the social consequences of the declining importance of national borders? What is the significance of the transformed conditions of work? Are there different forms of oppression and exclusion in late modernity as compared to early modernity? Has the meaning of democracy changed in contemporary society? How should we understand gender and sexuality after their denaturalisation? Is there a 'post-modern family' or 'post-modern sexuality'? Which are the general social consequences of the emergence of multicultural societies? Only after such a discussion is it possible to deal with the general social logic behind these various transformations of modern society. If it is true that society is radically changing in all these respects, are we entering a new epoch of modernity? Is there a new kind of social logic which can explain all these changes? Are we experiencing a transformation of the logic of social change? Have the classical conceptions of modernisation as class struggle (Marx), rationalisation (Weber), or differentiation (Durkheim) become obsolete? Is a transformed social logic to be found on the same general level or is contemporary modernity rather characterised by the lack of such a general social logic?

To be able to deal with these purposes and themes the transformation of modernity must be investigated on different levels, in different aspects and from different perspectives. The conference will include micro, macro, meta-theoretical, sociological, philosophical and historical attempts to come to grips with the changing social and cultural world in which we are living today.

The Contributions of the Book

Many, but not all the topics suggested in this preamble were subsequently taken up in the papers of the conference. The papers, not the preamble, have of course determined the scope of the present volume. In reviewing the contributions, we quickly discovered that they touched upon different aspects and levels of the transformation of modernity. We have therefore - as mentioned above - divided the book into three parts in order to present related topics and discussions in close connection to each other. These are: *Part I: General Aspects*; *Part II: Identity, Sexuality and the Intimate Sphere*; and *Part III: Globalisation, Knowledge and Democracy.*

Part I: General Aspects

The first contribution in this section is the most philosophical of the volume. Nikolas Kompridis takes his point of departure in Jürgen Habermas' conception of modernity's time consciousness as a special relation between past, present and future. The most fundamental trait of modernity, according to this view, is that modernity finds itself - in Augustine's words - 'in the shadow of the future'.[3] Kompridis points out that modernity's typical openness to the future should not be understood as certainty, but as confidence. He then goes on to investigate what this involves on an ethical-existential level, observing that we are experiencing a decline in confidence in the future. He quotes Marlene Dietrich who, in *Touch of Evil*, is reading the future of a corrupt police detective: 'You haven't got any left', she says, 'your future is all used up'. In Kompridis' text, Dietrich, in the role of fortune-teller, thus symbolises the end of an era that found its first expression already in the work of the Saint Augustine. But Kompridis does not leave us standing in the graveyard of historical epochs gazing down at the coffin of modernity. He concludes his chapter with a discussion of the conditions required for a revival of confidence - 'the problem of beginning anew'.

Ulrich Beck is probably the most influential sociologist discussing the transformation of modern social institutions. His *Risk Society* (Beck, 1992) has already become a classic in the field. In the second contribution of Part I, Klaus Rasborg critically discusses Beck's central thesis that we are leaving industrial society and entering risk society. Rasborg reviews the ongoing debate about Beck's book, including Beck's responses to his critics in his later works. Rasborg also contrasts Beck's theory with other influential conceptions of risk promulgated by Niklas Luhmann, Anthony Giddens and Francois Ewald. Rasborg ends with a rather critical assessment of Beck's theory, due to its ambivalent realist notion of risk. Perhaps, he concludes, we should think beyond risk society.

Rasborg is not critical of the idea that we are in some sense experiencing a transformation of modernity. Rather, he criticises Beck's conceptualisation of this transformation. In the third contribution, Gorm Harste takes one step further and contests a more general conception of social transformation that we find - in different versions - not only in Beck's work but also in Anthony Giddens and Scott Lash; that is, the idea that modernity is currently undergoing a 'reflexive turn'. Harste argues that this idea underestimates the impact of reflexivity during the initial emergence of modernity. He supports his critique by going back not only to intellectual discussions in France and Germany during early modernity but also by an examination of the state institutions of the time. Harste acknowledges that reflexivity in early modernity was limited to a small elite. But his thesis is that since then, reflexivity has neither really evolved in depth, nor in institutional importance, but only in scope. Harste's contribution is profoundly critical of the thesis that modernity is undergoing a fundamental transformation.

The next chapter, by Bo Isenberg, can be used to support Harste's criticism of the transformation thesis, although here the critique takes a different route. This time we are dealing with intellectual, not institutional history. Isenberg claims that we should not see late modern or postmodern ideas as standing in opposition to the discourses that we find in - what he calls - classical modernity. When using this term, he refers to thinkers like Max Weber, Georg Lukács, Siegfried Kracauer, Georg Simmel, Sigmund Freud, Friedrich Nietzsche and especially Robert Musil. Postmodern thinkers claims Isenberg, are directly indebted to classical modernity. Classical modernity is the archive of postmodernity. Isenberg finds this archive, for instance, in conceptions like Musil's 'principle of insufficient reason' and Lukács' notion of our 'transcendental homelessness'. Both formulations remind us for instance of Richard Rorty's concept of 'anti-foundationalism'. Isenberg concludes that modernity is neither transforming itself nor being transformed. Modernity *is* transformation.

Isenberg's assertion is related to the point of departure for Mikael Carleheden's contribution. In this last chapter of the first part, Carleheden asks if there have been any transformations of the logic of modern social change. He looks for an answer in some parts of the canon of grand social theory. In the classic part (Marx, Weber and Durkheim), he finds several different conceptions of the logic of social change. Carleheden investigates Habermas' reconstruction of these classic conceptions. He argues that Habermas is convincing in his criticism of the classics, but that - like Hegel's owl of Minerva - he only managed to take off at the moment when the epoch he paints ('*mit Grau in Grau*') already has grown old. Carleheden then rejects the suggestion - occasionally heard - that Manuel Castells would be the new Marx or Weber of our times. Instead he turns to Peter Wagner. Wagner has agued that it is possible to differentiate between three historical epochs of modernity. Carleheden claims, however, that Wagner is rather inconsistent, and that he has next to nothing to say about the third epoch of modernity. Carleheden attempts to reconstruct Wagner's theory in order to develop a conception that distinguishes between three different social logics of social change during modernity. He concludes with an effort to find those signs, which could help us understand our elusive position in third modernity at the threshold of the 21st century.

Part II: Identity, Sexuality and the Intimate Sphere

There is little doubt that the general transformations of modernity are in some way related to changes in the more intimate and personal aspects of social life, such as identity, sexuality and relations within the family. Part II contains contributions that focus on such aspects and of how they are connected to the kind of wider social transformations examined in Part I. In the first contribution, Steven Seidman discusses homosexuality in the United States. His thesis is that in the last decade we have experienced a transformation from overt social repression to normalising controls of the homosexual minority, which has in turn led to a shift from gay to queer politics. Supported by empirical examples, Seidman argues that today's homosexuals appear to find it easier to disclose their sexuality than previously. However, this does not mean that oppression has disappeared entirely. What has occurred is a transformation in the social logic of oppression. Seidman argues that at least since the 1950s up to quite recently, heteronormativity has been reproduced primarily through a pollution logic. Such a logic establishes a moral division between heterosexuality and homosexuality. Heterosexuality signifies a pure and good human status in contrast to the dangerous homosexual. In the 1990s, however, a new social logic operating by means of normalisation has emerged. Normalisation entails incorporation of homosexuals into the national community with equal civic status to the heterosexual. However, the normalised homosexual is compelled to exhibit what is considered to be 'normal' behaviours, traits or identities. Seidman concludes with a discussion of how this transformation of heteronormativity is related to the general transformation from modernity to postmodernity.

Following up on the sexual aspect of modernity and late modernity, Michael Hviid Jacobsen in his contribution examines the historical roots of contemporary sexual morality. Taking his point of departure in the writings of Zygmunt Bauman, Jacobsen traces these roots back to the bifurcated Biblical notions of *conformity* and *choice*. Armed with these notions, he then examines the social scientific construction of sexuality throughout the late 19th century and early 20th century, showing how a heteronormative and moralistic perspective has been prevalent in most parts of this field. Moving on from morality and science, he then shifts perspective to politics and is critical of the notion, advanced by some scholars, that sexual politics is determined by either libertarian or communitarian positions. Instead, he proposes that so-called *fair-weather liberals* who, in large part, hold the key to the decision-making process and who maintain a certain morality of conformity which continue to dominate the general sexual political climate in most parts of today's Western world. Jacobsen then takes a closer look at the Danish debate, where he finds support for both the liberation as well as the repression thesis. He concludes by proposing an understanding of contemporary sexual morality by advancing a third viable option between the Scylla of the morality of conformity and the Charybdis of a morality of choice. This he terms 'the conformity of choice' or 'the choice of conformity'- a new type of social disciplination of sexuality.

The next two contributions of Part II, by Catharina Juul Kristensen and Lars Dencik, focus on identity construction in contemporary Scandinavia. The Scandinavian empirical background is of particular interest in the context of the subject matter of this book, because today's Scandinavians - according to Ingelhart's research (1997) - seem to be the most 'postmodern' people in the world.

Juul Kristensen describes how younger adult men and women use self-perception as a strategy in everyday life to gain a feeling of empowerment. Assisted by theoretical and conceptual arsenal of Giddens and using findings from her own in-depth interviews, Juul Kristensen agues that women in late modernity utilise a strategy found in the modern notion of the individual and formerly reserved primarily for white middle-class men which holds that individuals are capable of planning their own lives and that they are the ultimate sources of their own destinies. In doing so, these women are capable of creating a meaningful and coherent existence in a world marked by uncertainty, radical doubt, transition and anxiety. Juul Kristensen's contribution thus discusses the prevalent discourse of independence among younger adult men and women in contemporary Denmark, i.e., the prevalent self-perception and how these men and women articulate themselves as independent individuals able to influence their own lives. One of her conclusions is that particularly women utilise this subjective strategy of self-reliance when faced with objective conditions and circumstances that might otherwise hamper action and individual choice. This strategy creates a mental foundation in a transformative social environment.

Dencik, in the following chapter, continues the investigation of how identities are shaped and maintained in an increasingly global and rapidly changing world. Dencik asks about the kind of self individuals have to develop when they must become 'turbonomads in postmodernity'. Do mobile people need mobile identities? And how will these transformations of personal life affect the self-image of established nations-states? To answer these questions, Dencik uses three different empirical examples. First, he reviews his own investigations of the daily life of children in contemporary

Scandinavia; children experience the 'dual-socialisation' of the family and the day-care institution. Secondly, he shows that Sweden and Denmark are interesting cases in this context, because few countries have had such a high degree of ethnic homogeneity and are now experiencing rapid 'post-modernisation'. Finally, Dencik discusses if the diaspora Jewish experience could be understood as prototypical for living under conditions of postmodernisation. He concludes that the postmodern self exists only as 'the movement he or she produces in the social situation in which the individual lives and operates'.

Part III: Globalisation, Knowledge and Democracy

Changes in the macro and the micro spheres of society are intrinsically linked. These relations are often either understood structurally, inter-actionally or with the help of some kind of combination of structural and action theoretical approaches. We certainly need to be cautious so as not to extrapolate transformations on the microlevel directly to transformations on the macrolevel and vice versa. We need to elaborate and apply what Erving Goffman (1983, p.11) called a 'membrane of transformation rules' to understand such complicated relations. The reader of this book will find different - implicit or explicit - attempts to do just that, but our main focus is not on this unavoidable problematic.[4] As editors, we have simply used the micro-macro division to distinguish between the second and the third parts of the book. Hence part three deals with such macrophenomena as globalisation, democracy, development of professions and organisation.

We have already noted that globalisation is often understood as the single most important feature of the transformation of modernity.[5] Hauke Brunkhorst begins the third section with a chapter that deals with the increasingly urgent question of whether the ongoing globalisation of economics and politics will mean the death of democracy. He focuses on the fact that different kinds of transnational law follow in the footsteps of global capitalism, but that we also increasingly have to deal with law without states. Transnational law lacks a constitutional and democratic basis. This 'de-statification' of law and politics can be understood as the re-feudalisation of society on a global level. Brunkhorst examines the UN as an example of this transformation of politics. We are witnessing a de-positivisation and re-moralisation of human rights, at the same time as the Security Council is gaining interpretive authority vis-à-vis the General Assembly. This chapter makes clear how dramatically the social conditions for democracy have changed during the last decades. It also shows how difficult it is to find any signs of a 'third democratic transformation' (Robert Dahl) after the rise and fall of the city-state democracy of the Greek *polis* and of 20th century nation-state democracy in the West.

The conclusion to be drawn from Brunkhorst's chapter is that the significance of nation-states and democratic publics is decreasing in the new global society. This decline of influence seems to open up for a rise of influence of other groups. In the second chapter of the third section, Margareta Bertilsson investigates whether the professions could constitute a new type of group gaining in power under present social conditions. She chooses the legal profession as her example, asking whether a global class of jurists will emerge as a new dominant class. Bertilsson points out that the market in legal services has become global. Lawyers are liberating themselves from their earlier dependence of the nation-state. An army of grey-suited experts follows in the footsteps of global capitalism. There is an emergence of 'mega-law' and global law firms, which operate on a transnational level. However, Bertilsson is sceptical about the proclamation of a global class of jurists as a new dominant class. To be sure, jurists play an increasingly important role on the global scene, but we cannot talk about a single class with a common interest. Bertilsson doubts whether the difference between private and public law and the different interests these two types of law represent will disappear. Furthermore, she questions the thesis that we should understand globalisation as cultural homogenisation. We will, for instance, also in the future see different types of capitalism. Bertilsson concludes that there will also be legal pluralism at the global level.

In the last contribution we turn from globalisation to the legitimation of economic and political power. Øjvind Larsen argues that the bureaucratic-legal form of legitimacy in early modernity - described by Max Weber - does not work in contemporary organisations. Larsen is defending the idea of a reflective turn in late modernity. However, Larsen relies more on Habermas' critique of Weber's theory of legitimation than on Beck, Giddens and Lash, who were the objects of Harste's critique in the first part of this volume. Larsen argues that global communication society necessitates a new type of leadership, what he calls 'reflexive leadership'. Communication in Habermas' sense would then play the crucial role. Larsen sees this transformation of the conditions for legitimacy of power as a chance to further develop modern democracy. He ends with a more optimistic conclusion than Brunkhorst and lends support to Bertilsson's assumption that public interest cannot completely lose its significance in global modernity. Thus, the book seems to end with the rather ambiguous conclusion that economic and political globalisation, on the one hand, and the transformation of the social conditions of legitimacy, on the other, currently work in opposite directions. This ambiguity is not only theoretical. It is rather an expression of our contemporary social situation. If this is true, then Marlene Dietrich's words in *Touch of Evil* are a bit premature. The future seems, after all, still to be open. Modernity seems still to survive its self-transformations.

Notes

1 That is not surprising, for Giddens' suggestion is hardly a bold one, but rather, an assemblage of major trends in social theory of modernity.

2 Giddens' theory of modernity is too indistinct to be easily categorised in any one of these positions. On the one hand, he sticks to the classic distinction between tradition and modernity at the institutional level. On the other hand, he stresses how radically modernity has changed in depth and weight (self-identity) and in extension and scope (globalisation). The question he leaves open is whether this *radicalisation* of modernity should be understood as changes only in degree or also in kind. Giddens seems very indecisive on this point. Can one really stick to the classic distinction at an institutional level and at the same time claim that modernity is changing radically in depth and scope? This book comprises different attempts to answer just such questions.

3 This quotation has its origin in Augustine's *Confessiones*, but we have borrowed it from the title of Sven-Eric Liedman's (1997) book about the intellectual history of modernity. Liedman held a stimulating lecture on this topic during our conference, but unfortunately could not participate in this volume.

4 Charles Wright Mills (1958) distinguished between what he called 'drift' and 'thrust'. Where the former concept denotes changes that happen almost without human interference and with no obvious source of origin or intent, the latter, on the contrary, denotes wilful changing of the world. Mills regarded drift as fortuitous or entirely guided by fate. Thrust, in contrast, was regarded as the outcome of intentionally planned and orchestrated activities and the outcome of human deliberation. Hence, we can ask whether the transformation of modernity is the outcome of forces of thrust or of drift? However, even if there are several attempts to answer this question in this volume, this has not been the main task. Rather, the task has been to determine whether we should talk about a transformation of modernity at all.

5 Despite the variety and diversity of the contributions in this volume, we are well aware that not all the aspects of the transformations of contemporary societies can be covered here. However, in a recently issued collection of contributions edited by Will Hutton and Anthony Giddens (2001), a wide range of perspectives is dealt with and among others are the impact of global transformations on technology and information, finance and economy, care and emotion, individualisation and identity, and also culture.

References

Bauman, Z. (1987), *Legislators and Interpreters: On Modernity, Post-Modernity and Intellectuals*, Cornell University Press, Ithaca, New York.

Bauman, Z. (1998), *Globalization: The Human Consequences*, Columbia University Press, New York.

Beck, U. (1992), *Risk Society: Towards a New Modernity*, Sage Publications, London.

Beck, U. (2000), *What is Globalization?*, Polity Press, Malden, Mont.

Beck, U. and E. Beck-Gernsheim (1995), *The Normal Chaos of Love*, Polity Press, Cambridge.

Castells, M. (1996), *The Rise of the Network Society*, Blackwell, Oxford.

Giddens, A. (1990), *The Consequences of Modernity*, Polity Press, Cambridge.

Giddens, A. (1991), *Modernity and Self-Identity: Self and Society in the Late Modern Age*, Polity Press, Cambridge.

Giddens, A. (1992), *The Transformation of Intimacy: Sexuality, Love and Eroticism in Modern Societies*, Stanford University Press, Stanford, CA.

Goffman, E. (1983), 'The Interaction Order - American Sociological Association, 1982 Presidential Address', *American Sociological Review*, vol. 48, pp.1-17.

Held, D. (1995), *Democracy and the Global Order: From the Modern State to Cosmopolitan Governance*, Polity Press, Cambridge.

Held, D. and D. Archibugi (1995), *Cosmopolitan Democracy: An Agenda for a New World Order*, Polity Press, Cambridge.

Hutton, W. and A. Giddens (eds.) (2001), *On the Edge: Living with Global Capitalism*, Vintage, London.

Inglehart, R. (1997), *Modernization and Postmodernization: Cultural, Economic and Political Change in 43 Societies*, Princeton University Press, Princeton, NJ.

Liedman, S-E. (1997), *I skuggan av framtiden: Modernitetens idéhistoria*, Albert Bonniers Förlag, Viborg.

Mills, C. W. (1958), *The Causes of World War Three*, Simon and Schuster, New York.

Ritzer, G. (1999), *Re-Enchanting a Disenchanted World: Revolutionizing the Means of Consumption*, Pine Forge Press, Thousand Oaks, CA.

Sztompka, P. (1993), *The Sociology of Social Change*, Blackwell, Oxford.

Part I

General Aspects

1 Time-Consciousness and Transformation: On Modernity's Relation to the Future

NIKOLAS KOMPRIDIS

That modernity is an enormously protean is unquestionable; yet, it is not altogether clear what makes it so transformable. Why is modernity so amenable to incessant and, apparently, relentless change? What can explain its readiness to submit to massive, abrupt, deeply unsettling change? One might attempt to answer this question simply by pointing to the symbiotic dynamics of capitalist growth and technological innovation. Obviously capitalism and technology are very powerful vehicles of change. For some, that would be the end of the story, but it is hardly the whole story. Another essential part of the story involves the role that the political and legal framework of modern democracies plays in dramatically enlarging the scope of individual and collective initiative, both in the culture of everyday life and in the specialized cultures of science, morality, and art. But this too does not count as a sufficient explanation. Neither of these answers, alone nor in unison, sufficiently explains just what makes modernity so immensely transformable, since they fail fully to explain what it is about the nature of modernity that not only enables, but also renders it inordinately receptive, to self-transformation.

In order to arrive at a richer explanation we need to incorporate into our explanation the outlook, the stance, the attitude or orientation that makes radical change possible in the first place. To explore the nature of this outlook or orientation I want to turn to the characterization of modernity's relation to the future offered by Jürgen Habermas in *The Philosophical Discourse of Modernity*. This characterization owes a great deal to Reinhard Koselleck's *Begriffsgeschichten* of modern concepts of time and movement, and to Walter Benjamin's critical meditations on the philosophy of history.[1] Although Habermas' immediate purpose is to identify what is distinctive about modernity as an historical epoch, his characterization also succeeds in clarifying an essential piece of modernity's self-understanding. By unintentionally answering a question that Habermas does not pose, however, it does even more: it provides the basis for a more adequate answer to our question by linking modernity's receptivity to change to its epoch-defining relation to the future: Modernity 'is the epoch that lives for the future, that opens itself up to the novelty of the future' (Habermas, 1987, p.5). Thus, in my view, it is primarily in virtue of modernity's openness to the novelty of the future that radical processes of change can first get going. Furthermore, it is largely because of this openness to the novelty of the future that such processes of change can acquire the status of self-justifying processes.

Habermas introduced the term of art, 'modernity's time-consciousness', in order to elucidate modernity's distinctive orientation to the future (Habermas, 1987, p.13). The expectations that guide this orientation, disclose a horizon of possibility that keeps perpetually open the promise of a future different from the past: it contains the promise of a break with the past, and the promise of a new beginning.

Taking advantage of Koselleck's historical investigations, Habermas shows how modernity's open, expectant stance to the future, reconfigures the relationships between past, present, and future, opening up the meaning of history to ongoing reinterpretation. Through this reconfiguration, the present emerges as the narrow arena where new and old collide. It is an unavoidable consequence of this future-oriented stance that the present will be subject to crisis-experiences which arise from the disorienting collision of old and new: the more open to discontinuity we are - the more open, that is, to the possibility of beginning anew - the more we will have to wrestle with the issue of continuity. Thus, on each occasion in which modernity's time consciousness intensifies, we are pressed into evaluations and decisions 'concerning the proportion of continuity and discontinuity in the forms of life we pass on' (Habermas, 1989, p.263).

That the present is experienced as a time of crisis, is not only due to modernity's openness to the novelty of the future, but also to the way in which the future functions as a source of pressure brought to bear on unsolved problems, on unrealized or unnoticed possibilities. In light of this reconfiguration of past, present, and future, 'there arises an existentially sharpened consciousness of the danger of missed decisions, and neglected interventions. There arises a perspective from which the present state of affairs sees itself called to account as the past of a future present. There arises the suggestion of a responsibility for the connection of one situation to the next, for the continuation of a process that sheds its nature-like spontaneity and refuses to hold out the promise of any taken-for-granted continuity' (Habermas, 1987, p.58).

Echoing Hegel, Bernard Williams put this state of affairs just right: 'There is no route back from reflectiveness' (Williams, 1985, p.163). Modernity's time-consciousness enjoins each generation to respond to the question of how to 'go on', how to continue, and that question is tightly entwined to the question of how self-critically to inherit (or reinherit) the past. Both of these questions belong to a larger problem that modernity's openness to the novelty of the future engenders. Habermas refers to this problem as the problem of 'self-reassurance'.[2] The reassurance in question concerns the legitimacy of modernity - a legitimacy that is supposed to be grounded on reason alone rather than on external authority. Of course the kind of legitimacy that reason confers upon modernity will depend on what reason is taken to be, on what capabilities are ascribed to it. And so the problem of modernity's self-reassurance is entangled with the meaning and capabilities of modern reason. If, for example, we were working with a Cartesian understanding of reason, self-reassurance would require certainty in order to reassure convincingly. In Habermas' view, this kind of reassurance is simply not on. We should not look for self-reassurance in a form that is incompatible with modernity's consciousness of time - in a form that 'closes off the future as a source of *disruption*' (Habermas, 1987, p.12). While the kind of self-reassurance that Habermas thinks modernity should aim for is much weaker than Cartesian certainty, it should be somewhat stronger than the kind Bernard Williams recommends. Williams uses a more ordinary term to capture - accurately, I believe - what Habermas means by the need for self-reassurance: *confidence* (Williams, 1985, pp.169-173). For Williams, confidence refers to a mode of conviction very different from certainty. Confidence, in contrast to certainty, is a social good that must be renewed continuously by the social practices and cultural traditions to which it lends itself. In this respect, Williams' understanding of modernity's need for self-reassurance entails, is quite close to Hegel's. Although Habermas derives his understanding of modernity's need for self-reassurance from Hegel, he derives his answer to that need from Kant, in the form of a procedural conception of the unity of reason.

Unfortunately, Habermas' procedural conception responds only to one dimension of the problem of self-reassurance: the legitimacy of the normative order of modern societies. But this one-sided response does not answer the need for self-reassurance, for the problem of self-reassurance does not reduce to the problem of the legitimacy of our legal and political institutions. The need for self-reassurance has an 'ethical-existential' dimension that is just as important as the legal-political dimension. Our need for reassurance, our confidence, must be answered, secured, in both dimensions.[3] That our time - the time of modernity - is a time in which this need is very intensely and palpably felt, is something that has been said many times by various philosophers and theorists. Today, it is very difficult not to notice the widespread decline of confidence, the pervasive doubt among the members of late modern societies concerning their capacity for self-determination - which is to say, their capacity to understand and shape, as self-consciously as possible, their individual and collective reality, and to change for the better, themselves and their world. The 'mood of the times' is one that manifests a considerable fatalism in the face of massive change - change that is experienced as happening *to* us, rather than initiated *by* us. Now this certainly heralds a shift in modernity's orientation to the novelty of the future, for it is no longer clear whether the future will bring anything new - where, new means something both new and better. It had been an essential feature of modernity's time-consciousness since the Enlightenment that the future held the promise of both something new and something better. It appears that this is no longer the case. Although we still expect something new, we are no longer confident that the new promises something better. Habermas already identified this shift in modernity's time-consciousness some time ago: 'Today it seems as though utopian energies have been used up, as if they have retreated from historical thought. The horizon of the future has contracted and changed both the *Zeitgeist* and politics in fundamental ways. The future is *negatively cathected* [...] What is at stake is Western culture's *confidence in itself* '(Habermas, 1989, pp.50-51, my emphasis).

Given that our orientation to the novelty of the future is deeply anchored in the self-understanding of modernity, its cultural practices, and political institutions, it should come as no surprise that our confidence should be drastically undermined by the exhaustion of utopian energies, by doubts about the future. In what follows, I want first to explore the decline of confidence that arises from our relation to a negatively cathected future, beginning with a few lines from a song by Leonard Cohen. I will then engage more directly with the *problem of beginning anew*, which is my way of describing the problem of how to 'go on', how to continue, how to deal with the question of 'the proportion of continuity and discontinuity in the forms of life we pass on'.

I. The Problem of Confidence

Everybody knows the war is over
Everybody knows the good guys lost
Everybody knows the fight was fixed
The poor stay poor
The rich get rich
That's how it goes
Everybody knows[4]

What do we make of these words? Do they ring true or false? Are they the expression of suspiciously hip cynicism, or do they capture, in their own peculiar way, a prevailing cultural mood that it might be an egregious error to mistake for mere cynicism? Before I proceed any further with the import I wish to attribute to these words, I should state immediately that I'm using the term 'cultural mood' to mean much more than an ephemeral and surface phenomenon of cultural life, changeable as the look of fashion. By cultural mood, I mean a cultural sensibility - that self-defining way by which a culture lets itself be *affected* by the world, the way in which it *receives* its understanding of the world. By world, of course, I do not mean the physical world but our social world, a world structured by cultural meanings rather than by physical laws. Following Heidegger, I think of cultural moods or cultural sensibilities as defining the stance, open in some ways, closed in others, that we take up towards our social world. So while a cultural mood in this sense is historically variable, it is nothing ephemeral or transient. Indeed, it may take a half-century or much longer before the emergence of a new cultural mood can become discernible, before what it portends can become visible.[5]

Cohen wrote the song from which these lines are taken shortly before the tumultuous, dizzying events that took place in the fall of 1989. Certainly I am not alone in thinking poets and artists are often much better and much faster at registering social and cultural change, at registering shifts of cultural mood than are philosophers and social scientists. That said, to justify why I choose to ascribe time-diagnostic significance to the words of a poet/troubadour. So what is the mood that I think these words capture, and what is the significance of their being written shortly before the year 1989? What is it that 'everybody knows'? I'll take up this last question first.

If we take the act of knowing intended by these words not in a strictly epistemological sense, but in a much more ordinary, pre-reflective sense, then we can get a clearer sense of the status of their knowledge claim. The kind of knowledge at issue here is not that of a mind-independent object, or of some sentence-shaped fact. The knowledge at issue is a 'knowing one's way around' rather than a 'knowing-that'. And in this case, what 'everybody knows' consists in the discovery that something that was a familiar and essential part of one's world until just yesterday is no longer a part of it today. What has vanished, gone missing, or become obsolete are not things, say, record players or statues of Lenin; what has vanished from one's world are certain possibilities. A new boundary has been drawn, contracting substantially, the space of possibility. No sooner is the space of possibility contracted, than the horizon of the future is reset. As a consequence, some of our former hopes and expectations appear to be deleted from what the future once held. Rendering Cohen less poetically, we could say that what we now 'know' makes us much less confident that one day the good guys might win, that poverty might be eliminated, that the rules governing our common social, political, and economic life might finally be fair *and* just.

Perhaps, all this sounds just a touch arbitrary? Perhaps I am trying to make too much of these words, putting more time-diagnostic pressure on them than they can actually bear? Let me broaden somewhat the *Zeitdiagnose* I am exploring here.

I mentioned there was some significance to the fact that Cohen's song was written prior to 1989. The significance I ascribe to Cohen's song consists in this: it *anticipates* the crushing disappointment that followed from the realization that the meaning of 1989 turned out very different from what many of us had first hoped. It anticipates the disillusionment that this 'belated' revolution would not be the one that would at last 'redeem' the promise of the French Revolution (Ackermann, 1992, p.123) - a promise that then appeared not to have lost any of its power to reawaken our imaginations and to reanimate utopian energies. For a moment, a truly transient and ephemeral moment, when it was still unclear in which direction events would unfold, the space of possibility expanded dramatically, the horizon of the future opened wide, becoming an exceedingly generous receptacle of projected hopes and expectations.

In 1992, when Francis Fukuyama enthusiastically proclaimed that the 'end of history' had arrived, bearing 'glad tidings' for all men and women, he was not being just a little premature.[6] In any case, the most pathetic feature of his announcement, not only for him but for us too, clearer now in retrospect than it was then, is the ironic twist of history with which his prognosis would become 'true'. By this ironic twist I mean more than the way in which the horrors of Bosnia and Rwanda dampened the effect of the 'good news', to more than the technologically sanitized warfare that constituted the West's ill-timed response to 'ethnic cleansing' in Kosovo. And to more than the 'creative destruction' set loose upon our defeated Cold War foes in Russia, Eastern Europe, as well as selected sites in the Third World; for, as everybody knows, we have set this 'creative destruction' loose upon ourselves as well (although with rather different material consequences). What more do I mean? What then is the truth-candidate contained in Fukuyama's ill-timed and presumptuous pronouncement? Between 1989 and today, the connotations of the claim have changed through a kind of temporal inversion, such that we can now think of the 'end of history' as referring not to the closure of the past, but to the closure, or rather, the foreclosure, of the future. So the 'end of history' does not mean the end of the future so much as the recognition that it no longer appears to be a source of disruption, a source of new and unexpected possibilities: our possibilities seem to be fixed in advance.

Let me clarify this point by referring to the dramatic climax of Orson Welles' masterpiece, *Touch of Evil*. The climax comes at the point when the main character, a corrupt police detective facing imminent exposure, takes a brief time out from his inescapable predicament to ask his former girlfriend and occasional fortune-teller to read his future. Played by Marlene Dietrich, she dryly replies, as only Dietrich can: 'You haven't got any left. Your future is all used up'. By this Dietrich does not just mean that this corrupt cop, played by Welles, does not have any time left to live; he could, like the homeless and dispossessed have time left to live without enjoying the prospect of a future. Having time ahead of us and having a future are not the same thing. So if Dietrich were to say to us, that our future is all used up, she would be saying that our possibilities are exhausted. That is not to say that we do not have *any* possibilities; only that we cannot count on any *new* possibilities. To say that we no longer have a future is to say that our future can no longer bear the promise of something genuinely new, the promise of future different from, better than, the past.

Of course, one can never really be in a position to say that (any more than one is in a position to say that history has come to an end), at least not if one is intending to state an empirical truth. Possibility is not an 'object' of empirical knowledge; it is not an object at all. So it cannot be something about which 'empirical' truths can be stated. But one can say that there is an empirical connection between the having of confidence and the having of possibilities. If my *interpretation* of our cultural mood is not wildly inaccurate, the exhaustion of possibilities should be cause for alarm. Habermas is right: our confidence is at stake.

In order to show why this state of affairs should be of considerable concern to philosophers and social scientists, I'd like to connect what I've said thus far to a phenomenon that already is: globalization. A complex topic, to be sure, and one far beyond the parameters of this paper to treat it in a manner that even begins to do justice to its complexity. Nonetheless, I shall wade into this debate rather deeply and rather abruptly, making some very strong but largely unsupported claims. I want first to distinguish between the globalization of markets, on the one hand, and the globalization of human rights and democratic self-government, on the other. While acknowledging the wisdom of the experts that we must take into account both of these aspects of globalization if we are to render this phenomenon as perspicuous as possible, I want to point out that we experience and understand these two aspects in strikingly different ways. Above all what is distinctive in this respect is that the globalization of markets is almost universally experienced and almost universally described as a quasi-natural process - a process we cannot stop, reverse, or master. Our only 'realistic' option, if it can properly described as an option, is successful adaptation to an ineluctable evolutionary process. While the process propelling the globalization of markets enjoys this quasi-natural status, the globalization of human rights and democratic self-government does not. Its status is much more tentative and fragile. Not easily reversible by any means, but not exactly the 'fact of life' that many 'experts' take the globalization of markets to be.

If we now consider this 'fact of life' in connection with our discussion of the future, with what I have described as the experience of the foreclosure of the future, we need to ask how we stand in relation to the future towards which globalization processes hurl us? Is this a future we wish to claim as our own, under suitably appropriate conditions of reflection and debate? Or is it a simply a fate we must accept and endure because we have no other choice?

It has been said, quite correctly, that the globalization of markets has eroded democracy, in so far as democratic decision-making has heretofore been anchored in the nation-state, whose power itself has been eroded. What has been singled out in particular, is the profound acceleration of the flow of world-wide capital, and the new ways in which national economic conditions are indexed to the assessments of capital markets (Habermas, 1999). So once again, in their antagonistic but purportedly interdependent and inseparable relationship, it is capitalism and not democracy that ultimately sets the pace, the direction, and the terms of cultural and political change. Democracy is always placed in the role of catching up, or more optimistically, of trying to lead from the back. The hope of some now seems to reside in the possibility that we might once again democratically constrain the anonymous systems of money and power in whose hands our fate seems to rest. However, until such time as democratic practices and institutions of self-government - at the local, national, and international level - can restore, in some meaningful sense, our sense of agency, our hopes of truly becoming the authors and addressees of the laws that govern us, the ongoing erosion of democracy will only intensify the feeling that our future is fixed in advance, not truly ours to decide, thereby undermining our confidence, both in our ideals and in our agency.

In my view, the renewal of that confidence in our ideals and in our agency will depend on the renewal of possibility, the possibility that we can *begin anew*. Political philosophers and social scientists have failed adequately to understand, let alone respond, to this problem. It is a problem not only central to political philosophy, but to the life of democracy. Failure properly to understand and to respond to this problem will mean that democracy will no longer have a life. Recognizing the need for, and successfully instituting a new beginning, is precisely that upon which the life of democracy depends. The failure to institute a new beginning can be disastrous for any form of life is, I believe, an empirical truth for which there is plenty of historical evidence. It would be a particularly bitter failure for democratic forms of life in so far as their existence depend on this human capacity - a capacity that Hannah Arendt has called 'miraculous'. If it is so miraculous why have we failed to appreciate its importance? Why are we suspicious of it? Why do we resist its call?

II. The Problem of Beginning Anew

While there is no route back from reflectiveness, there is no clear, uncontestable route forward. 'You must go on', urges the narrator of Samuel Beckett's *The Unnameable* (Beckett, 1958, p.3). Most surely, we must go on. But if we are to 'go on' reflectively rather than blindly, how do we 'go on'? To where do we go on? What do we take, what do we leave behind? What of ourselves do we continue, what discontinue? Where or to what do we look for orientation? Do we look to the past? Or do we look to other forms of life? As Hilary Putnam puts it: 'Our problem is not that we must choose from among an already fixed and defined number of optimal ways of life; our problem is that we don't know even one *optimal* way of life' (Putnam, 1994, p.194). In so far as 'we don't know even one *optimal* way of life' which could serve as a secure normative standard, we shall have to solve that problem all by ourselves. But whatever we determine to be the 'right' proportion of the continuity and discontinuity in the forms of life we pass on, will be a determination that is neither final nor indefeasible. The 'right' proportion will have to be reviewed and revised *as* we 'go on'. But even if we don't *know* one optimal way of life, can we not *hope* for and work toward something better than what we now have? The question then arises as to whether our expectations of, and hopes for, the future can in any way guide our efforts to make sense of the 'the proportion of continuity and discontinuity in the forms of life we pass on'. But how does our culture open itself up to the future? How does its openness to the future render intelligible (or unintelligible) the ever-shifting constellation of relationships between past, present and future? Are there better or worse ways to be open to the future - which, is to say, are there better or worse to be open to something new?

Something quite important is missing from Putnam's otherwise perceptive characterisation of our situation, and that is the way in which the unavailability of a normative standard for determining how we are to go on is intensified by the peculiarly modern experience of time. We must go on - not knowing how or to where - under the vertiginous pressure of modern time. As we are hurled forward into the future at an unprecedented speed, there is less and less time and, therefore, more and more pressure to bring into some intelligible pattern the often obscure and ambiguous relationships between the past, the present, and the future. There is also evidence that as the pressure mounts to render intelligible the discontinuity and change that these relationships undergo, so does the pressure to abandon or regard as useless the effort to make sense of relentless discontinuity and change.

There is perhaps nothing more common today than the insistent, compulsively repeated exhortation to embrace the new, to embrace the future - a future into which we headlong rush as much as into which we are headlong pushed. Perhaps, there is nothing more characteristic of the culture of modernity. Whether it is in the name of 'globalisation', the 'new economy', or the 'digital age', no matter how familiar, no matter how transparently ideological or strategic, it is an exhortation with an almost irresistible appeal. Because the source of its power is deeply and inseparably anchored in modernity's self-understanding, the appeal to the 'new' retains its power to be a highly persuasive, perhaps the most persuasive, rhetorical device of modern culture. It is an appeal so powerful that it can render pointless demands to justify itself. Yes, asymmetries of power, various kinds of domination (over human beings, nature, and things), unchecked capitalist growth, and the erosion (at least, according to some 'crisis thinkers') of institutions and practices of democratic self-government do play a mighty powerful role in bringing about changes in the name of something 'new'. But all by themselves these forces do not sufficiently account for the appeal, for the *seductiveness* of the new. Little wonder, then, that Adorno and Benjamin regarded the recurrent appeal of the 'new' as an appeal possessing a power equivalent to, if not identical with, myth - tellingly instancing the reversion of 'enlightenment to myth'.[7] No wonder, too, that such change as we are exhorted to embrace is change whose 'inevitability' we are forced to experience as our fate rather than as the outcome of our agency. 'Keep going, going on, call that going, call that on' (Beckett, 1958, p.3).

We can't stop the future. We must go on. But why must we go on *unreflectively*? What presses us to go on towards what we have had neither the time nor the opportunity to question, reject, or endorse under appropriately reflective conditions? There are different answers that can be adduced. For one, the new is not just seductive; it also arouses fear. Thus, one reason why we go on as unreflectively as we do, is simply because we are afraid to be left behind, afraid of being rendered obsolete, the fear of which is perhaps internal to the seductiveness of the new. But as we have already averred, this is not the only meaning of the new, not the only source of its appeal. The new also contains the promise of something better, a promise of happiness. And it can only be exploited for ideological purposes or for profit because it contains this promise: the promise of something better than what we have known. It is this promise that also brings the new into the proximity, if not the domain, of myth.

Is there not a more reflective way for us to be open to the future and to the new - a way that is less inviting of myth? Only as architects of the future who also comprehend the needs of the present can we make sense of the past, suggested the young Nietzsche (Nietzsche, 1983, p.94). He may be right, but it is not self-evident just what his suggestion entails. At the very least, making sense of our past and present seems to demand a way of imagining our future in terms of some utopian project or set of projects that respond to the needs of the present - which supposes, of course, that we have correctly interpreted our present needs. Nonetheless, Nietzsche's suggestion remains a gnomic one, raising as many questions as it is meant to answer. Must we be architects of a *determinate* future if we are properly to comprehend the present and make sense of the past? The lately departed 20th century saw the rise of some truly monstrous architecture created by self-appointed 'architects of the future'. Evidently, they suffered from no lack of confidence: either about their architectural talents or about the legitimacy of the utopia they wanted to build. The architecture of horror that enveloped the

20th century is surely not what Nietzsche had in mind. But there is no way of getting around the fact that without some explicit normative constraints his suggestion appears to be a recipe for disaster. It comes alarmingly close to the most dangerous of modernist fantasies in which the architecture of the future becomes a license to annihilate rather than to understand the past.

In Nietzsche's defence, however, it should be said that a determinate future would not, on his view, be a future to which we ought to say *yes*, for it is precisely the demand that the future conform to the determination of our will that leads to nihilism and destructiveness. To imagine the future with complete determinacy would be to deny the indeterminacy essential to the future - essential to the openness of the future. Thus, this stance to the future would consist not in its affirmation but in its negation. Yet, in spite of the inherent dangers of such an undertaking, Nietzsche insists that we must nonetheless engage in imagining the future differently. Why? Is it simply to satisfy the modernist craving for the new, for which the name 'Nietzsche' serves us a convenient abbreviation? Certainly this is one way to understand Nietzsche's insistence on the new - but it would not be the best way, not least because it would be untrue to Nietzsche. Nietzsche's insistence on the new has little - if anything - to do with the satisfaction of a desire for the new for its own sake (in fact, he regarded this desire as a pathological manifestation of the 'ascetic ideal'); rather, it is motivated by the idea that making sense of how to we are to 'go on' requires that we think from a *new stance*. 'Architect of the future' in Nietzsche's sense, then, names an attitude or stance which one is required to assume in order to think anew 'the proportion of continuity and discontinuity in the forms of life we pass on'. To *think anew* the question of 'the proportion of continuity and discontinuity in the forms of life we pass on' is not just one way to make sense of this question, one possible way to be responsive and responsible to it. On Nietzsche's view, it is the *only* way: to make sense of it, to be responsive and responsible to it, *is* to think it anew.

This orientation to the new, to the affirmation of a future different from the past, is the distinctive mark of the 'philosopher of the future'. Taking Emerson and Nietzsche as exemplars of this type of 'philosopher', Stanley Cavell helps us to identify why they arouse our suspicion; why the new itself arouses another kind of anxiety and fear: '[I]f we are to think anew it must be from a new stance, one essentially *unfamiliar* to us; or, say, from a further perspective that is *uncontrollable* by us' (Cavell, 1995, p.6). Various and diverse sorts of explanations have been offered to explain why we prefer, or cling to ways of life, patterns of belief, and action orientations with which we are already familiar, and in which we are already at 'home'. While the explanations themselves may be contestable, the tendency they aim to explain is not. The value of Cavell's remark, however, does not consist in serving as one more reminder of this tendency, but in pointing to a link between the unfamiliar and the uncontrollable. It is the latter, so I claim, that best explains why the new makes most philosophers, particularly moral and political philosophers, suspicious and anxious. From a purely cognitive standpoint, the new arouses fear and anxiety because it is not something whose effects we can predict and control. We cannot master what we do not know. From a moral and political standpoint, we are understandably suspicious about any stance or perspective that is uncontrollable. Our suspicion here arises from the assumption that a stance that is uncontrollable is a stance that cannot be made accountable. And so it is quite unclear how thinking anew can be thinking responsibly. Affirming an indeterminate future seems to be no less risky, no less dangerous, then, than affirming a determinate one. Whatever the relevant reasons, it would seem that neither the 'architects' of a determinate or an indeterminate future can be held accountable for the future they wish to build.

Although Nietzsche's suggestion may not be altogether 'untimely', not quite as existentially remote from and politically incompatible with the pluralistic, multicultural nature of our 21st century modernity as first appeared, it still remains disturbing. If thinking anew from a new stance means thinking in a way that cannot be held accountable, it would seem to involve an evasion rather than an acceptance of the responsibility we must bear for 'the proportion of continuity and discontinuity in the forms of life we pass on'. But perhaps we can save Nietzsche's (and by implication, Emerson's and Cavell's) suggestion from leading to this conclusion if we recall that to think anew from a new stance arises from an objective not a subjective need. And so it is possible to evaluate the new stance according to the degree to which it illuminates both past and present. To the degree to which it helps make better sense of the problem of how to go on, the new stance demonstrates responsiveness and responsibility to the problem to which it represents an answer.

The challenge, then, is to see how a stance that cannot be controlled can be made accountable. Given the nature of the task, how could we ever reassure ourselves that we have got *right* the proportion of continuity and discontinuity in the forms of life we pass on? How could we confidently - but not blindly - affirm the future we are aiming to build? To what would we owe that confidence? How could we make it accountable? Here is a provisional answer to these questions. We would be entitled to our confidence - ethically and epistemically, speaking - only if our change of orientation to the future made us insightfully aware of a previously uncritical relation to the past. In other words, a change of orientation to the future in light of the new stance we assume would have to make us more accountable to, more responsible for, the proportion of continuity and discontinuity in the forms of life we pass on. We could not justify any orientation to the future - new or old - which made us inconstant to or forgetful of the obligation reflectively and critically to renew our traditions and forms of life. On the other hand, if we were to abandon the continuous, never-ending task of integrating continuity and discontinuity, we would disown our responsibility to those who came before us, and to those who will succeed us.

There is, unfortunately, a deeply-entrenched way to think of this wholly modern idea of beginning anew as involving the complete dismantling of all our previous beliefs and commitments, and beginning radically anew from scratch. This is the way common to Descartes and 17th century epistemology, to a popular (one-sided, if not erroneous) reading of Nietzsche, to the avant-garde mentality of modernism, and to the standard understanding of 'progress'. Returning to Habermas' characterization of modernity's time-consciousness, we can see the normative outline of another way to think of beginning anew. Less willful, less self-undermining, and less misguided, it requires neither the negation of the past nor the glorification of a self-creating or self-constituting subject; rather, it requires the recognition of the past as the prehistory of the present, with which, moreover, it is interconnected 'as by the chain of a continual destiny' (Habermas, 1987, p.14). If we are to make any coherent sense of the present as a potential new beginning, as a difference that can make a difference to our practices and self-understanding, we will need to relink it accountably to a reinherited, to a reappropriated, past.

The stance towards the future which constitutes modernity's time consciousness not only places possibility ontologically higher than actuality (Heidegger, 1962, p.63); it also places an almost unbearable sense of responsibility upon the present. If we are to respond authentically to our consciousness of historical time, we are compelled to take the ethical perspective of a historically accountable 'future present'. From this projected ethical perspective we come to recognize the past as the 'prehistory of the present', to which the present is connected 'as by the chain of a continual destiny'. Within this ethically-reinterpreted historical horizon we bear a special responsibility: we are the ones who must self-consciously renew and correct our forms of life, who must repair what is broken, or break with what seems irreparable. We are the ones who must remake our languages and practices, and make something new out of something old.

By drawing on modernity's consciousness of time to clarify the responsibility we must bear for the proportion of continuity and discontinuity in the forms of life that we pass on, Habermas has outlined a highly suggestive picture of how we can 'go on' reflectively and self-critically. This picture suggests that every rupture, every break with the past calls for both a cognitive and an ethical response. From a cognitive standpoint, the activity of making the difference between past and present intelligible demands that it be regarded against a background of continuity which itself cannot be taken for granted; rather, it must be continuously re-evaluated and remade. Furthermore, such re-evaluation and remaking is normatively guided by the obligation to get right the proportion of continuity and discontinuity in the forms of life we pass on. This cognitive standpoint presupposes the ethical *and* existential standpoint from which we come to see that the problem of getting right the proportion of continuity and discontinuity in the forms of life we pass on, is *our* problem. Coming to see it as our problem means, of course, that our sense of responsibility for self-critically renewing our traditions must have a very strong affective component. Lacking such an affective component, our relation to the past would be marked by inconstancy as much as by denial of responsibility. And so it has typically been, and continues to be, the acute insights of Walter Benjamin's critique of the philosophy of history notwithstanding.[8]

Notes

1 Cf. especially Reinhard Koselleck *Futures Past: The Semantics of Historical Time* and Walter Benjamin 'Theses on the Philosophy of History' in *Illuminations*.

2 For Habermas, the problem of self-reassurance constitutes the philosophical discourse of modernity: 'Since the close of the eighteenth century, the discourse of modernity has had a single theme under ever new titles: the weakening of the forces of social bonding, privatization, and diremption - in short, the deformations of a one-sidedly rationalized everyday practice which evoke the need for something equivalent to the unifying power of religion' (Habermas, 1987, p.139).

3 See Nikolas Kompridis *In Times of Need: Habermas, Heidegger and the Future of Critical Theory* for a more elaborate and critical account of Habermas' treatment of the problem of self-reassurance.

4 Leonard Cohen 'Everybody Knows' from *I'm Your Man*, 1988.

5 Of course I am not of the view that a historical period can be defined by or understood in terms of a *single* cultural mood, for a historical period can manifest multiple, shifting cultural moods, each of which reveals a different aspect of the cultural totality.

6 We've not so completely lost our grasp of intellectual and cultural history to forget that such announcements are always premature; nor are we so morally disoriented to ignore the fact that Fukuyama constructs his Kojevian-cum-neo-liberal philosophy of history from the standpoint of the victors.

7 Cf. Walter Benjamin (1999) *The Arcades Projects*, Theodore Adorno (1974) *Minima Moralia*, and Max Horkheimer and Theodore Adorno (1972) *Dialectic of Enlightenment*.

8 I'm thinking of insights such as the following: 'For every image of the past that is not recognized by the present as one of its own concerns threatens to disappear irretrievably' and 'To articulate the past historically does not mean to recognize it *the way it really was* (Ranke). It means to seize hold of memory as it flashes up at a moment of danger [...] The danger affects both the content of the tradition and its receivers' (Benjamin, 1969).

References

Ackermann, B. (1992), *Liberal Revolution*, Yale University Press, New Haven.

Adorno, T. (1974), *Minima Moralia*,Verso, London.

Beckett, S. (1958), *The Unnamable*, Grove Press, New York.

Benjamin, W. (1969), 'Theses on the Philosophy of History', in *Illuminations*, Schocken, New York.

Benjamin, W. (1999), *The Arcades Projects*, Harvard University Press, Cambridge, MA.

Cavell, S. (1995), 'Time After Time', *London Review of Books*, 12 January.

Habermas, J. (1987), *The Philosophical Discourse of Modernity*, MIT Press, Cambridge, MA.

Habermas, J. (1989), *The New Conservatism*, MIT Press, Cambridge, MA.

Habermas, J. (1999), 'Europe and Globalization', *New Left Review*, no. 235.

Heidegger, M. (1962), *Being and Time*, Harper and Row, New York.

Horkheimer, M. and T. Adorno (1972), *Dialectic of Enlightenment*, Continuum, New York.

Kompridis, N. (forthcoming), *In Times of Need: Habermas, Heidegger and the Future of Critical Theory*, Northwestern University Press, Evanston.

Koselleck, R. (1985), *Futures Past: The Semantics of Historical Time*, MIT Press, Cambridge, MA.

Nietzsche, F. (1983), 'On the Uses and Disadvantages of History for Life', in *Untimely Meditations*, Cambridge University Press, Cambridge.

Putnam, H. (1994), *Words and Life*, Harvard University Press, Cambridge, MA.

Williams, B. (1985), *Ethics and the Limits of Philosophy*, Harvard University Press, Cambridge.

2 From Industrial Modernity to Risk Modernity? A Critical Discussion of the Theory of the 'Risk Society'[1]

KLAUS RASBORG

Do we live in a risk society? Has the production and distribution of risks today become so predominant in relation to the production and distribution of welfare that we have become part of a new type of society that differs fundamentally from classic industrial society? A society the understanding of which makes new demands on the fundamental concepts of sociology - or maybe even necessitates the construction of a new sociological paradigm. This is undoubtedly the most fundamental question that has been raised by the German sociologist Ulrich Beck, who has coined the phrase of the 'risk society' and who has established himself as a leading theorist within the sociological discussion of risk.

There can hardly be any doubt that Beck (1992 [1986]) claims to have put forward a new theoretical model for understanding our times. It emphasizes that contemporary society has changed radically compared to the 'classic industrial society' which was the object of Marx', Weber's and Durkheim's analyses. At the same time Beck repudiates the idea that this shift should lead to a relativistic, postmodern cultural and social condition where all binding standards erode.

I am working on a new and optimistic model for understanding our times. My argument interprets what others see as the development of a postmodern order in terms of a stage of *radicalized* (second phase) modernity, a stage where the dynamics of individualization, globalization and risk undermining the first phase of industrial nation-state modernity and its foundations. Modernity becomes *reflexive*, which means concerned with its unintended consequences, risks and their implications for its foundations. Where most postmodern theorists are critical of grand narratives, general theory and humanity, I remain committed to all of these, but in a new sense. To me the

Enlightenment is *not* a historical notion and set of ideas but a process and dynamics where criticism, self-criticism, irony and humanity play a central role (Beck, 1999c, p.152).

Beck's (1992 [1986]) basic idea seems to be quite simple: Today a new set of problems and conflicts, relating to the production and distribution of risks, has become at least as dominant as the traditional problems and conflicts relating to the distribution of welfare. In earlier times risks primarily originated from nature, whereas today they originate from ourselves. Risks, according to Beck, are a product of industrial modernization; they are the unintended consequences of the rapid development of science and technology in modern capitalist society (Rasborg, 1997).

However, if one considers the implications of this simple hypothesis, things soon become more complicated. Beck's subsequent work bears witness to this, in so far as it can be seen as an attempt to address the many questions that have been raised by the original hypothesis. Moreover, Beck develops his theory in a permanent dialogue with the ideas of other prominent (risk) sociologists of our time - not least Anthony Giddens and Niklas Luhmann.

In this article I will try to sketch out some of the main ways in which Beck has developed his theory since *Risk Society* was first published in 1986. As my point of departure for the discussion of Beck's theory, I will analyse three alternative views on risk (and insurance) that can be found in recent German, French and American social theory. On this basis, I will discuss some fundamental problems with Beck's diagnosis of contemporary society as a 'risk society' or a 'reflexive modernity'.

Risk and Danger

One of the most obvious objections to the hypothesis of a 'risk society' is that we have always been confronted with risk: earthquakes, floods, plague, cholera etc. And not only have we always been confronted with risk, one can even claim that in some respects our existence today is *less* risky than it was just a hundred years ago.

Thus, average life expectancy has increased significantly in all modern industrialized countries in the 20th century which is not at least due to better living conditions and improvements within medical science (Giddens, 1991, p.114ff). Moreover, we take many significant risks in modern life, voluntarily, so to speak; these include smoking, driving, drinking, junk food, extreme sports, unsafe sex etc. (Greenfeld, 1999, pp.54-62). Taken together such things cause not an insignificant number of deaths, increased hazards and health care expenditure.

In 1986 Beck had already anticipated some of these objections by arguing that it is the nature of risk that has changed. Whereas risks were previously more 'accidental' and 'individual' (that is bound to the actions of a single agent e.g. the hunter who goes out hunting), they are today systematically produced by modern industrial-capitalistic forms of production. In late modern society risks are 'systems immanent' and universalizing (increasingly global) (Beck, 1992 [1986], pp.21, 32, 62).

In his more recent writings, however, Beck (1993, p.278, note 10a, 1995 [1988], p.77ff) has attempted to clarify the differences between old and new respectively voluntary and involuntary risks, and in this he has adopted Niklas Luhmann's (1997) distinction between risk and danger.[2]

In Luhmann's systems theory risks are analysed as 'second order observations, that is as 'observations of observations' (Luhmann, 1997, p.162, cf. Kneer and Nassehi, 1997, p.176). In Luhmann's (1997, p.65) opinion, observations are related to social systems that operate from a distinction between system (self-reference) and the surrounding world (other-reference). The observations of social systems always take place on the basis of certain guiding differences (binary codes), with the result that some aspects of the observed matter are manifest while others are not. Social systems are self-referential, that is, they are not able to communicate but can only make a surrounding world for, or 'irritate', each other (Luhmann, 1997).

According to Luhmann there is a close connection between risk and decision. Risk must be seen as decisions observed with respect to the future (ibid., pp.161, 166). But as decisions are always made towards a contingent future, the possibility, or risk, of unintended consequences of action is always present. Thus, all decisions, that is also decisions concerned with safety, are connected with risk (ibid, pp.159, 190). The only thing that is certain, is that there is no definite certainty. Therefore risk must be opposed to *danger* rather than to safety (ibid., p.158ff).

The way to determine whether the consequences of a given action constitute a risk or a danger has to do with the question of who makes the decision. For the one who decides the consequences of the action appear as *risk*; for the one who is affected the consequences appear as *danger* (Luhmann, 1997, pp.162, 177). Thus, depending on the perspective, the same phenomenon can be observed as risk or danger: If I am a smoker, I run the risk of getting lung cancer, whereas those who due to my smoking become passive smokers are exposed to danger.

Hence in Luhmann's constructivist approach risk and danger are seen as relative phenomena closely linked with the observations and decisions of social systems; risks do not exist 'as such', but must be seen as symptoms of the way in which modern society observes itself with respect to the consequences of an increasing complexity of decisions.

Danger, Risk, Large-Scale Hazards

Now, in the course of his writing Beck has developed his notion of risk in a way that bears a certain resemblance to the Luhmannian notion of risk.

In *Risk Society* (1992 [1986]) Beck speaks indiscriminately of risk and danger; in addition he points out the difficulties in connecting given risks with certain causes (*Urheber*) (cf. above). However, in his more recent writings Beck (1996, 1993, 1995 [1988]) adopts the Luhmannian distinction between risk and danger, and at the same time he emphasizes the dependence of risks on decisions. Thus, Beck now says, one has to distinguish between:

> [...] pre-industrial hazards, not based on technological-economic decisions, and thus externalizable (onto nature, the gods), and industrial risks, products of social choice, which must be weighed against opportunities and acknowledged, dealt with, or simply foisted on individuals (Beck, 1995 [1988], p.77; cf. Beck, 1996, p.11).

Within modern society one has also to distinguish between:

> [...] (industrial) risks and the return of incalculable insecurities in the form of large-scale hazards of late industrialism. The latter also emerged historically out of human deeds, so they cannot be palmed off on extra-societal forces and influences; but they simultaneously undercut the social logic of risk calculation and provision (ibid.).

Thus, in Beck's version the distinction between risk and danger seems to be identical with a historical distinction between pre-modern *dangers*, which are due to the vagaries of *nature* (earthquakes, floods, epidemics etc.), and modern *risks* that result from modern civilization and thereby, ultimately, from human decisions (ibid., p.77ff). Whereas Beck in his earlier writings tended to oppose risk to safety (Nielsen, 1999), this distinction is now - in line with the general trend in the sociological literature on risk - given up in favour of the distinction between risk and danger (Grundmann, 1999, p.48).

In this way Beck (1992, p.98) is able to point out that modern risks not only differ from pre-modern dangers by virtue of their magnitude, but also by virtue of their origin in decisions - although, of course, we are dealing in this case with complex decision-making processes taking place within the framework of organizations, enterprises, state organs, political parties etc. (ibid.)

The new large-scale hazards - nuclear disasters, holes in the ozone layer, global warming etc. - that seem to be even more dominant in a highly developed risk society, are in Beck's view characterized by the fact that they are so extensive and complex that: first they cannot be limited temporally, spatially and socially; second it is difficult with any degree of certainty to identify the person causing the loss and thereby to hold him responsible; third, it is not possible to compensate the victims economically by way of insurance (Beck, 1995 [1988], pp.76, 109; cf. Beck, 2000 [1998], p.41ff).

Thus, Beck now distinguishes between pre-modern *dangers*, that were uncontrollable, modern (industrial) *risks*, that can in principle be compensated for by insurance, and the highly developed risk society's increasing number of *large-scale hazards* that are not possible to insure against (Rasborg, 1999).

Of course the analogy between Luhmann's and Beck's view on risk should not be taken too far, in as much as Beck (1997, p.57; 1997 [1993], p.180, note 16) generally distances himself from Luhmann's systems theory. Beck (1993, p.278ff, note 10c) thus criticizes Luhmann's version of the distinction between risk and danger for being much too relative (in relation to themes and situations) and thereby making difficult the demarcation of social lines of conflict in relation to risks. Furthermore, Beck (1997 [1993], pp.27, 112, 124, 157) criticizes the notion of self-referentiality for failing to acknowledge the increasing interdependence of social systems in reflexive modernity. Finally, Beck (1997, p.55ff) emphasizes that social systems are not 'subject-free' but, on the contrary, are constituted by individuals and therefore also dependent on their consent.[3]

External Risk, Manufactured Risk, High-Consequence Risk

Anthony Giddens (1999, 1998a, 1998b, 1994, 1991, 1990) is another prominent sociologist who has based part of his analysis of late modernity on a notion of risk. And in recent years Giddens and Beck seem to have been increasingly inspired by each other's work (cf. Beck, Giddens and Lash, 1994).

Early modernity, according to Giddens, was dominated by 'external risks', that is risks that could somehow be perceived as independent of the actions of the individuals, that could fairly well be calculated, and that could therefore also be subjected to actuarial tables (e.g. unemployment, sickness etc.):

> We should distinguish risk from hazard, but we must also make a distinction between two kinds of risk. The first two hundred years of the existence of industrial society were dominated by what one might call *external risk*. External risk, expressed in down-to-earth terms, is risk of events that may strike individuals unexpectedly (from the outside, as it were), but that happen regularly and often enough in a whole population of people to be broadly predictable, and so insurable. There are two kinds of insurance associated with the rise of industrial society: the private insurance company and public insurance, which is the predominant concern of the welfare state (Giddens, 1998a, p.27).

In late modernity, however, we are increasingly confronted with new types of risk, namely 'high-consequence risks' and 'manufactured uncertainty' (Giddens, 1994, pp.78, 152, 219). Whereas the first refer to global threats to the environment caused by human intervention in nature, the second refer to an existential uncertainty found in societies where traditional certainties are eroded as a consequence of the 'end' of tradition and nature:

> A world which lives after nature and after the end of tradition is one marked by a transition from external to what I call *manufactured risk*. Manufactured risk is risk created by the very progression of human development, especially by the progression of science and technology. Manufactured risk refers to new risk environments for which history provides us with very little previous experience. We often don't really know what the risks are, let alone how to calculate them accurately in terms of probability tables (Giddens, 1998a, p.28ff).

Giddens (1998a, p.26ff) thus, in line with Beck, distinguishes between three different 'stages' in the development of risk: a pre-modern stage dominated by 'hazards'; an early modern stage (industrial society) dominated by 'external risks'; and a late modern stage (risk society) dominated by 'manufactured uncertainty' and 'high-consequence risks' (Rasborg, 1999). And one of the most important characteristics of the new types of risk that occur in the highly developed risk society is, according to Beck and Giddens, that they are not calculable and therefore not manageable.

Risk and Insurance

For this reason, risk society in Beck and Giddens's view is not simply an 'insurance-society' (Ewald, 1991 [1989]). As long as risks were rather confined and could fairly well be calculated, they were insurable (e.g. health insurance, unemployment insurance, industrial injury insurance etc.); in this respect the risk society and the insurance-society, of course, are two sides of the same coin. However, 'high-consequence risks' and 'manufactured uncertainty' indicate the breakdown of the principle of insurance, in as much as it becomes difficult to identify, predict and calculate risks (Beck, 1995 [1988], pp.85, 106-110).

Consequently, the highly developed risk society's 'low probability, but high consequence risks' lead to a paradox. Even though technicians, experts and political decision-makers claim that the risk of a given damage is minimal, it nevertheless cannot be insured; thus the technical risk assessment and the principle of insurance collide in the highly developed risk society (cf. Beck, 1994a, p.11ff).

If one wants to make a clear cut distinction, one can say that the highly developed risk society, in Beck's and Giddens's opinion, is a '*post-risk-calculation-society*' (Dean, 1998, p.29ff, my italics), and therefore it is also a '*post-insurance-society*'.

The question is, however, whether it is possible to uphold Beck's and Giddens's assumption of the existence of one historical stage (industrial society) where risks could be fairly well calculated, and another (risk society) where it becomes more difficult to calculate and thus insure risks. This opposition seems to be based on a *realist* assumption of the existence of different historical stages that are dominated by different types of 'real risks'.

The Critique of the Realist Notion of Risk

The French social theorist Francois Ewald (1991, 1991 [1989]) has criticized the realist, or essentialist, interpretation of risk. Risk, Ewald points out, does not exist as such: 'Nothing is a risk in itself; there is no risk in reality. But on the other hand, anything *can* be a risk; it all depends on how one analyses the danger, considers the event' (Ewald, 1991, p.199ff).

Thus, risk or 'riskiness' is not an inherent property of the given phenomenon. On the contrary, risk is a way of *observing* given phenomena (damages). One might say that whereas risk according to Luhmann is a way of observing decisions with respect to the future, risk according to Ewald is a way of observing given phenomena (damages) from an insurance point of view.

Hence there is an inner connection between risk and insurance. Insurance is simply the technology of risk, as it is insurance that makes it meaningful at all to speak of something as a risk: 'Insurance can be defined as a technology of risk. In fact the term 'risk' [...] has no precise meaning other than as a category of this technology' (Ewald, 1991, p.198ff). From an insurance point of view three distinctive features characterize risks.

Risk is *calculable*. For something to be a risk, it must be subjectable to actuarial principles, that is statistics and calculations of probability: 'For an event to be a risk, it must be possible to evaluate its probability. Insurance has a dual basis; the statistical table which establishes the regularity of certain events, and the calculus of probabilities applied to that statistic, which yields an evaluation of the chances of that class of event actually occurring' (ibid., p.201ff).

Risk is *collective*. If risks are to be calculated, it must be possible to survey their distribution across a given population; therefore insurance against risks can be seen as a way of equalizing risks where the 'insurance community' sets off the individual loss (ibid., p.202ff).

Risk, lastly, is a *capital*. Insurance is an economic compensation for damages that cannot in principle be priced (e.g. the loss of a bodypart because of an industrial accident) (ibid., p.204). The economic compensation for a given damage (e.g. the degree of disablement) is determined on the basis of actuarial tables, wherefore insurance must be seen as '[...] an attempt to make the incalculable calculable' (Dean, 1998, p.29ff).

Thus, if risk is defined in terms of insurance, it follows that it is not possible to speak of risks that cannot be insured (cf. below).

Taking this actuarial notion of risk as his point of departure, Ewald (1991 [1989], pp.288, 291, 1991, pp.207, 209) conceives of the modern welfare state as a collective system of insurance against the risks of industrial society (unemployment, sickness etc.). As a system of insurance the welfare state socializes risk; thus insurance can be seen as constitutive of the social contract, and hence solidarity, in modern society.

Three Questionable Assumptions Concerning Beck's Theory

Taking Ewald's notion of risk as his point of departure, Mitchell Dean (1998) has argued that the theory of the risk society can be said to be based on three basic assumptions that reveal the problematic nature of Beck's approach to the analysis of risk.

The assumption of uniformity of risk: '[...] that it is possible to make a general and abstract characterization of risk in a given type of society, i.e. that risk has fundamentally the same characteristics in all spheres' (ibid.). This refers to Beck's (and Giddens') assumption that it is possible to categorize risks in general types that are predominant in different historical periods (cf. above).

The realist assumption: '[...] that the reason why risk is a feature of quotidian existence in this risk society, and a component of individual and collective experience and identities, is that real riskiness has increased so much that it has outrun the mechanisms of its calculation and control' (ibid.). This refers to Beck's view that risks are not pure constructions but have a real content; a content that even changes in the highly developed risk society (incalculability).

All in all these are the assumptions that can be said to lie behind Beck's and Giddens' 'realist' idea that it is possible to distinguish between one historical stage where risks were, in principle, calculable, and another where risks increasingly become incalculable. Thus, in Beck's (and Giddens') theory '[...] risk is viewed within a general schema and narrative of *phases of modernity* and as a feature of *the ontological condition of humans* within current social forms' (ibid., p.25, my italics).

Seen from Ewald's point of view, though, this idea proves to be wrong. If risk is defined in terms of insurance, it follows that it must be calculable (if it were not, it would not be a risk): 'It is [...] not possible to speak of incalculable risks, or of risks that escape our modes of calculation, end even less to speak of a social order in which risk is largely calculable and contrast it with one in which risk has become largely incalculable' (ibid., p.25).

As making the incalculable calculable is what insurance is all about: '[...] it is not possible to contrast calculable risks and incalculable risks. For insurance rationality, everything can be treated as a risk and the task of insurers has been both to 'produce' risks and to find ways of insuring what has previously been thought to be uninsurable' (ibid., p.29).

Consequently, Beck and Giddens' view of risk as rooted primarily in the development of science and technology seems to be much too simple: 'It is clear that the genealogy of risk is much more complex than the theory of risk society allows' (Dean, 1998, p.34). Instead Dean suggests a more differentiated theoretical model where risks are analysed as connected with '[...] specific types of risk rationalities and practices' (Dean, 1998, p.28). Important sources of inspiration for such an approach to the analysis of risk are the theories of Foucault and Ewald where '[...] risk is analysed as a component of assemblages of practices, techniques and rationalities concerned with how we govern' (ibid., p.25).

Thus, all in all, it seems to be much too simple to analyse risk as connected only with science and technology; they also have to do with modern forms of 'governmentality', that is certain forms of governing practices concerned with the regulation and control of human conduct (cf. Dean, 1999).

Risk as a Social Construction

However, Dean's critique of Beck's 'realism' seems to ignore the fact that from the very beginning Beck's theory contained a rather significant constructivist train of thought; and in recent years Beck (1999b, 1996) has explicitly distanced himself from 'naive realism'.

In *Risk Society*, Beck (1992 [1986], pp.22, 26-34, 51-84) emphasized the dependence of risk on knowledge. As risk often cannot be experienced directly (e.g. pesticides in the drinking water, holes in the ozone layer etc.), the role of science in detecting risk becomes of tremendous importance. Consequently, it could be claimed that risks only 'become risks' due to our (scientific) knowledge of them. And sometimes Beck (ibid., pp.22, 27, 55) actually goes as far as to claim that risks only exist *in our knowledge*. However, at the same time Beck (ibid., pp.26, 62, 177) again and again, in a realist way, refers to the *fact* that risks are increasing rapidly in contemporary society.

Hence the theory of the risk society seems to be burdened by a basic inconsistency with respect to the epistemological and ontological status of risk. Are risks hard, material facts? Or are they rather to be seen as cultural and social constructions? Are risks increasing rapidly in late modernity? Or are we rather to speak of an increasing awareness of risk? In *Risk Society*, Beck (1992 [1986], p.55) seems to answer these questions in a quite ambiguous way: Our *awareness* of risk is increasing, because of *the fact* that risks are multiplying.

In his recent writings Beck (1999c, 1996) seems to take a more explicit stand on the question of constructivism versus realism. His position can be described as a rejection of 'naive realism' as well as of 'naive constructivism'. Whereas a naive realism claims that risks exist in a hard, material way and thus can be determined independently of the observer (e.g. in the form of threshold values), a naive, or radical, constructivism conversely claims that risks are cognitive, scientific, social and cultural constructions that cannot be determined independently of the observer.

In Beck's (1996) opinion neither of these alternatives is tenable. A naive realism ignores the fact that risk assessments, threshold values etc. are dependent on definitions, and are determined in a highly complex game of knowledge, power, political and economic interests etc. (cf. Beck, 1992 [1986], pp.22, 26-34, 51-84). On the contrary, a radical constructivism leads to a total relativism that 'deprives' risks of any real content. Yet this is problematic.

For, among other things, we know that people in the Stone Age did not have the capacity for nuclear and ecological annihilation, and that the dangers posed by lurking demons did not have the same political dynamic as the man-made hazards of ecological self-destruction (Beck, 1996, p.4).

Instead Beck (ibid., pp.4-7) advocates a '*reflexive realism*', that is an 'intermediate position' between the two extremes. Beck's reflexive realism can be described as a conditional, or modified, constructivism that insists that even if risks are interpreted differently at different times and places, they, nevertheless, have a real - objective, if you like - content that cannot be reduced to interpretations (cf. Adam and van Loon, 2000, p.2ff).

Thus, Beck in a peculiar way wants to claim that risks are at one and the same time 'real' and socially constituted: '[...] risks are at the same time 'real' *and* constituted by social perception and construction' (Beck, 1999c, p.143). In late modernity risks must be seen as highly complex factors that at one and the same time are related to mathematical calculations, technical knowledge, culture and norms:

> As mathematical calculations (probability computations or accident scenarios), risks are related directly and indirectly to cultural definitions and standards of a tolerable or intolerable life. So in a risk society the question we must ask ourselves is: how do we want to live? This means, among other things, that risk statements are by nature statements that can be deciphered only in an interdisciplinary (competitive) relationship, because they assume in equal measure insight into technical know-how and familiarity with cultural perceptions and norms (Beck, 1999c, p.138).

Because of the 'real' as well as 'constructed' character of risk it is not possible to make a decision as to whether a realist or a constructivist approach is more adequate:

> I consider realism and constructivism to be neither an either-or option nor a mere matter of belief. We should not have to swear allegiance to any

> particular view or theoretical perspective. The decision whether to take a realist or a constructivist approach is for me a rather *pragmatic* one, a matter of choosing the appropriate means for a desired goal. If I have to be a realist (for the moment) in order to open up the social sciences for the new and contradictory experiences of the global age of global risks, then I have no qualms about adopting the guise and language of a ('reflexive') 'realist'. If constructivism makes a (positive) problem shift possible and if it allows us to raise important questions that realists do not ask, then I am content (for the moment at least) to be a constructivist [...] I find it insufficient today, especially in the area of risk, to restrict my analysis to one perspective or conceptual dogma only: I can be both a realist and constructivist, using realism *and* constructivism as far as those meta-narratives are useful for the purpose of understanding the complex and ambivalent 'nature' of risk in the world risk society we live in (Beck, 1999c, p.134).

Consequently, in Beck's opinion, the choice between one or the other approach seems to be a purely pragmatic one that depends on the analysed object, or on what one wants to emphasize. However, the question is whether this purely pragmatic and deeply ambivalent 'both-and'-attitude can be said to contribute to a clarification of the problem of the epistemological and ontological status of risk.

The Idea of 'Reflexive Modernization'

Beck's reflexive realism, of course, is closely related to his idea of 'reflexive modernization'. For Beck, Giddens and Lash the notion of reflexive modernization is launched as an alternative to the unfruitful debate on modernity versus postmodernity.

For all of us, the protracted debate about modernity and postmodernity has become wearisome and like so many such debates in the end has produced rather little. The idea of reflexive modernization, regardless of whether or not one uses that term as such, breaks the stranglehold which these debates have tended to place upon conceptual innovation (Beck, Giddens and Lash, 1994, p.vi).

Contrary to Lash (1994a, 1994b), for whom the reflexivity of late modernity primarily seems to be a cultural and aesthetic phenomenon, and Giddens (1994a, 1994b) who in a wider sense prefers to speak of an 'institutional reflexivity' that can be said to be an effect of the post-traditional society, Beck's (1994a, 1994b) notion of reflexive modernity refers to an epochal differentiation between different *stages* in the process of modernization.

In Beck's (1997 [1993], pp.11-19, 1992 [1986], pp.10, 19, 153) theory of modernity the transition from industrial to the risk society is seen as a transition from a *simple* to a *reflexive* modernity. In the early, 'simple' stage of modernity progress and science were still able to legitimate risks, whereas in the reflexive stage - corresponding with the emergence of the risk society - belief in progress and science erodes as it becomes clear that the productive forces become destructive and that science 'participates' in the production of risks; hence risks can no longer be legitimated by science and progress.

The loss of legitimacy forces modernity to see itself in a matter-of-fact way; modernity, as Beck puts is, '[...] becomes a theme and a problem for itself' (Beck, 1994a, p.8; 1992 [1986], p.19). And it is exactly this 'self-confrontation' that makes modernity reflexive (Beck, 1994a, p.5ff).

However, what is characteristic of Beck's notion of reflexivity is that the reflexivity of late modernity does not necessarily lead to an increasing *reflection* on the 'self-destructive potentials' of the risk society. Thus, Beck (1999b, p.109, 1994b, p.175ff) is critical of Giddens' and Lash's inclination to conceive of reflexive modernization as a conscious process mediated by *knowledge* (reflection).

Beck (1999b, p.110) does not disagree with Giddens and Lash in that knowledge plays an important role in reflexive modernity. However, contrary to Giddens and Lash, Beck emphasizes that the 'medium' of reflexive modernization to a large extent is *un*awareness, in as much as risk must be seen as the *un*intended consequences of industrial modernization (reflexivity):

> What distinguishes my concept of reflexive modernization from those of Giddens and Lash? To put it briefly and pointedly: *the 'medium' of reflexive modernization is not knowledge, but - more or less reflexive - unawareness*. It is this aspect of the distribution and defence of unawareness (*Nicht-Wissen*) that opens the horizon of inquiry for *non*-linear theories (of reflexive modernization). We live in the age of unintended consequences, and it is this state of affairs that must be decoded and shaped methodologically and theoretically, in everyday life and politically (Beck, 1999b, p.119).[4]

Beck (1999a, p.73, 1999b, p.109ff) thus wants to distinguish between on the one hand *reflexivity*, seen as the confrontation of modernity with its own results (risk), and on the other *reflection*, seen as the awareness of the 'self-destructive potentials' of the risk society. Whereas the first notion refers to a 'structural reflexivity', the second refers to individual (self)reflection.

In this way Beck (ibid.) is able to point out that the transition from industrial to the risk society occurs in a 'reflex-like' way, that is not as a conscious and intentional process that the agents are fully aware of. In other words, the *reflexivity* of the risk society does not necessarily, in Beck's opinion, imply an increasing *reflection* in the sense of an increasing *awareness* of risk.

Nevertheless, with this peculiar notion of reflexivity Beck seems to entangle himself in rather serious contradictions. On the one hand Beck assumes that risks are real (but systematically excommunicated) in the risk society. It is, Beck says, an '[...] interesting 'law' of the risk society', that '[...] *the less risks are publicly recognized, the more risks are produced*' (Beck, 1999c, p.144; Beck's italics). On the other hand Beck, in a radical constructivist way, claims that risks exist only in our knowledge of them: 'So ultimately: *it is cultural perception and definition that constitute risk.* 'Risk' and the '(public) definition of risk' are one and the same' (Beck, 1999c, p.135; Beck's italics). Thus, at one and the same time, Beck seems to claim that risks are real and purely discoursive phenomena (cf. above).

In an attempt to solve this contradiction Beck develops a 'two-stage-model' of knowledge and unawareness in relation to risks. Thus, Beck (1999a, p.72ff) distinguishes between two stages in the development of the risk society. A primary stage where risks are still latent, wherefore '[...] the self-identity of industrial society' is still dominating (ibid., p.72); a secondary stage where risks become so extensive and manifest, that '[...] industrial society sees and criticizes itself *as* risk society' (ibid.). Beck, in other words, introduces a hypothesis of a 'time lag' between (objective) production and (subjective) perception of risk (Alexander and Smith, 1996, p.254ff).

This hypothesis, however, seems to be based on a simple 'reflection theory' according to which it is the factual multiplication of risk that creates an increasing awareness of them:

> Beck wants to portray the risk society as an objective fact, both ontologically, in the sense that it exists as such, in a cold, hard and material way, and epistemologically, in the sense that these objective facts are perceived directly and accurately in the minds of citizens themselves (ibid., p.255ff).

Beck thus seems to ignore, or at least to play down, the impact of cultural factors in the perception of risk: 'The questions of when, and how, a 'risk' is detected, and of how these risks are placed on the social agenda, are not raised. It is simply the sheer enormity of risk that creates its apperception' (ibid., p.254). In a similar way Beck has been criticized for his overly 'rationalist' or 'cognitivist' approach to risk and reflexivity that tends to ignore the impact of lay knowledge of risk as well as more cultural or hermeneutic forms of reflexivity (Wynne, 1996; Alexander, 1996; Lash, 1994a).[5]

However, Beck's objectivist line of argument seems to be totally contradicted by his aforementioned hypothesis within the fields of a sociology of knowledge, saying not only that risks exist only in our knowledge of them, but also that they are systematically excommunicated in late modern society (cf. above) (Alexander and Smith, 1996, p.255). The contradiction seems to be almost total. Risk is real and objective, and yet it exists only in our knowledge. Thus, the question of the relation between knowledge and unawareness in relation to risk still must be said to be completely unsettled in Beck's theory.

If Beck were to address the problem of perception of risk in a more consistent way, he would have to take the cultural factor much more explicitly into consideration:

> Ontologically, he would have to acknowledge that the very production of a risk society rest upon a massive, if largely tacit cultural commitment to solving the problems of the world through the introduction of rationalizing, science-based technology. Epistemologically, he would have to recognize that the perception of this technological society as highly risky itself involves a fundamental shift in the social referents of this overarching cultural scheme (Alexander and Smith, 1996, p.256; cf. Wynne, 1996).

Beck's Concept of Rationality

Taking the theory of reflexive modernization as his point of departure, Beck (1997 [1993], pp.20-40) wants to claim that most of the sociological tradition - from Marx, Durkheim and Weber via Parsons to Luhmann, Habermas etc. - has been theorizing within the paradigm of simple modernization. In other words, we have to do with 'linear' theories of an advancing modernization and rationalization.

It might seem as if Beck himself outlines a linear theory, in so far as risk society is conceived of as an (apparently) new 'stage' in the development of society that necessarily follows from the previous stage (industrial society).[6]

However, Beck emphasizes that reflexive modernization must be seen as a dialectic between modernization and '*counter*-modernization'.

'Counter-modernity' refers to phenomena that can be seen as regressive in relation to modernity's ideals of reason, freedom and liberty (Beck, 1997 [1993], pp.61-93; 1992 [1986], pp.108, 192, 214). 'Counter-modernization' is not a *de*-modernization but, on the contrary, is a product of reflexive modernization (Beck, 1997 [1993], p.90). Religious fundamentalism, neo-nationalism, neo-racism, neo-tribalism etc. are, in Beck's sense, counter-modern phenomena that can be seen as reactions to a widespread reflexivity and as indicating a need for simple fixed points in a detraditionalized lifeworld (*Fraglosigkeit*). Hence the process of modernization is not necessarily equivalent to an irreversible change for the better; on the contrary, the risk of repercussions and re-emerging irrationalism is always present.

Beck's (1997 [1993], p.161) critical encounter with a linear concept of progress in many ways bears resemblance to Horkheimer and Adorno's (1993 [1944]) diagnosis of the 'dialectic of Enlightenment' as a fatal and unrecoverable process ending up in that the 'project of Enlightenment' turns into its opposite and becomes barbaric. Horkheimer and Adorno's metaphor for rationality's becoming irrational was *Auschwitz*; Beck's is *Chernobyl*.

Beck, like Horkheimer and Adorno, attempts to demonstrate that modern rationality contains a latent irrationalism. The modern 'project of the conquering of nature', which was meant to liberate us from the forces of nature, paradoxically, leads to a new dependency, in so far as we become subjected to the risks produced by modern civilization.

If the vicious circle is to be broken, modernity must 'come to its senses' (Beck 1994a, p.54, note 19). However, in Beck's opinion, the prevailing irrationality can be overcome only *by way of rationality*. Whereas Horkheimer and Adorno wanted to 'enlighten Enlightenment', Beck wants to 'radicalize (rationalize) rationality':

> It is not an excess of rationality, but a shocking lack of rationality, the prevailing irrationality, that explains the ailment of industrial modernity. It can be cured, if at all, not by a retreat, but only by a radicalization of rationality, which will absorb the repressed uncertainty (Beck, 1997 [1993], p.126; 1994a, p.33).

Thus, Beck's theory of reflexive modernization can be seen as an attempt to reformulate and develop Critical Theory's critique of rationality and science within a new social and historical context - the risk society (Beck, 1994a, p.53, note 12).[7]

However, with the rather vague notion of a 'radicalization (rationalization) of rationality', Beck seems to end up with the same basic problem as Critical Theory, that is the question of how critique is possible if one is located within the same space as the matter which is criticized.

This is the problem that Habermas (1981) attempts to solve by developing a concept of a communicative rationality that functions as a critical 'counter-rationality' towards instrumental rationality.

The step into a communicative paradigm of society is not made by Beck. Indeed, Beck (1992 [1986], pp.29, 58, 61) refers to a 'social rationality', which is counterposed to the technical and scientific rationality; furthermore he (1997, p.59; 1997 [1993], pp.128), with general reference to Habermas, speaks of reflexive modernization as a 'discursive modernization'. But these small steps towards a conceptualization of other forms of rationality than the instrumental risk-producing rationality do not become much more than rather vague hints that are never really developed.

Thus, seen from a Habermasian point of view, Beck undoubtedly must still be said to theorize within a subject-philosophical paradigm with its monological subject-object-logic; that is the paradigm that, according to Habermas, has dominated the whole tradition of thought up to the linguistic turn within philosophy and social theory. One can therefore assume that it is Beck's theoretical roots in a monological concept of reason that makes it difficult for him to conceive of and identify alternatives to instrumental rationality.

Conclusion

In this article I have called attention to some basic problems and inner contradictions in Beck's theory of the risk society. The lack of clarification of the epistemological and ontological status of risk; the questionable view of the relation between knowledge and unawareness in relation to risks; the rather vague and opaque notions of 'social rationality' and 'discursive modernization'.

A main thread in the critique has been that of addressing the limitations of Beck's 'realist' notion of risk. In recent years Beck, as shown, has tried to solve the problem of the relation between realism and constructivism by advocating a 'reflexive realism'; in his most recent writings he also advances a deeply ambivalent and purely pragmatic 'both-and'-attitude. However, the relation between realism and constructivism must be said be completely unclarified in Beck's theory.

A more emphatic constructivism would not seem be a solution to Beck's dilemma, in as much as the question of the risk society as a 'social fact' would dissolve into a purely discourse-theoretical question as to why in the second half of the 20th century there has apparently been a change in the 'semantics of crisis' of the highly developed industrial society - from an observation of the 'legitimation crisis' of late capitalism (Habermas, 1975 [1973]) to an observation of the 'ecological crisis'. Conversely, realism totally contradicts Beck's central hypothesis of the dependence of risks on knowledge and definitions; a hypothesis which is clearly anti-realistic and based on a sociology of knowledge.

In his most recent writings Beck (1999a, 1999b, 1999c) tries to solve this theoretical dilemma at a purely conceptual level by introducing still more distinctions and ad-hoc hypotheses, whereby his theorizing ends up in a more and more abstract construction of concepts. Instead of testing his hypotheses empirically in order to see if this could bring new life to the concepts, Beck chooses the role of a 'theory constructor', whereby his theory becomes rather speculative. Hence Beck's diagnosis of the 'risk society' is still mainly to be seen as a set of theoretical hypotheses and assumptions that are put forward on a general, macro-theoretical level with rather weak empirical foundations (Grundmann, 1999; Seippel, 1999; Alexander, 1996).

With the alternative positions discussed in this article some indications have been given as to how one could in a more fruitful way elaborate on the problem of risk. It has been suggested that risk should, perhaps, be seen as relating to the self-observation of modern society (Luhmann), to modern forms of governmentality (Dean), or to the general structures of meaning that regulate the self-understanding of a society (Alexander and Smith). A common characteristic of these alternative positions is that they avoid an exclusive focus on technology as well as a realist notion of risk. Thus, rather than a hard, ontological fact, the 'risk society' is to be seen as indicating a new 'semantics of crisis', the emergence of new problems of governmentality, or a changing cultural self-understanding of late modern society.

It is in the confrontation with such alternative conceptions that Beck's argument has to stand the test. In its present state of development Beck's theory, as shown, seems to be burdened with serious theoretical and empirical problems, wherefore the question has to be left open as to whether the notion of a 'risk society' can be said to be fruitful as a key category in a sociological diagnosis of the new century - or if, perhaps, we should rather think beyond the 'risk society'.

Notes

1 In the present article I elaborate on my previous work on the subject (cf. Rasborg 2000, 1999, 1997). I would like to thank Finn Hansson for comments on the article.

2 Beck (1993, p.278, note 10a) explicitly refers to Niklas Luhmann in connection with the distinction between 'risk' and 'danger' and calls attention to the fact that this distinction, in different versions, has become widely accepted within the sociological litterature on risk (cf. Giddens 1999, 1998a, 1998b; Luhmann 1997; Ewald 1991 [1989], 1991; Castel 1991).

3 Thus, in Alexander's view, Beck's theory can be seen as offering '[...] an alternative to Luhmann's exaggerated emphasis on fragmentation and self-referentiality, a conservative and technocratic vision that has exercised, at least until recently, such a great influence over continental general theory' (Alexander, 1996, p.134).

4 Because of the incalculability and unpredictability of risk, Beck (1994a, p.9) sometimes describes the risk producing rationality as a '*Post*-Zweckrationalität'.

5 Wynne, however, notes that '[...] in his accounts of the ways modern expert institutions tacitly construct self-serving and socially disorientating versions of responsibility for the risks of modern science and technology, and in his focus upon the unanticipated, Beck comes closer to avoiding a rationalistic framework than Giddens. However, the mechanisms of self-dissolution or self-refutation, and thus the reflexive transformations of modernity, are still conceived by Beck solely in terms of uncontrolled 'out-there' aspects of the unanticipated – of risks, side-effects, etc. out there in nature or technology' (Wynne, 1996, p.79, note 8).

6 Therefore one can also ask whether Beck really succeeds in liberating himself from the philosophy of history way of thinking of the German Marx/Hegel-tradition (Nielsen, 1999); although, of course, it should be added that in Beck's case we have to deal with a 'negative philosophy of history'.

7 Of course, I do not claim that there should be a general agreement between Beck and the early Frankfurt School. Beck (1994b, p.l77), for instance, explicitly distances himself from the pessimism of the late Horkheimer og Adorno (but, conversely, thinks that Giddens' view of late modernity is much to optimistic).

References

Adam, B. and Loon, J. van (2000), 'Introduction: Repositioning Risk; The Challenge for Social Theory', in Adam, B., Beck, U. and Loon, J. van (eds.), *The Risk Society and Beyond: Critical Issues for Social Theory*, Sage, London, pp.1-31.

Adorno, T. W. and Horkheimer, M. (1993) [1944]), *Oplysningens dialektik* [The Dialectic of Enlightenment],Gyldendal, Copenhagen.

Alexander, J. C. (1996), 'Critical Reflections on 'Reflexive Modernization', *Theory, Culture and Society*, vol.13 no.4, pp.133-38.

Alexander, J. C. and Smith, P. (1996), 'Social Science and Salvation: Risk Society as Mythical Discourse', *Zeitschrift für Soziologie*, vol.25 no.4, pp.251-62.

Beck, U. (1992) [1986]), *Risk Society: Towards a New Modernity*, Polity Press, Cambridge.

Beck, U. (1992), 'From Industrial Society to the Risk Society: Questions of Survival, Social Structure and Ecological Enlightenment', *Theory, Culture and Society*, vol.9 no.1, pp.97-123.

Beck, U. (1993), *Die Erfindung des Politischen. Zu einer Theorie reflexiver Modernisierung*, Suhrkamp, Frankfurt am Main.

Beck, U. (1994a), 'The Reinvention of Politics: Towards a Theory of Reflexive Modernization', in Beck, U., Giddens, A. and Lash, S. (eds.), *Reflexive Modernization: Politics, Tradition and Aesthetics in the Modern Social Order*, Polity Press, Cambridge, pp.l-55.

Beck, U. (1994b), 'Self-Dissolution and Self-Endangerment of Industrial Society: What Does This Mean?', in Beck, U., Giddens, A. and Lash, S. (eds.), *Reflexive Modernization: Politics, Tradition and Aesthetics in the Modern Social Order*, Polity Press, Cambridge, pp.74-83.

Beck, U. (1995) [1988]), *Ecological Politics in an Age of Risk*, Polity Press, Cambridge.

Beck, U. (1996), 'World Risk Society as Cosmopolitan Society. Ecological Questions in a Framework of Manufactured Uncertainties', *Theory, Culture and Society*, vol.13 no.4, pp.1-32.

Beck, U. (1997) [1993]), *The Reinvention of Politics: Rethinking Modernity in the Global Social Order*, Polity Press, Cambridge.

Beck, U. (1997), 'Subpolitics: Ecology and the Disintegration of Institutional Power', in *Organization and Environment*, vol.10 no.1, pp.52-65.

Beck, U. (1999a), 'Risk Society and the Welfare State', in *World Risk Society*, Polity Press, Cambridge, pp.72-90.

Beck, U. (1999b), 'Knowledge or Unawareness? Two Perspectives on 'Reflexive Modernization'', in *World Risk Society*, Polity Press, Cambridge, pp.109-32.

Beck, U. (1999c), 'Risk Society Revisited: Theory, Politics, Critiques and Research Programmes', in *World Risk Society*, Polity Press, Cambridge, pp.133-52.

Beck, U. (2000) [1998]), *What is Globalization?*, Polity Press, Cambridge.

Beck, U., Giddens, A. and Lash, S., (1994), *Reflexive Modernization: Politics, Tradition and Aesthetics in the Modern Social Order*, Polity Press, Cambridge.

Castel, Robert (1991), 'From Dangerousness to Risk', in Burchell, G., Gordon, C. and Miller, P. (eds.), *The Foucault Effect: Studies in Governmentality*, Harvester Wheatsheaf, Hermel Hempstead, pp.281-98.

Dean, M. (1998), 'Risk, Calculable and Incalculable', *Soziale Welt* (49), pp.25-42.

Dean, M. (1999), *Governmentality: Power and Rule in Modern Society*, Sage, London.

Ewald, F. (1991)[1989]), 'Die Versicherungs-Gesellschaft', in Beck, U., *Politik in der Risikogesellschaft: Essays und Analysen*, Suhrkamp, Frankfurt am Main, pp.288-301.

Ewald, F. (1991), 'Insurance and Risk', in Burchell, G., Gordon, C. and Miller, P. (eds.), *The Foucault Effect: Studies in Governmentality*, Harvester Wheatsheaf, Hermel Hempstead, pp.197-210.

Giddens, A. (1990), *The Consequences of Modernity*, Polity Press, Cambridge.

Giddens, A. (1991), *Modernity and Self-Identity: Self and Society in the Late Modern Age*, Polity Press, Cambridge.

Giddens, A. (1994a), 'Living in a Post-Traditional Society', in Beck, U., Giddens, A. and Lash, S. (eds.), *Reflexive Modernization: Politics, Tradition and Aesthetics in the Modern Social Order*, Polity Press, Cambridge, pp.56-109.

Giddens, A. (1994b), 'Risk, Trust, Reflexivity', in Beck, U., Giddens, A. and Lash, S. (eds.), *Reflexive Modernization: Politics, Tradition and Aesthetics in the Modern Social Order*, Polity Press, Cambridge, pp.184-97.

Giddens, A. (1994c), *Beyond Left and Right: The Future of Radical Politics*, Polity Press, Cambridge.

Giddens, A. (1998a), 'Risk Society: The Context of British Politics', in Franklin, J. (ed.), *The Politics of Risk Society*, Polity Press, Cambridge, pp. 23-34.

Giddens, A. (1998b), *The Third Way: The Renewal of Social Democracy*, Polity Press, Cambridge.

Giddens, A. (1999), *Runaway World: How Globalisation is Reshaping our Lives*, Profile Books, Cambridge.

Greenfeld, K. T. (1999), 'Life on the Edge: Is Everyday Life too Dull? Why Else Would Americans Seek Risk as Never Before?', *Time Magazine*, September 6, 1999, vol.154 no.10, pp.55-62.

Grundmann, R. (1999), 'Wo steht die Risikosoziologie?', *Zeitschrift für Soziologie*, vol.28 no. 1, pp.44-59.

Habermas, J. (1975) [1973]), *Legitimationsproblemer i senkapitalismen* [Legitimation Crisis], Fremad, Copenhagen.

Habermas, J. (1981), *Theorie des kommunikativen Handelns*, Vols. 1 and 2. Suhrkamp, Frankfurt/M.

Kneer, G. and Nassehi, A. (1997), *Niklas Luhmann - introduktion til teorien om sociale systemer* [N. Luhmann - An Introduction to the Theory of Social Systems], Hans Reitzels Forlag, Copenhagen.

Lash, S. (1994a), 'Reflexivity and its Doubles: Structure, Aesthetics, Community', in U. Beck, A. Giddens and S. Lash (eds.), *Reflexive Modernization: Politics, Tradition and Aesthetics in the Modern Social Order*, Polity Press, Cambridge, pp.110-73.

Lash, S. (1994b), 'Expert-Systems or Situated Interpretation? Culture and Institutions in Disorganized Capitalism', in Beck, U., Giddens, A. and Lash, S. (eds.), *Reflexive Modernization: Politics, Tradition and Aesthetics in the Modern Social Order*, Polity Press, Cambridge, pp.198-215.

Luhmann, N. (1997), *Iagttagelse og paradoks: Essays om autopoietiske systemer* [Observation and Paradox: Essays on Autopoietic Systems], Gyldendal, Copenhagen.

Nielsen, T. Hviid (1999), 'Risici - i teknologien, i samfundet og i hovederne: Apropos risikobegreberne hos Beck, U., Giddens, A. og Luhmann', N. [Risks – in Technology, Society and the Mind. The Notions of Risk in the Work of Beck, U., Giddens, A. and Luhmann, N.], in Rasborg, K. et.al. (ed.), *Risiko, politik og miljø i det moderne samfund*, Forlaget Sociologi, Copenhagen, pp.40-62.

Rasborg, K. (1997), 'Refleksiv modernisering i risikosamfundet' [Reflexive Modernization in the Risk Society], *Dansk Sociologi*, vol.8 no.2, pp.7-20.

Rasborg, K. (1999), 'Sikkerhed, fare, risiko - et forsøg på en afklaring af det sociologiske risikobegreb' [Security, Danger, Risk - An Attempt to Clarify the Sociological Notion of Risk], in Rasborg, K. et.al. (ed.), *Risiko, politik og miljø i det moderne samfund*, Forlaget Sociologi, Copenhagen, pp.17-39.

Rasborg, K. (2000), 'Velfærdsstat og civilsamfund i risikosamfundet' [The Welfare State and Civil Society in the Risk Society], Roskilde, Roskilde University Press, pp.1-30 (forthcoming).

Seippel, Ø. (1998), 'Risikosamfunnet - en teoretisk og empirisk kritikk' [Risk Society - A Theoretical and Empirical critique], *Tidsskrift for Samfunnsforskning*, vol.39 no.3, pp.411-45.

Wynne, B. (1996), 'May the Sheep Safely Graze? A Reflexive View of the Expert-Lay Knowledge Divide', in Lash, S., Szerszynski, B. and Wynne, B. (eds.), *Risk, Environment and Modernity: Towards a New Ecology*, Sage, London, pp.44-83.

3 Early Reflexive Modernity: The Differentiation of Political Reflexivity

GORM HARSTE

This chapter analyses the political reflexivity of modern society in the form of historical questions. It discusses modern political and social theory on the touchstone of historical sociology and conceptual history. If modern democratic states can be defined as states determined by the reflexivity of a self-determinant autonomous will-formation, two questions arise: Is the reflexivity of autonomous will-formation a recent modern phenomenon? Or is political reflexivity in the strong autonomous form a much earlier phenomenon predating the democratic form of modern states?

The central these of Ulrich Beck's theory is, firstly, that we actually experience a de-differentiation of functional sub-systems because of problems emerging in risk society; and secondly, that de-differentiation dissolves politics in a classical modern sense but paves the way for a new politics of reflexivity (Beck, 1993, 1994, 1997). This conception presupposes strong notions about what is meant by the notions of 'modernity', 'reflexivity' and 'differentiation'. However, I feel uncomfortable with the rather unanalysed historical presuppositions inherent in Beck's analysis.

I will therefore contest Beck's much-discussed thesis of 'reflexive modernization' (Beck, 1994). The problem is not that it overestimates the concept of reflexivity. Rather I will argue that it underestimates the constitutive impact that reflexivity has had on the construction of modernity. Hence, it also underestimates the concept 'modern'. Modernity without reflexivity is the more narrow notion implied in the term 'modernization', according to which social processes could be conceived as non-reflexive and external to human action, as if instrumentality and technological growth were the central factors leading to contemporary society.[1] This conception, however, underestimates the social and cooperative organisation of modernity.

In his demonstration of 'reflexive modernization', Ulrich Beck displays a criticism of the unilinear modernization thesis. The term 'reflexive modernization' has become widely known following its use as the title of the influential book he edited together with Anthony Giddens and Scott Lash after the World Congress of Sociology in 1994. In the first pages, he quotes the context of the famous phrase: 'All that is solid melts into air', a phrase used as the title for an influential diagnosis of modernity written by Marshall Berman in 1984. Karl Marx wrote this phrase in 1848; similar citations are common to the founding fathers of sociology and can, for instance, be found in the writings of Émile Durkheim (1930, p.405.). In fact, similar quotations can be found all the way down in history back to Homer's description of Thebes.

Since the so-called 'Querelle entre les anciens et les modernes' at the end of the 17th century, the idea that reflection and reflexivity went along with modern history has been influential: Temporality entered in time as change.[2] Change implied contingency, new decisions and thus, new possibilities for perfection, reasonable ordering and reflexivity.

Kant referred to the way ideas about 'reason of state' were transformed into a new kind of reflexivity of the legal form of society paving the way for modern democratic states. Thus, if, reflexivity is an extremely recent social phenomenon, as Beck suggests, then we can hardly speak of a reasonable democratic state formation. Classical state construction would be purely absolutist, if not despotic, completely dependent on a non-reflexive sovereign lawgiver. If, however, reflexivity was constitutive of the institutional build-up of European states as well as reinforced by it, then we should not expect a reflexive transformation to follow a new kind of de-differentiation of modern society, as does Ulrich Beck.[3]

In this article, I address the question when modernity turned reflexive, what it meant and for whom? First, I will contest the conventional wisdom, i.e. that reflexive modernity is a very recent phenomenon evolving since the 1960s. At the end of the article, I shall balance the account: what kind of reflexivity has changed? Let me begin, however, with a more in depth description of the reflexive modernization thesis.

I. Beck's Critique of Luhmann's 'Differentiation' Thesis

Ulrich Beck and Anthony Giddens has advocated the term 'reflexive modernization'. Beck, as usual, defines the concept in several ways:

> 'Reflexive modernization' means the possibility of a creative (self-) destruction for an entire epoch: that of industrial society [...] Reflexive modernization means first the dis-embedding and second the re-embedding of industrial social forms by another modernity (Beck, 1994, p.2).[4]

Beck's use of Luhmann's classic distinction between *reflection* and *reflexivity* is important insofar as the concept 'reflexive modernization'

> does not imply (as the adjective 'reflexive' might suggest) *reflection*, but (first) *self-confrontation* [...]This type of confrontation of the bases of modernization with the consequences of modernization should be clearly distinguished from the increase of knowledge and scientization in the sense of self-reflection on modernization. Let us call the autonomous, undesired and unseen, transition from industrial to risk society *reflexivity* (to differentiate it from and contrast it with *reflection*) (Beck, 1994, pp.5-6).[5]

Now Beck tries to use this Luhmannian distinction *against* Luhmann's theory of a modernity of functional differentiated systems:

> Why should modernity be exhausted in autonomization and culminate, of all things, in 'self-referentiality' as Luhmann argues? And why should it not find new and fertile grounds in focusing on the opposite, i.e. specialization on interrelationships, on contextual understandings and on cross-boundary communication? (Beck, 1994, p.24).

The differentiations between the functional sub-systems of law, economy, research, mass-media, art, love, military, religion, etc. constitute, according to Luhmann, the risky undertaking upon which modernity is based. These subsystems are structurally coupled, but they are not symmetrical, they are paradoxical, even conflictual, and they are what we have, thus, they are risky: We cannot dismiss them; and we can only change them by their own means, or make new sub-systemical self-referential codes. They are like a convoy of supertankers, their speed is high and their weight enormous, they cannot turn easily, and they are probably not sailing in the same direction, perhaps their course is even catastrophic (cf. Luhmann 1986, 1991, 1993). According to Luhmann, 'reflexivity' is bound to the reaction of the sub-systems against their own destinies, while 'reflection' is the operation internal to the single sub-system towards its environment.

Beck questions this and proposes, that the rules of the sub-systems might be altered when confronted with their own fate; across or between the sub-systems, rules are reflected whenever they confront the way in which particular disasters do not fit into their categorically pre-determined treatments. This especially applies to the case of ecological politics, which, still according to Beck, is a kind of politics 'reinventing' politics in the sense, that the rules, codes and categories we use in distributions of goods and risks are re-activated and altered. Hence, such politics is turned into sub-politics which questions pregiven classifications over and over in daily life, as well as in thousands of sub-governmental committees, specialized in bringing together *different* experts (engineers, biologists, politicians, journalists, priests and even sociological experts in the point of view of everyday-life). This sub-governmental neo-corporatism re-invents politics in the sub-systems of modern society:

> The distinction between official politics and sub-politics, which is oriented to the systemic structure of society, must therefore be contrasted with the distinction between simple (rule-directed) and reflexive (rule-altering) politics (Beck, 1994, p.36).

These sub-political activities form a (de)central *locus* of reflection, thus re-entering into the reflexivity, hence the concept of 'reflexive' modernization. Policies, rules and regulations are reflected, i.e. reorganised, reformed and readapted in the particular situations of everyday decisions questioning the individuality of how to do what by whom and why.

II. Reflection and Reflexivity in Early Modernity

Now we may ask, is all this correct? And to what degree? Is it a new phenomenon that modernity turns reflexive? Is it a recent phenomenon that the distinctions operating *in* society are reflected by society, or, are not the distinctions themselves conditions for the 'operation of reflection'?[6] Were not reflexivity, reflection and re-entered reflection built into the construction of modernity? In this perspective let me briefly discuss a classical experience of reflection followed by a classical experience of reflexivity.

The experience of reflection

Reflection is defined as 'an operation by which the system indicates itself in contrast to its environment' (Luhmann, 1995, p.444). As such, reflection was selected, stabilised and institutionalised (Luhmann, 1975, p.153) in the form of a social system by the interpretations of a central perspective learned by

Europeans since the days of Colbert, Louis XIV and Vauban (cf. Foucault, 1966; Mukerji, 1997). Today, we hardly have these possibilities to project our ordered systems and central perspectives on an ordered or disordered environment: We observe disorders; which was in fact, what Colbert, too, observed when he read 'ordered' reports from the 'disordered' landscapes of France (d'Ormesson, 1975, pp.93-119).

Colbert and the state elites around him formed a(n) (e)state within the state; they invented a new kind of 'state reasoning' used to observe the environment of the state from the central perspective of Versailles (Mukerji, 1997). These observations were constructed in sociological, economical, juridical and especially military dimensions; and in Versailles their reflection even had an aesthetic dimension. Standardisations, measurements, reflections and codes of observation were placed not only on the observed, but also in the observer: The architecture of Versailles and especially its gardens and the imitated state-architecture in France and in Europe was an ordered invention of the observer as a reflection of forms: a reflexive actor.[7] It was no accident that the perspective of central state actors as Colbert and before him Richelieu followed the Renaissance subjectivisation of the observer. In philosophy, God was replaced by Descartes, and sacral knowledge by doubt.

The classical Kantian problem of judging situations (Kant, 1974 [1790], pp.87-88 (A XXIV),§§69; Guyer, 1997, chap.2) is not only, and especially not anymore, and not even at the dawn of modernity, in 1790, as much a lack of rules as it is an overwhelming set of aesthetic, legal, passionate, scientific, mediatized, economic and ecological rules and representations present in the interpretation of situations.[8] Not only the objects, the facts, are contingent on observation and interpretation, but the interpretations themselves were contingent as well (Jouanna, 1996; Harste, 2000c).

Today, we have no standards of judgement outside the already reflected standards inherent in modern society. No new norms, behaviours or social orders can emerge which can be judged according to present criteria of pre-reflexive traditions. No traditional experience is left, everything has become reflected in a movement, which began perhaps 250 years - 350 years ago, or, according to other criteria 500 years or 2800 years ago.[9]

The experience of reflexivity

Sociologically, the reflection as well as the reflexivity of social events concerns learning processes. How is learning to be learned? How will we cope with new events giving them a new form we do not yet know? And how will we know that this is known? In his classic article on 'Reflexive

Mechanism' from 1966 Luhmann elaborates the a) material as well as the b) temporal dissolution of these questions (Luhmann, 1970b, pp.92-112). One of Luhmann's most elegant, however difficult, articles is his analysis of reflexivity in the educational sub-system (Luhmann, 1981b pp.105-194).

Objectively or materially ('sachlich'), we can cope with the question of how to reflect in the old Cartesian way of questioning our thinking by means of our thinking ending up with methodological doubt. Reflection emerges in all kind of functional social systems. Religion described the complexity of the world; operating this distinction between itself and the world, it had to describe how it described the world and how it described itself; in religion this reflection should be established without losing sight of the whole world, thus turning (w)holiness into itself, leading to still more specialised reflections about ways to manage this operation.

Temporarily, the description of descriptions should be distinguished from the way in which a description stabilises itself. The learning of new learnings is a temporal procedure learning about the contingency of the world as well as the contingencies of learnings and interpretations. Before I discuss the political learning processes, I will shortly describe what is meant by learning and reflexivity in the organised learning of emerging educational systems: New semantics were invented in the 18th century in order to obtain another criterion than the upper/lower criterion of the strata which could not generate a sufficient number of well-formed and educated young men to make their way to the growing and increasingly complex administrations of the military states. However, examinations were reflected by a new set of temporal distinctions because the temporal distinction before/after re-entered in preparatory courses before the final threshold, the final before/after. Furthermore, entire systems of temporalised reflexivity invented hierarchies of learning processes and programmes in educational systems (Stichweh, 1989, 1994, pp.174-245; Green, 1990, pp.111-170).

In the educational system, the theological semantics of reflection re-entered as a question of the 'perfect' or total formation of the pupil in his reflection of the different disciplines. At the turn of the 18th century, the reflexive debate on education in Germany and France was transformed into an opposition between philanthropists' focusing on the perfection in spite of the disciplines, and the 'neo-humanists' trusting the pupils' own formation as a distanced reflection over disciplined validity claims. This opposition emerged however in the form of different proposals to the temporal reflexivity of learning systems. The philanthropists strove for an integration of the pupil as a whole human being as model for a society, while the more Kantian neo-humanist scholars advocated programmes which left the reflexivity of the pupil to his own experience of learning and his own autobiography. Their idea was that the programmes and themes could more easily be reflected, accepted and changed in the reflexivity process of the pupil, if he, as a human, was at distance to the programmes. According to them differentiation was a condition for reflexivity.

III. The Reflexivity of Differentiation

The great filtration of 'all that was solid' no doubt occurred at the end of the 18th century. Society was invented between, beyond, above and under the 'societé d'ordres', the ancient orders of the estates. Society was administered and governed, formed and reformed: The forms of Versailles penetrated everywhere. Above all, society began to be organised and reorganised. In fact, the concept 'organisation' was invented at that moment, and quite interestingly, from the beginning it was structured as a conceptual redoubled idea, as 'organisation et reorganisation'.[10]

An organisation happened to be an organisation only to the extent it could reorganise itself (Luhmann, 2000, p.327). Societies had form if they were governed and organised, in the sense that they could be reformed and changed. The most spectacular reforms known to all observers at that moment, not only in France, were the French municipal reforms introduced by the general controller François de Laverdy, in 1764 immediately after the enormously expensive Seven Years War. However, these reforms decreased the taxes even more than the ancient, basically centrally governed systems of intendants, which already in 1771 led to new reforms, proposed by Terray and Maupeou, who virtually tried to destroy the old corporations of the towns by buying their offices.

In short, the French state tried to own itself, i.e. own its offices, not only at a central but also at a local level, in the city halls and in the local courts (Chaussinand-Nogaret, Constant, Jouanna, 1994).[11] Of course, if the aim was to govern the state more effectively, i.e. to increase taxes to pay the still more expensive wars, then the paradox was that money should be dispensed in order to receive more money. Thus, offices were bought too cheaply, and local resistance among influential office-holders became too strong (Collins, 1995).

On a more general level, the almost evolutionary functionally increasing military competition in Europe, emerging in the middle of the 16th century, led to a still more intense awareness of reforms, military, financial, juridical, educational, infrastructural etc. A large number of people lived in and off the still more complex state-centred system, which evolved in order to organise and reorganise all those sub-systems. More and more civilians, the new state-citizens, were employed in the more and more numerous and still bigger departments of the state. Logistics and supply functions spread welfare initiatives to a still better governed, i.e. tax-financing, population.

Of course, when the main reason behind the increasing complexities was military, then it was not possible to lean back against tradition. The political dilemmas as to accept sacral semantics and sacral forms of legitimation as fundament to the emerging state can be observed in the writings from the Protestants Jean Bodin, François de la Noue and the Catholics Jean de Lucinge and Richelieu, who at the end of the 16th and beginning of the 17th centuries searched for new ways to reason about the state, although their method still remained a theological argumentation mixed with empirical analysis.[12] In his chapter on 'Die Reflexionstheorien der Funktionssysteme' in *Die Gesellschaft der Gesellschaft* Luhmann comments on the semantic developments in reason of state since 1600:

> The concepts of economic or scientific rationality or for a self-critical reason turn explicitly away from any binding through tradition - indeed without remarking that in this way they themselves motivate a tradition (Luhmann, 1997, p.961; my translation).

At that time, France was the superpower, militarily, politically and culturally. What happened in France was to become copied or somehow repeated in other states. Even the words, the concepts, the modes of discourse, were to be repeated and reformulated. Military systems are copy-machines, and that is probably the decisive factor in explaining and understanding the evolutionary character of the 18th century. Over and over concepts of reform, reshaping, reorganisation, *reflection* and - in the end - revolution found their place in public discourses. Reason, reflection, 'raison d'état', analysis, 'les memoires' and 'Denkschrifte' were intrinsic parts of the constitutive construction of Europe's self-organising state-systems.[13] With all the extensive written 'remonstrances' following each meeting of the estates (Jouanna, 1989, pp.281-368, 1996) and the writings of authors as - just to mention a few - Claude de Seyssel (1961 [1515]), Jean Bodin (1961 [1576]), Réné de Lucinge (1984 [1588]) and François de la Noue (1967 [1587]) at the end of the 16th century, and later on the analyses of officials such as Cardin le Bret (1631) and first-ministers such as Richelieu (1990 [1638]) and Colbert (1664, pp.69-82) or even Vauban (1988 [1709]), detailed analysis as well as methodologically reflected political science and political theory were important measures for the observations of the estate of the state. Especially in France the discussions of reform continued for decades, financial, juridical and municipal reforms were one after the other not sufficiently radical to solve all the constraints which the role as a dominating world power implied (Bordes, 1970, pp.254-345; Richet, 1973, pp.127-182; Tilly, 1994, pp.161).[14] A decade later the reformative Prime Minister of Bayern, Montgelas, even coined the term 'reorganisational fever'.

The Luhmannian distinction between 'reflection' and 'reflexivity' is adequate to describe this reform period, precisely because it distinguishes the gigantic projects of reflection as the state's internal description of society, for instance, in cartographic projects or statistics, on the one hand, and on the other hand, reflexivity as the way in which the present moment is bound to the past and react on it by reflecting new projects and plans to alter the future. This is also the reason why we see so many conceptions of 'l'esprit de corps', 'l'esprit des loix' (Montesquieu) and 'l'esprit des institutions'. Denis Richet argues that the spirit of whatever was happening always interpreted and reinterpreted events in order to filter, moderate and react in new ways. 'L'esprit' means construction, interpretation and reinterpretation of the observer. 'L'esprit' means interpretation and reinterpretation in a reflexive community of communication (Richet, 1973).[15]

So, what was reflexive social order in that period of enlightenment? It was order as re-order, by means of violence and discourse. Order was re-order, and order was to re-order. No 'belief system' could stay outside the massage of what happened to be known as 'public opinion'. Consciousness, human reflection, become swallowed and filtered by an all-penetrating discourse and conceptual reformulation of everything from laws to love. To my mind the best description of this conceptual revolution during what Reinhart Koselleck calls 'Die Sattelzeit' is this passage from his first dissertation, *Kritik und Krise*:

> Without becoming conscious about it the spirit of the 18th century civil society transformed history into a process. Inaugurating modernity, this appearance is identical with the genesis of the philosophy of history [...] Self-confidently the rising elites counted themselves among the natural assessors to the high court of reason, and they adduced evidences at different stages for all spheres of life in their proceedings. Theology, art, history, law, state and politics, eventually even reason itself were all sooner or later quoted to the bar and had to undertake the defence and justify. The spirit of civil society functioned in that court as attorney, as final court judgements - and as party which had decisive importance for philosophy of history. Progress was always already at the side of the civil judge. No one

> and nothing could escape the new justice and what did not stand up to the judgement of the civil critics was to be condemned by a moral censorship which did what had to be done in order to discriminate, thus fulfilling the judgement [...]The subjective self-justice does not count the given evidence but transforms everything historically given and history itself into an open-ended process as long as the private categories of judgements never enable to overhaul the events they helped to release (Koselleck, 1973 [1959], pp.6-7; my translation).[16]

This is all extremely Kantian, of course. Since its early days beginning around 1770 Kant's theory of judgement was extremely intertwined with the enlightenment process. Kant was the autonomous son of the reinforced reforms of Frederick the Great, with all its extreme attention on legal reforms, welfare reforms and military armament and disaster. Königsberg was the centre of the world's first wave of welfare reforms during the 're-establishment'. Kant's university was the result of these reforms, beginning in the aftermath of the Northern War (1700-1720) which lead to complete disaster in East Prussia. Everything was to be rebuilt in that peripheral part of Europe, which was also a transition camp, to a still more reformed Russia.

Enlightenment was somehow the functional implication of the increasing complexities of what later came to be called 'absolutism'.[17] The term 'absolutism' is not very adequate. Was Sweden absolutist, was England, was France?[18] I will propose the more appropriate concept of 'self-organising state-systems'. Such systems were systems of still higher reflection. They operated with descriptions of their environment inside their systems. They had environments not only external to them but also internal. The environments were codified and recodified according to standards, descriptions, classifications of tax-levels, needs, quality of soil, age of population.[19] According to philosophies of reasonability the environment was codified as 'common good', as 'bien ordonée' and 'heureux', as perfectibility or imperfectibility of human beings, desires, language and principles of language. New codes, principles and problems emerged as to hold a person together as one who is 'in-divided' and divided between reason, duty, passion, between citizens equal to and different from others, between 'moi' and 'moi-même'.

These reflexive concerns were not only peripheral to those who ruled in the name of absolute eternity. They were also written, studied and discussed by some of the most central figures even in the early Enlightenment period, above all, of course, King Frederick the Great,[20] the court president Charles Montesquieu and chancellor Henri-François d'Aguesseau.

The way many of these reflexive writings operated could, according to Beck and Luhmann, be described with the concept of reflexivity: They reacted with systematic descriptions of past social evolutions in order to rearrange and reform. Let me take d'Aguesseau as an example. His considerations constituted legal meta-communications about the organisational construction of Early Modern France. Above, reflection was understood as a cognitive description of societal descriptions. Reflexivity is a temporal attempt to reform given forms. This is exactly what d'Aguesseau intended, planned and began to implement.

D'Aguesseau's philosophy, 100 years before Hegel, seems quite Hegelian. He describes societal reflexivity in an ideal form in a reaction against all the wars of the self-organising state-system in Europe. His younger writings, such as his annual speeches at the opening of the high courts in Paris, held from 1693-1716, proposed the ideal-type of the 'Magistrate', the judicial officer. As if a morally complete official could interpenetrate the war-machine of the state super powering gigantic wars as the War of the Spanish Succession. After having organised a number of penetrating supply- and food-programmes during the starvation years 1709-1710 and important tax-reforms doing some distributive justice to the sheer inequalities of wealth d'Aguesseau might have become somewhat disillusioned facing the weight of almost despotic power. Hence, when he became chancellor in 1717, after a few years of conflicts, he renounced the political role, but began to elaborate the foundations of the later so famous legal reforms, which was concluded many years later with the 'Code Civil' in 1804. He drew the basic constitution of a differentiated 'droit public' and described the way adequate civil servants should be educated. The philosophical character of his endeavours also probably seems to recognise the need for a reflection at distance from contingencies. He was chancellor 1717-1751 and dominated legal differentiation in the French super-power through early Enlightenment. His 600 page *Metaphysical Meditations* are lengthy, elaborated analyses of forms of reflexive reasoning, written between 1722 and 1726, in early Enlightenment and followed by a shorter and elegant philosophical treatise on natural law, *L'institution du droit public*.

When chancellor d'Aguesseau began his project of a recodification of the French 'état de justice', morally according to natural law and politically to balance the financial departments, he had to investigate how committed reasonable humans could be in their duties towards themselves. Were they supposed only to follow interests, as Hobbes thought? Or, could they rely on pregiven customs and manners? Could they rely on principles of free will, distancing every passionate interest? Were they alone, and was will a particular phenomenon?

D'Aguesseau's central argument of rule-following in will's commitment to itself - and will is always committed if will is in fact willing - is that the 'fright of judgement' is always asking for witnesses and is in principle open to a universal 'Peuple entier'. This is simply because humans are 'instructed by nature itself to frighten the inner judge' (d'Aguesseau, 1759, p.506) and because:

> He will owe justice to himself & not in order to have some reputation in the spirit of others. If he frightens censorship, he doubts even more that of his consciousness; & he will never put himself into a state in which he could not *without horror face himself* to speak with one of our great poets (d'Aguesseau, 1759, p.505).[21]

Of course, this comes close to Kant's argument for an autonomous morality. Both reflect what in contemporary philosophy is known as the later Wittgenstein's 'private language'-argument: Is it possible to follow a rule alone (Kant, 1790, §§6-22; Harste, 1994, pp.56-68). No, so what does it mean to be alone? As to D'Aguesseau, the 'moi-même' transcends the 'moi' with the help of God - and speech, 'la parole':

> The use of speech, which has not been accorded only to man, will itself suffice to demonstrate that he is born for society. That is the channel through which God has given him the mean to communicate his thoughts and sentiments to his associates [ses semblables] (d'Aguesseau, 1759, p.468).

God is present in d'Aguesseau's writings, but it is Malebranche's God, i.e. a God who serves as a principle to structure nature and life as some object possible to understand for man.

The model of the judge, the judicial court and the discourse of the court was central. As King Louis XV was minor, D'Aguesseau was, *de facto*, the supreme judge in the French superpower, his career proceeded all the way through all the highest institutions. He was the leader of the formally most central institutions, the seldom but powerful meetings of the 'lit de justice' and the more regularly meetings in 'les conseil du roi'. However, he was under strong pressure from the financial and military departments as well as from ancient privileged nobles. According to d'Aguesseau, court language was to be regulated, it should follow principles, valid to all. So rhetoric, intrigues and interests might play their game, but the game could find its' laws, positive laws and behind them the constitutive laws of natural law.

At that time, this court-model was central to the enlightenment in France; and the reason is simple. The lawyers and the court officials formed an enormous stratum of citizens rising to nobilising positions. Remember, that Ulrich Beck located 'sub-politics' into decentred governmental agencies, committees, thousands of meetings and expert-groups. In the period of early reflexive modernity, administration was not divided into specific jurisdictions, administration was rarely departmentalised; rather, administration was exercised in collegial groups, small bodies of 5 to 20 persons. Here deliberation followed procedures of argumentation and above all intrigues, rhetoric, alliances, jokes and moralising norms of what was communicable and what was not communicable. Courtesy was as intriguing as it was polite and respectful.

It was into that undifferentiated mess of communication that d'Aguesseau - 25 years before Montesquieu! - interfered with the idea of a constitution separating and departmentalising the powers, not only according to their material communication or to validity claims of truth, but also to social validity claims of justice and morality. D'Aguesseau's formula was this:

> It is evident that three kinds of sentiments concur to form the impression of fear that the consideration of the legislator as such makes on our mind.
>
> 1. The knowledge we have of the constant and recognised truth of his power.
> 2. The idea we form of the justice with which he exercises power.
> 3. The persuasion we have of the extension of the power or its force and the impossibility of resisting it.
>
> In one word, certitude of authority, justice of authority, extension of authority; these are the three characters which unified make the legislator really redoubtable and the efficacity of his laws are always proportional to the degree in which he possesses these three characters (d'Aguesseau, 1759, pp.485-486).[22]

These powers could only unify at an infinite, unlimited creature, God; but men as well as kings are limited creatures and have to separate powers.

In my reading, d'Aguesseau's idea and plan was that courts and administrative bodies should follow procedures of truth and justice. Administrative financial constraints on the one hand and ancient aristocratic politics of privileges on the other reduced the courts' political conditions for manoeuvres. By withdrawing the juridical reflections of central court from the political scene a new space opened for a more pure political debate at the centre between administrative, financial, juridical and intellectual circles.[23] Later this became a space for both a new public opinion and for a completely new institution which was not an assembly of the estates nor a politically reformed high court ('parlement') but the national assembly.

The members of the juridical bodies formed the core of the public opinion and knew how to address that opinion. They formed what Karl-Otto Apel, talking about developments of public opinion in our present time, has called 'the public sphere of the thousand conferences'. Displaying another aspect of the rather aesthetic picture drawn by Habermas in *Strukturwandel der Öffentlichkeit,*[24] the courts were centres of rhetoric *and* procedural deliberation and argumentation. During the 18th century their procedures reflected less and less noble manners of interaction and still more the universal morals of the two general maxims, 'deux maximes générales', in 'la société civile', which thus becomes the whole society of mankind, 'la Société entiere du Genre humain'. D'Aguesseau expressed the well-known 'golden rule' of morality in this way:[25]

> Don't do unto others as you wouldn't they should do unto you. Do unto others as you would they should do unto you (D'Aguesseau, 1759, p.551).

The more constitutive form of the second maxim includes a principle of communication between 'men as equal to me' ('les hommes comme mes semblables'):

> Equally I should always act for their advantage, as I desire that they always act for mine, as we reciprocally are obliged to do when we consult only our mutual needs (D'Aguesseau, 1759, p.477).

This is a reciprocal principle of commitment. Remark that d'Aguesseau talks about the form of the *will* as a phenomenon beyond the power subject but not only subject to God. Will is objectively committed to an empire of reason ('l'empire de la raison' (D'Aguesseau, 1759, pp.529, 530) to be distinguished from everybody's will ('les volontés de tous les membres').[26] However 'reason itself has no power to establish & conserve a state to which only the path of authority can lead.'(D'Aguesseau, 1759, p.532).

D'Aguesseau's point was that the departmentalisation of government led to a free reflexivity of another order, in individuals, among individuals, in society as such, because reflexivity as reflexive 'raisonnement' was differentiated from the strict juridical positive codes, administrative codes and political codes.

IV. The Self-Reference of Reflexivity: Immanuel Kant

I will not discuss whatever reflexive notions signified during the culmination of the French Enlightenment. From Montesquieu and Voltaire to Diderot and Rousseau, this is all well known and forms the core of most analyses of Enlightenment thought.

The later, more known and still unsurpassed philosophies of reflexive thought were elaborated during the short and extremely intensive break-up from about 1770 to 1820. Still, reflexive judgement is to be defined with Immanuel Kant in his theory of judgement from 1790:

> Judgement is the capacity to think the particular contained in the universal. If the universal (the rule, principle, or law) is given, then the judgement which subsumes the particular under it is determinant. Meanwhile, if only the particular is given to which a universal is to be found, then the judgement is only reflective (Kant, 1974, p.87) (A XXIII-XXIV).[27]

Reflexive judgement is a capacity; and it is a capacity to think and to find. Find what? Find universality in the particular. Reflexive judgement is the capacity to invent possible concepts for a given particular. In the earlier published introduction, Kant defines what it is to reflect, it 'is to compare and combine a given representation either with other representations or with one's cognitive faculties, with respect to a concept thereby made possible' (Guyer, 1997, p.35).

Now Kant does not only define reflexive judgement, such definitions are well known since antiquity. He elaborated a theory of judgement in particular situations.[28] Central to Kant is that the 'reflexive operation' (§40) is bound to communication without allowing the sense of communication to stop inside the prison of communication. Judgement is free because of communication and beyond communication. Judgement is bound to reasonability, but reasonable communication never exhausts the particular *form* of a situation. That form, however, is only revealed because of communication, but also never emptied by communication. 'Sense' is 'sense of' and 'sense that'. Today, these methods of analysis are well known from the aesthetic theories of the sublime, from theory of discourse, from philosophy of common sense and culture and from sociological theories of taste and judgements, such as those of Elias and Bourdieu.

According to Kant's social and political theory much can be said about reflection and reflexivity if we take into account his philosophy of history and consequently his theory of teleology of natural history and civilisation history. When we observe history, i.e. first, throwing a glance at the present by separating it from the past, we not only classify and register, we also have reflexive ideas about the complexities and the entire situations we observe. This, of course, is an indispensable hermeneutic fact. We can also call it a fact of functional self-reference: Reflexivity is here, now, and how would reflection in history have been if it should have given way to such a reflexivity?[29] Which forms have been present in history? How was judgement possible in history? Which self-references were possible in history? How could communication refer to itself in history, with the risks and reflections embedded into all kinds of communications being blind to their own blind spots? With these few methodological devices to conceptual history, I make my standpoint clear, there is *no* opposition between a critical hermeneutic method and a systemic method, they both have to rely on the way the reflexivity/reflection distinction observes itself in history. For instance, such a fusion between functional and hermeneutic methods seems obvious in the conceptual history undertaken by Koselleck and Luhmann.[30]

A very clear analysis of the implications of Kant's (later) authorship is demonstrated by Ingeborg Maus in her Luhmannian and Habermasian approach 'Zur Theorie der Institutionalisierung bei Kant'. Her analysis follows three steps '1. From reflection to reflexivity', '2. Moral reflexivity' and '3. Reflexivity of political institutionalisation'.

From the outset, Maus demonstrates how reflexivity is built into history. 'Kant outlines a theory of institutionalisation and not of the institution' (Maus, 1992, p.249). Kant analyses the form, the structuration of the rules, because social institutions are valid and have meaning as socially important and reflected institutions. Institutions are made. 'Organisation' is probably a more suitable word. Maus conceptualises 'institution' in a manner far more precise than what is used in contemporary sociology. D'Aguesseau, however, used 'institution' in such a constitutive way. In Kant's time, 'organisation' would have been the word, and it is also the one he uses from 1790 and onwards. Organisations are organised.

'Organisation as the form of the medium social coordination' (Luhmann, 2000) implies that organisation does things. Organisation changes. And according to Maus, Kant wants to elaborate his 'Copernican revolution' in his analysis of organisation in order to observe social organisation as a social form which changes and is changed: 'Kant's philosophy makes evident that neither the phenomenal world nor the institutions are made of 'materials'

['Sachen'], but are themselves accounted to performances of a subject (Maus, 1992, p.251; my translation). Thus, Kant dismisses traditionalist views of institutions or organisations, 'bodies' as they were named up to the end of the 18th century. The idea is that organisations are *only* constituted, and thus obligatory to their members, if they are reflexive. What is undertaken in organisations is constituted as obligatory commitments *because* commitments are reflected.[31]

One could ask, what sense could it have if an organisation organised and no one observed it, no one reflected it, thought about it, felt it, attached some kind of meaning to it, etc.? Nevertheless, conservative privileged institutions could have exactly such a constitution, they could be privileged by God or tradition and thus have claims to right of resistance, as claimed by the defenders of the ancient regime at the time of Kant. In fact, detailed historical studies tell us how commitments and obligations were more discussed, more object for reflexivity and resistance at the dawn of modern ways to organise than later on, when expectations to executives were more formalised and more conventional (Jouanna, 1989, 1996). Of course, this is also why it is possible to observe an enormous literature originating from the middle of the 16th century reflecting about necessities and contingencies in all kinds of official commitments among officers and commissioners. From Jean Bodin to d'Aguesseau, the central question was how it is possible to bind officers into the obligatory form of a legal system.

Thus, Kant as to Bodin and D'Aguesseau earlier, organised modernity is only possible as reflexive modernity because modern (republican) social order is organised in a 'well-orderly' way.[32] Radically reorganised modernity can be well ordered if reflexive judgement learns from past reflections of reform, what to do, and what *not* to do. Legal and organisational reforms are in principle - i.e. after a transformative period - complete reconstructions: Perhaps past principles were well alive here and there, already reflecting past reforms in a sufficiently reasonable way; but the critical judgement is here and now in the present reformative situation filtering everything inherited from the past, and asking, 'Do we have rules to coordinate future's social order?' We know from the past that reform and reorgansation *is* possible, but the present situation is new and has to be reflected upon once more. From Kant to Luhmann, we have learned that the sense of change implies that we cannot socially change everything material at one single temporal moment. Complexities have to be reduced using, for instance, legal forms.

According to Kant, legal reforms have to be constituted as modern in the strong, modernist, sense: That is, constitutions should not stay unchangeable forever in any eternity (Brandt, 1995, pp.69-86). This is one of two great differences from D'Aguesseau's plan for a constitution. For D'Aguesseau, constitution was rooted in an eternal 'droit naturel' with the constitutive mark that it consists in the difference between principles of morality and positive law. D'Aguesseau still had the Christian idea that a constitution should be the final response to an eternal perfectibility. The other difference is that d'Aguesseau was not democrat. The monarch was to be constituted, but it was still the monarch who gave the laws. This differs from the Kantian republican government. Nevertheless Svarez, the reformative author of the path-breaking Prussian general Code from 1790, was less radical than D'Aguesseau, who, contrary to Svarez, founded his constitutional plan in the idea of complete equality and freedom according to Descartes philosophy of the equality of reasoned subjects:

> Everyone has a body similar to all others: Everyone has a mind that contains equally in itself an intelligence and a will. The difference of talents, of education and of reflections might result in some kind of inequality; but there is none in their essence (D'Aguesseau, 1759 [1723], p.467; Langer, 1986, pp.86-87).

In Prussia, several of the later higher officials were, what Kant, in *Streit der Fakultäten*, called, 'good Kantians'. The ministers, von Altenstein and von Schön, pleaded for an ever reconstituting constitution. A constitution should not only lay the groundwork for a new constitution, it should even commit itself to still more reformed constitutions, as to throw itself into complex learning processes (Altenstein, 1931, p.501; Koselleck, 1967, pp.160-161; Langer, 1986, pp.81-94).

Maus' analysis of 'reflexive institutionalisation' demonstrates how Kant coped with 'reflection' and 'reflexivity' in a way parallel to the double concept of 'organisation and reorganisation' mentioned above. Luhmann claims that a basic democratic condition is that there is a kind of 're-entry' (Luhmann's term) of organisation into reorganisation, and of reorganisation into organisation (Luhmann, 2000, p.327). According to Maus, this form of modern 'reflexive' order of politics, legitimacy and state building was basic to Kant's theory. The constitutive embeddedness of reflection and reflexivity might be easier to observe as part of the organisation of differentiation during the formative process of modernity than today when we are used to observing differentiated modernity as conventional.

V. Use and Abuse of 'Reflexive' Semantics

We have now analysed reflection and reflexivity at the beginning of the Enlightenment (d'Aguesseau) and at the end (the later Kant). In both cases, the reasonability inherent in the very form of a still more complex state building was that organisation presupposed that rules and organisations could and should change. This is indeed the basic democratic idea, which gives legitimacy to legality, i.e. to the possibility that positive and, thus, changeable law had its take off during the 18th century. The paradoxical rationality herein is that stable rules can be changed, unstable rules cannot (Habermas, 1992; Luhmann, 1981a; Langer, 1986, esp. p.55ff).

Beck defines reflexive politics as 'rule-altering' politics, whereas an examination of the co-constitution of modernity and reflexive reforms reveals that there is a paradoxical plus-sum between stabilisation and change, involution and evolution, ordering and reflexivity. 'Well-ordered' society gave way to reflexivity, i.e. to society's competence to reflect upon itself by means of differentiated thematisation, criticising, planning and acting.

Why presume, as Beck does, that organisations should be single ordered classifications if they organise themselves in such a way, that they reflect themselves. This reflection is not neutral. According to Durkheim, a morally structured reflexivity is inherent in modern social order inasmuch as it leads to cooperation and coordination in organisations in which labour is divided (Durkheim, 1930 [1893]; Harste, 2000). Modern persons are bound to reflexivity whenever they have to cooperate with other persons with different specialisation, coming from different backgrounds and using different norms. Maus is perfectly correct that a normative procedure claiming the application of moral universal principles is not empty. It is, rather, a social construction of reality forming social reality into a rationalised order open to thematisation, reflection, criticism and reform.

Today, reflexivity, reflection etc. are hardly adequate concepts for these procedures. Communication, meta-communication, discourses, codification and re-codification are more suitable terms. It is too difficult to figure out exactly the theme, the criterion and the judgement if we use concepts of reflexivity and reflection in an inflationary way. Clear distinctions are necessary.[33] Perhaps it is possible to make clear distinctions between the concepts of reflection and reflexivity as does Luhmann in *Social Systems* (chap.11). However, in spite of Ulrich Beck's interesting observations, his idea of a new reflexive rule-altering politics fails dealing with history.

Notions of reflection, the reflexive and of reflexivity - with or without 'x' - might very well re-introduce what Luhmann calls old European semantics into a description of modern social order as if unity in form of reflexivity is possible. Luhmann himself defines reflexivity as the double negation of contingency in order to analyse societal self-thematisations: 'Both the necessity and the possibility of thematising society emerge as a result of society's own development' (Luhmann, 1982b, p.332). A part of a societal whole is different from that whole, in the sense that it can reflect the reflexivity of the whole into itself, - and it cannot avoid this reflection. Kant describes how the culture of reflexive judgement is part of natural history in exactly the same way, i.e., through difference rather than unity. Reflexivity is based on a differentiation between reflection and reflectivity. Relations are handled by relations.

The magic of Early Modern reflexivity is that such a harsh thing as the complex growth processes of those military states, called 'war-machines' by Charles Tilly (1992), reformed and reflected themselves so as to give way to positive law, a separation of powers, a well-ordering of their populations and a still more public opinion as to reform themselves completely. Insofar, this separation of powers or functional differentiation of early modernity is the in-between in Kant's famous statement which even serves as his epitaph: 'Two things fill my mind with still new and growing admiration and veneration the more persistently it occupies the reflection: The heaven's stars above me and the moral law in me' (Kant, 1974 [1788], A 288).

VI. What is Left? What is New?

From the beginning to the end of the Enlightenment, reforms were 'reform from above'. As Alexis de Tocqueville was the first to remark, even the French Revolution can hardly be reckoned as a 'reform from below'. Rather, it was a series of radical and for decades expected reforms to come, plus a number of uprisings and discursive restructurations of what was meant by a political society, and it is this last part that can most precisely be referred to as 'revolutionary' (Woloch, 1994; Behrens, 1985; Furet; 1989, p.16ff).

Since that moment, 'reflexive' sub-politics has not as much been a change in quality. On the contrary, observers such as Rousseau, Kant and Hegel, who were witnesses to the 'Sattelzeit', could often easier grasp the depth of what was going on than we can. Rather, I will suggest that 'reflexive' modernization is a quantitative phenomenon to the extent that 'reflexive' reorganisation, reform and reconsideration today involve far more extensive groups of people than the Enlightenment's small elite of a few thousand people. In that quantitative sense, 'reflexive' modernization has become more democratic. However, it often *seems to be the case* that the opposite applies: The size and complexity of today's state leaves the impression 'that everything can be changed, and there's nothing I can do' (Luhmann, 1970a, p.44).

Sub-politics is implied in the functional differentiations of policies, inasmuch as differentiated reflexive sub-systems open space to decentred reflexivity. The experience of instability and contingency in the reflexivity of everyday life has paradoxically become possible *because* of the systemic stabilisation of the way modern social order continues to change at a still increasing speed. Thus, we may also say: 'I can make changes to everything, and that will not change anything'.

Today, we probably have a new kind of hyper-complexity and hyper-differentiation, implying reflexive individualisation or particularisation (Luhmann, 1995, p.471). Individuals, firms and organisations striving towards recognition in social interaction or on markets have to find their own particular niche, different from all others. However, the endeavours and the learning-processes in which persons and organisations learn to find their own identity are fulfilled in the same kinds of courses offered by the same kind of consulting teams which, every second year, teach a new mode (Harste, 1997).

Nevertheless, whether striving for still more inclusion in a world without final safety or striving to escape from exclusion, each social agent turns into a decision-maker, not so much as a decision-maker who chooses but more as someone who binds him or herself into systems of commitments. To say 'choice' is just to say that societies since Odysseus have had to cope with binary poles (between Scylla and Charybdis), or even since ancient Egypt have had to say that we do things by day or by night. Decision is a binding of contingencies and commitments, that is, a binding of the social bond, 'les liens sociaux', as French thinkers and state-planners told us 300 years ago. Compared to urban enlightenment, our contemporary hyper-differentiation of everyday life is probably, on the one hand, the quantity of people involved and, on the other hand, the complexity of signs, discourses and semantics overloading the reflexive commitment in particular situations.

Finally, what about risk society? According to Beck, 'reflexive modernization' is a confrontation with the destructions of risk society. During the Enlightenment, the risk was not so much pollution, as we know it, as it was epidemics, illness and sudden death. In that sense, the risk was not an endogenous risk contingent to human decisions, but exogenous 'danger'. The risk was therefore rather lack of sub-systems. However, the extremely real risky sub-system was rather the military system (Porter, 1994;

Downing, 1992). In his brief 1784 article, 'Ideen zur einer allgemeinen Geschichte in weltbürgerlichen Absicht', Kant mentioned a danger that the military systems of his time could evolve into monsters beyond that political control beginning to be framed in phrases such as von Clausewitz' famous principle of war and politics. As is well known, the long peace after the Congress of Vienna was both stable and unstable. It continued the forced armament which had already had been a motor in European state-building for centuries, and it led to a disaster echoes of which still reverberate.

Do ecological disasters change the structure of modernity? There is no reason to believe that the ecological disruption experienced or discovered since the late 1960s will not lead to new differentiations of sub-systems. Elsewhere, I have argued that it is easy to observe a construction of a sub-system of waste. Garbage is a code, re-coded by sub-systems of, first, sewerage systems and waste containers in the middle of the 19th century, then from the 1970s still more sophisticated systems of waste disposal and waste treatment. This in turn changes our daily notions of what garbage is and is not; it selects our selections - a strong criterion for systemic stabilisation. Waste systems make room for some kinds of pollution and not for others. Furthermore, environmental law, ministries, experts, journalists, values, departments, industries etc. become ever more established. This, of course, creates yet another risk-filled system: It observes what it observes, and does not observe, that it does not observe what it does not observe (three times, - not two, not four, but three!) (Harste, 1999c, pp.158-188).

Thus, ecology might as well concern the emergence of still another sub-system than the breakdown of the whole modern construction of functionally differentiated sub-systems.[34] Environmental politics might even strengthen other sub-systems, such as the European-wide sub-systems.

There is no doubt that Beck has simply not taken into account the importance of the so-called 'communicative turn' in methodology, undertaken by, among others, Luhmann. Nor has Beck analysed the consequence of that turn for the theory of the emergence of modern functionally differentiated society: sub-systems are self-referential and autonomous to the extent that they have been able to codify their communicative codifications. Self-referential systems are not simply ordered bunches of classifications trying to regulate their environments as first level systemic institutions. They are only self-referential *and* autopoietic if their codifications are codified on a second order level.

In that sense, the emergence of functionally differentiated self-referential sub-systems is an empirical historical process in which communications are codified, and furthermore, these codes are *reflected* upon by means of second order constructions. Garbage is only poison if it cannot be coped with in sub-systems of waste disposal: That is, if garbage is defined as something which is in its wrong place - which most observers do - then it could find its place being recycled in a waste disposal system recycling it. Such a sub-system stays blind for what rests, as poison. However, perhaps even waste systems can learn how to codify dangerous waste, and perhaps even learn to learn, i.e. develop differentiated 'reflexive mechanisms'.

Money was *reflected* and codified as money to be paid for in the banking systems of Renaissance Italy and the Low Countries, as rent, interest and profit. Law was discussed, analysed, *reflected* upon and recodified as rights to have the right status. Science was subject to research and *reflected* in description of what science was and was not. These reflec*tions* were certainly reflexive, in the sense that they reflected upon their way of changing things: They confronted what had happened with new ways to let it happen.

Today, the reflexivity of modern society can be observed as a feed-back relation of a society reacting upon itself. However, reflexivity is a different phenomenon and not just a simple causally induced loop of inputs and outputs extended in time. Even the more simple reflection of society is bound to a self-observation and to the emergence of codes of self-observation and self-description. Reflexivity is the temporal condition for the stabilisation of such codes. Luhmann calls this, the temporal bindings of expectations (1991, pp.59-82). Today, we can observe such temporal bindings in economic, legal, scientific, military, waste-treatment sub-systems and other sub-systems. The actual differentiation we have obtained as a result of historical events and processes is a risky one. The risk is that the differentiation is as it is; it could be different, but it is not.

Reflexivity is part of the functional differentiation of modern society. Reflexivity as change of codified time-binding was an essential part of the separation of powers that emerged as a reaction to the risky military colonisation of Early Modern Europe.[35] That battle was not won with the Enlightenment; still, two hundred years of risky self-referential military armament should leave 'politics as the continuation of war, but with other means' (Foucault, 1997). However, the possibility to invent completely new codes structured on other premises than those dominating the, seemingly endless, military and organisational competition in the 17th and the 18th centuries was essential to the differentiation process undertaken in the 18th century. This invention and transformation of codes was undertaken by those who could observe new possibilities to form society and state in ways that made room for both new roles, positions, earnings, careers and new and more universal moralities (Bourdieu, 1998, pp.373-389). Reflexivity was essential to the structuring of modernity as reform even before democratic reflection and reflexivity emerged in the aftermath of the French revolution.

The claim that modernity experiences a reflexive turn in our contemporary decades might be correct in the simple and certainly important quantitative sense that more people get education, that more books are being published, etc. But it is a different claim to suggest that the structure of modernity turns reflexive in a manner that it has not been before. It is not a new phenomenon that social order reacts on its own structures in order to reform, reorder and reconstitute its own premises. As demonstrated with the case of some central reformers and transformers in early Enlightenment, those premises not only concern the specific codes and programmes of the sub-systems. They also concern the forms used to reflect in every sense of that word.

Notes

1 One might argue that the discussions of differences between 'modernity' and 'modernization' in the course of theoretical developments since the 1960s, has changed the concept of 'modernization' from one which included only aspects concerning an industrial revolution and not also a democratic revolution. Both were included in Parsons' (1971) rather ignored *The Systems of Modern Societies*. Broader discussions of the 'modernization' paradigm is Østerud (1978, pp.12-60) Eder (1985). Eder and with him, Habermas, have demonstrated, that the 'Moral der Kooperation', as already analysed by Durkheim, conceptualises agency in a way in which evolution and 'le fait moral' go hand in hand. However, with the instrumentalisation of 'modernization', agency is left out and opens the way to new combinations and concepts re-including agency. 'Reflexive modernization' is such a concept.

2 Jauss (1974, pp.11-66) (probably the best account of the concept 'modern' ever written). See also Gumbrecht (1983).

3 I shall use the term reflexive in a broad undefined way and stick to the conceptual distinction between reflection and reflexivity elaborated in the beginning of section I. Later, I will criticize possible abuses of term.

4 The article is more elaborated in Beck, 1993, p.57ff.

5 Luhmann describes the distinction in his 'The Self-Thematization of Society' (1982, pp.324-362).

6 Kant (1974 [1790]) coined the term 'the operation of reflection' in §§ 39-41. Cf. Kant (1974 [1781] B 316-348).

7 This should be compared to Kant's classical definition of reflection as consideration ('Überlegung') not only of the objects of knowledge but on the subjective conditions of judgement, cf. Kant (1974 [1781] p.B 316ff).

8 Before early modern states standardized social order, what counted as rules, legal jurisdictions and authority was manifold, complex without homogeneous and codified reductions of codes. Historians such as Reynolds (1996) and Jouanna (1996) are among those who have recently demonstrated how non-standardized pre-modern social (dis)order

was conceived. Remark: Order was observed disordered! The most significant exposition of this disorder of crosscutting jurisdictions is Bodin (1961 [1576], chapter 9, pp.161-211).

9 The long period is proposed by authors as divergent as Durkheim, in his sociology of tribal religion, or Adorno and Horkheimer going back to Odysseus in their *Dialektik der Aufklärung* from 1944, or Derrida in his *Grammatology*. Luhmann too, suggests that there is no way back to judgements before written media; however, he furthermore claims that evolution since that moment is improbable and, empirically, open to historical contingencies.

10 The classic reference is Sieyès (1982 [1789]). The best general documentation of this, which I know about, might be Winter (1931) and also Knemeyer (1983). The conceptual history is described by Böckenförde and Dohrn-van Rossum (1978, pp.519-622). Cf. Eder (1985, pp.329-356). However, Eder's analysis, brilliant as it is, does downplays the importance of organisational and military undertakings in favour of legal reforms. Unfortunately, this has become extremely common among leading German political theorists, especially since the Nazi period.

11 The most important studies of this process are Mousnier's (1971, 1974, 1980) magistral works.

12 Jouanna (1989, pp.28-368); commentaries to Bodin usually take a position either in favour of or against his modernity; even the turn in his writings towards absolutism give way to opposite interpretations.

13 Cf. some of the best studies of the 'reflective' so-called absolutism; Stolleis (1990); Mandrou (1997); Chaunu (1982).

14 Tilly (1994, p.161ff), however, is far too brief in his elaboration of the reform movements, see rather Collins (1995, p.180ff).

15 Concerning the term 'esprit' cf. Kantorowicz (1957).16 Koselleck's description could also serve as a summary of Cassirer's *Die Philosophie der Aufklärung*, (1998 [1932]) in which especially the first chapter is one long discussion of the French Enlightenment as a reflective period. The difference between Koselleck and Cassirer is that Cassirer stays inside a history of ideas and reflection, while Koselleck's conceptual history is a more sociological analysis of reflexivity.

16 Koselleck's description could also serve as a summary of Cassirer's *Die Philosophie der Aufklärung*, (1998 [1932]) in which especially the first chapter is one long discussion of the French Enlightenment as a reflective period. The difference between Koselleck and Cassirer is that Cassirer stays inside a history of ideas and reflection, while Koselleck's conceptual history is a more sociological analysis of reflexivity.

17 Generally I find the best account in Behrens (1985).

18 Bonney's (1994) account *Absolutism* demonstrates how the concept 'absolute' emerged as a theological concept used to legitimate a certain kind of monarchical government and a specific position of the monarch towards law, but it did not describe central administration as such.

19 For instance Vauban (1988) [1709]) who of course also reflects his tax proposals in a theological part considering their constitution. The most classic administrative 'reflections' are probably Colbert's (1975) [1698]) instructions, for instance *Les mémoires des intendants pour l'instruction du duc de Bourgogne* The most famous analysis of all this is, at the moment, Foucault's (1991, pp.87-104) article 'Governmentality'.

20 Cf. Hauser (1987), esp. pp.1-93; cf. the two short examples of Friederich's (1987, 1986) works.

21 For a further introduction to D'Aguesseau's position among French elites, see Harste (1999). and more extensive: Storez (1996). I have not found any translations of d'Aguesseau into English, thus the citations are all translated by me.

22 John Locke's idea of a division of power is hardly a division based on an autonomous legal sub-system in the sense of d'Aguesseau, Montesquieu and Kant. The English Common Law tradition gave no material background to such an idea, and Locke even restricted any possibility of a symmetric division when he wrote that 'Between an Executive Power in being, with such a Prerogative, and a Legislative that depends upon his will for their convening, there can be no judge on Earth...', (1963)[1680/1689], pp.425-426). As well documented by Hintze, O., it must be added that the division between chambers, chancelleries and high courts of estate representatives has long traditions, although the chambers increased in still more complex systems with the so-called 'military revolution' from the 16th century onwards. Thus, the traditional system of checks and balances has to be distinguished from a formal separation of powers.

23 This probably unintended consequence of the transformation of law for a pure modernity of political reflection is not observed in Campbell's, P. (1996) (perhaps too) detailed book.

24 Habermas (1962, spec. chap.2). Note how much Habermas was inspired by Koselleck's analysis of reflexivity.

25 Cf. Luhmann (1980, pp.72-161); Elias, N. (1981). Detailed descriptions of the procedures can be found in Mousnier, R. (1974, 1980) and Bluche, F. (1960).

26 Riley has not observed the role of d'Aguesseau in the philosophical development between Malebranche and Rousseau (Riley 1978). By the way I have found no other commentary to the philosophical developments in early Enligthenment which has observed the philosophical substance in d'Aguesseau' writings, for instance neither in Derathé (1950) nor Cassirer (1932).

27 I have elaborated my interpretation at length in Harste (1994, pp.49-116). Cf. Harste, Mertens, Scheffer (1996).

28 A recent exposition of Kant's theory of reflective judgement is found in Guyer (1997), see the conceptual discussion pp.29-59. A brilliant actualisation of Kant's theory is Ferry (1990), esp.chap.III, pp.111-160.

29 This is, I would say, the pure classical form of the distinction reflection/reflexivity.

30 For a more detailed discussion see Harste (1999); still hesitating about the identical pre-conditions of functionalism and hermeneutics Harste (1996, pp.169-183).

31 This was why the concept of 'spiritus corpus' was so important to the medieval church. It was the notion used to commit its delegates at a moment when other mediums of trust, such as power, money, law and war, were impossible or too costly.

32 Another excellent treatment of this part of Kant's social philosophy is Langer (1986).

33 Cf. Habermas' critique of 'Reflection' as concept in the *Nachwort* (1973, pp.411).

34 This breakdown is postulated by Beck (1997, pp.52-65), (for a less interesting Luhmann-critique see also Beck (1988, pp.166-176). A Danish version of the article is published as 'Subpolitik' in Aagaard, K. (1999), in which my somewhat more substantial defence of a Luhmannian approach to risks also appears (pp.158-188).

35 Death numbers are often estimates; the War of Spanish Succession are by some calculated to have cost France 4 million lives of which by far the major part was due to starvation an epidemic diseases as result of war. In East Prussia about 40% of the population disappeared and farms and lands began to suffer severely.

References

Aagaard, K. et al. (eds.) (1999), *Risiko, politik og miljø i det moderne samfund*, Forlaget Sociologi, Copenhagen.

Aguesseau, H.-F. (1759), *L'institution au droit public*, in *Oeuvres T.1*, Paris.

Altenstein (1931), 'Denkschrift, 1806', in G. Winter (eds.), *Die Reorganisation des Preussischen Staates unter Stein und Hardenberg*, Verlag Hirzel, Leipzig.

Beck, U. (1988), *Gegengifte: Die organisierte Unverantwortlichkeit*, Suhrkamp, Frankfurt am Main.

Beck, U. (1993), *Die Erfindung des Politischen. Zu einer Theorie reflexiver Modernisierung*, Suhrkamp, Frankfurt am Main.

Beck, U. (1994), 'The Reinvention of Politics', in Beck, U., A. Giddens and Lash, S., *Reflexive Modernization*, Polity Press, Cambridge.

Beck, U. (1997), 'Subpolitics, Ecology and the Disintegration of Institutional Power', in *Organization and Environment*, vol.10, no.1.

Behrens, C.B.A. (1985), *Society, Government and Enlightenment: The Experience of 18th Century France and Prussia*, Thames and Hudson, London.

Bluche, F. (1960), *Les Magistrats de Paris au 18ieme siecle*, PUF, Paris.

Böckenförde, E.-W. and G. Dohrn-van Rossum (1978), 'Organ, Organismus, Organisation, politische Körper', in Brunner, O., Koselleck, R. (eds.), *Geschichtliche Grundbegriffe Band*, Klett-Cotta, Stuttgart.

Bodin, J. (1961 [1576]), *Les six livres de la République*, Scientia, Aalen.

Bonney, R. (1994), *Absolutism*, PUF, Paris.

Bordes, M. (1970), *L'Administration provinciale et municipale en France au XVIIIe siecle*, SEDES, Paris.

Bourdieu, P. (1998), *The State Nobility*, Polity Press, Cambridge.

Brandt, R. (1995), 'Das Problem der Erlaubnisgesetze im Spätwerk Kants', in Höffe, O. (ed.), *Immanuel Kant. Zum ewigen Frieden*, Akademie Verlag, Berlin.

Campbell, P. (1996), *Power and Politics in Old Regime France, 1720-45*, Routledge, London.

Cassirer, E. (1998 [1932]), *Die Philosophie der Aufklärung*, Meiner Verlag, Hamburg.

Chaunu, P. (1982), *La Civilisation de l'Europe des Lumieres*, Flammarion, Paris.

Chaussinand-Nogaret, G., Constant, B. and Jouanna, A. (1994), *Histoire des élites en France*, Pluriel, Paris.

Claude de Seyssel(1961[1515]), *La Monarchie de la France*, Librairie d'Argences, Paris.

Colbert, J.-B. (1975 [1664]), 'Mémoire pour messieurs les maitres des requêtes' in Comité des Travaux historiques', *Les mémoires des intendants*, Bibliothèque Nationale, Paris.

Colbert, Jean-Baptiste (1975 [1698]), *Les mémoires des intendants pour l'instruction du duc de Bourgogne*, Bibliotheque Nationale, Paris.

Collins, J. (1995), *The State in Early Modern France*, Cambridge University Press, Cambridge.

Derathé, R. (1988 [1950]), *Jean-Jacques Rousseau et la science politique de son temps*, Vrin, Paris.

Downing, B. (1992), *The Military Revolution and Political Change*, Princeton University Press, Princeton, N.J.

Durkheim, E. (1930 [1893]), *De la division du travail*, PUF, Paris.

Eder, K. (1985), *Geschichte als Lernprozeß? Zur Pathogenese politischer Modernität in Deutschland*, Suhrkamp, Frankfurt am Main.

Elias, N. (1981), *Die höfische Gesellschaft*, Luchterhand, Berlin.
Ferry, L. (1990), *Homo Aestheticus. L'invention du gout à l'Âge démocratique*, Grasset, Paris.
Foucault, M. (1966), *Les mots et les choses*, Gallimard, Paris.
Foucault, M. (1991), 'Governmentality', in Burcell, G. et al. (eds.), *The Foucault Effect*, University of Chicago Press, Chicago.
Foucault, M. (1997), *'Il faut défendre la société'*, Seuil, Paris.
Furet, F. (1978), *Penser la Revolution française*, Folio, Paris.
Furet, F. (1988) *La Revolution*, Hachette, Paris.
Friedrich, the II (1986), *Friederich der Große und die Philosophie*, Reclam, Stuttgart.
Friedrich, the II (1987), *Das politische Testament 1752*, Reclam, Stuttgart.
Giddens, A. (1994), 'Living in a Post-Traditional Society', in Beck, U., Giddens, A. and Lash, S. (eds.), *Reflexive Modernity*, Polity Press, Cambridge.
Gumbrecht, H.-U. (1983), 'Modern, Modernität, Moderne' in Brunner, O., Conze, W. and Koselleck, R.(eds.), *Geschichtliche Grundbegriffe* Band 4, Klett-Cotta, Stuttgart.
Guyer, P. (1997), *Kant and the Claims of Taste*, Cambridge University Press, Cambridge.
Habermas, J. (1962), *Strukturwandel der Öffentlichkeit*, Luchterhand, Berlin.
Habermas, J. (1973), 'Nachwort', in *Erkenntnis und Interesse*, Suhrkamp, Frankfurt am Main.
Habermas, J. (1981), *Theorie des kommunikativen Handlens Band 1*, Suhrkamp, Frankfurt am Main.
Habermas, J. (1985), 'Die Normative Gehalt der Moderne', in Habermas, J., *Der philosophische Diskurs der Moderne*, Suhrkamp, Frankfurt am Main.
Habermas, J. (1992), *Fakticität und Geltung*, Suhrkamp, Frankfurt.
Harste, G. (1986), *Kann das Diskursprinczip mit einem Organisierungsprinzip verbunden werden? Über Demokratie und Komplexität*, Paper to NopSa-conference, Finland.
Harste, G. (1994), 'Kommunikation, naturtelologi og politik i Kants 'Kritik der Urteilskraft'' in Harste, G. (ed.), *Kompleksitet og Dømmekraft: Immanuel Kant om politik, æstetik og natur*, Nordisk Sommeruniversitet, Aalborg.
Harste, G. (1996), 'Kant und Luhmann über Teleologie in politischer Kommunikation und Natur', in Harste, G. et al. (eds.), *Immanuel Kant über Natur und Gesellschaft*, Odense University Press, Odense.
Harste, G. (1997), *Modernitet og Organisation*, Politisk Revy, Copenhagen.
Harste, G. (1999a), 'Efter oplysningen - om autonomi og autopoiesis hos Habermas og Luhmann', *Philosophia*, vol.26 no.3-4.
Harste, G. (1999b), ''L'État c'est nous'', Paper, Department of Political Science, University of Aarhus.
Harste, G. (1999c), 'Risikosamfundets systemdifferentiering', in Nielsen, K. Aa. et al. (eds.), *Risiko, Politik og Miljø i det moderne samfund*, Forlaget Sociologi, Copenhagen.
Harste, G. (2000a), 'Post-industrialism, Cultural and Contemporary Diagnosis' in Andersen, H. and Kaspersen, L.-B. (eds.), *Classical and Modern Social Theory*, Blackwell, Oxford.
Harste, G. (2000b), 'Introduktion og fortolkning', in Durkheim, E., *Om den sociale arbejdsdeling*, H. Reitzel, Copenhagen.
Harste, G. (2000c), 'Samfundsteoriens rolle i samfundet' in *Distinktion*, nr. 1, Aarhus.
Hauser, O. (ed.) (1987), *Friederich der Grosse in seiner Zeit*, Böhlau, Köln.
Jauß, H. R. (1974), 'Litterarische Tradition und gegenwärtiges Bewußtsein der Modernität' in *Lieteraturgeschichte als Provokation*, Suhrkamp, Frankfurt.
Jouanna, A. (1989), *Le devoir de la révolte*, Fayard, Paris.
Jouanna, A. (1996), *La France du XVIe siècle*, PUF, Paris.
Kant, I. (1974 [1781]), *Kritik der reinen Vernunft*, Suhrkamp, Frankfurt am Main.

Kant, I. (1974 [1788]), *Kritik der praktischen Vernunft*, Suhrkamp, Frankfurt am Main.

Kant, I. (1974 [1790]), *Kritik der Urteilskraft, Werkausgabe Band X*, Suhrkamp, Frankfurt am Main.

Kantorowicz, E. (1957), *The King's Two Bodies*, Princeton University Press, Princeton.

Knemeyer, F.-L. (1983), 'Beginn der Reorganisation der Verwaltung in Deutschland', in Jeserich, K. et al. (eds.), *Deutsche Verwaltungsgeschichte Band 2*, Klett-Cotta Stuttgart.

Koselleck, R. (1967), *Preussen zwischen Reform und Revolution*, Klett-Cotta, Stuttgart.

Koselleck, R. (1973 [1959]), *Kritik und Krise. Eine Studie zur Pathogenese der bürgerlichen Welt*, Suhrkamp, Frankfurt am Main.

Langer, C. (1986), *Reform durch Prinzipien. Untersuchungen zur politischen Theorie Immanuel Kants*, Klett-Cotta, Stuttgart.

le Bret, C. (1631), *De la souverainité du roi*, Paris.

Locke, J. (1963 [1680/1689]), *Two Treatises of Government*, Cambridge University Press, Cambridge.

Lucinge, R. de (1984 [1588]), *De la naissance durée et chute des estats*, Droz , Genéve.

Luhmann, N. (1970a), 'Komplexität und Demokratie', in *Politische Planung*, Westdeutscher Verlag, Opladen.

Luhmann, N. (1970b), 'Reflexive Mechanismen', in *Soziologische Aufklärung*, Band 1, Westdeutscher Verlag, Opladen.

Luhmann, N. (1975), 'Evolution und Geschichte', *Soziologische Aufklärung*, Band 2, Westdeutscher Verlag, Opladen.

Luhmann, N. (1980), 'Interaktion in den Oberschichten: Zur Transformation ihrer Semantik im 17. Und 18. Jahrhundert' in Luhmann, N.,*Gesellschaftsstruktur und Semantik Band 1*, Suhrkamp, Frankfurt am Main.

Luhmann, N. (1981a), 'Die Positivierung des Rechts', in Luhmann, N., *Differenzierung des Rechts*, Suhrkamp, Frankfurt am Main.

Luhmann, N. (1981b), 'Theoriesubstitution in der Erziehungswissenschaft: Von der Philanthropie zum Neuhumanismus', in *Gesellschaftsstruktur und Semantik*, Band 2, Suhrkamp, Frankfurt.

Luhmann, N. (1982b), 'The Self-Thematization of Society', in Luhmann, N., *The Differentiation of Society*, Columbia University Press, New York.

Luhmann, N. (1986), *Ökologisches Kommunikation*, Westdeutscher Verlag, Opladen.

Luhmann, N. (1991), *Soziologie der Risiko*, De Gruyter, Berlin.

Luhmann, N. (1993), *Beobachtungen der Moderne*, Westdeutscher Verlag, Opladen.

Luhmann, N. (1995), *Social Systems*, Stanford University Press, Palo Alto.

Luhmann, N. (1997), *Die Gesellschaft der Gesellschaft*, Suhrkamp, Frankfurt am Main.

Luhmann, N. (2000), *Organisation und Entscheidung*, Westdeutscher Verlag, Opladen.

Mandrou, R. (1997), *L'Europe 'absolutiste'. Raison et raison d'État 1649–1775*, Fayard, Paris.

Maus, I. (1992), 'Zur Theorie der Institutionalisierung bei Kant', in Maus, I., *Zur Aufklärung der Demokratietheorie*, Suhrkamp, Frankfurt am Main.

Mousnier, R. (1971), *La venalité des Offices*, PUF, Paris.

Mousnier, R. (1974/1980), *Les institution françaises sous la monarchie absolue T.1-2*, PUF, Paris.

Mukerji, C. (1997), *Territorial Ambitions and the Gardens of Versailles*, Cambridge University Press, Cambridge.

Noue, F. de la (1967 [1587]), *Discours politiques et militaires*, Droz, Genéve.

Ormesson, Le Fèvre d' (1975), 'Mémoire concernant la province d'Auvergne' Comité des Travaux historiques: *Les mémoires des intendants, T. xxvi*, Paris, Bibliothèque National.
Parsons, T. (1971), *The Systems of Modern Societies*, Prentice-Hall, Englewood Cliff.
Porter, B. (1994), *War and the Rise of the State*, Free Press, New York.
Reynolds, S. (1996), *Fief and Vassals*, Oxford University Press, Oxford.
Richelieu, A. (1990 [1638]), *Testament politique*, Complexe, Paris.
Richet, D. (1973), *La France Moderne. L'esprit des institutions*, Flammarion, Paris.
Riley, P. (1978), 'The General Will before Rousseau'; *Political Theory*, vol.6.
Sieyès, E. (1982 [1789]), *Qu'est-ce que le tiers état?*, Quadrige, Paris.
Stolleis, M. (1990), *Staat und Staatsräson in der frühen Neuzeit*, Suhrkamp, Frankfurt.
Storez, I. (1996), *Le Chancelier Henri-François D'Aguesseau (1668 - 1751)*, Publisud, Paris.
Tilly, C. (1992), 'War Makes States and States Make War' in Tilly, C., *Coercion, Capital and the European States 1990 - 1992*, Blackwell, Oxford.
Tilly, C. (1994), *European Revolution, 1492 - 1992*, Blackwell, Oxford.
Vauban (1988 [1709]), *Projet d'une dixme royale*, Association des amis de la Maison Vaban, Saint-Léger-Vauban.
Winter, G. (eds.) (1931), *Die Reorganisation des Preussischen Staates unter Stein und Hardenberg*, Verlag Hirzel, Leipzig.
Woloch, I. (1994), *The New Regime*, Norton, London.
Østerud, Ø. (1978), *Utviklingsteori og historisk endring*, Norsk Gyldendal, Oslo.

4 Modernity and Its Archive: The Principle of Insufficient Reason

BO ISENBERG

This chapter discusses two major theoretical discourses of modernity: Classical modernity and postmodernity. I will suggest a possible *historical relation* between those two discourses of crucial importance to modernity's intellectual history, a historical connection founded upon what I call *the principle of insufficient reason*.

The principle of insufficient reason tells us that a historical process, event, or action could have been otherwise - or not at all - since it lacks a sufficient, absolute reason or foundation, such as God, tradition, myth, or man's reason, so much stressed by the Enlightenment. From what we learn from the discourses of classical modernity and postmodernity, the principle of insufficient reason may be invoked when outlining the logics of transformation of the modern epoch. In fact, postmodern understanding of modernity appears as a recurrence of classical modern theory and philosophy. (I will return to a more extensive definition of the notion of the principle of insufficient reason later on. In order to avoid any misunderstandings, let me state that reason does not refer to man's reason in general (German: *Vernunft*) or his judgment, but rather to foundation (German: *Grund*), to indubitable origins, or to motives).

Classical modernity - represented by figures such as the early Lukács, Kracauer, Simmel, Weber, Freud and Musil, and above all Nietzsche - continues to constitute the horizons of contemporary philosophy and theory. In it, we discover the *archive* of postmodern thinking, to use an image first outlined by Foucault.

In consequence, postmodern theory does not break off that cultural self-understanding expressed and indeed heightened by classical modernity. Rather, it varies already discussed themes, through different ideological currents.

Let me make clear what I mean by the three main notions used in this paper - classical modernity, postmodernity, and the principle of insufficient reason. The concepts of classical modernity and postmodernity should be understood in a Weberian ideal-typical sense. After having defined the paper's main concepts, I will go on to present four typical examples of positions of classical modernity and contemporary discussions on the culture of modernity.

The term *classical modernity* has its origins in aesthetics and more specifically in the history of art. Here, it signifies the shift from art as representation to abstract art, a shift which took place during the decades before and after 1900. In the works of the German historian Detlev Peukert, the notion has been extended into a cultural historical conception designating the period between 1890 and 1933 in Germany, a time of massive social, economic, and political change (Peukert, 1987).

I will argue that classical modernity can also be translated into an *intellectual discourse* within philosophy, sociology, literature, essayism, and critique.[1] As Europe was characterised by excessive social and economic transformation, these changes were accompanied by extraordinary reflection.

Fundamentally, it was a transformation that concerned the crisis and ongoing loss of the significance of religion in everyday life, and the increasing role of the secular - and secularising - forces of science and politics.

In Tönnies' words, it was the shift from *Gemeinschaft* to *Gesellschaft*. In Weber's vocabulary, the world was increasingly *disenchanted.*

Classical modernity as intellectual and critical discourse was the exceptional reflexive consciousness of an exceptional epoch. In the words of Max Weber's brother Alfred, sociology - as *the* knowledge of modernity - was the 'daughter of crisis', 'the most profound crisis that the occidental world had experienced so far' (Weber, 1955, p.496). The name of that crisis was modernity itself. It was the crisis which consisted in losing that sufficient and absolute reason of all being that was God.

Crisis is one recurrent theme of the discourse of classical modernity, a theme which ties together different perspectives, ideologies, and scientific disciplines. Indeed, ideology and a scientific approach appear to be subordinated matter, as 'progressive' and 'reactionary', 'leftist' and 'rightist' positions demonstrated similar views of modern society.

The main dividing line rather was drawn between on the one hand those tolerating or even affirming the plurality of new orders and realities and on the other hand those cultural understandings which longed for either that which was now lost or for new unambiguous orders and realities.[2] These understandings were politically realised in the two main ideological currents of the time, the two main *social* or *political religions*, which Eric Voegelin spoke of: Communism and National Socialism. The installing of these regimes also signifies the end of classical modernity (Voegelin, 1938; cf. Gurian, 1954).

I will return to a few voices of classical modern critique shortly. Let me first present a very brief catalogue of conceptions that were commonly used. 'Progressive' as well as 'reactionary' writers frequently described their modern world as 'fragmented', as 'relative' or 'relativistic', as 'vastly confused', as an 'empty space' (the favourite image in the works of Kracauer), as 'artificial', 'contingent', 'provisional' or 'ambivalent'.

Indeed, the notions that emerged in order to come to terms with World War One, Weimar, The Russian Revolution, depression and inflation, and the vanishing Christianity constitute a catalogue which would be just as useful to any postmodern writer.

As was the case with the concept of classical modernity, the notion of *postmodernity* had its origin in art, but also in architecture. Only later was it imported into philosophy and social science.

Today postmodernity appears to have passed its prime. One explanation - and there are certainly others - might be that we have not been bothering to trace our own historical past.

I understand postmodernity as an intellectual disposition or intellectual discourse, that is, the same type of understanding which I apply to the notion of classical modernity. As intellectual discourse, it brings together approaches within several fields - social science, philosophy, literature, and architecture.

Unlike classical modern critique, the works of Foucault, Lyotard, Deleuze, and in other directions Zygmunt Bauman and Bryan Turner, have not so much been a reflection of contemporary fundamental social transformations and uncertainties. Rather, I would argue that they have constituted a *reaction* against what it regarded as a dominant kind of modernity, a modernity which stressed progress, social engineering, technology, and scientific management.[3]

Postmodernity, too, was an attack against those totalising projects of social order and unambiguous reality which were put on the agenda by the political and intellectual avantgarde, that avantgarde which was to end up in the secular religions of the twentieth century. Postmodernity may be seen as *the end of avantgarde,* indeed *of the* very *possibility of the avantgarde*.

In reacting against its culture, postmodernity reoccupied positions that were already that of classical modernity. Occasionally, it explicitly referred to classical modern approaches, to Nietzsche, Simmel, Valéry, and Freud. And occasionally, it did not.

Thematically as well as conceptionally, there is a striking continuity between classical modernity and postmodernity. Accordingly, the brief catalogue of images presented earlier is that of postmodernity, too. Descriptions of contemporary society in terms of 'fragmentation', 'relativity', 'heterogeneity', 'contingency', and 'ambivalence' may all be found in that *archive* which classical modernity constitutes toward postmodernity.

In other words: The principle which was that of classical modernity - the principle of insufficient reason - was to become that of postmodernity.

Postmodernity thus extensively shares classical modernity's *diagnosis* of modern culture. On the other hand, it shares its *attitude*, its *normative approach* with a mere *minority* of classical modern writers. Those include, although the picture is not unequivocal, writers like Weber, Mannheim, Musil, Valéry, and Helmuth Plessner. It is a standpoint characterised by tolerance, acceptance, even affirmation of the modern principle of insufficient reason - of contingency, relativity, of the absence of God and tradition. In the words of German philosopher Hans Blumenberg, it is the affirmation of modern culture as 'culture of contingency' (*Kontingenz- kultur*)(Blumenberg, 1987, p.57).[4]

Postmodernity signifies *minority currents of classical modernity having become mainstream today.* Indeed, descriptions of contemporary culture as 'ambivalent' or 'relativistic' now constitute elements which are not only present in postmodern jargon.

As a basic element of the very definition of being postmodern, there is *already* the acknowledgement, the affirmation of the principle of insufficient reason.

As for the very latest revisions of understanding of contemporary modern culture, there is a strong tendency to incorporate the positions of postmodern critique - and, accordingly, to rework the archive of classical modernity. By way of emphasising notions such as 'risk', 'uncertainty', 'contingency', and 'plurality', the 'late modernity' of Giddens and the 'second modernity' of Beck, signify a *modernisation of the modern project*, a *modernisation of modernity as project*.

Let me now turn to the concept of the principle of insufficient reason. *The principle of insufficient reason* - as far as I know an image conceived by Austrian novelist Robert Musil and used throughout his novel *The Man Without Qualities* (*Der Mann ohne Eigenschaften*) - has its origin in its very opposite, in the principle of *sufficient* reason.[5]

The principle of *sufficient* reason has been discussed within philosophy by Leibniz, Schopenhauer, and Heidegger. Very briefly, it might be described as a reason or foundation (German: *Grund*) which makes something necessary or conditional. The order of things has an absolute, sufficient, and absolutely sufficient reason from which it may be derived and which in itself is, or is understood as, universal and eternal. In Christianity, God is the ultimate, sufficient reason. The Enlightenment perceived the reason of Man (German: *Vernunft*) as the sufficient foundation of human culture. In antiquity, the cosmos was the reason of all being. This is the principle of *sufficient* reason.[6]

The principle of modernity is different. It states that a historical process, an event, an action *could have been otherwise*. Or - not at all. No reason, no foundation is necessary or sufficient in itself. The principle indicates that almost any reason might be used, or many different reasons simultaneously; and different manifestations could be derived from the very same reason.

The principle of insufficient reason thus allows that good and evil have the same reason, and that the reason of good and evil, respectively, could have been different.

Modernity experiences no sufficient reason, God is no longer sufficient, nor tradition, nor myth. That which exists in modernity exists for the time being, conditionally, temporarily. Briefly, it exists *historically*.

This would also be the case for that foundation of man and society which was inaugurated by the Enlightenment, that is, man's own reason and its derivatives in science and philosophy.

To be sure the Enlightenment was an endeavor to abolish ambiguity and contingency by way of declaring man's reason as a new foundation. In Gehlen's words, it sought to install man as *maître et possesseur de la nature et de la société*, man as master and possessor of nature and society (Gehlen, 1986, p.221).[7]

But the Enlightenment lived by its conception of contingency, of a world being at disposal - indeed that world which included man himself, his subjectivity, as well as his very reason.

As Kant tried to define man's reason, it was a compelling reaction to the suspicion that man's intellectual ability was a highly problematic question. Blumenberg writes that the critique of pure reason was the 'overall plan of confinement' (Blumenberg, 1989, p.796).

Let me exemplify four positions of classical modernity and contemporary discussions on culture which can be seen as (ideal-) typical examples of four standpoints: (1) mainstream classical modernity, (2) classical modern minority, (3) postmodernity, and (4) late modernity. These standpoints may in turn be seen as standpoints which all use *the principle of insufficient reason as the main logic of modernity*.

First, however, I would like to return to Nietzsche, *the* modern critic of modernity. Nietzsche furnishes modern reflection with some of its fundamental concepts and images. The image of 'the death of God' was impossible to reject. If God were dead, then society no longer had a sufficient reason for what is good and what is bad, what is true and what is false. In the absence of that indubitable, sufficient, and absolute reason which was God, the characteristics of modernity became contingency, ambiguity, and irresoluteness. Man's search for certitude, Nietzsche writes in one of his early theoretical texts, turned into 'a fumbling game on the back of things'. Man, he says, 'hangs on the back of a tiger'.[8]

To Nietzsche, the death of God - a death caused by man himself - was the greatest of all events. Maybe it was *too* great, since man has so far not been able to establish a new, sufficient reason. This was Nietzsche's problem.

The image of 'the death of God' was widely accepted and developed in philosophy, literature, and the emerging cultural sociology - by Weber and Simmel, Mannheim and Scheler, Kracauer and Benjamin, Musil, Kafka and the essayistic literature of what has been called 'the generation of 1905' (cf. Luft, 1980).[9]

(1) One of those who most certainly read Nietzsche was the young Georg von Lukács, in many ways a typical critic of modernity. His critique could have been that of Benn or Kracauer, Benjamin or Schmitt as well.

At the time of World War One, Lukács formulated his theory of the novel.[10] This typical modern genre, he says, is the reflection of a world 'without God', a world where 'the last foundations of creating have become homeless'. The fact that the novel rests on the conception of sovereign subjectivity in itself demonstrates that modern culture lacks foundations. Everything remains temporary, as does the object of the novel, that object which consists of the more and more dissolved human subject.

The modern world, Lukács writes, is a world whose main characteristic consists of the indeed precarious relation between 'contingent world and problematic individual', which constitute 'mutually conditional realities'. Man's soul, Lukács states, is marked by 'transcendental homelessness' (*transzendentale Heimatlosigkeit*), an image which was repeated and elaborated in his following works inspired by Marxism.

(2) A typical representative of the classical modern *minority* current which generally accepted or affirmed the new, modern experience of contingency is Robert Musil. His great novel could of course be read 'merely' as a novel. But this extensive interpretation of modernity, which has never been surpassed, might also be understood as an essayistic reworking of the possibilities and problems of an epoch.

At the same time, affirmation of contingency is conditional, not programmatic. There is a great sensibility to religion and tradition, a sensibility which only by way of exception has survived into postmodernity. The works of Foucault, Lyotard, and others seek to do away with religion altogether. In this respect, Blumenberg would be an exception.

To Musil, the society of modernity is in a state of chronic crisis. Modernity is per definition crisis. It lacks a superior idea or ethics to lead its culture, its individuals. And it is not only the hero of the novel who is without qualities, but modern man in general. Modern subjectivity is extremely problematic; man's problematic subjectivity affects culture, which, as problematic culture, in turn affects man. Modernity lacks given foundations, and the result is a cultural collective lethargy combined with individual vitality. Modernity, Musil states, turns into an overall 'nervousness' (Musil, 1978, p.969).

This is Musil's critique. But this is the impetus to those possibilities of which Musil speaks as well. The man without qualities is imaginable only in modern culture. He stands for extraordinary reflexivity, for scepticism, indeed on the verge of self-destruction. To Ulrich, there is nothing in modern culture which cannot be relativised. Everything is perceived as constructions in the widest sense, as cultural products. Ultimately, reality itself is called into question: Why should there be anything real at all if there is nothing to sanction it, if it lacks foundation?

(3) The uniting factor of the rather heterogeneous postmodern circle of philosophers and social scientists might be their *post-metaphysical* efforts. Above all, postmodern writers turn against specific *modern* attempts to create sufficient reasons, that is, in their view, and paradoxically, *modern metaphysics*. For instance, in his paradigmatic critique, Lyotard speaks of the Grand Narratives of human Reason, of Progress, of the Emancipation of the working subject, and so forth (Lyotard, 1979).

Foucault's analysis of modernity has also become paradigmatic to postmodern, or poststructuralist thinking. It concerns, for instance, his understanding of Man, of the human subject. Man, Foucault states, is a conception that emerges only in the modern regime of knowledge. Man appears as a 'figure of knowledge', as an 'epistemological figure' (Foucault, 1973, pp.xxiv, x). Being a historical product, Foucault in a now famous passage says, it will one day disappear 'like a face drawn in the sand at the edge of the sea' (ibid., 387). In other studies, Foucault demonstrated how the conception of man and his subjectivity was produced by different mechanisms of power and knowledge. In his discussion of the two specific modern forms of power, bio-power and the disciplines, Foucault designates man as a 'plenitude of the possible' (Foucault, 1976, p.191).

To Foucault, the modern era meant that the order of things - but also, and in particular, man himself - was at man's disposal. The prison, the asylum, psychiatry, criminology, and the sexual science were responses to a historical problem. Foucault analyses these responses, these solutions. The problem, however, basically remains tacit. My answer would be: *Contingency*, an increasing experience of contingency, contingency as something *problematic*.

For Foucault too, the principle of modernity is that of insufficient reason, since that which is contingent, that is, that which could have been different, is precisely that which lacks sufficient reason.

(4) The fourth variation on the principle of insufficient reason as the logic of modernity is represented by Beck and Giddens, whose interpretations appear to resemble each other.[11] In both cases, there is an emphasis on what was considered to be 'typical' postmodern conceptions - on contingency, uncertainty, and so forth. Contrary to postmodern interpretations, however, the 'late modernity' of Giddens and the 'second modernity' of Beck stress politics and economics rather than ethics and aesthetics. In this sense, they also remain within a more traditional discussion on modernity, represented by, for example, Jürgen Habermas.

Beck and Giddens aim at a *modernisation of the modern project*, a *modernisation of modernity as project*. In Becks understanding, globalisation could be understood *as the modern principle of insufficient reason becoming global*. The encounter and the compound of different politics, moralities, and so forth means that no single polity, no single ethics, will have a dominant impact on everyday life.

Globalisation, therefore, is the diffusion of the chief characteristic conferred to the modern *metropolis* in the classical modern discussion: Different, often heterogeneous things exist at the same place at the same time.

With the exception of Simmel and Musil and a few others, the metropolis was considered by classical modernity to be mainly a *problem*. Globalisation is considered by Beck and others as a *possibility*. The globalised world, says Beck, is populated by 'children of freedom', individuals who are free to work, to communicate, to move (Beck, 1997). Or - forced to do so.

Beck's 'second modernity' focuses on the *possibilities* of contemporary culture. Its dangers, its contingency, Beck translates into *risk*. Risk appears as a notion signifying that uncertainty will always be there; it appears as sublimation of vague perils through reflexivity. Here, Beck and for that matter Giddens, clearly incorporate positions of postmodernity.

In the conceptualisations of Beck and Giddens, modernity emerges as a *culture between uncertainty and possiblity*. It is a culture becoming aware of its uncertainties as well as emphasising its possibilities.

The discourses of late modernity and second modernity abandon the relentless critique of postmodernity. They retain postmodernity's affirmation of contingency. Also, they are not lost to the modern belief in progress, to the attitude where the world is at the disposal of politics and science.

Late modernity and second modernity remain, however, within those conceptual categories established by classical modernity, categories summed up in the principle of insufficient reason.

The underlying problematic of this chapter is the question of whether the logic of transformation of the modern epoch has changed and whether contemporary social theory has been able to express this matter adequately.[12] For some time now, social theory and philosophy have been under suspicion of suffering a standstill while society as well as its underlying structures change without respite.

Indeed, one fundamental characteristic of modernity is that its culture, its social relations, undergo permanent change. To be modern does not merely mean to be new in a trivial sense, but *modernity as epoch signifies the novelty*. Modernity's contingent nature not only means the *prerogative* to do or perceive things differently, but has come to *force* us to do so: The very possibility has turned into necessity, the necessity to change, to destruct, and to construct. In his novel, Musil writes that the specific modern attitude towards the world is the *structive* attitude (Musil, 1978, p.453).

Musil's image of the structive may in turn be understood as a complementary image to that of the principle of insufficient reason. The principle makes it possible, indeed forces man to destruct and to construct, but at the same time it makes it impossible for him to focus his efforts in certain directions. At the end, the principle therefore means disorder, change, confusion.

I have argued in this paper that the principle of insufficient reason is the uniting element of different discourses on the modern epoch. Postmodernity, but also the discourses of late modernity and second modernity, find their *archive* in classical modernity.

Accordingly, modernity is still our epoch. Its logic of transformation tells us that modernity *is* transformation.

What I would like to suggest is that postmodernity and other contemporary discourses may be conceived as *revisions* of modernity, but also that they *remain modern*. They revise existing conceptions, permute them, and in this limited sense they constitute novelties. To revise, to vary, to combine anew what already exists, is, however, something distinctly *modern*. To revise and vary one's concepts, one's interpretations, also signifies that which Weber, in his famous lecture on *Science as vocation*, calls 'science surpassing itself' (Weber, 1992). For Weber, to surpass oneself means to be modern, and accordingly to remain within modernity. Indeed, for Weber there seems to be nothing beyond modernity.

Classical modernity, and in particular its minor currents which stressed their affirmation of modernity as culture of contingency, is the future's past, the past of postmodernity. The history of postmodernity demonstrates the latter's very possibilities of being different.

Notes

1 This argument has been made by the German sociologist Michael Makropoulos, to whom I express my gratitude. See Makropoulos (1991, 1997). Both works have been of great importance to my understanding. Cf. Raulet (1984).

2 A similar view is expressed in Makropoulos, *Modernität und Kontingenz*, pp.101.

3 Swedish intellectual historian Sven-Eric Liedman refers to this dominant kind of modernity as the 'hard' side of modernity of the Enlightenment. Their 'soft' side consists of art, ethics, and religion (Liedman, 1997).

4 On Blumenberg, see Isenberg (1998).

5 The title of chapter 35 of the second part of the first volume of Musil's 1930/1932 novel *Der Mann ohne Eigenschaften* (*The Man Without Qualities*) is 'Direktor Leo Fischel und das Prinzip des unzureichenden Grundes'.

6 The principle of sufficient reason is referred to in several philosophical dictionaries. *Reason*, however, may be exchanged for foundation or indubitable origin or motive.

7 In a forthcoming book, I elaborate on the conception of the principle of insufficient reason as a main characteristic of modernity at length (Isenberg, forthcoming).

8 Gehlen is, of course, referring to Descartes, who talked of man as *maître et possesseur de la nature*.

9 Nietzsche speaks of 'the death of God' in *Die Fröhliche Wissenschaft*, #125 (*KSA* 3, pp.480). The 'irresoluteness' of modernity is discussed in *Der Fall Wagner*, Epilog (*KSA* 6, pp.50). The two quotations are from 'Üeber Wahrheit und Lüge im au*ß*ermoralischen Sinne' (*KSA* 1, p.876ff).

10 Luft includes Kahler, Kraus, Mannheim, Hofmannsthal, Thomas Mann, Hesse, Döblin, Spengler, Benn, Kafka, Musil, Broch, Zweig, Rilke in 'the generation of 1905'. On the relation of the early German cultural sociology to Nietzsche, see Lichtblau (1996).

11 Quotations in this and the following paragraph from Lukács, 1994, pp.82, 31, 47, 52, 107. Lukács also uses the less pregnant expression *transzendentale Obdachlosigkeit* (p.32). A few years later, Lukács, now a Marxist, expresses similar thoughts in his *Geschichte und*

Klassenbewußtsein: 'the need for an understanding of totality, at least with regard to knowledge, cannot be eradicated' (Lukács, 1970, p.199). In 1921, Lukács' theory of the novel was positively reviewed by Siegfried Kracauer (Kracauer, 1992).

12 Related texts by Beck include Beck (1986, 1997); Giddens formulates his view on modernity in Giddens (1991, 1998).

References

Beck, U. (1986), *Risikogesellschaft: Auf dem Weg in eine andere moderne*, Suhrkamp, Frankfurt am Main.

Beck, U. (1997) (ed.), *Kinder der Freiheit*, Suhrkamp, Frankfurt am Main.

Blumenberg, H. (1987), *Die Sorge geht über den Fluß*, Suhrkamp, Frankfurt am Main.

Blumenberg, H. (1989), *Höhlenausgänge*, Suhrkamp, Frankfurt am Main.

Foucault, M. (1973), *The Order of Things: An Archaeology of the Human Sciences*, Vintage, New York.

Foucault, M. (1976), *Histoire de la sexualité. 1. La volonté de savoir*, Gallimard, Paris.

Gehlen, A. (1986), 'Sozialpsychologie. Sozialpsychologische Probleme in der industriellen Gesellschaft', in *Anthropologische und Sozialpsychologische Untersuchungen*, Rowohlt, Reinbek bei Hamburg.

Giddens, A. (1991), *Modernity and Self-Identity: Self and Society in the Late Moderns Age*, Polity Press, Cambridge.

Giddens, A. (1998), *The Third Way: The Renewal of Social Democracy*, Polity Press, Cambridge.

Gurian, W. (1954), 'Totalitarianism as Political Religion', in Friedrich, C. J. (ed.): *Totalitarianism*, Harvard University Press, Harvard.

Isenberg, B. (1998), 'Answering the Question: What is Culture? A Sociological Reworking of the Philosophy of Hans Blumenberg', in Yamamoto, T., Andrew, E. G., Chartier, R. and Rabinow, P. (eds.): *Philosophical Designs for a Socio-Cultural Transformation. Beyond Violence and the Modern Era*, Rowman & Littlefield, Tokyo, Boulder.

Isenberg, B. (forthcoming), *Struktivitet och abundans. Essä om det moderna.*

Kracauer, S. (1992), *Der verbotene Blick. Beobachtungen, Analysen, Kritiken*, Reclam, Leipzig.

Lichtblau, K. (1996), *Kulturkrise und Soziologie um die Jahrhundertwende. Zur Genealogie der Kultursoziologie in Deutschland*, Suhrkamp, Frankfurt am Main.

Liedman, S.-E. (1997), *I skuggan av framtiden. Modernitetens historia*, Bonnier Alba, Stockholm.

Luft, D. (1980), *Robert Musil and the Crisis of European Culture 1880-1942*, University of California Press, Berkeley.

Lukács, G. (1970), *Geschichte und Klassenbewußtsein. Studien über marxistische Dialektik*, Luchterhand, Darmstadt, Neuwied.

Lukács, G. (1994), *Die Theorie des Romans: Ein geschichtsphilosophischer Versuch über die Formen der großen Epik*, dtv, München.

Lyotard, J.-F. (1979), *La condition postmoderne: rapport sur le savoir*, Minuit, Paris.

Makropoulos, M. (1991), 'Tendenzen der Zwanziger Jahre. Zum Diskurs der Klassischen Moderne in Deutschland'. *Deutsche Zeitschrift für Philosophie*, vol.39, pp.675-687.

Makropoulos, M. (1997), *Modernität und Kontingenz*, Fink, München.

Musil, R. (1978), *Der Mann ohne Eigenschaften*, Rowohlt, Reinbek bei Hamburg.

Nietzsche, F. (1988), Sämtliche Werke. Kritische Studienausgabe (=*KSA*), dtv/de Gruyter, Berlin/New York.

Peukert, D. J. K. (1987), *Die Weimarer Republik. Krisenjahre der Klassischen Moderne.* Suhrkamp, Frankfurt am Main.

Raulet, G. (1984), 'Pour une archéologie de la postmodernité', in Raulet, G. (ed): *Weimar ou l'Explosion de la Modernité*, Anthropos, Paris.

Voegelin, E. (1994), *Die politischen Religionen*, Fink, München.

Weber, A. (1955), 'Der Mensch und die Zeiten', in Weber, A. (ed.): *Einführung in die Soziologie*, Piper, München.

Weber, M. (1992), *Wissenschaft als Beruf*, Duncker & Humblot, Berlin.

5 Rethinking the Epochs of Western Modernity

MIKAEL CARLEHEDEN

Introduction

Academic sociology emerged with the transformation from traditional to modern society. The founding fathers of the discipline were, to a great extent, all preoccupied with trying to come to grips with this dramatic historical event and the new social problems attached to it. Classical sociology was first and foremost an institutionalised reflection on the causes, significance and consequences of the emergence of 'modernity' (even though the term was not in use at the time). After this first phase of sociology, however, the discipline's emphasis on diachronic aspects of sociality tended to fade. Concern with the transformation from pre-modernity to modernity was typically replaced by the study of the synchronic dimensions of modernity itself. To the extent that dynamic processes were investigated, it was the development *up to*, not *of*, modernity. According to the dominant evolutionist view, the 'developed' countries had more or less finished their route to modernity. 'Modernisation theory' was relevant only in studies of 'developing' countries, i.e., societies which were still on their way to becoming 'modern' (Tiryakian, 1991; Wallerstein et al., 1996). This new rigidity of sociology after its classical phase was not simply ideology. This second phase, too, reflected the society it investigated.[1] It was a child of its times. During this period, Western society was undergoing a process of consolidation rather than transformation. And social science does not stand above its research object in any divine fashion. It is always socially situated in a more fundamental way than it can grasp itself. The mistake made during this second phase was not primarily that of underestimating social change, but rather, that a particular form of modernity was universalised. Today, however, we seem to be entering a new form of modernity, and contemporary sociology is struggling to liberate itself from the universal claims of its second phase.

For more than 30 years, sociologists have been talking about some kind of new groundbreaking and dramatic social change. Ever since the end of the

1960s, concepts such as 'post-industrial' and 'postmodern' society have been in use (for an overview see Kumar, 1995; Reese-Schäfer, 1999). Today we are practically inundated with terminological variations on that theme: 'another modernity' (Beck, 1986; Lash, 1999), 'second modernity' (Seel, 1986, 1989; Beck, 1993), 'late modernity' (Giddens, 1990), 'Modernisation II or neo-modernisation analysis' (Tiryakian, 1991), 'postmodernization' (Crook, Pakulski and Waters, 1992), 'reflexive modernisation' (Beck, Giddens and Lash, 1994), 'new modernity (Beck, 1992), 'extended liberal modernity' (Wagner, 1994), 'supermodernity' (Augé, 1995; Jacobsen and Chatterjee, 2001), 'the great disruption' (Fukuyama, 1999), 'liquid modernity' (Bauman, 2000) etc., etc. One of the most popular rhetorical strategies in contemporary sociology is to proclaim some kind of new society. Apart from the above mentioned concepts of a post-industrial society (Bell, 1973) and postmodern society (Etzioni, 1968), we have witnessed the proclamation of the following types of societies: 'information society' (Bell, 1973), 'risk society' (Beck, 1986), '*Erlebnisgesellschaft*' (Schulze, 1993), 'service society' (Häusermann and Siebel, 1995), 'network society' (Castells, 1996) and now even 'dream society' (Jensen, 1999). The many suggestions indicate that something important is happening. If contemporary sociologists are not worse in reflecting their own society than their forerunners, not only sociology, but also modernity is entering a third phase.

The proposal that I am going to develop in this chapter is that these three different phases of sociology are reflections of three different epochs of modernity. My main purpose is to explicate the meaning of these three epochs.[2] Thus, I will use the transformation of sociology as an indication of social change. I will, in other words, work metatheoretically (Ritzer, 1996, p.622ff). Of course, there is no guarantee that the transformation of sociology actually mirrors social change. However, social scientific discourse does not exist outside the empirical social world, but is rather a part of it. It both influences it and is influenced by it. I believe that such a metatheoretical investigation can give us a preliminary idea of contemporary social change which can be used as a point of departure for empirical investigations.

The idea that we are entering third modernity does not imply that 'postmodernists' have in some sense triumphed in their debate with the 'modernists'. Rather, I would argue that the debate has ended in a draw. Or perhaps better, the two sides have learned from each other. Postmodernism has certainly not 'won' the debate on a normative level. Moral and epistemological relativism or contextualism are simple negations of Enlightenment normativity, rather than alternatives.[3] And on a sociological level, some of the above mentioned concepts - e.g., 'another modernity' and 'late modernity' - were from the start already intended to go beyond this polarised debate. Today, few scholars actually take the term 'postmodernity' literally.[4] We have not left modernity. We have not been witnessing a transition from modernity to postmodernity. We are not living in an epoch which is as different from modernity as modernity is different from what classical sociologists called traditional society. On the other hand, nor are we living in the same type of society as did Parsons. Modernity has not ended, but it is transforming itself in a fundamental sense. What we are dealing with are epochal distinctions *within* modernity (Beck, 1986, p.13). This is one of the most important results of the modernist-postmodernist debate. This debate was itself a reflection of a period of social transition. The third phase of sociology appears not only after modernism, but also 'after postmodernism' - to use another popular title of books in social theory in the end of the first whole century of sociology.

The inflation in concepts, intended to capture the current transformations within modernity, can be seen as a sign of the immaturity of the third phase of sociology. We do not have any contemporary equivalent to Marx, Durkheim and Weber of the first phase or to Parsons and Merton of the second phase. The only grand social theoreticians after Parsons - Habermas and Luhmann - seem to have lived their intellectually formative years too early to have been able to thematise the fundamental importance of current transformations.[5] In Habermas' case, his *normative* criticism of post-modernism seems to have prevented him from taking the *sociological* concept of postmodernity seriously. His sociological *magnum opus* - *Theorie des kommunikativen Handelns* - is more a critical reconstruction of Parsons' conception of second modernity rather than a conceptualisation of third modernity (Reese-Schäfer, 1999). This impressive work is a perfect example of Hegel's owl of Minerva, which only takes off when an epoch has already grown old.[6] Manuel Castells has sometimes been suggested to be the Marx or Weber of our time. But his *Information Age* has been criticised for being theoretically underdeveloped and giving too much weight to technological and economical levels to be able to take up the vacant *sociological* mantle of Grand Theory. I will come back to this critique.

What do we then lack, when we lack a grand social theory of the present? We lack an overall picture which can bind together the thousands of observations made at so many different levels. We lack that which Lyotard (1979) rejected as a 'meta-narrative'. In his rejection, however, Lyotard committed the fallacy of universalising something particular just as much as did Parsons - although in a critical version. His criticism of totalitarian meta-narratives is - at best - applicable only to theories of second modernity

(Reese-Schäfer, 1999, p.440). It cannot be universalised to meta-narratives in general. Actually, Lyotard's own conception of the postmodern condition is the beginning of meta-narrative. Third phase sociology cannot avoid grand social theory in its attempt to understand the meaning of the many observations of a new epoch of modernity.

Grand theory involves what we might call a conception of the social logic of society. Such a conception can be divided into three parts: (1) the logic of social structure, (2) the logic of social reproduction, and (3) the logic of social transformation. Let me try to explain what I mean by these terms.

Conceptions of a social logic have often implied evolutionism and the privilege of structure over action. Today, however, most versions of social science try to overcome both structuralist and action theoretical reductionism. Actors find themselves '*immer schon*' in a social world and can thus only change it from within. Action changes the same society, which has constituted the actor. Under such theoretical conditions, what we call 'social logic' refers to a pattern, system or structure of relations of social institutions, which can be identified for a period of time in a certain place. In every historical epoch there is a prevailing structure of social institutions, which is more or less abstract and which make up the common conditions for action, creativity and change. To talk about the logic of the social structure, then, means not more than to say that the social institutions have a specific character and that they are related to each other in a specific way. Social logic concerns, secondly, social reproduction. This kind of social change occurs within the general structure given by the dominant institutions of a particular society. It is what Sztompka (1993, pp.6, 20) calls 'changes *in* the system'. 'Changes *of* the system', in contrast, involves a change in the logic of the social structure (and thus subsequently also a change of the logic of reproduction). Following Sztompka, we can call change of the system a 'transformation'. However, it follows from what we have argued that social change can never be truly revolutionary. Revolutionaries are formed by the societies which they overthrow. The antithesis is not independent of the thesis. The causes and reasons, which explain transformation are always related to the specific social institutions of the past. That means that the transformation of the logic of social structure can involve its own logic. Grand theory thus, thirdly, involves the logic of social transformation, which concerns the world historical development of human kind and its institutions. According to this terminology, the epochal change within modernity seems to fall in between reproduction and transformation. It is neither simply a reproduction, because then we could not be talking about different epochs of modernity. Nor is it a question of a transformation of modernity, because that would mean that we are leaving modernity behind us. I will therefore suggest that we talk about a transformation *within* modernity. It is the nature and significance of this particular type of social change, which will be the focus of this chapter.

Sociology has been much too dependent on the grand theories of its founding fathers to be able to make sense of such a transformation. As long as we remain faithful to the founding fathers of sociology, we run the risk of universalising their particular experiences of first modernity. It is still very hard to find any alternatives to the master concepts of classical Grand Theory. I am thinking of Marx' idea of class struggle, Durkheim's theory of social differentiation and Weber's concept of social rationalisation or disenchantment. The best alternatives which contemporary social scientists can offer are mostly conceptions like 'beyond class' (Beck, 1986, p.121ff), 'de-differentiation', (Beck, 1986, p.369), 're-feudalisation' (Maus, 1992) and 'de-rationalisation' or 're-enchantment' (Bauman, 1992, pp.x-xi; Ritzer, 1999). Such simple negations are not very helpful if we want to demonstrate that modernity has not ceased to exist, but has been internally transformed. We need what the classics could not have given us for the simple reason that they lived too early. We need a conception of the social logic of modernity which allows for internal transformations. We need a general and abstract concept of the reproduction of modernity, along with particular conceptions of social transformation able to identify different epochs of modernity without contradicting the general logic of the reproduction of modernity. We need, in other words, a conception of the social logic of modernity, which can simultaneously uphold the contrast to traditional society and grasp fundamental change *within* modernity. Such a conception would allow for different historical and cultural forms of modernity but without placing these forms in any sort of evolutionist scheme. The purpose of this chapter is to make a preliminary attempt to develop such a conception. It takes 'Western modernity' as its point of reference, but only as an example, not as a model. I will therefore present some theoretical conditions and empirical observations which support the idea of transformation within modernity. I will proceed in three steps. First, I will begin with climbing up on the shoulders of Habermas, the theorist who has developed Marx, Weber and Durkheim's grand theories the furthest. Habermas offers us the best account of what we, from the perspective of third phase sociology, should understand as old modernisation theory. Second, - following a brief critique of Castells' conception of our epoch as an information age - I discuss what I believe to be the most illuminating historical and sociological theory of transformation within modernity: Peter Wagner's *A Sociology of Modernity*. In comparing

Habermas and Wagner, I then offer a possible solution to how we might reconstruct classical and neo-classical conceptions of the logic of modern social change if sociology is to accurately understand the rapid changes of contemporary society. This leads us, in conclusion, to a very preliminary conception of third modernity.

Habermas' Reconstruction of the Classical Conceptions of Social Change

Habermas (1981a) had without doubt the same ambition as did Parsons a generation before him. Both of them took what they thought to be the most convincing parts of the competing major traditions in sociology and transformed them into a coherent theory meant to grasp the social logic of modern society. It is thus difficult to say which one of the classical sociologists was most important to Habermas. He used them all - and Parsons - extensively. His ambition was to 'reconstruct' sociology from Marx to Parsons, that is, to improve their conception of Modern society (Habermas, 1976, p.9):

> It has become conventional for sociologists to distinguish the stages of social evolution as tribal societies, traditional societies, or societies organised around a state and modern societies (where the economic system has been differentiated out) (Habermas, 1981a vol.2, p.230, Engl., 1987, pp.153-154).

This classical sociological convention does not thematise different epochs within modernity, and Habermas follows that convention. He even himself calls his sociological theory 'a neo-classical concept of modernity' (Habermas, 1998, p.231).[7] As we can see in the quotation above, this sociological convention includes social evolutionism. In some sense or the other social change in classical grand social theory has always meant social evolution, and social evolution has in turn always implied social progress. We are here dealing with some kind of mixture of Enlightenment philosophy of history and social Darwinism. A reconstruction of classical sociology cannot avoid this aspect, which thus means that Habermas retains evolutionist thinking while improving it (Habermas, 1976, pp.154-157). If we believe, as I do (Carleheden, 1996), that Habermas actually succeeded in his ambition to improve classical sociology, our task becomes much easier. We do not have to wade through the whole history of classical sociological theory to locate the best version of the classical idea of the social logic of modernity. Habermas has already done the job for us.

Marx, Durkheim and Weber did not deliver three completely dissimilar concepts of social evolution. They had all learned from Kant and Hegel.[8] Social differentiation played a crucial role for all three thinkers, even though Marx developed a more dialectical and Durkheim a more functionalistic version of it. And in Weber's famous foreword to his *Gesammelte Aufsätze zur Religionssoziologie* (1934), where we find his idea of modernisation in its most coherent form, social rationalisation includes the neo-Kantian differentiation between cognitive-instrumental, moral-practical and aesthetic-expressive value spheres (Habermas, 1984a, p.441ff). But something more is at stake in Weber's work than just increasing differentiation and specialisation. It allows us to capture the crucial role of intellectualisation and disenchantment in a way that a pure concept of social differentiation hardly does - neither in Marx' nor Durkheim's version. Weber, as is well known, stressed the cultural side of modernisation. Habermas is a typical Webermarxist. Like Weber, he criticises the Marxian tendency to reduce the significance of the cultural sphere of society to the functional demands of economy or technology. On the other hand, he retains the Marxian idea of the possibility of social critique in contrast to Weber's Nietzschian ethical relativism:

> [T]he species learns not only in the dimension of technically useful knowledge decisive for the development of productive forces but also in the dimension of moral-practical consciousness decisive for structures of interaction. The rules of communicative action do develop in reaction to changes in the domain of instrumental and strategic action; but in doing so they follow *their own logic* (Habermas, 1976, pp.162-163; Engl. 1984b, p.148).

Against Weber, Habermas holds that rationalisation does not simply mean that the bureaucratic institutionalisation of instrumental-strategic action destroys the validity of traditional norms. Rationalisation also means that norms are recreated in a communicative way. And against Marx, Habermas claims that this communicative rationalisation is of fundamental importance for modernisation. This theoretical fusion of Marxian and Weberian intentions forms the basis for Habermas' criticism of the Durkheimian account of modernisation as differentiation.

Social differentiation does not simply mean separation. It not only means that social institutions become more specialised and individuals more individualised, but also that they are re-integrated in a new way.

Differentiation as modernisation means that modern social integration - in contrast to pre-modern - should be understood in terms of integration of difference. Increasing difference actually means increasing mutual dependence, but this takes place in what Tönnies would call a *Gesellschaftliche* form rather than a *Gemeinschaftliche*. We can capture Habermas' criticism of this theory if we ask ourselves why modernisation in this sense should be understood as some form of evolution. Habermas finds the most explicit answer in Luhmann's radicalised version of the Durkheimian sociological tradition. Luhmann's answer builds on the idea of self-maintenance by means of increased complexity. Hence, 'the more states a system can assume, the more complex the environment with which it can cope and against which it can maintain itself', the more secure is the survival of the social system (Habermas, 1976, pp.155-156; Engl. 1984b, p.141). Habermas argues that this answer, while partially correct, is not sufficiently comprehensive. Society can be complex in infinitely different ways. What kind of increasing differentiation is to be understood as modernisation? Let us take two examples. According to Durkheim and Parsons, differentiation of gender roles is a sign of social evolution. However, today the increased equality between men and women has meant that the differentiation into an instrumental and an emotional gender role is of ever decreasing significance. Increased equality here seems to lead to de-differentiation. Is this to be understood as de-evolution? And - just to give another example - how should we understand globalisation? It is possible to interpret the decreasing importance of the nation state as a de-differentiation of the international world system. Does this constitute de-evolution as well? The answer to such questions depends on which aspects of differentiation and complexity we choose to focus on. Habermas (1976, p.156; Engl. 1984b, p.141) argues that history shows us that some forms of increased complexity 'turn out to be dead ends'. The basic weakness of differentiation theory is its tendency to naturalism. The theory found its point of departure in Herbert Spencer's sociological translation of Darwinism. Society is understood as a special kind of organism. However, while the success of natural organisms can be judged according to their physical survival, the evolution of societies must be measured 'in terms of securing a normatively prescribed societal identity, a culturally interpreted 'good' or 'tolerable' life' (Habermas, 1976, p. 156; Engl. 1984b, p.142). Social theory must thus be able to grasp the moral-practical dimension of the modernisation of society.

Durkheim - like Hegel before him - actually criticised the idea that modern society is possible without a modernisation also of ethical life. If modernisation is not to involve a state of general anomie, it has to be more than, what Spencer called, 'industrial society', that is, more than '*Gesellschaft*'. There is no immanent guarantee in the logic of social differentiation that society becomes integrated. This point is also the beginning of Habermas' two-level concept of modern society as both lifeworld and system. Differentiation in the realm of the systemic material reproduction of society does not necessarily lead to social integration or solidarity. It does not lead to the symbolic reproduction of the lifeworld.[9] Durkheim saw the problem, but - according to Habermas (1981a vol. 2, pp.173-180) - he was too caught up by the logic of differentiation theory to be able to conceptualise its solution.

Habermas criticises Marx in a manner similar to Durkheim. We find the beginning of a two-level theory of modern society also in Marx. His criticism of alienation was a moral-practical based criticism. But like Durkheim, Marx lacked a theory of modern social integration or normative modernisation. It is at this point that Habermas re-introduces Weber's conception of modernisation as social rationalisation. By means of a reconstruction of this concept, Habermas claims to be able to explicate the modernisation of social integration in terms of the rationalisation of the lifeworld. Actually he turns Weber's theory of disenchantment on his head. It is not less but more social rationalisation which makes possible a distinctly modern form of ethical life. Of course, Habermas then uses a different concept of rationality than did Weber. As is well known, he not only sees instrumental-strategic rationality as fundamental for modern life; he also stresses the role of communicative rationality.

Social differentiation is a condition for social rationalisation, also according to Habermas. Fundamental importance is given to the differentiation of society into lifeworld and system, and to the further differentiation between the two subsystems of 'state' and 'economy' - each working according to their own specific code (power and money). The further differentiation of the lifeworld into 'culture', 'society' and 'person' is just as significant. The differentiation, between lifeworld and system is both a precondition for an increase of complexity in the subsystems and for an increase of communicative rationality in the lifeworld. The differentiation of the lifeworld into culture, society and person is related to an increase in reflectivity, universality and individuality. His concept of communicative rationality enables Habermas to liberate himself from neo-Darwinist conceptions of social evolution and relate modernisation to processes of *cultural* learning (1981a vol. 2, pp.218, 482). Communicative rationality is neither about a solitary actor's effectiveness in reaching goals, nor about the systemic integration of non-intended consequences of instrumental-strategic actions. It is about mutual understanding and social co-operation. Modernisation of the lifeworld in the realm of culture means that mutual understanding depends less on both traditions and social institutions and more on argumentation, good reasons and reflective insight. In the realm of society, it means universalisation and formalisation of norms, while in the realm of the person it means more abstract, 'post-conventional' self-identities (Habermas, 1998, p.226). This process presupposes, in turn, that we moderns have learned to differentiate between the different kinds of 'value claims' and reasons that are inherent in all communication. Here Habermas follows the neo-Kantian distinction, between truth, rightness of norms and truthfulness.

I cannot go further into Habermas well known concept of communicative rationality (Compare instead Carleheden, 1996, 1999, pp.21-27). My purpose in this brief exposition has been to make clear the general meaning of Habermas' reconstruction of classic modernisation theory. The most important theoretical innovation in this reconstruction is the concept of communicative rationality. We find no real parallel to communicative rationality in the classical sociological tradition - although Mead did play a role. On this point Habermas had to go outside sociology to philosophical hermeneutics and speech act theory. But still, it is a reconstruction of classical sociological theory of social evolution. This reconstruction has four aspects.

First, Habermas understands modernisation as social differentiation. Not only does modernisation mean the 'differentiation out' of systems from the lifeworld, but also that differentiation plays a crucial role both in the lifeworld and in the systems. I have already mentioned the structural differentiation of the lifeworld into culture, person and society and the differentiation between validity claims. Habermas' systems theory not only differentiates between state and economy; these subsystems also rest on the logic of integration of non-intended consequences of action on which differentiation theory has focused ever since Adam Smith in *The Wealth of Nations*.

Second, Habermas is indeed even more an Enlightenment type of modernist than Weber when he claims that more rationality liberates us from the 'iron cage'. Habermas' concept of communicative rationality allows him to claim that he can overcome Weberian doubts about modernity while solving the theoretical contradictions in Durkheim and Marx's theories of modernisation. The 'pathologies' of modern society are not necessary consequences of modernity per se, but of an unfinished modernity, that is, a type of modern society in which the logic of the systems has colonised the communicative logic of the lifeworld.

The third aspect of Habermas' reconstruction is that Marx's concept of class struggle has survived. The central conflict in a modern welfare state, however, is no more to be found in the relation between the working class and the bourgeoisie or the capitalist economical system, but is rather *aufgehoben* in the attempts of the citizens in the public sphere to escape the colonising effects of the political system.[10]

Finally, Habermas sees differentiation and rationalisation in terms of an evolutionist logic, which he calls 'developmental logic'. This logic must be distinguished from the empirical development of modernity. It provides us with a kind of yardstick with which we can judge empirical modernisation according to its degree of communicative rationality. The yardstick is not purely normative. It gives us a 'logical space', which is based on 'anthropologically deep-seated general structures' and which 'arose to the extent that the cognitive and motivational potential of the anthropoid apes was transformed and reorganised under conditions of linguistic communication' (Habermas, 1976, pp.154-155; Engl. 1984b, p.140). This symbolic logic has empirical force by means of learning and can be used to understand the cultural development of both individual human beings and human societies. Like the founding fathers of sociology, Habermas wants to grasp the social evolution of mankind in its totality. Modernity thus becomes the end-state which is achieved through the right combination of differentiation and rationalisation processes. For Habermas, Modernity is, the end of history.

Excursus about Castells' 'Information Age'

In my account of transformation within modernity which follows, I will focus on the moral and ethical side of social life, not the economic or technological. This focus does not imply that the former aspect is more important than the latter, but, rather, that it is just as important. I agree with Habermas that the '*Eigengesetzlichkeit*' - to use Weber's term - of the moral-ethical sphere is of crucial importance for an understanding of social change.[11] My point of departure is that this focus could turn out to be very helpful for investigating transformation *within* modernity. This is why I will argue that Castells is unable to provide us with the grand social theory for third phase sociology. Castells might be our new Marx or Weber, or both at the same time (although I doubt that, too), but he revitalizes sociology using a huge amount of globally collected new empirical data rather than any sort of theoretical innovation. Theoretically, he actually falls behind Habermas' reconstruction of classical sociology. Castells sometimes take pains to avoid a historical materialist type of reductionism, but there is no doubt that he accords fundamental significance to the microelectronics-based information and communication technologies and genetic engineering:

> In the last quarter of this fading century, a technological revolution, centered around information, has transformed the way we think, we produce, we consume, we trade, we manage, we communicate, we live, we die, we make war, and we make love (Castells, 1998, p.1).[12]

Castells gives perhaps more significance to culture and social identity than did Marx, but the non-technological and non-economical parts of the information age are clearly the dependent rather than the independent variable in his work. By simply adopting Weber's analysis of the fading importance of the Protestant ethic for capitalism (Castells, 1996, pp.195-200) - a rather confusing move in view of the fact that Weber wrote about modernity while Castells claims that we are living in an age after modernity - Castells can combine Weber with materialist reductionism without any significant theoretical reconstructions. Apparently, ethics once had crucial influence on social change, but no more. Today it is the logic of information technology and global capitalism, which have 'induced a new form of society' (Castells, 1997, p.1). Thus, the metaphor of the iron cage seems to fit the information age just as well as it did the modern age. In parallel to Weber's analysis, we find in Castells' understanding of the world a situation whereby isolated, fragmented and powerless selves are trying to ride a Juggernaut - to use Giddens' (1990) term. While for Weber (and Kafka) the Juggernaut was the bureaucracy, for Castells it is the network. Networks, Castells writes - in a perhaps more Luhmannian than Weberian fashion - 'value-free or neutral. They can equally kill or kiss [...] a network is an automaton' (2000, p. 16). And just as in Weber's modern world, there are only two options in the information age. Either we 'bear the fate of the times like a man' (Weber, 1991, p.155) - which for Castells' (1997, p.355) means having no identity, only 'basic instincts, power drives, self-centered strategic calculations' - or we return to the 'arms of the old churches' (Weber, 1991, p.155). Global networks rule our world. If we are lucky and are born at the right time in the right place (that is, if we are connected to the right node in the right network), they can temporarily provide us with power and money, but they cannot provide us with meaning: 'The search for meaning takes place, then, in the reconstruction of defensive identities around communal principles' (Castells, 1997, p.11) Castells finds four types of such identities in the Information age; religious fundamentalism, nationalism, ethnic identity and territorial identity. All of them can be seen as variations on Weber's 'return to the old church'.

However, Castells stresses that these two options are not really open for choice. The first option - money and power, but no identity and no meaning - is for those included in the network society. The second option - a traditional type of identity and meaning, but no money and no power - is for the excluded. Defensive collective identities have the character of 'the exclusion of the excluders by the excluded' (Castells, 1997, p.9). This analysis might very well be true. But, on the other hand, one will hardly find, what one not is looking for. Castells writes (1997, p.3), 'that for me social theory is a tool'. However, perhaps he has picked out the wrong tools from the sociological toolkit. A theory that has 'the net and the self' as its fundamental components (Castells, 1996, pp.22-23) is not a two-level concept of society. It is not a distinction between two types of sociality, but between the society and the individual. It lacks an idea of modernisation of the moral-ethical sphere. It takes its point of departure in Marxian materialism, on the one side, and Weberian ethical relativism, on the other, ending up with a concept of network society that ultimately reminds us of pure differentiation theory à la Luhmann. If we find Habermas' reconstruction of classical sociology convincing, then we should at least look for signs of a transformation - and not only a fragmentation - of the moral-ethical sphere within modern society. If it is this kind of investigation we are interested in, I suggest that we discard Castells' *Information Age* and turn to Peter Wagner's *A Sociology of Modernity*.[13]

Wagner's Theory of the History of Modernity

Wagner is not a Habermasian. His sociology is not neo-classic. Rather, he is a good example of someone who has learned from both camps of the modernist-postmodernist debate. He does not see modernity as a question of liberty *or* rational discipline (Wagner 1994, pp.xi, 5ff). Modernisation cannot simply be understood as progress and liberation, which Enlightenment thinkers (including much first and second phase sociology) tend to believe, nor can it be understood as more or less tacit disciplining, as - for instance - Foucault and Bauman tend to believe. Rather, modernity, Wagner claims, has always been and always has to be - although in different constellations - at the same time *both* liberation *and* rational discipline. These two aspects are actually interdependent. The logic of autonomy in itself, that is the logic of self-rule, does not give us the substance of these rules. Freedom needs boundaries to be realised. Modernisation cannot simply mean liberation; it must necessarily also mean setting new rules and thus new boundaries. Wagner's theoretical point of departure is that *autonomy has to be bounded to exist at all.* And boundaries, of course, immediately limit freedom. Thus, modernity is an inherently ambivalent project. It is both freedom and discipline. The fact that new rules - after liberation from tradition - are not pre-given, but set in a more or less reflective or rational way does not at all mean that the disciplinary side of modernity tends to vanish. This fact is connected to the social conditions of self-rule. Autonomy is not and cannot be solely a private matter. It is - and more problematically so - always a public matter as well.

When we talk about a specific modern society, we are thus referring to a society that is founded upon - not simply autonomy - but *realised autonomy.* Such realisation of autonomy is always achieved in a special way. Realised modernity can thus never be something exclusively universal, as Enlightenment thinkers argued at times. Nor can realised modernity be purely contingent, as postmodern thinkers have sometimes suggested. Realised modernity is always an institutionalised, historic modernity. It is facticity, not simply contingency. Realised modernity is always *particular facticity.* Every modern society thus necessarily excludes - to some degree and in one way or the other - those who have tried to realise their freedom in a manner different from the dominant manner. The possibility of a modern society depends on the institutionalisation of common norms and values following the liberation from tradition. In this context, Wagner uses terms such as 'conventionalisation', 'collectivisation' or 'reembedding'. Realised modernity is always more than what Habermas and Rawls call 'justice'. It always includes more substantial and at the same time more particular conceptions of the collective good. Every modern society has some kind of disciplinary institutions to support these collectivisations. If this is true, a theory of modernity after postmodernism should draw the following conclusion: To understand discipline as darkness and liberty as light is too simple. What is crucial, rather, is the particular combination of these two inescapable sides of modernity.

If we accept Wagner's theoretical point of departure, it becomes clear that there can be different modernities. Modern society has not been - and can never become - a state of universal freedom. The recognition of this fact leads a theory of modernity in the direction of sociology and history. Wagner's point of departure can explain how we at the same time can have a general concept of modernity and talk about different epochs within modernity. The 'dialectic' between autonomy and rational disciplining provides us with the foundations of the general social logic of modernity. The particular ways in which this dialectic becomes realised in processes of conventionalisation and de-conventionalisation give us the different epochs of modernity. A society in which autonomy has no institutionalised significance is not modern. Habermas is thus correct in emphasising the importance of this kind of normativity for a theory of modernity. Castells, who does not give moral and ethical autonomy any significance in network society, is thus also theoretically consistent when he claims that the information age comes after the modern age. On the other hand, modernity must also include some type of institutionalised disciplining to be realised. Postmodern thinkers from Foucault to Judith Butler have all stressed that disciplining is normative. In this tradition, the concept of normativity primarily implies 'policing'. Norms normalise, regulate, govern and thus exclude 'the other' (Butler, 1999). Modern normative disciplining is distinguished from pre-modern normative disciplining by its use of individualised and therapeutic methods and by its use of rational methods - in a strategic-instrumental sense. As is well known, Foucault has - most explicitly in *Surveillir et punir* and in the first part of *Histoire de la sexualité* - shown how dominant modern social institutions use science, knowledge and various types of individualising technologies to govern in a distinctively modern normative way. No system can - beyond analytical distinctions - simply be understood as 'norm free sociality' (Fraser, 1989, p.113ff). Systems have specific normative consequences. Of course, it makes a normative difference whether systems 'kill or kiss'. But the criticism of systems theory (including Habermas' use of it) goes further. Systems use existing norms as their social material. Therefore, the transformation of social systems cannot be understood independently of the ongoing transformation of normative beliefs and technologies (Honneth, 1985, pp.279ff, 328ff; Wagner, 1994, p.188ff; Carleheden, 1996, p.37ff).

In my, rather free interpretation of Wagner, we have found the beginning of a general logic of modern social change, a logic which - in contrast to (neo-) classic modernisation theory - seems able to grasp social transformation within modernity. The stress on the normative - in the double sense just mentioned - means furthermore that this conception focuses precisely on the social dimension, which Castells neglects. Let us now proceed from this idea of a general logic of modernity to the particular epochs within modernity. It is this transformation within modernity that forms the main part of Wagner's book. The question is whether we can identify particular modern social logics that work in special ways in each different epoch of modernity and still remain within the general modern social logic. The idea of a transformation within modernity presupposes that this is the case.

According to Wagner, there have existed in the West the two historical epochs of realised modernity, with a third one now on its way. In chronological order, Wagner calls these three epochs 'restricted liberal modernity' (roughly during the 19th century), 'organised modernity' (roughly from the beginning the 20th century until the early 1970s) and 'extended liberal modernity'.[14] Between these epochs of modernity are two periods of crisis of modernity, both of which are characterised by contingency and uncertainty. The first crisis can be dated to around the turn of the 19th century, while the second is still with us. It is thus difficult to make any definitive statement about the third epoch of modernity. Wagner has more to say about the crisis of organised modernity, that is, the de-conventionalisation or de-collectivisation of the rules of organised modernity.

Before we go on, we should look more closely at a conceptual ambiguity in Wagner's book. Every now and then his division into three epochs of modernity appears to be a historical rather than sociological division. If we examine his conception from a sociological perspective, it seems to allow us to speak of only two epochs, the liberal and the organised. He sometimes gives the impression that organised modernity only interrupted the development from restricted to extended liberal modernity.[15] When I distinguish between a sociological and a historical approach, I mean the following: If we are to differentiate in a sociological sense, we should identify different social logics. If we find only gradual differences, interruptions, radicalisations and so on, then we are rather dealing with historical differences. Where this is the case, we do not really need a new grand *social* theory. It is unclear if Wagner at all wants to differentiate between a sociological and a historical account of modernity. In any case, he does not talk about any sort of social logic. However, the implication of Wagner's theoretical point of departure is that *each* epoch of modernity should be understood as a qualitatively different mixture of liberty and disciplining. This point of departure does not fit with the fact that Wagner's terms 'liberal' and 'organised' come very close to the terms 'liberty' and 'discipline'. In contrast to his point of departure, in his actual elaboration of his conception he inclines to 'either liberty or discipline' rather than different constellations of 'both liberty and discipline'. Or perhaps better, he indicates an understanding of the differences between the epochs as differences in degrees of liberty and discipline. More of the one entails less of the other. The second epoch of modernity, for instance, is characterised as a period where 'liberal practices were decreasingly important' and where 'the setting of boundaries and social production of certainties is generally privileged' (Wagner, 1994, p.68). Such a description contradicts his theoretical point of departure and means that his historical distinction between three types of modernity must be 'bent' such that it corresponds to a sociological distinction that only allows two types of modernity. I would rather like to retain Wagner's point of departure, where he speaks about three particular combinations of liberty and discipline. This would be a more promising and more consistent attempt to break away from old modernisation theory. If we are to clarify this idea, we must not simply find more or less autonomy and more or less discipline in the three historical epochs. Rather, we must find different social constellations of discipline and autonomy in each epoch. Each of these social constellations must be shown to have a particular social logic. In the following I can only describe the outlines of such a conception. I will then use Wagner's historical account of the three modernities while ignoring his ambiguities and contradictions. I will favour what I take to be the better side of his argument. Hence, I choose a different terminology than Wagner: I will refer to first, second and third modernity.

First modernity was based on the rule of law and on civil rights. This foundation provided opportunities for economical and political autonomy to only a small bourgeois and intellectual elite. Other formal or informal institutions created boundaries that excluded workers, women and those who were categorised as mad or perverse, that is, 'the masses'. In practice, 19th century modernists only partly trusted the revolutionary conception of universal human rights. In this sense, the masses were the objects and victims of modernisation rather than its agents. In another sense, the modern revolutions of science, production, economics and politics did indeed liberate large parts of the population from the contingencies of nature and from pre-modern conventions. However, as Marx showed with his ironic concept of the free worker, this liberation immediately turned into a harsh discipline. The traditional forms of discipline were replaced by the rational discipline of the market and the factory. This discipline is in turn related to the emergence of a new work ethic, which Weber examined in *Die protestantische Ethik und der Geist des Kapitalismus* and later Foucault in *Surveillir et punir* (compare also Bauman, 1998, p.5ff). The struggle against this particular form of modernity - most importantly in the movements for universal suffrage and workers' rights - should first and foremost be seen as a struggle against the harsh discipline of the market and the factory and against the unequal distribution resulting from capitalist production. Representative democracy, trade unions and the welfare state became the means for masses to constitute themselves as a class, to tame capitalist economy and thus to achieve economic autonomy. This process involves what Esping-Andersen (1990) calls the 'de-commodification' of the workers.

From what has already been discussed, it follows that second modernity cannot be understood as a simple increase in autonomy. A gain of autonomy in some form presupposes new conventions, boundaries and exclusions.

Autonomy has to be re-embedded. The main instruments of this social re-embedding process in second modernity were the institutionalisation of the imaginary ideas of not only class but also nationality. The 'masses' were included in modernity within the boundaries of class and nation.

If we reconstruct Marshall's (1964) conception of the evolution of citizenship, we can use it to capture some aspects of social transformation within modernity. The elitist character of first modernity shows that *civil rights* are not enough to realise autonomy for the masses. In second modernity, *social rights*, administered by a welfare bureaucracy, supplemented civil rights. This presupposes a strong collective agent, the nation state. But this state cannot simply be seen as an instrument of the will of an autonomous people. Rather, this state had to take an active part in creating an autonomous people. In other words, it was a paternalistic state and thus exerted a bounded autonomy at the very moment of its emergence. The political form that suited this kind of modernity was representative democracy. The representatives of the working class, i.e., politicians, intellectual legislators and experts of all kinds, allocated to themselves the right to work out the true will of the 'people' (Bauman, 1987). They did not simply try to interpret what individual citizens actually wanted. Rather, they presumed to know what the collective subject 'people' (the class or the nation) *should* want, if the people - as one of the more important avant-garde intellectual legislators of Swedish second modernity, Gunnar Myrdal (1954, p.201) put it - 'knew all that is actually known by contemporary experts.' This co-operation between scientists and politicians above the heads of ordinary people became what we now call 'social engineering'. The consequence of this kind of modernisation goes against the evolutionist picture of the development of citizenship given by Marshall. The institutionalisation of civil rights in first modernity was complemented in second modernity by the realisation of social rights rather than by the realisation of political rights. If we follow Habermas (1990), the inclusion of the masses went hand in hand with the decline of the public sphere. The difference between first and second modernity concerning political autonomy is therefore a difference between depth and scope, rather than between less or more.[16] Social order and mass loyalty to the state and its representatives was created through class and nation identifications. A good illustration of this paternalism comes from an interview with a high-ranking Swedish social democratic politician (Lars Stjernkvist), who states: 'In earlier days people joined the party out of loyalty to our ideas. Today they join because they want to influence and to change' (*Dagens Nyheter*, 16th June 2000; compare also Hirdman, 1990).[17] Stjernkvist's statement says quite a lot about what democracy meant in second modernity. Representative democracy, the welfare state and union struggles tamed the discipline of the market and the factory. These major institutions of second modernity were all expressions of general inclusion and autonomy in modern society. However, it was to a high degree a kind of paternalistic collective autonomy. It was an autonomy that presupposed belonging and loyalty to the imaginary institutions of class and nation. This belonging and loyalty involved the appearance of a new kind of rational discipline. I will illustrate that with an example from the Scandinavian model of second modernity - a model that in many senses comes close to the ideal typical case. The Icelandic pop star Björk has expressed this claim perfectly when she sings: 'Thought I could organise freedom/ how Scandinavian of me/' ('The Hunter', 1997).

In Scandinavia there has been little tension between class, nation and party identifications (Wagner, 1994, p.159). In Sweden, the national welfare state, which was largely constructed by the social democratic party, was called the 'people's home' (*folkhem*). In Norway the concept 'the workers-party state' (*arbeiderpartistaten*) has been suggested to grasp a similar social-political constellation (Slagstad, 1998, p.191). And in Denmark the still very influential philosopher and priest Nicolai Frederik Severin Grundtvig had already in the 19th century coined the term 'people's community' (*folkefælleskab*) and 'the Danish people's tribe' (*den danske folkestam*).[18] There were several ways to strengthen these identifications and thus integrate the masses into second modernity. One method was the afore-mentioned paternalistic form of democracy. The clearest case of the disciplinary character of second modernity, however, was the naturalisation of nationality and its methods. If one takes a closer look at how modernity managed to overcome its first crisis, it becomes clear that a more or less scientific kind of racism was used as a sort of social lever. Second modernity is partly built on the imaginary signification of nationality in terms of race (cf. Foucault, 1990; Bauman, 1991, p.32ff). Sweden actually had the first institute of eugenics (1922-1958) in the world. German scientists who later became important in the Nazi regime travelled to this institute to study (Zaremba, 1999, p.35). Today we can say that the aim of eugenics was literally to draw social boundaries of autonomy in the physical body. There was a concern for the 'population quality', for the physical and moral health of the 'human material' of the nation (Myrdal, 1968). In North America and Northern Europe - and most frequently in Scandinavia - sterilisations were utilised as instruments to improve not only the physical, but also the moral health of the population.[19] It is possible to claim that sterilisation at the time was seen as a rational instrument to physically create an autonomous people. I believe that the Scandinavian countries are interesting cases here, because they went very far in the direction of rational disciplining in their attempt to achieve autonomy. However, they never abandoned, as in Nazi Germany, the imaginary institution of autonomy. According to the theory of modernity which we have elaborated here, Bauman (1989, 1991) is wrong when he implies that National Socialism was the ultimate logical extreme of modernity (or, in our terminology, second modernity). Rather, Nazi Germany was modern only in the sense of its rational disciplining, but hardly in the sense of autonomy. During the years of National Socialist rule, Germany in fact broke with the general social logic of modernity. Now Bauman might rejoin that the racist idea of the *autonomy* of the 'German people' was crucial to Nazi politics. I would, however, claim that a modern conception of autonomy must in some sense be related to individualism. A state that completely abolishes the individual rights of some of its citizens crosses the moral-practical border of modernity. The rights of the citizens of modernity are individual rights. However, they are also formal rights and have in some way to be materialised and embedded. In second modernity, this embedding was typically accomplished via the collective identities of class and nation. This collective manner of materialisation limited individual rights in a special way, but it did not abolish them. The Scandinavian countries never left the dialectic of autonomy and rational disciplining. On the contrary, they probably worked through the possibilities of second modernity more thoroughly than any other countries.

The Scandinavian case demonstrates the value of using both 'modern' (individual rights) and 'postmodern' (rational discipline) concepts if we are to understand the complexity of the different epochs within modernity. In order to realise the private and public autonomy that is implicit in the moral-practical dimension of modernity, the masses had to use different forms of collective action. This presupposed their self-transformation, by means of a collective identity from a mass to a collective subject. However, the extensive use of sterilisations in Scandinavia is a clear indication of the importance of also using Foucault and Bauman's thesis of rational disciplining, normalisation and exclusion to achieve the full picture of this kind of modernisation. To a high degree, it affected those who were categorised as Gypsies. And a majority of those who were sterilised - at least in Sweden - were women diagnosed as 'feeble-minded'. This was a term with a medical aura but which also had an undoubtedly moral content. By means of sterilisation, a morally clean race was to be created. To be a sexually active woman without being married could be reason enough for sterilisation (Runcis, 1998). The example of sterilisation is used to show how autonomy in second modernity was rationally bounded. Private and public autonomy were realised through individual citizens' identification with a *particular* collective subject - be it the nation, the race, the society, the working class or simply the people. Such identification presupposes disciplining and normalisation, and those who could not or refused to adapt were excluded.

Today, all the characteristic components of second modernity have been in a situation of crisis for a couple of decades. For a rather long period, we have been living under the social conditions of de-conventionalisation and dis-embedding, that is, in the second crisis of modernity. Let me just mention some of the more well-known aspects of this crisis (compare the introduction to this volume):

- Paternalistic social engineering and representative democracy is losing legitimacy.
- Class identification has to a large extent disappeared due to the relative success of the welfare state and its individualising methods.
- The nation-state and national identities have declined in importance due to globalisation.
- The welfare state is in crisis due to globalisation and the 'legitimation crisis'.
- We are witnessing a general 'deconstruction' of fixed identities, which is supported by the above-mentioned general social trends (Sennett, 1998; Bauman, 1998, p.23ff; Wagner, 1994, p.154ff). Under these 'flexible' social conditions, Queer Theory's celebration of 'fluid identities' seems to be losing its critical edge and is beginning to reflect these new conditions.[20]

Wagner has much more to say about this crisis of second modernity than about third modernity. He even writes that today 'no major reembedding is recognizable' (1994, p.170). The last part of the book has therefore the cautious title 'Towards Extended Liberal Modernity?'. However, if we are correct in our claim above that autonomy has to become bounded to exist at all, we cannot stay in the contemporary situation of contingency and uncertainty for long. Either we are departing from modernity, as Castells implies, or, *pace* Wagner (1994, pp.175, 182) despite his hesitancy seems to be claiming, we are entering a third epoch of realised modernity. However, Wagner has a tendency to see this new epoch in terms of increased liberty and less discipline. Hence, he highlights the return of the idea of a public sphere, which Habermas saw declining with first modernity. This return is related both to the 1989 'revolutions' in East-Europe and the legitimation crisis in the

West (Cohen and Arato, 1992). Nevertheless, on the last page of his book, Wagner refers to a second 'reorganisation of modernity':

> The record of organised modernity [what we here would term 'second modernity'] is a very mixed one. Any of its strong institutions and discourses was enabling and constraining, liberating and disciplining at the same time. The same would almost inevitably be true for another attempt at institution-building (Wagner, 1994, p.193).

Thus, he returns to what I have called his theoretical point of departure. However, we find no conception of any sort of third modernity here. We must seek elsewhere. Before we do, however, let me just make an intermediate conclusion of what we have found out so far about modernity and its transformation.

Intermediate Conclusion

We have located a general social logic of modernity. The dialectic of liberty and rational discipline has generally reproduced itself in the West since the end of the 18th century. This theory of modernity is in many ways related to the master concepts of (neo-)classic sociology. First modernity can be understood, at least partly, as the outcome of the struggles of the bourgeois class, while the welfare state of second modernity can be seen as a compromise between the interests of the working class and the bourgeoisie. In both cases, we need notions of liberation and autonomy to understand this development. On the other hand, Marx's concept of alienation and exploitation, Weber's concept of the 'iron cage' and Habermas' concept of 'colonisation' clearly specify different types of rational discipline. Yet in contrast to these types, our concept of discipline, like postmodern concepts in general, stresses the normative aspect. Habermas' idea of communicative rationalisation seems on first sight to be compatible with Wagner's conception of autonomy. The difference is that Wagner's history of modernity shows that processes of normative conventionalisation and collectivisation play crucial roles also in modern times. This points us in a partly different direction than the concepts of class struggle, rationalisation and differentiation. The emergence of the Weberian type of work ethic or collective identities like class and nation cannot simply be understood as effects of social processes of differentiation and individualisation. As Habermas has shown, we cannot explain processes of social integration solely in terms of differentiation. Habermas' theory of communicative action fails, however, to satisfy our theoretical needs for two reasons. First, his conception of modern morality comprises a concept of right or justice (norms), rather than a concept of the good (values).[21] Habermas has developed a Kantian idea of post-conventional, universal norms. Such a theory of necessarily formal and abstract norms is important for understanding the meaning of private and public autonomy in general but has nothing to say about how autonomy is realised in the different epochs within modernity. The concept of justice is much too thin for our sociological purposes. We also need conceptions of distinctly modern values to be able to understand the significance of normative conventionalisations, collectivisations and disciplining for the realisation of autonomy.[22] Because Habermas does not really see this need, he cannot see any justification for a social theory that makes space for the self-transformation of modernity.[23] This leads us directly over to the second explanation as to why Habermas' social theory cannot be the Grand Theory of our times. We have said that Habermas misses the importance of modern normative collective identities as class and nation. Some other parts of his social theory, however, are rather thick, notably his colonisation thesis. This shows that Habermas sociological work perhaps should be seen as a reflection of the decline of second modernity, rather than of second modernity at its height. In any case, his social theory does not go beyond the particular social logic of second modernity. His social theory deals with a nationally bounded society in which the welfare state plays the crucial role. It is a society where the political system colonises the public sphere and turns political autonomy into a mere formality. To be sure, Habermas claims that such kind of modernity is unfinished, but the main structure of this society would not change with its unlikely completion. What would change is only the balance between the lifeworld and the system. We cannot understand a completion of modernity in Habermas' sense as a transformation within modernity, but rather, as second modernity's idealisation of itself.[24]

As a second intermediate conclusion, we may note that, we have so far found that the dialectic between liberty and discipline in the West has historically realised itself in at least two distinct ways. In first modernity, this general social logic took its main form in the dialectic between individual liberation from nature and traditional power, on the one hand, and the immediate discipline of the market and the factory on the other. In second modernity, we found the same general social logic in the dialectic between, on the one hand, the collective power of a nationally bounded working class freeing itself, by means of the trade union, the party and the democratic social state, from material hardship and commodification and, on the other, the paternalistic, bureaucratic and normalising consequences of this type of liberation. Furthermore, between first and second modernity and after second modernity we found two different types of crisis of modernity. This suggests that the loss of meaning noted by Weber - experiencing the first crisis - and by Bauman and other postmodernists - experiencing the second - that this loss of meaning is not the destiny of the inhabitants of modernity in general. This leads us to the final question to be asked in this chapter. Is a third modernity presently being constituted? And if so, how should this new emerging epoch be understood?

Contours of a Third Modernity

To be able to answer these questions, we need to search for a new kind of realised dialectic between autonomy and rational discipline. This task requires a much deeper discussion than what can be described in these concluding remarks. My aim here is only to demonstrate that if we stand on the foundation of the theory of modernity developed above and examine some of the recent findings in social science, we will find more than contingency and uncertainty. Rather, modernity has already started to realise itself in a third way.

There can be no doubt about which point of departure we should chose for this investigation. Contemporary social scientists seem to more or less agree that the most important topic today is 'globalisation'.[25] Third modernity is a global modernity, not only in an economic, but also in a political, a cultural and a social sense.

At the *economic* level, globalisation has meant the liberation of capitalist forces from the relatively firm grip of the nation-state. In this sense, we seem to be experiencing a return to first modernity, but now on a global level. This involves, on the one hand, a widening of the free market and an increase in civil autonomy (cf. Bertilsson, 2001). On the other, this revitalization of capitalism means a re-commodification of workers or better - in view of the post-industrial character of third modernity in the wealthiest parts of the globe, - of employees (Castells, 1996-1998, Sennett, 1998).

In *political* terms, globalisation seems, on the one hand, to have increased the distance between those who represent and those who are represented to such an extent that some political scientists have begun to speak of the end of democracy (cf. Brunkhorst, 2001). While the welfare bureaucracy is shrinking at the national level, an army of global bureaucrats - appointed by national governments, multinational companies or other non-governmental organisations - has suddenly appeared, carrying out their deliberations and taking decisions at a secure distance from the nationally bounded citizen. On the other hand, the declining significance of national sovereignty has enlarged the political terrain. With the end of the Cold War, transnational and, to some extent, democratic organisations like the EU[26] and the UN have started to play a global role. Social movements for environmental protection, human rights and anti-global capitalism have at the same time created the rudiment of a transnational civil society and a public sphere.[27] This re-emergence of the public sphere is related to the legitimation crisis of second modernity. Just as the emergence of second modernity must be understood in relation to the social dialectic of first modernity, the emergence of a third modernity must be understood in relation to the social dialectic of second modernity. As we have seen, the citizen of second modernity - as a result of paternalistic political organisations and the colonising effects of the political system - has in practice never played the political role that was formally given to the citizen in the democratic constitutions of the Western countries. If we believe that classic (Weber) and neo-classic (Habermas) social theory were correct in their claims that power has to have legitimacy and that, in modernity, legitimacy - at least to some extent - presupposes democracy, then third modernity cannot mean the end of democracy (cf. Larsen, 2001). Rather, we would expect third modernity to be a reaction against the paternalistic democracy of second modernity. The new social movements, which evolved during the crisis of second modernity, could thus be seen as an indication of the meaning of public autonomy in third modernity. The struggle against political inequality has become at least as important as the struggle against inequality in material welfare.[28]

The *cultural* dimension of globalisation has provided us with clear indications of what third modernity involves. The ethnic homogeneity which was a pre-condition of 'the Scandinavian model', belongs to the past (cf. Dencik, 2001). On the one hand, this means intensified ethnic struggles. In third modernity, struggles for recognition, identity politics or politics of difference are more significant than class struggle. On the other hand, the idea that globalisation is producing a cultural homogenisation can, at the most, be defended from a view from nowhere, from God eye's view. The everyday experiencing of foreign lifestyles, values and beliefs among ordinary people is without doubt more frequent today than in any other epoch of world history. And while racism and crude nationalism was national state policy at least during the construction of second modernity, criticism of the universalisation of the experiences of the Western, white, middle-class, heterosexual male has today become 'politically correct'.

At the *social* level, globalisation means, on the one hand, a 'stretching process' of the time-space distance (Giddens, 1990, p.64); i.e., a radicalisation of the separation of time and space, which, according to Giddens, is typical of modernity in general. Social integration has thus to take place over larger time-space distances. However, Giddens claims that this stretching process does not simply mean that social relations are getting 'colder' and that a fragmentation of the social has taken place. Strategic relations to global and technical systems or networks make up a considerable part of sociality in third modernity. On the other hand, we have also experienced an intensification of other social relations. There is, Giddens writes, 'a turning inward toward human subjectivity, and meaning and stability are sought in the inner self' (Giddens, 1990, p.115). Intimate relations today increasing depend on the ability of opening up this inner self to the other, on 'a mutual process of self-disclosure' (Giddens, 1990, p.121). We find support for such an analysis of the growing significance of inner life in Habermas' (1981a) thesis of the differentiation of the subjective world from the objective and the social worlds. However, it is Charles Taylor (1989) who most significantly has developed this understanding of the modern self with his emphasis on the concept of authenticity. Third modernity should in this respect be understood as 'the age of authenticity' (Ferrara, 1998).[29] Let us conclude by developing this conception a bit further. This transformation of intimate life has not only consequence on a micro level, but for social life in general.

Like Habermas, Taylor has no notion of transformations *within* modernity. In his conception, the invention of the inner self is Modern. His conception is too philosophical and too dependent on a history of ideas to be directly useful for us. It is difficult to see how a conception of inner self could help us understand the significance of civil rights and of the work ethic during first modernity or the importance of social rights and loyalty to a class or a nation during second modernity. Giddens, on the other hand, acknowledges changes within modernity. For Giddens, however, it seems to be a question of radicalisation rather than transformation. We find more support for our thesis of a transformation of the formation of personal identity among 'postmodern' thinkers. On the one hand we have the well-known theory of the emergence of narcissism (Lasch, 1991) and consumerism. Bauman (1998) actually calls one of his chapters 'From the Work Ethic to the Aesthetic of Consumption', omitting, however, the class, nation and loyalty ethic of second modernity. And Foucault, towards the end of his life, claimed that 'for a whole lot of reasons, the idea of morality as obedience to a code of rules is now disappearing, has already disappeared. And to this absence of morality, must correspond, the search for an aesthetics of existence' (Foucault, 1988, p.49). It is surely this Foucauldian idea that Richard Rorty (1989, p.23ff) is relying upon in his understanding of selfhood as an aesthetic invention - 'life-as-poem'. Postmodern thinkers would, of course, not use the term 'authenticity' because they associate it with essentialism. This association, however, is fallacious in the case of Taylor, Habermas and Giddens, who use 'authenticity' in a Heideggerian sense. However, all of them would probably agree with Taylor (1991, p.35ff) when he claims that 'defining myself means finding what is significant in my difference from others'. While this is not the place for detailed discussion of the differences between these thinkers, I believe that we can use their ideas to develop a concept of personal identity which is distinctly different from the kind of personal identities that existed in the earlier epochs of modernity.

Personal identity is not something that simply emerges in an isolated individual. Rather, it is socially constituted and needs recognition. Identity formation in third modernity is a social process where we open up our inner selves and are accorded recognition by the other. We cannot limit this kind of sociality to love and friendship relations. Identity is built upon values which we share with people who are like us. Together with them we create communities, cultivate these values and struggle for recognition. There is nothing suggesting that such values must be traditional. The typical form of disciplining of identity formation in third modernity is the market and consumerism rather than tradition. Value construction in modernity in general is post-traditional (cf. Joas, 1999). However, we are talking about another kind of community than the communities of second modernity. Communities in third modernity are not paternalistically organised. Authenticity-seeking selves and paternalism do not go well together. I cannot develop this point further here. I just wanted to demonstrate that social relations in third modernity are neither limited to strategic relations to global systems and consumerism, nor to distant respect for the human rights of strangers. There are also social relations which demand authenticity and which are organised in non-hierarchical communities.[30]

In this last section, I have tried to indicate that there exist dialectics between autonomy and rational discipline in all these four aspects of globalisation. In the economic sphere, there is the dialectic between global civil autonomy, on the one hand, and global material inequality and commodification of work, on the other. In the political sphere, there is the dialectic between a global political bureaucracy and a global public sphere. In the cultural sphere, there is the dialectic between homogenisation and heterogenisation within global society. And in the social sphere we finally found the dialectic between a distanciation and an intensification of social relations. Surely these four spheres are interrelated. To fully distinguish third modernity from earlier epochs of modernity, we should be able to grasp how these different dialectics merge into one main dialectic. I have not found any convincing attempt to do this yet. On the other hand, it would be surprising if the owl of Minerva was already about to take off.

Notes

1 We can also call this second phase of sociology the American phase. Compare Wagner (1994, p.111) who describes Merton's sociology as a synthesis between Lazarsfeld and Parsons' sociology. Neither sooner nor later has sociology come closer to Kuhn's conception of science, with only one prevalent paradigm at any given time, as during the governance of this Mertonian synthesis.

2 Beck (1993, 1997) and Carleheden's (1996) distinction between first and second modernity is too broad to catch the transformations within Western modernity. Rather, I will follow Wagner (1994) on this point.

3 I am here only discussing the social theoretical part of the debate. In Carleheden (1996, 1998) I have dealt with the moral and ethical part and in Carleheden (1999) with the epistemological part of that debate.

4 Compare, for instance Lyotard, Bauman and Lash. Already in 1982, Lyotard - in contrast to his 1979 book - claimed that postmodernity is a part of modernity. Bauman (2000, p.2) - in contrast to Bauman (1992) - talks about 'liquid modernity' as 'the present stage of the modern era' and the present 'phase in the history of modernity'. Lash (1999) uses Beck's term 'another modernity' as the title of his latest book. This is a term that Beck (1986, p.12) used as an attempt to find a way beyond the - at the time - very polarised modernist-postmodernist debate. Unfortunately, this fact is concealed for the reader of the English version of Beck's book because here '*eine andere Moderne*' for some strange reason is translated into 'new modernity'. Castells is one of the few important contemporary exceptions to this theoretical trend, even though he does not use the term 'postmodernity'. Castells apparently believes that 'the information age' comes *after* modernity (cf. Castells, 1997, pp.10-11).

5 Actually Habermas admits this himself in an interview with Frederik Stjernfelt in the Danish newspaper *Weekendavisen* (26 September - 2 October, 1997). Habermas here talks about 'my own lacking ability to create conceptual tools which can capture the present' and 'I have participated in the public debate for 40 years. The next generation must take over' (my translation).

6 I hereby partly revise my earlier account of Habermas (Carleheden, 1996, pp.166-175), where I tended to blend the normative advantages of Habermas' theory with his less successful sociological attempt to understand contemporary society. In the mid-1970s, Habermas had still not closed the door to the idea of a postmodern society (Habermas, 1976, p.182). Since his normative critique of postmodernism, in his famous article on the so-called 'unfinished project of modernity' (1981b), the door seems to be closed for good. There is a confusing theoretical relationship between Habermas and Beck in this context. Beck claims to have been inspired by Habermas' 1981-article when he developed his conception of 'second modernity' (Beck, 1997, p.25). This seems to be a creative misunderstanding, because Habermas' argumentation - in contrast to Beck's - is rather normative and implies that Modernity might be completed. It is not an idea about different epochs within modernity. Habermas, in turn, refers to Beck and the idea of a post-industrial

society (Habermas, 1998, pp.229-230; cf. also 1988, pp.234-241). Here he uses Beck's terminology of industrial societies as 'semi-modern' societies (Beck, 1986, 1993, pp.99-96). Such a terminology better fits Habermas' second-phase sociology than Beck's own sociology. It is true to the logic of 'modernisation theory I', even though it partly changes its substance and postpones the end of history. Beck cannot develop such an idea without endangering his position as one of the leading figures of the third phase sociology. The concept 'semi-modern society' implies stages on the route *to* Modernity, while concepts such as 'another modernity' and 'second modernity' imply the possibility of different epochs *within* modernity. The academic relationship between Habermas and Beck is thus a sign of uncertainty in Beck's own work. In it we also find the idea that the first modernity was in fact not completely modern. This explains why a second-phase sociologist such as Habermas can at all use Beck.

7 Habermas (1998) also makes clear that he has not changed his sociological thinking in any significant way since 1981.

8 Compare Kant's differentiation between theoretical, practical and aesthetic reason in his *Critiques*, and Hegel's distinction between family, civil society and state in his *Rechtphilosophie*.

9 Symbolic reproduction is more than reproduction of solidarity and ethical life, but here I will focus on the moral-practical dimension.

10 Habermas rejects the Marxian kind of Hegelian reconciliation, that is, that class struggle will finally end with the socialist revolution. Habermas does not believe that modern society can manage without systemic integration. We can only hope for the right balance between social and systemic integration.

11 I will return to Habermas' distinction (1991, p.100ff; compare also Habermas, 2000 - his latest comment on this subject) between moral (norms) and ethics (values). Both are in turn to be distinguished from preferences or private interests, which is the action-theoretical basis for most economic theories and for those sociological theories inspired by economics (e.g., rational choice).

12 Compare Castells' most recent pronouncements on this subject. He writes that 'while technology is not the cause of the transformation, it is indeed the indispensable medium. And in fact, it is what constitutes the historical novelty of this multidimensional transformation' (2000, p.14).

13 Wagner (1994, p.21) investigates modern practices, institutions and technologies of material allocation, authoritative power and signification (or symbolic representation). Here I will particularly utilize his general conception of modernity and the different aspects of authoritative power and signification. Signification connotes forms of modern self-understanding, for instance, in a moral-ethical sense.

14 These periods must of course be dated slightly differently in different Western countries.

15 Compare, for instance, Wagner (1994, p.158). Here he talks about organised modernity as a period, which 'could temporarily arrest modernity'.

16 I believe that this early historical work of Habermas - in contrast to his later works - is immediately useful for our attempt to develop a conception of transformation within modernity. However, Habermas speaks only about the bourgeois public sphere and its decay in the mass democracy of the 'social state', that is - in our terminology - it is only a distinction between first and second modernity. In this historical context, we can also understand Habermas' later theory of colonisation and clientisation as a theory of rational discipline in second modernity.

17 Actually, people also join less and less. Membership in political parties in Sweden is shrinking dramatically - especially membership in the Social Democratic Party.

18 For a more comprehensive account of the Swedish and Danish case, see Dencik (2001). For

similar concepts used in other Western countries during second modernity, compare Wagner (1994, p.66ff).

19 If we make adjustments for difference in population size, this instrument has been used more frequently in Norway, Finland and Sweden than anywhere else in the world, including Nazi-Germany.

20 For an opposite view on this last point, compare Seidman (2001).

21 This was not always the case. In the 1970s, Habermas had still not made any systematic distinction between norms and values (compare for instance Habermas, 1976, p.63ff). The systematic split between norms and values was made only after *Theorie des kommunikativen Handelns*, which is a work that is very indecisive on this point. Soon after, however, Habermas (1983, p.189) explicitly claimed that only norms, not values, can be post-conventional. This means that only norms, not values can be modern. We have here a notion of pure autonomy which is still caught up in the logic of Enlightenment thinking and old modernisation theory.

22 In this sense Parsons' theory, due to its focus on norm-regulated action, is a better reflection of second modernity than Habermas' theory.

23 During the 1990s, he began to develop a conception of ethics (i.e., a theory of values) in contrast to morality (i.e., a theory of norms), but the former is very underdeveloped and his aim is to say what morality is not, rather than to say what ethics is.

24 It is true that since the early 1990s, Habermas has been attempting to incorporate the fact of globalisation into his theory. But he does this on a strictly political level rather than on a sociological one. Compare Beck (2000, p.91), who criticises Habermas for only having 'extended national politics, one historical size bigger'.

25 The programme of the last world conference of the International Sociological Association in Montreal, for instance, shows globalisation to have been the most popular topic.

26 There cannot be any doubt about that the EU is talking small steps towards becoming a less international and a more transnational (federal) organisation.

27 Jaatinen and Hultman (2000) call tellingly their study of the demonstrations against WTO in Seattle 'Our opposition is as global as the capital'.

28 Compare Inglehart (1997), who claims that a shift from materialist to postmaterialist values has occurred in 'the advanced industrial society' in the period 1970-1994.

29 It is rather surprising to see that Habermas once (1976, p.182) actually saw the coming of a 'postmodern society' in this sense.

30 Different kinds of new social movements, subcultures and shared lifestyles are examples of such communities.

References

Augé, M. (1995), *Non-Places: Introduction to an Anthropology of Supermodernity*, Verso, London.

Bauman, Z. (1987a), *Legislators and Interpreters*, Cornell University Press, Ithaca, New York.

Bauman, Z. (1987b), *Modernity and the Holocaust*, Polity Press, Cambridge.

Bauman, Z. (1991), *Modernity and Ambivalence*, Polity Press, Cambridge.

Bauman, Z. (1992), *Intimations of Postmodernity*, Routledge, London.

Bauman, Z. (1998), *Work, Consumerism and the New Poor*, Open University Press, Buckingham.

Bauman, Z. (2000), *Liquid Modernity*, Polity Press, Cambridge.

Beck, U. (1986), *Risikogesellschaft: Auf dem Weg in eine andere Moderne*, Suhrkamp, Frankfurt am Main.
Beck, U. (1992), *Risk Society: Towards a New Modernity*, Sage, London.
Beck, U. (1993), *Die Erfindung des Politischen*, Suhrkamp, Frankfurt am Main.
Beck, U. (1997), *Was ist Globalisierung?*, Suhrkamp, Frankfurt am Main.
Beck, U. (2000), 'The Cosmopolitan Perspective: Sociology of the Second Age of Modernity', *British Journal of Sociology*, vol. 51 no. 1, pp.79-105.
Beck, U., Giddens, A. and S. Lash (1994), *Reflexive Modernization*, Polity Press, Cambridge.
Bell, D. (1973), *The Coming of Post-Industrial Society: A Venture in Social Forecasting*, Basic Books, New York.
Bertilsson, M. (2001), 'Professions on the Road to Global Power: The Case of the Legal Profession', in this volume.
Brunkhorst, H. (2001), 'Global Society as the Crisis of Democracy', in this volume.
Butler, J. (1999), 'Preface (1999)' in Butler, J.: *Gender Trouble: Feminism and the Subversion of Identity*, Routledge, New York.
Carleheden, M. (1996), *Det andra moderna: Om Jürgen Habermas och den samhällsteoretiska diskursen om det moderna*, Daidalos, Göteborg.
Carleheden, M. (1998), 'Another Sociology: The Future of Sociology from a Critical Theoretical Perspective', *Dansk Sociologi*, vol. 9 special issue, pp. 55-75.
Carleheden, M. (1999), 'Reconstructing Epistemology: Toward a Post-Positivist Conception of Social Science', *Sociologisk Arbejdspapir*, no. 3, University of Aalborg.
Castells, M. (1996), *The Rise of the Network Society*, Blackwell, Oxford.
Castells, M. (1997), *The Power of Identity*, Blackwell, Oxford.
Castells, M. (1998), *End of Millennium*, Blackwell, Oxford.
Castells, M. (1998), 'Materials for an Exploratory Theory of the Network Society', *British Journal of Sociology*, vol. 51 no. 1, pp.5-24.
Cohen, J. and A. Arato (1992), *Civil Society and Political Theory*, M.I.T Press, Cambridge, Mass.
Crook, S., Pakulski, J. and M. Waters (1992), *Postmodernization: Change in Advanced Society*, Sage, London.
Dencik. L. (2001), 'Transformations of Identities in Rapidly Changing Societies', in this volume.
Esping-Andersen, G. (1990), *The Three Worlds of Welfare Capitalism*, Polity Press, Cambridge.
Etzioni, A. (1968), *The Active Society: A Theory of Societal and Political Processes*, Collier-Macmillan, London.
Ferrara, A. (1998), *Reflective Authenticity*, Routledge, London.
Foucault, M. (1988), 'An Aesthetics of Existence' in Kritzman, L. (ed.), *Michel Foucault: Politics, Philosophy, Culture: Interviews and Other Writings 1977-1984*, Routledge, London.
Foucault, M. (1990), *The History of Sexuality Vol. 1: An Introduction*, Random House, New York.
Fraser, N. (1989), *Unruly Practices*, Polity Press, Cambridge.
Fukuyama, F. (1999), *The Great Disruption*, Profile Books, London.
Giddens, A. (1990), *The Consequences of Modernity*, Polity Press, Cambridge.
Habermas, J. (1976), *Zur Rekonstruktion des historischen Materialismus*, Suhrkamp, Frankfurt am Main.
Habermas, J. (1981a), *Theorie des kommunikativen Handelns*, 2 vols., Suhrkamp, Frankfurt am Main.

Habermas, J. (1981b), 'Die Moderne - ein unvollendetes Projekt', in Habermas, J.: *Kleine politische Schriften I-IV*, Suhrkamp, Frankfurt am Main.

Habermas, J. (1983), *Moralbewußtsein und kommunikatives Handeln*, Suhrkamp, Frankfurt am Main.

Habermas, J. (1984a), *Vorstudien und Ergänzungen zur Theorie des kommunikativen Handelns*, Suhrkamp, Frankfurt am Main.

Habermas, J. (1984b), *Communication and the Evolution of Society*, Polity Press, Cambridge.

Habermas, J. (1987), *The Theory of Communicative Action: vol.2*, Polity Press, Cambridge.

Habermas, J. (1990), *Strukturwandel der Öffentlichkeit*, Suhrkamp, Frankfurt am Main.

Habermas, J. (1991), *Erläuterungen zur Diskursethik*, Suhrkamp, Frankfurt am Main.

Habermas, J. (1998), 'Konzeptionen der Moderne: Ein Rückblick auf zwei Traditionen', in Habermas, J.: *Die postnationale Konstellation*, Suhrkamp, Frankfurt am Main.

Habermas, J. (2000), 'Werte und Normen', *Deutsche Zeitschrift für Philosophie*, vol.48 no.4, pp.547-564.

Häusermann, H. and W. Siebel (1995), *Dienstleistungsgesellschaften*, Suhrkamp, Frankfurt am Main.

Hirdman, Y. (1990), *Att lägga livet till rätta - studier i svensk folkhemspolitik*, Carlssons, Helsingborg.

Honneth, A. (1985), *Kritik der Macht*, Suhrkamp, Frankfurt am Main.

Inglehart, R. (1997), *Modernization and Postmodernization: Cultural, Economic and Political Change in 43 Societies*, Princeton University Press, Princeton, NJ.

Jaatinen, J. and P. Hultman (2000) 'Vårt motstånd är lika globalt som kapitalet – en fallstudie av demonstrationerna i Seattle', Institutionen för Freds- och Utvecklingsforskning, University of Gothenburg.

Jacobsen, M. H. and N. Chatterjee (2001), 'The Fall of Public Place: Sociological Reflections and Observations on a Supermodern American Ghost City', *Sociologisk Arbejdspapir*, no. 9, University of Aalborg.

Jensen, R. (1999), *The Dream Society*, McGraw-Hill, New York.

Joas, H. (1999), *Die Entstehung der Werte*, Suhrkamp, Frankfurt am Main.

Kumar, K. (1995), *From Post-Industrial to Post-Modern Society*, Blackwell, Oxford.

Larsen, Ø (2001), 'Modern Reflexive Leadership', in this volume.

Lasch, C. (1991), *The Culture of Narcissism*, W.W. Norton & Company, New York.

Lash, S. (1999), *Another Modernity: A Different Rationality*, Blackwell, Oxford.

Lyotard, J-F. (1979), *La condition postmoderne: rapport sur le savoir*, Éd. de minuit, Paris.

Lyotard, J-F. (1982), 'Reponse a la Question: Qu'est-ce que le postmoderne?', *Critigue*, no. 419, pp 357-367.

Marshall, T. H. (1964), 'Citizenship and Social Class', in Marshall, T. H., *Class, Citizenship, and Social Development*, Garden City, New York.

Maus, I. (1992), *Zur Aufklärung der Demokratietheorie*, Suhrkamp, Frankfurt am Main.

Myrdal, A. (1968), *Nation and Family: the Swedish Experiment in Democratic Family and Population Policy*, M.I.T Press, Cambridge, Mass.

Myrdal, G. (1954), *The Political Element in the Development of Economic Theory*, Harvard University Press, Cambridge, Mass.

Reese-Schäfer, W. (1999), 'Die seltsame Konvergenz der Zeitdiagnosen: Versuch einer Zwischenbilanz', *Soziale Welt*, vol.50 no 4, pp.433-448.

Ritzer, G. (1996), *Sociological Theory*, McGraw-Hill, New York.

Ritzer, G. (1999), *Re-Enchanting a Disenchanted World: Revolutionizing the Means of Consumption*, Pine Forge Press, Thousand Oaks, CA.

Rorty, R. (1989), *Contingency, Irony and Solidarity*, Cambridge University Press, Cambridge.

Runcis, M. (1998), *Sterilisering i folkhemmet*, Ordfront, Stockholm.

Schulze, G. (1993), *Die Erlebnisgesellschaft*, Campus, Frankfurt am Main.

Seel, M. (1986), 'Eine zweite Moderne?', *Merkur*, vol. 40 no.3, pp. 245-251.

Seel, M. (1989), 'Plädoyer für die zweite Moderne', in Kunneman, H. and Hent de Vries (eds.), *Die Aktualität der 'Dialektik der Aufklärung': Zwischen Moderne und Postmoderne*, Campus, Frankfurt am Main.

Seidman, S. (2001), 'Modern and Postmodern Themes in American Sexual Politics', in this volume.

Sennett, R. (1998), *The Corrosion of Character*, W.W. Norton & Company, New York.

Slagstad, R. (1998), *De nasjonale strateger*, Pax, Oslo.

Sztompka, P. (1993), *The Sociology of Social Change*, Blackwell, Oxford.

Taylor, C. (1989), *Sources of the Self: The Making of the Modern Identity*, Harvard University Press, Cambridge, Mass.

Taylor, C. (1991), The Ethics of Authenticity, Harvard University Press, Cambridge, Massachusetts.

Tiryakian, E. (1991), 'Modernisation: Exhumetur in Pace', *International Sociology*, vol. 6 no.2, pp.165-180.

Wagner, P. (1994), *A Sociology of Modernity: Liberty and Discipline*, Routledge, London.

Wallerstein, I. et al. (1996), *Open the Social Sciences*, Stanford University Press, Stanford, CA.

Weber, M. (1934), *Gesammelte Aufsätze zur Religionssoziologie I*, J.C.B. Mohr, Tübingen.

Weber, M. (1991), 'Science as a Vocation', in Gerth H. H. and C. W. Mills (eds.), *From Max Weber: Essays in Sociology*. Routledge, London.

Zaremba, M. (1999), *De rena och de andra*, Bokförlaget DN, Stockholm.

Part II
Identity, Sexuality and the Intimate Sphere

6 Modern and Postmodern Themes in American Sexual Politics

STEVEN SEIDMAN

Since at least the 1950s, a social division between a dominant heterosexual majority and a subordinate homosexual minority has been central to American society. This hierarchy has been maintained, until recently, by primarily repressive practices. These practices create the idea of the heterosexual and the homosexual as antithetical human types and enforce the normative status of heterosexuality by polluting the homosexual. I will argue that in the last decade or so, the norm of heterosexuality has been sustained less by social repression than by normalizing controls. Moreover, I suggest that if we understand gay identity politics as a response to a repressive social logic of normative heterosexuality, a historically unique type of sexual politics, so-called queer politics, can be viewed as a response to gay normalization.

In the course of sketching this shift from the 'gay' to the 'queer', and from homosexual pollution to normalization, I will comment on its broader social meaning. Specifically, I raise the question: are these shifts in sexual politics indicative of a movement from modernity to postmodernity? The answer is, I think, mixed. On the one hand, if we take gay identity politics as an indication of modernity, then the rise of queer politics suggests a postmodern event. On the other hand, identity politics is still, at least in the United States, the dominant mode of politics. This suggests that the modern/postmodern dichotomy is perhaps appropriately viewed in analytical rather then linear, temporal terms.

Contemporary American gay culture can be dated from the 1950s. Two events occurred. First, there was the dominance of a view of homosexuality as a deviant minority identity. Second, there occurred, perhaps for the first time historically, a national campaign to enforce normative heterosexuality by enlisting the state and other social institutions to control the homosexual. This societal mobilization, deploying strategies of repression and pollution, gave birth to the era of the closet and identity politics.

Central to this logic is the exclusion of the homosexual from public life. Constructing the homosexual as defiled justifies her exclusion from public life. Symbolically degrading the homosexual contributes to creating dominated gay selves - that is, individuals for whom shame and guilt are at the core of their sense of self. Public invisibility becomes partly self-enforced. The exclusion of the homosexual from public life is reinforced by civic disenfranchisement - the denial of civil rights and political representation. Socially segregating the homosexual from the heterosexual is so basic to the repressive logic that everyday anti-gay violence is tolerated in order to protect the purity of the heterosexual. To the extent that the exclusion of homosexuals from public life fails, policing strategies focus on enforcing their social isolation and sequestration. Quasi-public gay spaces, well-policed and removed from heterosexual public life, are permitted on the condition of their social segregation and containment. An example are gay bars, which are often tolerated but only on the territorial and social margins of cities, and only on the condition that this semi-public concentration of homosexuals remains unseen by the respectable heterosexual citizen. A repressive logic enforcing heteronormativity thus operates via strategies of cultural pollution and censorship, criminalization and civic disenfranchisement, sequestration and violence.

Repressive strategies do not aim to eliminate the homosexual, but to preserve the division between the pure heterosexual and the polluted homosexual. Indeed, we might say that the polluted homosexual was invented in the 1950s and 1960s in order to maintain the purity of particular patterns of heterosexuality. It is not, in other words, the homosexual in general that is polluted, but a specific idea of the homosexual: for example, the homosexual as compulsively hedonistic and promiscuous. Accordingly, it is not just the homosexual who is defiled, but specific sexual-intimate practices such as pleasure driven sex or multiple partner sex. Heterosexuals who engage in such practices will experience something of the polluted status of homosexuals. Polluting homosexuality thus purifies a particular normative heterosexual order; e.g., sex that is person-and love-centered and monogamous. Hence, regimes of heternormativity not only regulate the homosexual but control heterosexual practices by creating a moral hierarchy of good and bad sexual citizens.

One unintended effect of a repressive social logic has been the development of gay social worlds. In these socially circumscribed private spaces, individuals can be recognized as homosexual. However, through at least the 1970s, these worlds survived on the margins of American society, largely hidden from the heterosexual public. To say it differently, a repressive social logic imposes on individuals the condition that we have come to call the closet - a pressure to compulsively project a public heterosexual identity by confining one's homosexuality to a private world of desire or sequestered gay enclaves. Living in the closet entails such intensive and extensive daily efforts at self-management that homosexuality often becomes the basis for a distinct social identity and way of life. This is the irony of the closet: intended to contain homosexuality, the closet transforms homosexuality into a primary identity and produces a desire to come out.

Thus, repressive strategies not only produce the closet; they also generate politics aimed at gaining recognition. Gay identity politics has often been oriented to reverse a logic of homosexual repression. Thus, against the social imperative to make a secret of homosexuality, gay politics champions coming out; against the shame induced by pollution, gay pride is affirmed; against a fragmented, double life, gay politics pursues an ideal of an integrated and public gay life. Gay politics has not, however, challenged the construction of homosexuality as a minority identity. It has not contested the separation of sexual from gender, racial, or class politics, and it has not politicized social norms that regulate gay selves apart from the norm of heterosexuality, for example, norms of sexual monogamy or public sex. In short, gay identity politics has challenged a repressive politics but largely on the terms set by this regime of normative heterosexuality.

Gay identity politics has had considerable success: the achievement of a wide range of civic rights, the decline of polluting representations in many sectors of public culture, the intermingling of straights and gays in public life, and the entry of gays into the political arena indicate a blurring of the boundary between the heterosexual and the homosexual and, accordingly, a weakening of a repressive heteronormative logic.

I have found evidence for the changing social status of the homosexual in interviews I conducted. Targeting individuals who identify as gay, but who are not part of a public gay culture, and hence individuals I expected to be closeted, I found that most of them described lives beyond the closet.

Consider Clara, an 18-year-old Black lesbian. Clara disclosed to her entire family when she was 14. Today, she says, 'I talk about everything with my mother and my sisters and one brother. They know about my lover [...] and just about everything about my lesbian life'. Her comments on disclosing to her father, a Jamaican described as less tolerant, illustrate the extent to which Clara has normalized her homosexuality. 'He had the biggest problem with it, but it didn't matter to me because I just told him to be telling him. I wasn't telling him for approval.' The way Clara deals with peers also points toward normalization. As a freshman living in a college dorm, Clara had to confront issues of disclosure. She reports being invited to a fraternity party. Clara declined. 'I'm not going, and they were like, 'Why?' I told them that I'm a lesbian'. Clara's relatively painless integration of homosexuality into her life is exceptional. It was more common for respondents to narrate a change from a double life to a life beyond the closet.

For example, Bill is a White, 40 year old, middle-level civil servant who grew up in a working-class neighborhood in a small town. Bill was aware of his homosexual feelings as a child. These became more vivid when dating began in adolescence. Comments made by family, friends and his minister describing homosexuals in demeaning ways led Bill to follow the straight pattern of his peers. By early adulthood, he had married, joined the Marines, and started drinking to manage what he described as a closeted life. Perhaps triggered by the end of his marriage and his decision to get sober, Bill, now in his late-30s, decided to integrate his homosexuality into his life. He disclosed initially in the gay world and gradually to his entire family and indeed to his hometown, as Bill was interviewed by a local newspaper on being gay and Christian. Today, his homosexuality is conventionalized to such a degree that his life should not be described by the concept of the closet. For example, when his son was 10, Bill tried to explain that he was gay. His son didn't respond. From time to time, Bill would reintroduce this topic, but his son showed little interest. Bill decided to be relaxed about it. 'I would be completely myself in front of him, and that included conversations with gay friends, or talking about gay people or places [...] I was in a relationship and I let him see us hugging and kissing. I was just trying to show him that [...] it was natural for us.'

Like Bill, Mike concealed his homosexuality from family and friends until he was 40. Since 1991, Mike has been deliberate in disclosing his homosexuality: 'I'm very free about being gay and don't want anybody to assume that I'm not'. In this regard, Mike has a picture of his partner on his desk at work. However, Mike does not disclose to all his co-workers. This is not for reasons of fear or shame, which would be indicative of the closet. With co-workers, his decision to disclose 'depends on the way the conversation runs. If someone asks me if I'm married [...] I say that I'm with a man'. With some co-workers, Mike would not disclose because 'I probably would never have an opportunity to share anything personal with them'. Mike approaches his homosexuality as part of a class of 'intimate' or personal information, like, say, religion or financial matters. Disclosure decisions hinge on the degree of intimacy established or desired. In short, like Clara and Bill, Mike has normalized his gay identity (for a more elaborated statement of this argument, see Seidman et al., 1999).

Social resistance to normalizing gay identities remains strong. Many Americans still feel compelled to live closeted lives. Moreover, acceptance by family, friends and co-workers does not necessarily translate into institutional integration. Key social institutions, from families to schools and the military, continue to be organized by a norm of heterosexuality that is enforced by repressive strategies. My claim, though, is that for many individuals today, while managing homosexuality may involve episodic practices of concealment, these do not create a primary gay identity or a distinctive gay way of life. This argument suggests the end of the era of the closet, but not the end of normative heterosexuality as an institution.

If heteronormativity is sustained today less by repressive strategies, how is it maintained? To address this question, I studied American films between 1960 and 1997. I found that a shift is occurring from a dominant pollution logic, which pivots around a rigid social and symbolic division between the pure heterosexual and the defiled homosexual, to a normalizing logic. The latter recognizes gay identities, but only on the condition that every other key aspect of the gay self exhibits what would be considered 'normal' gender, sexual, familial, work, and national practices. Ultimately, normalization is a strategy to neutralize the critical aspects of a gay movement by rendering sexual difference a superficial aspect of a self who in every other way reproduces an ideal of a national citizen.

Consider the film 'Philadelphia' in many ways a breakthrough movie as it brought the issue of homosexuality and AIDS to the American mainstream. You may recall that the story is about the firing of a lawyer (Andy played by Tom Hanks) ostensibly because he has AIDS. Andy sues and wins. The film is also about the pathology not of homosexuality but of homophobia. It is the homophobia of the law firm that fires Andy and the bigotry of Joe, the lawyer (played by Denzel Washington) who defends Andy that is presented as a social problem. In other words, 'Philadelphia' asserts the normal status of the homosexual. From the very first scene,

Andy is 'out' and reveals no moral anguish over his gay identity. If there is a coming out story, it is Joe's struggle to normalize Andy's gay identity.

Through the figure of Joe, the film narrates a story of a shift in the logic of normative heterosexuality from pollution/repression to normalization. Joe initially pollutes homosexuals. Consider the scene where Andy approaches Joe for legal representation. As they are shaking hands, Andy tells Joe that he's seeking representation in an AIDS suit. Joe abruptly withdraws his hand, steps back, watches everything Andy touches on his desk, and declines to take the case for personal reasons, which he subsequently discloses as his hatred of homosexuals. In this scene, we can see normative heterosexuality operating as a repressive logic by establishing a hierarchical division between Joe - the normal, pure, and powerful heterosexual and Andy - the diseased, disgusting and disenfranchised homosexual.

As his relationship to Andy develops, Joe normalizes homosexuality as a minority identity. Anticipating his death, and the end of the trial, Andy has a party. At one point, Andy and Miguel are intimately embraced as they dance; Joe, who is similarly intimate with his wife, glances, then fixes on Andy and Miguel. Andy notices and smiles knowingly - as if he realizes in a way that Joe doesn't quite understand yet that he is beginning to normalize Andy by viewing Andy's love for Miguel as equivalent to his love for his wife. Joe's realization comes later that evening. After the guests leave, Joe and Andy are supposed to review Andy's anticipated testimony. Instead, in a poignant scene, Andy relates to Joe the story of a Maria Callas opera that is playing in the background. It's a sad tale of injustice, love, and tragic death. As Andy is fully absorbed in the operatic narrative, Joe is fixed intently on Andy. Tears begin to well up. No words are exchanged nor do we learn Joe's thoughts. My reading is that for the first time, Joe sees Andy as 'normal' or fully human. By the end of the film, Andy has ceased to be polluted for Joe. As Andy is dying in the hospital, he signals for Joe to sit next to him. This is a dramatic moment because such physical and emotional closeness marks the end of Andy's polluted status. Joe sits on the bed and touches Andy's face as he adjusts his breathing apparatus. This act signals for Joe - and presumably the viewer - the moral equivalence of the heterosexual and the homosexual.

If this film normalizes the homosexual, it still enforces a norm of heterosexuality. For example, homosexuality is confined to individuals whose lives in every way other than their sexual orientation fall within the realm of what American culture considers being 'the normal.' Thus, Andy is conventionally masculine; he's in a quasi-marital intimate relationship;

he is portrayed as hardworking and economically independent; and he is a champion of the rule of law - a core element of the American creed. Indeed, the figure of Andy not only reproduces the norm of heterosexuality by normalizing a binary gender order, but Andy epitomizes dominant American family, economic, and national values. As if to reassure the viewer that normalization does not threaten normative heterosexuality, Andy's parents' heterosexuality is portrayed in ideal terms. They have been happily married for 50 years, are lovingly involved with their children and grandchildren, and are unconditionally accepting of Andy. Likewise, Joe represents an idealized heterosexual figure - he's a masculine man, married, a father, homeowner, and a successful entrepreneur. The film's message is that only the homosexual who is a mirror image of the ideal heterosexual citizen is acceptable. To the extent that legitimation is conditional on the homosexual displaying dominant social conventions, normalization demands recognition only of a minority status, not the contestation of heteronormativity.

Normalization has been bravely fought for by the mainstream of the gay movement. A life beyond the closet, which is what normalization promises, affords a kind of personal integrity that has been unattainable for many individuals. However, legitimation through normalization leaves in place the polluted status of other marginal sexualities; it sustains the dominant norms that regulate our sexually intimate conduct apart from the norm of heterosexuality.

Two political responses to normalization stand out. First, new sexual identity movements have emerged. For example, marginal sexual groups within gay life have emerged advancing their own demands for rights based on claims of victimization. Indeed, their claims to sexual citizenship have been made against both the straight and the gay mainstream. For example, a bisexual and lesbian and gay S/M movement has had to struggle against the gay mainstream, which, in its quest for respectability, has echoed straight America's pollution of bisexuality and S/M. To the extent that bisexual and S/M politics aim at normalization they reproduce the identity political logic of the gay movement by claiming a distinct identity, by countering polluting with normalizing representations, and by aspiring to equal citizenship status.

A second response to normalization has been the rise of a queer politics. Whereas gay identity politics aims to change the status of homosexuality from a deviant to a normal identity, queer politics struggles against normalizing any identity. Queers are not against identity politics but aim to deflate its emancipatory narrative by exposing its exclusionary and disciplinary effects. For example, identity politics imposes a norm of sexual identification (e.g. to identify as gay, straight or bisexual) and projects a normative construction of this identity (e.g. of gays as white, young, lean-bodied men). Moreover, sexual identity politics is said to leave in place norms that sustain sexual hierarchies unrelated to gender preference, such as a norm that privatizes sex or a norm of monogamy. Queers are not in principle against normative regulation. They are against normalizing social controls.

A queer perspective holds that normalizing social controls assign a moral status of normal and abnormal to virtually every sexual desire and act. This creates a global division between good and bad sexualities and normal and deviant sexual citizens. Moreover, extensive institutional interventions into intimate life are justified for the purposes of preventing or minimizing the undesirable public consequences of sexual pathology. In short, by investing sexuality with heightened moral and social meaning, normalizing discourses justify and bring into being a wide network of controls that regulate sexual behavior. Queer politics is thus critical of any political strategy that aims only to redraw moral boundaries to include a deviant practice within 'the normal' - without challenging the regulatory power of the category of the normal.

The queer critique of normalization underscores its aim to defend the social de-regulation of sex. Movements such as Queer Nation, Sex Panic! and Lavender Menace have struggled to remove large stretches of sexual intimate life from institutional control. In order further to clarify the meaning of queer politics, a brief comment is necessary as to its normative grounds and political vision. As you will see, these aspects pointedly reveal its postmodern character.

Queer politics assumes what I would call a 'communicative' sexual ethic. In contrast to a normalizing ethic, which holds that sex acts have inherent moral significance or that sexual desires can be classified as either normal or abnormal or good or bad by virtue of their intrinsic qualities, a communicative ethic maintains that sex acts are given moral meaning by their communicative context. In other words, the qualities of a sexual desire or act per se cannot be the basis for determining its moral status. Accordingly, the focus of normative evaluation shifts from the sex act to the social exchange. Instead of determining whether a specific sex act is normal, critical judgement would focus on the moral features of a social exchange: Does it involve mutual consent? Are the agents acting responsibly and respectfully? Is there erotic-intimate reciprocity? In assessing the legitimacy of S/M the relevant consideration would be the communicative practice of the agents, not the particular qualities of S/M such as the use of pain or role-playing.

A communicative sexual ethic suggests that most sexual practices should be viewed as matters of personal or aesthetic not moral choice. It follows that many sexual practices would lose their moral, and hence, broader social significance. There would be less justification for social intervention beyond regulating behavior that involves coercion or minors. Accordingly, the range of legitimate sexual choice would expand considerably beyond what is permissible in a normalizing sexual culture. If S/M was to be viewed as lacking intrinsic moral meaning, there would be no warrant for controlling this practice beyond regulating the social exchange. S/M between consenting adults would become a matter of aesthetic taste, not a focus of morality and not a site of social regulation.

A queer politics advocates then shifting large stretches of bodily, sexual, and intimate practice from the sphere of morality to that of aesthetics. This de-legitimates extensive state and social institutional control over intimate life. At the root of queer politics is a libertarian standpoint.

In this regard, a queer politics draws heavily on liberal notions of bodily integrity and privacy. Sexual autonomy is said to presuppose individuals who can exercise a wide range of choice over bodily based pleasures and intimacies. Accordingly, a queer concept of sexual freedom involves a robust defense of a private sphere that is juridically and socially protected from interference by the state and other citizens. However, in contrast to liberal traditions, which often anchor notions of bodily and self-integrity in natural law traditions, queers deconstruct appeals to a transcendent order of nature or reason. It is this natural law grounding, with its essentialist ideas about self and sexuality, that partially explains the historic alignment of liberalism with a normalizing sexual politic. For example, if sexuality is assumed by nature to be heterosexual or procreative, the range of legitimate forms of sexual identity and intimacy are greatly restricted. As sexual practices are reinterpreted as belonging to the realm of social convention, establishing moral boundaries becomes a site of contestation involving arguments that lean more on the justificatory language of context, consent, and consequence than of nature and normality.

Yet libertarianism is limited as a politic. A concept of sexual autonomy assumes individual access to social resources (expertise, financial assistance, and information). For example, a condition of sexual autonomy for women would surely include access to family planning services, including abortion. Given the economic inequality among women, sexual autonomy would have to include state aid to lower income women as a condition of exercising their reproductive rights. Similarly, if a notion of sexual autonomy would presuppose that individuals have sexual knowledge to make informed choices, state enforced sex education in public schools should be part of a queer sexual politics. Hence, a queer politics would simultaneously advocate removing a wide range of sexually intimate practices from institutional regulation, and offer democratic justifications for state intervention to create the material and cultural conditions of sexual autonomy.

By way of a conclusion, let me revisit the question of whether the shift from identity to queer politics is indicative of a broader shift from modernity to postmodernity. It would, I think, be plausible to interpret identity politics as indicative of what we think of as modern. The dominant form of gay identity politics has assumed a modernist notion of the self - stable, internally coherent, characterized by a core, fixed identity. Furthermore, the agent's social interest and political aims are understood as grounded in this internally stable core identity. Finally, in classic modernist terms, gay identity politics has been primarily about agents gaining citizenship rights and full national inclusion. Hence, gay identity politics displays many of the key features of modernity - a stable self with an internal core identity, an agent who acts on self interest grounded in identity, and an orientation to rights and national inclusion.

By contrast, queer politics suggests postmodernity. First, queer politics is critical of an identity politics that assumes a coherent, clearly bounded self. Instead, it favors a view of the self as multiply identified and less internally unitary and stable than assumed by identity politics. Second, in place of a subject- based sexual politics, a queer politics is organized less around claims to identity than claims to be released from identity. That is, queer politics challenges the compulsion to announce a sexual identity and thereby to be regulated by a system of sexuality. Third, instead of pursuing a politics aimed at gaining rights and a normal identity status, queers seek to refashion the self, moral boundaries, and innovate new forms of self, pleasure, and relationships. Ultimately, an antinormalizing politics is less about rights than about de-regulating wide patches of social practice for the purpose of expanding choice, encouraging the flourishing of social differences, and reinventing forms of subjectivity and solidarity. Finally, its normative standpoint, as I see it, is quintessentially post- modern. A communicative ethic rejects appeals to a transcendental moral order or to unimpeachable foundations to resolve ethical conflicts in the sphere of sex.

Instead of appealing to notions such as the nature of sex or an idea of a normal, healthy sexuality, it abstracts from the sex act itself, from its content - its specific desires, feelings, and behaviors - to focus on the abstract formal qualities of the social exchange. A queer ethic offers only rough guidelines, not fixed principles to regulate behavior. Hence, a queer ethic exhibits one of the defining features of the postmodern - namely, postfoundationalism.

And yet, this simple dichotomization of identity and queer equals modern and postmodern needs to be qualified. On the one hand, identity politics remains dominant today, suggesting that the United States remains very much a modern society. Queer politics is still a marginal, counter current in American life. Moreover, identity politics cannot be reduced to a modernist politics of self, citizenship, and nationalism. For example, in the early 1970s, forms of identity politics flourished that understood the self as multiply identified and as deeply socially constructed; it framed politics as transgressive or about the remaking of self and society by decentering social and moral orders. On the other hand, queer politics doesn't abandon identity politics but, rather, contests the idea of a fixed, unitary sexual self in favor of a more open fluid contestable idea of identity. Queers still defend appeals to self and group identification and a politics organized around this identity. Finally, it is not at all clear that, while indicating a normative-political standpoint, queer doesn't implicitly aspire to its own identity standpoint.

In short, it is perhaps more useful to speak of the modern and postmodern as concurrent positions or sensibilities. In place of global theories about modernity and postmodernity, we perhaps need more concrete empirical analyses that avoid quick moves to index these developments in this meta register.

References

Seidman, S.; Meeks, C. and Francie Traschen (1999), 'Beyond the Closet? The Changing Social Meaning of Homosexuality in the United States', *Sexualities* vol.2 no.1, pp.9-34.

7 Private Sexuality, Public Morality and Modern Sexology: What Prospects of Sexuality in Times of Uncertainty?

MICHAEL HVIID JACOBSEN

Introduction

In a vein similar to that of the very capable analyst of modernity and post-modernity, Frederic Jameson (1991), who utilised Edvard Munch's *The Scream* as an artistic expression of the evils of the modern age, I too, also wish to begin this contribution with an observation on art as a signifier of contemporary social and sexual life. On a wall of a seminar room at the Department of Sociology at the University of Copenhagen, a marvellous painting by Poul Jupont is on display. The title of the painting, *Blinded by Hetero*, depicts the rather dramatic situation of a young naked male torso presumably suffocating from the violent facial embrace of two flamboyantly red stiletto clad female legs. Whether from pleasure, protest or pain, the young man seems to gesticulate silently to the sky, as in most paintings, such that the body position could be interpreted in numerous ways. Here I shall offer merely three possible interpretations. The first concerns the cry for help, the demand for a saviour descending from heaven above to release the young man from his agony. A second interpretation runs along the same lines, claiming that the man is pointing to the sky as if to signal that the truth or redemption should come from that direction, that only the ethereally unknown can provide the answers to life. The third interpretation is contrary to the two others, in that it proposes that the finger pointing to the sky is not a the physical gesture of a suppressed cry for help nor a demand for guidance, and thus is not made by a person looking for celestial insights or assistance, but rather, an act of overt defiance, an accusation of the truths and the rules stemming from above.

These interpretations are obviously marked by the fact that they are not the evaluative pronouncements of an art critic or someone claiming to hold either authoritative or esoteric knowledge of art, but they are instead the simple and trivial interpretations made by a sociologist. However, they can provide guidelines for the understanding of the following essay, which on its focussing on sexuality, has a fourfold purpose. First, to investigate the heteronormativity and dominance of the conformist heterosexual ideal in Western society - a heteronormativity whose roots exist prior to the advent of modernity, which is the theme of this anthology. Such heteronormativity is to certain degrees still prevalent in the West but is at the same time undergoing a transformation at the level of social practice. Second, this essay examines the heteronormative foundation of the social scientific interest in human sexuality, how this biased perspective evolved particularly during the modern epoch and how it has been transformed throughout the last century. Third, the essay paints a picture of our contemporary politics of sexuality as moulded by the sexual prescriptions of more than 100 years of heteronormative social science. Finally, the essay proposes a tentative alternative to this heteronormative bias in science as well as in society, in which individual freedom of choice is coupled with obligations and responsibilities, not to morality or social convention, but toward other individuals. We are indeed living in a society as well as practicing a social science, whose subject matter is exactly that society, where both are blinded by heteronormativity, as Jupont's painting suggested. This essay thus seeks to illustrate the historical backdrop for this social and scientific bias and aspires to point to new horizons in our understanding of sexuality.

The Rendezvous of *Homo Sexualis* with *Homo Sociologicus*

We are all subjected to the laws of nature, the pre-given characteristics governing and constituting our biology and anatomy, our body and hormones, and other physical aspects of our sexuality. Since every society is founded on the premise of continuous human procreation and sexual activity as one of the most common traits of being human, or a human being, we are all constituted, whether we like it or not, as a *homo sexualis*, as a sexual being in the analytical sense of the term. Simultaneously, we are also to various degrees subjected to the laws of society - the social and cultural logic governing our sociality, our minds, our behaviour and the more social and interactional aspects of our sexuality. Accordingly, since every society is founded upon the premise of human sociality as well as sociability as another fundamental feature of human beings we are all, whether we like it or not, equally constituted as a *homo sociologicus*, as social beings. This designation of man as a *homo sociologicus* was originally coined by Ralf Dahrendorf (1968), although the socialised conception of man is an ancient consideration in the social sciences (Wrong, 1961). This label intended to denote the non-randomness of human social existence, that being human is to be sited in the intersection of both individual desires and longings as well as collective constraints and expectations. In this way, we are from beginning to end social as well as sexual beings - products and bearers at one and the same time of social and sexual norms, roles, ideas, etc.[1] Norbert Elias (1994) termed such beings *homini aperti* which illuminates the fact that we acquire our identities not as completely self-contained, self-determined and secluded individuals, but through complex social figurations and networks that shape our personhood, identities, embodiments and conceptions of self and others.[2] The roles, morals, values and norms that mould us are the glue that holds society together, that which prevents it from falling apart and withering away. But where does morality, the very foundation for this sociality, stem from and what impact does it have on our construction as sexual human beings? How do morality and social norms interfere with our ability to construct a sexual identity from our own wishes and aspirations?

Polish sociologist Zygmunt Bauman recently published a diminutive but nevertheless rather powerful article titled *What Prospects of Morality in Times of Uncertainty?* from which I have borrowed and paraphrased the sub-title of this contribution. Bauman discusses the cultural foundation for morality by looking to the Biblical past, claiming that morality can be based on two different interpretations of the Biblical sources. The social and moral order of modernity was based on a primordial etiological myth which guide our actions according to specific and almost indispensable principles of right and wrong.[3] According to this so-called etiological myth, 'to be moral is to follow strictly the command - to obey unconditionally and never to deviate from the straight path, in deed or in thought' (Bauman, 1998a, p.13). The main source of this *morality of conformity* is, of course, the law-giving act on Mount Sinai and the bestowal of the Ten Commandments.[4] However, there is another option in the Bible for being moral, an option that has not come to dominate the course of morality in Western civilisation. The foundation for this kind of a *morality or drama of choice*, so to speak, was the moral transgression and subsequent expulsion of Adam and Eve from the Garden of Eden. It 'suggests that to be moral is to face a choice between good and evil, and to know that there is such a choice' (Bauman, 1998a, p.13). According to this rather different etiological myth, morality is a matter of personal choice, a choice that will inevitably lead to agony and desperation, since one can never know if one is a moral being or not. Accompanying this agony, however, is also the feeling of freedom from constraint and oppression; the knowledge that one can choose the road one believes will lead to happiness and personal fulfilment. Where the morality of conformity promises certainty mixed with fear, the morality of choice, on the other hand, promises uncertainty and anxiety mixed with freedom. This is the story, admittedly rather brief, of how the prevalent morality in society came to be the morality of conformity; a morality formation constructed, formulated and perpetrated by the powers that preside, and which was executed so as to make people abide by the letter of the Law and never to deviate from the absolute and universally binding top-down morality. The Ten Commandments are not about multiple choice but about limitations on choosing to do right. Those who dare dissent from the moral prescriptions will indeed be held accountable and be punished, as were the inhabitants of Sodom and Gomorrah; the latter-day imprisonment or stigmatisation of sexual deviants are equally illustrative examples. Hence even though 'prevailing concepts of sexuality vary according to the time, culture and most prominent moralities' (Gibbs, 1994, p.2), the morality of conformity has nevertheless held a hegemonic position in the discourses and politics surrounding sexuality for millennia which already Schelsky (1955) as a more reactionary observer noted.

Where morality supposedly had a bifurcated origin - understood as either conformity or choice - sexuality, according to the Bible and the subsequent dedicated followers of its orthodoxy, had only a single and unified birth - what shall subsequently be referred to as a *mono-genesis*. This mono-genesis spells out a sexuality determined by nature and maintained by nurture, the biological as well as social demands for endless breeding of the human race. The outcome of the dominance of the morality of conformity has thus been the equal dominance of a certain kind of sexuality, a sexuality tuned, as it were, to the moral as well as practical demands of the traditions of pre-modernity and the institutions of modernity. This historically and institutionally favoured sexuality is of course heterosexuality. Hence, the mono-genesis of a moral sexual identity and activity has since the Biblical prescriptions been supportive of monogamous heterosexual relationships, making heterosexuality a virtually moral imperative, if not compulsory. This is what we refer to when we talk about *heteronormativity*; that heterosexuality has become the sanctioned norm of sexual life. As Jonathan Ned Katz puts it:

> Heterosexuality is old as procreation, ancient as the lust of Eve and Adam. The first lady and gentleman, we assume, perceived themselves, behaved and felt just like today's heterosexuals. We suppose that heterosexuality is unchanging, universal, essential: ahistorical (Katz, 1990, p.7).[5]

Thus, sexual myth today leads to moral evaluation. In recent decades, however, radical changes have occurred at individual and societal levels which have challenged the almost God-given and erstwhile predominance of heterosexuality as the only legitimate pathway to social and moral grace.

The morality of conformity works extremely well in times marked by certainty and stability and in periods when society is integrated and cohesive. Times of uncertainty and increasing complexity, however, are marked by the advent of the morality of choice. These are indeed times of uncertainty - uncertainty about identity, sexuality, self, others, love and so forth (Weeks, 1995). These uncertainties relate as much to actions as to definitions of actions, discourses as it were, and these uncertainties have had a prolonged birth full of painful contractions and, as we shall see, were primarily instigated by the collapse of the social engineering of modernity and the resulting disappearance of a core of moral prescriptions, leading to what Bauman (1995) calls *the search for a centre that holds*. Writing on our uncertain post-modern or what I prefer to designate late modern phase, William Simon, the prominent theorist of contemporary sexuality, recently stated that 'the discourses of sexuality are invariably discourses about something else' (Simon, 1998, p.2). One is, of course, tempted to ask what is that something else then? In my view, discourses on sexuality centre around morality and social power in defining right and wrong. But whereas the sexual is fundamentally pre-social and primordial - existing in a natural and uncontaminated form prior to any kind of social arrangement and actually a prerequisite for sociality as such - the moral is necessarily social. The moral is culturally and historically determined. However, sexuality and morality are inextricably linked to each other on multiple levels, as this chapter will seek to illustrate, and the transformation of society also leads to transformations of sexual practices and the moral evaluations of these. Any alteration in sexual practices, therefore, is bound to lead to moral evaluations and sanctions, and any change in morality will in effect affect sexual practices. In this way, sexuality and morality mirror one another, being part and parcel of the very same discourses and lines of thinking. Hence, there exists a dialectical relationship between morality and sexuality and any appropriate and thorough understanding of the phenomenon of sexuality, will necessarily have to be connected to the issue of morality. Only in this way can we grasp this dialectic historically. In a period marked by a shift from a generally modern to a late modern phase of social development, academic discourses and discussions on issues so central to social life, are important and even indispensable. Although some social scientists claim that 'too much of the discussion of sexuality [...] today continues to be merely an adjunct of academics attempting to work through the potential logical implications of modernity' (Rival et al., 1998, p.315), the sexual must be analysed in connection with broader social developments.

Sexualised Civilisation and Civilised Sexuality

In the social sciences, our history has often been described as a process leading toward higher and more sophisticated forms of civilisation (Elias 1994) and as a process involved in the rationalisation of every single aspect of social life as Max Weber wrote.[6] Together, these two features of historical development - civilisation and rationalisation - could rather simplistically be termed *modernisation*. What have been the impact and the repercussions of this assumed modernisation of our society, of our actions, beliefs, mores and our lives on human sexuality? The conventional wisdom - though hardly ever spelled out in such rationalist terminology - is that we have moved from what might be termed *animalistic* or *primitive* to more *civilised and domesticated sexual practices*, and that the primary reason for this is due to a successful subjugation of human instincts and a sublimation of sexual desire and eroticism. Although a prevailing opinion amongst social scientists, this view is contested by the historian Theodore Zeldin (1994, p.86) who so wittingly noted, 'there has been more progress in cooking than in sex'. While there may be a grain of truth in Zeldin's remark - that the way we perform sex has not been altered radically throughout history - sexuality, at least within the discursive representations of sex and our self-understanding of tolerance toward it, has been depicted so as to present ourselves in a more advanced, more civilised position compared to pre-modern civilisations. The idea is propounded that throughout modernity and in an unprecedented fashion, we have sought to control sexuality: 'For earlier societies it may not have been a need to constrain severely the powerful sexual impulse in order to maintain social stability or limit inherently antisocial force' (Gagnon and Simon, 1973, p.17). It was only with the construction of social order, which happened particularly throughout the early stages of modernity, that sexuality and sexual variety became a problem. Just as our history of morality is coloured by etiological myths, or mythologies, so is the history of sexuality. The road to our present day late modern sexuality is indeed long and convoluted, full of change and paved with obstacles, recurrences and setbacks. Thus, it would be inappropriate to speak of a unilinear development or progress in connection with sexuality or our understanding of it.

Every human civilisation is fundamentally based on, even determined by, its members' continuous sexual activities; in other words, without sex, no civilisation. Sex is thus the prerequisite for establishing and maintaining culture. At the same time, every kind of social organisation, any society and any state, has its own notion of sexual correctness, what is considered right and wrong in sexual relationships, preferences and activities but, as suggested above, it is particularly the morality of conformity that has been a historical vantage point in commenting on sexuality and erotic activity. Therefore, a certain view on sexuality has been predominant in our Western hemisphere. As noted by two prominent analysts of sexuality: 'Sexuality is more than a domain in which history is enacted. It is constitutive of history itself. Society does not simply construct sexuality, society is constructed sexually' (Connell and Dowsett, 1999, p.190). Sex and society can thus be regarded as two sides of the same coin, as we saw in connection to *homo sociologicus* and *homo sexualis*. The natural is social and the social is natural, so to speak, and it is through the transformation of the natural into the social that we will eventually be able to control it: 'Sexuality's biological base is always experienced culturally [...] The bare biological facts do not speak for themselves; they must be expressed socially' (Ross and Rapp, 1983, p.51). As we shall see below, sexuality is the interplay of nature and culture and is really only revealed in the social being, what Boje Katzenelson (1994) termed *homo socius* as a contemporary counterpart to Ralf Dahrendorf's aforementioned notion of *homo sociologicus*. Katzenelson (1994, p.332) writes that the natural origin of humans

> does not present itself in a pure form, so to speak, but only in the form of 'homo socius'. Reality is not constructed in a way that we on the one hand have the natural human being, on the one hand, and, the cultural human being, on the other hand These two beings exist only as a single being; they are given in and by each other, and in a dialectical fashion they are conditional on each other [my translation].

Sexuality, then, is neither only a natural fact and perpetual facet of life nor is it merely an ethereal notion; it is the synergical effect of the combination of both society and nature. Somewhere betwixt and between these two poles of action and thought lies sexuality - but this location is never a stable and solid foundation. It is always rocked by action and reaction, short intervals of status quo erupted by evolutions and revolutions in ideas as well as practices. Nobody expressed this ambivalence in sexuality better than Michel Foucault (1978, p.152): 'Sexuality must not be thought of as a kind of 'natural given' which power tries to hold in check, or as an obscure domain which knowledge gradually tries to uncover. It is the name that can be given to a historical construct'. Thus, sexuality is – hardly surprising to scholars these days - a historical and social construction and representation; and it is always a representation from a particular moral standpoint, from a position of power and social interests. In this way, history is the battleground of sexual struggles. Sex is therefore also a social dynamic, a force which has the capacity to change things, to make a difference. But difference is exactly what cannot be accepted by a morality building on the aforementioned mono-genesis. The morality of conformity - what Freud (1974) termed *civilised sexual morality* - is, as the term suggests, constructed by and founded upon incontrovertible norms, and its ambition is the elimination of the doubting, misunderstanding and questioning of morality, a desire for human uniformity and accommodation within the pre-constructed categories of good and evil, righteous and sinful, right and wrong. Sexuality is a constant thorn in the side of this kind of moral authority.

Sexuality has both its repressive as well as its permissive potentials, but since sexuality has historically been subjugated to a civilised sexual morality, the latency of the subversive potentials of sexuality has always been present and has in recent years become more and more salient. The history of modernity - the period that most markedly relied on the morality of conformity (Bauman, 1991) to eliminate ambivalence and anxiety - is thus replete with attempts to repress and subjugate sexuality. Modernity was a project aimed at domination and control, categorisation and arrangement, regimentation and social engineering, and in the sexual sphere these instruments were deployed with a never-ending and tireless pertinacity. This is why modernity, which according to Anthony Giddens (1990, p.1) 'refers to modes of social life or organisation which emerged in Europe from about the seventeenth century onwards', is, not remarkably, that period on which most sociologists interested in the issue of sexuality have focused, since, it was the period throughout which the moral regulation and control of sexuality presumably reached its apex, although individual attention was not only paid to the sexual aspects of social life - what Max Weber (1948) termed *the erotic sphere* and Jeffrey Weeks (1991) denoted *the intimate sphere*. This regulatory preoccupation was particularly evident in the Victorian era marked by 'that damned morality' (Weeks, 1989, p.19), a morality aimed at a domestication of sexuality. The Victorian era was marked by the attempt to make the otherwise natural act of sexual activity unnatural, even perverted. Modernity, with its institutions of confession and interrogation, saw an unprecedented political regimentation and religious inculcation which more often than not converged to construct a powerful image of sexual dissidence and deviance. Where sex was initially regulated exclusively through the ecclesiastical doctrines of the Bible (Hawkes, 1996), as modernity progressed, and perhaps as a harbinger of the process of secularisation, there occurred a shift toward an almost purely scientific and medical regulation of sex but the consequences and repercussions of these two otherwise disparate regimes of power were rather similar: a reliance on a mono-genetic view of sexuality, a creation of perversion and perversity, the emergence of a surveillance system of and a moral iron grip on people's sexual activities in private as well as in public, and if not a religious damnation of certain sexual orientations then a social labelling and stigmatisation based on scientific discoveries.

If one believes in mono-genesis, as did people in modernity and particularly as did the Victorians, deviance will be regarded as sinful and as a human defect; in other words, as a perversion. But what if one believes in a *poly-genesis* of humans, the view that we are not all one and the same creation with the same desires and longings? Will there then be room for tolerance of deviance and human variability? Is this where we are heading in this historical and moral interlude between modernity and post-modernity? Although it is certainly advisable to look to the past to understand the contemporary, 'many of the uses of gender and sexuality, observable within the context of the rapidly changing present, may in fact be different than any that humanity has previously known' (Simon, 1996, p.3). This brings to the fore the problem of the persistence of pre-existing sexual ontologies as well as pre-given sexual adherences, many of which have been upheld in the name of morality by either religion or science, and many of which have subsequently been uncritically internalised by ordinary people in the sphere of everyday life.

In late modernity, contrary to the early modernity of the Victorian Age, we experience a loosening of the social control of sex and a democratisation of desire (Kaplan, 1997; Weeks, 1998). We are lulled and deceived into believing that we suddenly experience a feeling of being free to choose the object of our innermost desires and passions, that we can pursue exactly the sexual orientation we want. I suggest that we ought to be wary and critical of this delusion. What has happened in recent decades is not, however, necessarily a lowering of what Norbert Elias (1994) called the *threshold of repugnance* with respect to sexual activity but, on the contrary, a blurring of this point of moral fixity through the creation of many grey zones and morally uncharted waters - waters containing both uncertainty and anxiety. As I will argue below, we have actually become more prudish and morally judgmental in many respects, primarily in terms of our attitudes toward the actions of others. In the meantime, our own sexual life has remained as sacred as it is sacrilegious. The utilisation and deployment of double moral standards, as Freud noted, is perhaps the flamboyant sign of the times with regard not only to sexuality but also to morality, and the sciences, the media and politics are instrumental in promoting the kind of morality which rests on shifting sands.

The Emergence of a New *Scientia Sexualis*

In Umberto Eco's *In the Name of the Rose*, one of the medieval monks stated that there was no progress, no upheavals in the science of knowledge, that a cumulative progress in human insights was impossible. When it comes to the science of sexuality, this statement is particularly pertinent. Since the publication of Foucault's (1978, 1985, 1986) monumental trilogy on the history of sexuality, however, sociologists and historians have become increasingly interested in issues relating to love, sex and eroticism. In recent years, a veritable torrent of literature on these subjects has swept across the field of sociological theory and fertilised an otherwise barren soil. Nowadays, almost every sociologist with respect for himself and his discipline has contributed to the discussions surrounding sexuality and eroticism in contemporary society and have in this way contributed to the construction, maintenance and development of a body of knowledge on sex and a contemporary social science of sexuality. Yet, it would be inaccurate to speak of the occurrence of an entirely new phenomenon, since a scientific interest in issues relating to human sexuality can be traced back at least to the Enlightenment. It would also be utterly wrong to speak of the science of sex as a unified body of knowledge, since the content of sexological discourses has changed radically throughout the years. Thus, there appears to be some kind of progressive development.

The science of sex, like any scientific enterprise, has, throughout its relatively short life span, sought to demystify its object, sexuality - to subject it to the often rigid logic of scientific enquiry. One of the consequences of this effort may, in the long run, well be a disenchantment of sexual activity, as we shall discuss below. It is possible primarily to distinguish three, somewhat overlapping, phases in the development of these demystification attempts in the science of sex. In the first phase, scientists with an interest in social conditions, such as population control, began to theorise about sex, and in this fashion became the pioneers of sexology. This period lasted from the mid-18th century until the beginning of the 19th century, particularly in England and Continental Europe. The second phase, from the early 19th century to the 1970s, saw the interest in sex as an object of scientific scrutiny becoming increasingly dispersed across continents and throughout different disciplines. During this period, particularly cultural and psychological theories of sex flourished. In the third and current phase, that of the late modern era, we have become almost over-exposed to sex in the social sciences as in our everyday lives. Sex has become a topic for everyone to comment on, a commodity to be bought and sold, when tons of self-help books on sex are published faster than they can be read by the public, when sex and the erotic have become popularised in an unprecedented fashion, and when sociology has jumped on the bandwagon of this sexual and erotic carnival. Below I will spell out in more detail some of the scientific content of these three schematised phases since - as Giddens (1976, 1990) has illustrated - science tends to mirror society and vice versa through the working of a *double hermeneutic*; the continuous exchange between the language of laymen and scientific concepts, the fact that science, fortunately, is not secluded from social activity in general but reorganises and reinterprets an already organised and interpreted world. Changes in scientific enterprise, we thus assume, can tell us about social and political developments; where we come from, where we are going, and particularly important, why we are taking a particular route.[7]

Like society, the science of sex has undergone radical changes in the last centuries, and we shall now contrast some of the early, and some would say antediluvian, assumptions and routines of classical modern sexologists with more recent attempts to acquire knowledge about human sexuality. These initial studies, which were part of a significant expansion in the writings on sex from the early-19th century, were erected on a medical platform and were carried out primarily by people schooled in the medical sciences and not, as in the preceding centuries, in religious dogmatics. The transition from a religious to a scientific approach to human sexuality, however, did not immediately, as one would have expected, have liberating and emancipating consequences. Rather 'the result was not only a negative construction on sexuality, with an emphasis on the dangers rather than the pleasures, but also an emphasis on the deadly results of sexual over-indulgence and sensual voluptuousness' (Hawkes, 1996, p.53).[8] Apart from this, sexuality gradually lost its rooting in mental, and sinful, desire and pleasure and was eventually demystified and stripped of its carnal mystery only to be wrapped in a natural scientific discourse. As Robinson (1976) pointed out, sexuality - throughout its modernisation and medicalisation in the latter part of the 19th century - was thought of in purely anatomical and physiological terms and not in values and emotions that people hold for and about one another. Therefore, an inherent *nativism* (Connell and Dowsett, 1999, p.179) and *essentialism* dominated.[9] Sexuality was regarded as something innate to human nature, and the explanations offered by sexologists tended to be biologically reductionist.

As we are constantly taught, science and morals are often in conflict with each other. However, the early science of sex - what could be termed *the biological phase of sexology* - was, as Foucault (1978) also illustrated, heavily infused with moral prescriptions and normative biases. An illustrious example of the moral foundation of early sexology can be seen in the work of Richard von Krafft-Ebing, who in his notorious more than famous *Psychopathia Sexualis* overtly combined his medical views with political ones: 'The material and moral ruin of the community is steadily brought about by debauchery, adultery and luxury' (Krafft-Ebing, 1876, p.6). There was little doubt among these pioneering scientists of sex that sexual behaviour had destructive consequences for society. Sex had to be regulated and monitored. Therefore, their work often harmonised with the repressive efforts of the power elites and an almost spectacular suppression of sexuality followed. Among other contributors to the *fin de siecle* sexology, Havelock Ellis, also believed that the sexuality of the modern individual had been distorted and perverted by culture from its original and natural healthy constitution (Weeks, 1989, p.148). Like Krafft-Ebing, Ellis was interested in discovering the universal and natural laws governing human sexuality and his assumption was that this was to be achieved through in-depth investigations of human physiology.[10] Thus, the hallmark of early European sexology was the attempt *to decipher a naturally rooted sexual code in humans* in order to discover natural laws and uncover variations in sexual manifestations. As a result, the 19th century witnessed a transformation from religious dogmas and speculations about the sinfulness of sex to the scientisation of sex in which

> sexual behaviour was subjected to secular scientific scrutiny [...] The science of sex was [...] essentially a post-Enlightenment project. The centrality of nature in its discourse; the faith in human reason to tame the 'beast within'; the commitment to observe, classify and record, rather than judge and punish; and the search to establish universal fixed paradigms of 'normal' and 'abnormal' are all features evident in this endeavour (Hawkes, 1998, p.103).

Early sexology, like sociology itself a child of the Golden Age of modernity, simply had to rid itself of any associations with mystical and speculative notions about both divine as well as diabolical sexual orientations and try, albeit unsuccessfully, to restrain too obvious moral stances. The main concern of this kind of sexology, however, was to distinguish the moral from the amoral with respect to sexual orientation. Hence,

> words which designated sexual traits, such as nymphomania, narcissism, autoeroticism, kleptomania, urolagnia, and many others, began to seep into scientific discourse, by the end of the [nineteenth] century and the beginning of the twentieth century, indicating a new concern with detailing sexual variations, and with using sex as a distinguishing mark between individuals (Weeks, 1989, p.21).

In this way, the early sexology was marked, as well as marred, by attempts to segregate the socially and morally acceptable and prescribed from the unacceptable and perverse. Scientists of sex - either knowingly or unwittingly - became *moral mouthpieces*, so to speak, for the ideology of the modern state apparatus and its dominant morality of conformity. The vision that came to characterise sexology was that moral conformity and human uniformity were much coveted ideals for humans and societies alike.

The breakthrough from the early, somewhat obscure, science of sex to a more nuanced and complex understanding is, of course, the authorship and psychoanalytical practice of Sigmund Freud during the first decades of the 20th century. I will not focus too extensively on this period, as it is one of the most commonly described and analysed in the literature on the history of sexology. I will simply make some rather general comments on the dominant figures and their views during this second major phase in the development of the science of sex.[11] Freud's main mission in focusing on sexuality was, on the overall, to seek to map the *unconscious*. For Freud, sex thus became something of an epiphenomenon in the explanation of human mental disorders such as neurosis and hysteria. Freud also sought to try and understand - what Juliet Mitchell termed – the *tortuous* development of sexuality through the repression of human drives by society as well as the individual itself, a process beginning already in the years of early childhood. The single most important contribution of Freud to the science of sex was, although many may disagree on this postulate, his break with a rigid biologism and his introduction of a more psychological as well as historical perspective on human sexuality. Other prominent scholars of this second phase were William Masters and Virginia Johnson and, of course, Alfred Kinsey whose well-known theories I will, however, not dwell on in this paper.[12] Suffice it to say that this second period was marked by a heterogeneous understanding of human sexuality - both in the theories and methods aimed at mapping it. There was probably more dispute than consensus among sexologists than previously. All of them, however, sought to besiege sexuality theoretically since 'the expert-ridden world of the mid-twentieth century could not leave sex to take care of itself' (Hawkes, 1996, p.67).

The ambition of Freud and of those who followed in his footsteps in this second, *psychological phase of sexology*, which extends roughly from the early 20th century and until the early 1970s, was t*o decipher a psychologically - and in the final instance also culturally - rooted code in human sexuality*; though some still adhered to a biological reductionism). Like his predecessors in the first phase of sexology, however, Freud was also caught up in a moral evaluation, and eventually moral judgement, of people's sexual practices and desires. This is particularly evident in the dualism between the pathological versus the healthy and normal.[13] In order to construct what is normal, according to this approach, we must construct the abnormal, pathological and perverse. This binary distinction is a relic from a functionalist perspective on sex that never really left sociological theorising on sexuality and which psychoanalysis never successfully eroded. With the rise of symbolic interactionism in the sociology of the 1960s, this rather narrow and biological reductionist model of human sexuality was discarded, at least temporarily, and attempts at model-building based on the importance of socio-cultural moulding came to prominence (Stein, 1989). This was most exquisitely expressed in the pathbreaking work of John Gagnon and William Simon (1973), who even before Foucault proposed a model which saw perversion not as a manifestation of distorted individual psychology but as something created from without, so to speak, by society. This approach marked the transition from a modern science of sex to a more late modern style of sexology. However, this type of sexology still has its faults and traps - especially regarding sexual minorities such as the gay and lesbian movement or was somewhat biased toward a phallocentric perspective on sexuality. The morality of conformity, therefore, did not stop its inquisitive fervour regarding any phenomena related to sexuality but continued to circumscribe every single aspect of sexuality from choice of partner, time, place and frequency of sex and every single sexual utterance was dissected and analysed thoroughly. Although it has been humorously noted, that the 1960s and 1970s was certainly the period when 'the clitoris had been let out of the closet and would not be returned' (Hawkes, 1996, p.108), both sexology and public and popular discourse has reflected a tendency to focus on male stimulus in heterosexual intercourse. Hence, Woody Allen remarked that the idea and delusion of simultaneous orgasm, and thus a male-dominated perspective on sex, most feminists would agree, was the most tangible expression of sexual success and satisfaction in American society. In recent years, however, there has been a recognition - which the early sexologists neglected to emphasise in their work - that sexual theorising is inherently morally biased and a product of the time and place in which it is constructed and produced.[14] The second, psychological phase also marks the end of a long period of sex research, what Parker and Gagnon (1995) recently termed *the sexological period*, ranging from approximately 1890-1980. This was a period in which sexuality was subjected to a rigid scientific scrutiny and social and moral control. By the beginning of the 1980s, the perspective has changed radically, as we shall now see.

In the third, *sociological phase of sexology* sexuality has moved from the margins to the centre of attention, especially for sociologists. Instigated by Foucault's analyses some 25 years ago, prominent scholars in the social sciences have in recent years been lured to the field of sexuality as a fertile ground for theorising (Bauman, 1997, 1998a, 1998b; Beck and Beck-Gernsheim, 1995; Douglas and Atwell, 1988; Giddens, 1992; Luhmann, 1982; Seidman, 1991; Weeks, 1989, 1995). Sexuality has turned from an embarrassing and obscure interest to a career-promoting, mainstream occupation within sociology. Sexology has turned into an emporium for original as well as trivial ideas. There is therefore an acknowledgement that an understanding of sexuality and sexual practices will also inform us about society and social practices. What characterises late modern sexology compared to the modern attempts to create a science of sex is the focus on diffusion, and indeed confusion, instead of standardised and stereotypical images of man and his desires. An acceptance of diversity has replaced a preoccupation with perversion, an ambition to create a non-normative approach has replaced a judgmental gospel, and a sexuality of blurred genres has replaced a sexual straitjacket. Moreover, the proliferation of perspectives and differentiation of disciplines has resulted in a cascade of discourses on sexuality in which sociology has been one of the more productive, utilised and consulted disciplines within the social sciences. We have therefore seen a cognitive contraction, as it were, of sexuality, by which sociology has been able to attract many interesting bids from prominent sociologists. The mark of distinction of a late modern concern with sexuality, as opposed to the earlier paradigms within sexology, is therefore *to decipher a socially and culturally rooted code in human sexuality*, and thus examine the interplay of individual choice and social regulation. The contemporary sensitivity in studies of sexuality toward a social and cultural perspective has placed sociology in a particularly favourable position as the scientific interpreter *par excellence* of how we construct and maintain sexuality, how we negatively sanction certain sexual orientations while lending affirmation toward others, how relatively stable sexualities are at all possible in a world marked by rapid change and dissolution of 'all that is solid', where all the fixed reference points are disappearing, and how sexual theory is itself an ideological *expert system*, to use Giddens' notion (1990), which means that sexology is nothing but another ideological instrument and political representation from a particular vantage point, and thus not a value-neutral enterprise with no consequences for social structure and the everyday lives of individuals. This does not mean, however, that sociology has totally colonised the field of sexuality, that it is superior in comparison to the previous stages or any better equipped to function as an authority on sexual issues than other disciplines. Rather, it means that the discipline, due to its more general and broader perspective, is better capable of negotiating between perspectives and angles than earlier specialised, restricted and segmented attempts to theorise sexuality. Above, I have presented the science of sex almost solely as a restricting, authoritarian and powerful instrument for the use of control and repression of peoples' sexual desires. However, as Véronique Mottier (1998, p.114) has remarked, 'sexological discourse is not exclusively constraining; it can also be a reflexive resource for the active shaping of the sexual self'. Sexology is not merely, as Foucault seemed to claim, a source of top-down power but can thus also be regarded as an empowering sphere for a quotidian bottom-up discourse on sexuality and sexual relations, facilitating the expression of the desires of ordinary people practicing sex and reflecting upon it.[15] The development of the science of sex through the three stages has illustrated this.

The Politics of Sexuality

The construction of sexuality is, and always has been, a dialectical process between individual passions and desires, on the one hand, and societal expectations and demands on the other. In other words, the construction of sexual identity and a sense of sexual belonging goes on in a Heraclitean universe. This means, of course, that the individual and society are interrelated and mutually constitutive; the one cannot be analysed or thought of without the presence of the other. Basically, we can speak of two moral levels of sexuality in the social sphere, both of which in practice serve to reinforce each other. The first operates at the abstract level and can be termed the *moralisation of sexuality*. The second, which we shall return to below, may be called the *politicisation of sexuality* and operates at the more concrete level in the form of legislation. Since we have touched upon how sexuality is morally circumscribed and subject to moral constraints on behaviour and thoughts, this will merely be a further elaboration of those ideas. One of the keys to understanding the moralisation of sex lies in the so-called social *sublimation of desire*, i.e., that human sexual passion has to be directed and guided toward certain objects whilst being kept at bay of others, that some actions and the objects of those actions are regarded, to utilise Mary Douglas' apt terms, as symbols of sexual *purity* while others are imbued with sexual *danger*. Historically, this has meant that heterosexual, marital and coital intercourse performed for the sake of the production of progeny is regarded as the ideal against which to measure all other types of sexual activity. From this ideal construction of sex was derived a relegation of, for example, the sex performed by homosexuals, non-marital sex, adultery, non-coital sex, and sex-for-the-sake-of-carnal-and-mental-stimulation-and-satisfaction such as sado-masochism, necrophilia, paedophilia and nymphomania to the sphere of the perverse and obscene.

As we saw previously, sexology has been instrumental in a scientisation of this basically moral valorisation and juxtaposition of sexual practices for the purpose of judging, condemning or punishing. As a result, sexology has also been instrumental in moralising the otherwise purely scientific by lending support to often rather dubious ideas about human physiology and the psyche. Throughout its history the science of sex has created many myths about human sexuality, e.g. the myth of innate female frigidity and the asexual woman (Hawkes, 1998, p.103). Amazingly we never hear of frigid males! Early sexology was clearly plagued by misogynism and regarded the female as often nothing more than a simple instrument for the stimulation of male fantasies and as objects of male suppression - what C. Wright Mills' captured with the satiric phrase 'women, the darling little slaves'. Homosexuals, another popular category among late-19th century sexologists, were at best viewed disdainfully and at worst as carriers and transmitters of diseases; women with an overt appetite for carnal pleasure were regarded either as prostitutes or nymphomaniacs; onanism and auto-eroticism were seen as threatening to your mental and physical health; and people with passions that did not fit the mainstreamed ideal were thought of as threats to social cohesion and menaces to moral sanity. Generally speaking, sexology as well as society in general, was suspicious of what Foucault (1978) termed *peripheral sexualities*, sexual orientations other than the dominant heterosexual married couple. These *fringe sexualities*, so to speak, were thought of as vermin nibbling at the fabric of society and undermining the moral order. Today we find equally energetic attempts to separate the sexual minorities from the *normal* population, whoever they are, as the following will illustrate.

The obsession of medical sexology to categorise and segregate, analytically as well as physically, was evident in the works of Krafft-Ebing, Ellis, Kinsey and Masters and Johnson. As Michel Foucault has noted, this endeavour was a distinguishing feature of the mentality of the modern age. That this conglomeration of morality and science could also extend itself to our contemporary late modern era is rather surprising. This has to do with the fact that morality, science and politics have experienced 'a second coming', a new unexpected curtain call in regard to sexual matters due to the emergence of ever new uncertainties, and although the moralisation of sex was supposedly played down during the 1960s and 1970s it was revived with full strength during the 1980s and the decade known as the reign of the New Right. We are often led to believe that in the chaos of the 1960s sexual revolution people were liberated and emancipated in an unprecedented fashion. Paul Robinson (1976, p.xii) termed the 1960s and 1970s as the period 'before the lights went out', a period marked by a frivolous attitude toward sexual expressionism, erotic hedonism and a general moral turpitude. Following this, as a reactionary reaction, as it were, there emerged a new dogmatic regime which subdued our idea of sexual liberation. As the following decades and tragedies revealed, our emancipation and tolerance had hardly grown at all. Instead of a vigorous and powerful emancipation of sexuality, there occurred only an impaired and fragile sexual liberation. The *liberation thesis*, as the *repressive thesis* of Foucault (1978) demonstrated, is always to be understood in relative terms. It can be understood and accentuated only by asking critical questions such as, 'liberated from what into what?', 'liberated by purpose or by accident?', 'liberation for whom and with what consequences for others?' etc. The main factor behind the lack of complete sexual liberation, if this is indeed obtainable, and the continuing strict social regulation of sexual behaviour - as optimistically envisaged by writers such as Marcuse and Reich - fundamentally boils down to the emergence of the powerful discourse of the New Right, particularly in the United Kingdom and the United States, a discourse adopted in more diluted forms in Continental Europe as well as in the Scandinavian countries.

Social transformations are characterised by pushes and pulls and are therefore often accompanied by retrograde political allegiances that try to counter transformation. With the gradual transformation of the moral order into a more right-wing position, there occurred an accompanying transformation of one of the most conspicuous features of human nature and of our social organisation: a transformation of how we conceive of our *sexuality*. Simultaneously, uncertainties lurked below the surface, which meant that the dominant morality had to be re-attuned to contemporary conditions. This meant that the erstwhile old-fashioned moralisation was not applicable to the continuous control of new nuances of human instinct. More subtle, and at the same time more radical, measures had to be applied. The *politicisation of sexuality*, which is the willing henchman and inevitable outcome of the moralisation of sex, deals with how sex has to be practiced, that is, legally, regulated, which sexual orientations to sanction positively and negatively, who to promote as role models and who to imprison. It is a well known case, what Steven Seidman has eloquently, yet in a very concrete fashion, noted, that

> every society sets out rules regulating sexual expression. These rules tell us when to have sex, where, with whom, and how frequently. They regulate sexual representations as well as private behavior. These sexual rules presuppose basic ontologies of sex, i.e., definitions of sex that relate it to gender, self-identity and public life. These sexual concepts and rules are embodied in law, public representations, medical and scientific institutions as well as popular culture, everyday maxims and custom; they amount to a sexual regime. This sexual regime inevitably privileges particular desires and acts while disapproving and penalizing others. Individuals whose chief practices are transgressive will suffer while conformity will confer legitimacy (Seidman, 1992, p.205).

That sexuality is subjected to social control and regulation is probably one of the most commonly known truths in the history of sexology, and much has been written on the subject (DeLamater, 1981). Foucault was one of the first to point to the intimate connection between sexuality and power, the private and the public realm, and he used the term *bio-politics* (Foucault, 1978) to denote the regimentation and regulation of the singular human body as well as entire populations, designating the connection between sexuality and social power. Instruments of bio-politics, or what Weeks (1991, p.26) denoted *body McCarthyism*, included the Panoptikon, with its emphasis on constant surveillance and subsequent infliction of an equally constant fear of being observed, as well as more inquisitive measures. What has happened today is that protagonists of the New Right have been successful in monopolising vital parts of the discourse on sexuality and successfully re-accentuated the idea of bio-politics, of the necessity of a short leash on sexuality by the authorities, and a revitalisation of the morality of conformity. Political opposition to this monopolisation has been launched too half-heartedly resulting in a victory to the faction of the hawks in what Hunter (1991) termed the *moral civil war*.

What we quite often encounter in sociological theories about sexuality and politics is a rather limited view of the prevalent opinions in society about sexual practices and desires, an often artificially polarised conception of people's attitudes toward sex and about the performance of different kinds of sexual activity; in short, we encounter a rather conflict-ridden conception of the politics of sex. In our society, however, we are not merely faced with either *romanticists* or *libertarians* weighing down the poles of the sexual continuum, as Steven Seidman (1992, pp.187-209) seems to be suggesting, and which I read as an opposition between two different emotional rather than political positions. Although Seidman is quite aware that a third option is viable, namely his own more *pragmatic sexual ethic*, his focus on romanticists versus libertarians is an excessively polarised picture of reality and the pragmatic ethic is unfortunately reserved only for the enlightened avant-garde of academia. I therefore suggest another, less emotional and more political, typology of the prevalent ideologies of sexuality in contemporary Western society.[16] On the one hand we have the *reactionary conservatives*, who, rather like Seidman's romanticists, are quite hostile to sexual expressionism and politically active in promoting the true and pristine virtues. With a strange mixture of the darker sides of the New Right,[17] such as an orthodox reliance on State, Family and Church, this group is saturated with judgmental views and prejudices about sexuality that does not perform its reproductive role in the maintenance of society and culture. These people have common ground in those views Eskapa (1995) labelled as *sexual Fascism* - a notion tightly connected to that of moral fundamentalism. This group, at least in the Scandinavian countries, otherwise the avant garde when it comes to sexual politics, is presently a minority but their ideas are gradually and ceaselessly spilling over into larger segments of society. The other end of the continuum is occupied by the *emancipated expressionists* who, like Seidman's libertarians, are an equally strange mixture of the brighter sides of the New Right, exclaiming the right to individual choice, as well as leftish radicals with a flavour of the Reichian sexual philosophy. This group, however, is also quite easy to overlook, and their actions can more often than not have led to further restrictions instead of freedoms on sexuality as one of the proponents of radical sexual politics explained: 'Radical sexual politics may have created new spaces, but it has also opened new fissures, and generated new hostilities' (Weeks, 1991, p.24).

Instead of Seidman's aforementioned polarised perspective, one could propose a more nuanced understanding of public opinions on sexuality which, however, is not based on empirical observations but embedded in a desire to construct a viable analytical option. Such an option takes into account the fact that most people do not hold extreme opinions - not even in sexual matters. The vast majority of people, I will argue, therefore appear to be so-called *fair-weather liberals* who hold the key to changes in sexual attitudes, mores and beliefs. It is the beliefs and conceptions of this group that determine the course of the politics of sex. As the label indicates, these people are burdened with ambiguity and tergiversation. Like moral weathercocks, they constantly shift their allegiance. The fair-weather liberals are people who often have a predilection for freedom of choice and claim to be (oh, so) liberated from moral traditionalism and convention. However, their tolerance reaches only as far as their own doorstep, their own desires and their own preferences. They see a threat to public health and moral sanity in every sexual difference and deviance. These are indeed the incarnations of the subservient *little men* in Reich's (1974) caricature, the sanctimonious philistines of the late modern age. The fair-weather liberals disguise their intolerance as tolerance, and their celebration of sexual freedom often ends in an iron cage of right and wrong. On the surface, they are the ordinary citizens, the average people, the normal population, but in fact they are wolves in sheep's clothing, reactionary conservatives disguised as emancipated expressionists.

How did this group come to occupy such an important position in the discourse - morally as well as politically - on sexuality? What have been the consequences? Who have been the victims and who are the beneficiaries? Where do we draw the line and how bizarre does a sexual orientation have to be in order to be morally condemned and juridically criminalised? These are the unanswered, indeed unanswerable, questions arising in this late modern era, questions that sociologists, politicians and ordinary people are struggling to come to grips with.

As mentioned above, those who pose the greatest threat to sexual liberation are not groupings like the Salisbury Review in Britain or the Moral Majority in the United States. These variants of reactionary New Right ideology will probably never be powerful enough to set the sexual agenda at least in the Scandinavian countries. The danger lies in the possibility of their ideas being adopted by more moderate segments of the political spectrum. Having this in mind, those of us who in the face of the fair-weather liberals try to uphold a more genuinely nuanced and liberal sexual position - find it immensely satisfying when the moral hypocrites are caught with their pants down in the literal sense of the word. Some see the delicate disclosures in the mass media of the Monica Lewinskis and the Jessica Hahns as signs of the sexual hypocrisy and moral cancer festering at the heart of American society in particular and as a symbol of the tainted morality of Western capitalist societies in general. I would rather regard the sexual disclosures of the powerful as a natural outcome of a moral hypnosis of the media as well as the public in general, a society mesmerised by the spectacle of the private sexuality of other people, particularly those who claim to be immune to sexual seduction and stand as defenders of true family values. More than forty years ago, the media wallowing in sex and eroticism caught the concern of a far-sighted C. Wright Mills who wrote: 'All this public eroticism which floods the mass media in America is at once a reflection and a contributing cause of drastic changes in private morality' (Mills, 1972, p.326). Putting the private sexuality of moral hawks in the public limelight has always been a favourite pastime and sure-fire source of success for the media. Knowledge that scandalous disclosures are destined to be found among this group of people led Andrew Belsey to comment: 'The only three women in the life of the True Conservative are his Queen, his mother and his mistress, while his fantasy life is fully occupied by a vision of a 'willing' or even 'importunate' schoolgirl' (Belsey, 1981, p.5). In countries like Britain and the U.S. cases of sexual and moral infidelity have highlighted the fact that even the most vigorous protagonists of a return to the most traditional conservative values of sexuality - politicians, philosophers or tele-evangelists - cannot be trusted and that especially those people who have a vested interest in limiting the sexual freedom of others must have something to hide themselves. It also highlights that *moralism*, which is the evil stepmother and extreme and pathological variant of morality, ends up devouring even the most moral of otherwise immoral people, to paraphrase an old revolutionary saying.

Since politicians in liberal democratic societies are elected to office, their views and actions - admittedly only in the ideal case scenario - will mirror those of their electorate, and thus reflect the opinions of the majority of the people. Denmark is generally regarded as a haven for sexual dissidents and as spearheading an emancipated perspective on sexuality. However, as noted by Erik Albæk (1999, p.24), even in our liberal democratic paradise, limits necessarily have to be set and boundaries drawn:

> Liberal tolerance for others' right to live their lives according to cultural norms and values that deviate from one's own is great in Denmark, but is not boundless. A minority in the Danish population and in Folketinget [the parliament] draw the line at homosexuality. A majority of the MPs, and probably a majority in the population, draw the line at sexual relations with children.

Recent debates in the Danish media have highlighted the discussions about incest and paedophilia, illustrating the claim that tolerance is limited and that morality, in some form or other, still prevails. As Albæk further illustrates, there is a constant push and pull and give and take between liberal and communitarian - or what some denote *meliorist* - positions regarding tolerance in sexual matters. One of the victories, for example, has been the legalisation and general toleration of registered same-sex partnerships (Albæk, 1999). How amazing it is to recall that we do not have to go more than 40 years back in Danish history to discover that homosexuals were still prosecuted for violating the law on so-called *speculation in sensuality* stemming from the 1880s. This liberalisation, however, has been at the cost of other groups having been turned into sexual martyrs; other sexual minorities still, rightly or wrongly, remain in the closet. This is the result when the obscene and perverse is decided either by strict moral authorities or by submissive fair-weather liberals and not subjected to sound common sense and substantiated judgements. The personal consequences, and options, for people living in *fringe sexual relationships* as well as the established heterosexual couples may well be severe. But this is the topic for another article. Suffice it to say that for the moment, the politics of sex have not been morally slackened, if we ever believed so, but have instead been transformed and subjected to even further restrictive measures. This was affirmed by Connell and Dowsett (1992, p.123) who remarked:

> While such new ways of speaking of sexual politics in the past are beginning, the old ways still continue strongly into the present moment [...] What was then called wowserism and is now called moralism, whether expressed by doctors, clerics, politicians, feminists, or the populist right; what was then and is still called libertarianism, whether expressed by sexual radicals, pornographers, feminists, or the populist left: these discourses have survived at least a century and a half [...] That discourse is incapable of anything but condemnation of sexual behaviour that cannot be recuperated for worthy social ends, whether they be heterosexual reproduction or ideologically sound liberation politics [...] Such an official, public discourse is itself a sexual politics, one which denies other understandings of sexuality.

All talk about the continued existence of a morality of conformity, contrary to the notion that we are standing at the threshold to a morality of choice, appears to be without foundation. At best, we are transforming morality from an external and oppressive iron cage to an inner voluntary incarceration of desires and preferences. Thus, we should instead talk about the existence of a *choice of conformity* or *conformity of choice* in which people subject to persisting uncertainties and insecurities more or less voluntarily choose to embrace the old and rigid dichotomies of healthy and unhealthy sexuality. Michel Foucault, in an interview conducted close to his death, mentioned that the freedom of sexual choice was not a matter of necessarily deciding to choose. One also had the ability to manifest a choice or not at all (Foucault, 1983, p.12). That is the important lesson of living in the late modern society.

The Late Modern Cinderella Search for Morality and Sexuality

In this final part, let me conclude on the above discussion, if it is at all possible to conclude on such elusive subjects as morality and sexuality on such inconclusive grounds as those presented above. Moreover, I will finally attempt to state my own position regarding the issue of late modern morality and sexuality, which have been latent in many of the previous pages but which should now be presented as a more general, however, tentative position.

The era of modernity is on its way, slowly but surely, into the history books and annals of civilisation. However, many of the ideals modernity held so dearly have not completely disappeared, nor have they been fully replaced by others more appropriate to the problems facing the current times. One of the main proponents of a decisively post-modern understanding of our contemporary social condition, Zygmunt Bauman (1991), contends that the sign of the modern age was the quest for order and certainty. In times marked by the exactly opposite - chaos and uncertainty - the attempts to construct order and certainty are intensified at individual and collective levels. Bauman suggests that this is due to the desire to avoid the spectre of *ambivalence*, which is the thorn in the side of the grand modern project of streamlining, uniformity and conformity and which has not, and will never successfully be, entirely exorcised. Another equally capable analyst of modernity, Anthony Giddens (1990), described late modernity as a double-edged sword with one side of the edge representing choice and the opposite side representing limitation of choice, what he termed respectively the *opportunity side* and the *pessimistic side*. The simultaneous existence of both positive and negative consequences of life is probably universal to the human condition but in late modernity the dividing line between the opportunity side and the pessimistic side is becoming increasingly blurred and opaque. This is due to the fact that late modernity is an interlude, an intermezzo, between a distinctively modern and a post-modern age. As Paul Robinson noted:

> As moderns, we remain permanently divided between a Romantic past, whose repressions we would gladly rid ourselves of, and a deromantized future, whose emotional emptiness we fear even while we anticipate its freedom. It is precisely in this antithesis of Romantic and anti-Romantic impulses that the distinctly modern element in sexual modernism is to be located (Robinson quoted in Douglas and Attwell, 1988, p.17).

The sexual late modernism, however, is to be located in an entirely different though equivalent antithesis, that between a modern morality longing for security, certainty, and predictability and a post-modern morality's desire for freedom, dissolution and the infinity of choice.

Just as the late modern social order is marked by this duality, so is the contemporary sexual universe: 'The contemporary sexual landscape is haunted by a double-headed spectre: the irredeemable diversity of sexualities, the fact of otherness confronting us in all our dealings with individuals and collectivities; and the necessity of choice' (Weeks, 1995, p.58). Our freedom of choice necessitates that we, at one point, actually choose, that choice is only a temporary state awaiting final redemption and confirmation through the making of a choice. The contemporary predilection for diversity, reflexivity and choice appears as one of the dominant features of this late modernity and essential to achieving happiness. But choice has two sides to it: an opportunity side as well as a more harmful one. This was pointed out by the prominent sociologist Charles H. Cooley back in 1902:

> Choice is like a river; it broadens as it comes down through history - though there are always banks - and the wider it becomes the more persons drown in it. Stronger and stronger swimming is required, and types of character that lack vigor and self-reliance are more and more likely to go under (Cooley in Simon, 1996, p.70).

Choice, regarded by many as the supreme good, can therefore have devastating consequences personally as well as socially. The price - some would say too high a price - we have to pay for freedom of choice is the potentially harming and devastating effects of anxiety, insecurity and uncertainty pervading social life; insecurities about whether or not we made the right choice and whether or not the choice will be socially sanctioned and accepted. The moral limitations on choice have presumably been slackened, at least on the surface, and people appear to have ever more important choices to make - particularly in the sexual realm of life - and the choices seem to be made voluntarily and based on freedom, reflexive knowledge and a sense of personal meaning. As I have tried to demonstrate above, the individual as well as the social consequences may well be detrimental to the original intention of the craving for choice, namely self-constitution and autonomy. The immanent danger of choice may transform *homo sexualis* into what Norbert Elias (1994) termed *homo clausus* - the lonely, self-contained and almost solipsistic human being. The more positive aspects of living in a late modern age with uncharted areas waiting to be explored, with choice no longer as the highest, most unattainable good, with new horizons to appear, is that people today have a deep-rooted sense of and personal responsibility for the construction and maintenance of the project of the sexual self. As long as choice is coupled with responsibility, the positive sides of self-determination may well exceed the negative aspects.

Late modernity reveals 'a cacophony of discourses on sexuality - medical, religious, therapeutic, juridical and others - that tell us how to categorise our sex life, its problems and its prohibitions' (Mottier, 1998, p.115). These discourses, however important they may be for a sociological understanding of the historical transformation of sexuality, cannot provide the adequate means for a re-enchanted sexuality, for a liberation of sexuality from the moral bonds strapping it down, since they themselves are the tangible expression of moral evaluations, judgements and objectifications of sexual reality. This liberation can be achieved only through the subversive actions of people in their everyday lives, in the daily struggle to construct sexual selves and identities and in the attempts to influence the political decision-making on sexuality. But we have seen that the discourses are not separated entirely from social life. They play an active part in how people conceive of themselves and others. Thus, it is possible to find aid, inspiration and assistance in certain parts of contemporary sociological theory, from specific schools of thought oriented toward action, or *praxis*. I am thinking here of the valuable insights and practical impact of recent feminist theory, variants of critical theory and queer theory on contemporary discourses surrounding sexuality. These approaches have opened our otherwise tightly shut eyes and highlighted aspects of sexuality that we were heretofore accustomed to overlook.

These theories also contain overt political statements that offer some guidelines for achieving a liberation of sexuality. Looking at some of the most prevalent examples, I will briefly try to combine Sediman's (1991) *pragmatic ethic* with Weeks' (1998) *radical humanism*. This means orienting ourselves equally toward ideals of choice, sexual equality, tolerance, diversity, otherness, authenticity and autonomy. This approach has to be coupled with responsibility and solidarity in order not to become excessively concerned with individual self-expression and self-realisation. It entails a rejection of perversity as an acceptable descriptive term for the actions and orientations of others, a respect for sexual minorities, and a reliance on the social responsibility of people for themselves as well as for others. A sexual morality of the early third millennium must be based on the acceptance of continuous change, the assumption of the emergence of what has been characterised as a *moment of transgression* (Weeks, 1995), which is the moment when the previously repressed returns (Giddens, 1991), when the world is once again re-enchanted (Bauman, 1992), when the wonders of sex never cease to overcome us, when sexuality is not merely a clinical issue subjugated to a scientific logic and terminology but also an emotional sphere waiting to be discovered and continually rediscovered. From this follows that important questions arise, inasmuch as late modernity, with its radicalisation of the characteristics of modernity, poses new and unprecedented problems to be solved, territories to be explored, and issues to be confronted. For example, what is the impact of the postulated end of masculinity (MacInnes, 1998) and equally femininity on sexuality as well as morality? Which type of values will dominate in the decades to come - masculine or feminine values, or a hybrid of both? And with what consequences for identity formation? Are we, as we so loudly proclaim, finally free from the heterosexual phallocentrism of the past? And perhaps most importantly, where do we go from here? While answers to these questions cannot be explored further here, it is important to realise that answers to questions about social life - and especially about the erotic sphere - are never final and always open to conflicting interpretations.

In this chapter I have sought to present an alternative version of the recent history of sexuality. I have tried to explicate the link between private sexual preferences and public representations of sexuality, these being moulded by both moral constraint as well as moral encouragement in an age which, on the surface, is marked by freedom of choice, contingency and rapid change. These hallmarks of late modernity create both optimism and relief as well as pessimism and anxiety. To recapitulate some of my main points, as already Foucault (1978) noted, the history of sexuality is not a one-way street but is a continuously evolving story of the social push and pull mechanisms, of forces working to constrain as well as liberate sexuality. Second, that the science of sex in late modernity, as in those phases prior to this, has been unable to discover the universal laws governing human sexual conduct and has similarly failed to abandon a morally imbued position. Third, that the ability to accomplish and construct sexuality for human beings has not necessarily been enhanced by the supposedly more liberal attitude towards sex in contemporary society but rather, has created an illusion of choice and self-constitution. And finally that sexuality is, and always has been, a social construction created by supply and demand understood as the constant negotiation between private desire and the public moral and normative regulation of behaviour.

In this way, sexuality can be understood as a private construction sandblasted by the winds of change in wider society, a harness of individuality and choice *corroded* - to utilise Sennett's (1998) powerful term - by social demands, obligations and expectations. The negotiation of sexual identity and sense of belonging is not just a part of everyday life and politics. It is also present in the social sciences which have set their goal as the demystification of sexuality or, what Mottier (1998) echoing Guy Debord terms, *the spectacle of sex*. William Simon, an American proponent of sexual scripting theory, was optimistic to the prospects of finding the ultimate truth about sex in the near future: 'The sexual future in whatever form it is conceived may in fact be brighter than life today encourages us to expect. [Hence], the future of the sexual is only in the most minimal sense in the control of what presently constitutes the sexual' (Simon, 1996, p.19). Although we do not have an empty void ahead of us in our search for knowledge and understanding of sex, we are still far from the finish line - or more precisely, a receding horizon. There is no reason whatsoever to be excessively optimistic, or pessimistic for that matter, that the mystery of sex will eventually be solved in the years to come. This chapter has been but a preliminary attempt to theorise sporadically about the historical construction and deconstruction of the sexual. To believe that sexuality can ever be entirely cut loose from morality or social convention is a utopian fantasy. To borrow a phrase from Marx and Engels, sexuality today has nothing to lose but its chains. It still has, and always will have, a world to win.

Notes

1 The contemporary unease and confusion in social theory about how much determination in human behaviour is to be accorded to nature and how much to pin on culture was shown with clarity by Sheyla Benhabib who, although belonging to a constructivist position, still expressed implicit reservations about the social nature of the sexual by remarking that 'culture does not 'construct' everything, the human body is not a *tabula*

rasa on which all is inscribed by mechanisms of agency and socialization. The body is an active medium with its own dispositions and 'habits', which process, channel and deflect the influences which come to it from the outside, in accordance with its own accumulated modality of being toward the world' (Benhabib, 1992, p.236). The entire discussion about the primacy of nature or nurture is, as I see it, an academic dead end. Few would oppose a position, that by critics perhaps would be labelled *essentialism*, in which there is a natural core in human beings that is moulded as well as transformed throughout the span of a human life by social surroundings.

2 In his interesting discussion of Elias' and Foucault's views on the historical process of civilising and disciplining individuals and societies alike, Dennis Smith (1999) proposes several idiosyncratic and original perspectives.

3 An etiological myth is a story about the origin and perpetual continuation of a given phenomenon, its emergence and persistence. As Bauman more aptly puts it: 'Ostensibly, etiological myths are stories about the 'origins of it all', about the one-off event from which something started [...] they also spell out the conditions that must be met in order to ensure that the phenomenon in question does happen over and over again - that its happening was not a one-off event' (Bauman, 1998a, pp.11-12).

4 Although for many of us the Ten Commandments appear to be antediluvian, if not entirely irrelevant to contemporary sexuality and morality, I suggest a brief skimming of Kieslowski and Piesiewicz' brilliant filmic and literary masterpiece *Dekalog* (1990) in which present day stories from Poland are used to talk about the Ten Commandments and their influence on human behaviour regarding the harsh realities as well as fantasies and yearnings of sex, love and desire.

5 In Janet E. Halley's (1993) essay on the construction of heterosexuality, we also encounter the more legislative aspects of the classification of people as, respectively, homosexuals and heterosexuals. She shows how this is biased in favour on the latter and at the expense of the former.

6 In a brief, yet illuminating, comparison of the theories of Max Weber and Sigmund Freud on sexuality, Gail Hawkes (1998) focuses on the themes of civilising, modernising and rationalising, and their consequences for human sexual desire and pleasure.

7 Sagarin (1971), Gagnon (1975) and Weeks (1989) contain comprehensive discussions and illustrations on the history of *scientia sexualis*. One of the most illuminating pieces of work on the history of sexology, however, is Bullough's (1994) brilliant introduction to science in the bedroom and how sexual research has been conducted.

8 As Gail Hawkes (1996) illustrates, behind this negative construction on sexuality primarily lies the fact that the bourgeoisie, the class that presumably embodies and symbolises the modern spirit with its entrepreneurship, liberal-mindedness and sense of proportion, wanted to detach itself from the filthy sexuality of the lower classes as well as from the perversity and carnal pleasures of the decadent aristocracy. Therefore, the middle-position of the bourgeoisie turned out to be excessively restrictive. This is particularly interesting in connection to my conceptualisation of the so-called *fair-weather liberals*.

9 Connell and Dowsett (1999) rightly contend, that the nativism of the sexology of the 19th century started out as a religious variant and later, as I have illustrated, was replaced by a scientific nativism. Nativism implies that sexuality is pre-social making the impact of culture on sexuality rather limited.

10 As noted by amongst others Jeffrey Weeks (1989), Havelock Ellis actually combined a *cultural relativism* with a *biological determinism*. Therefore, Ellis' work cannot be regarded as a one-sided natural scientific approach to sexology.

11 A superb introduction to the ideas of Freud on sexuality and its rather dismal state in modernity can be found in Herbert Marcuse's (1956) *Eros and Civilization*.

12 Alfred Kinsey was one of the only sexologists to overtly claim that his ambition was to present a value-free approach to the study of human sexuality (Hawkes, 1996, p.64). Of course, like the rest of the sexologists, Kinsey was haunted by moral and normative ideals.

13 On several occasions, Freud mentions that perversion is not a unique but rather ubiquitous phenomenon. Hence, 'the disposition to perversions of every kind is a general and fundamental human characteristic' (Freud in Hawkes, 1998, p.103). The morality of Freud is most striking in his psychoanalytic practice, according to which it is possible to eliminate and cure, through confessional and therapeutic techniques, peoples' abnormal, yet natural, dispositions toward what he termed *polymorphous sexual perversions*.

14 If one takes a radical position and decides to follow Foucault to the extremes, it can be argued that any kind of theorising about sexuality is a violation of peoples' self-image and self-understanding and that sexology, no matter how liberally and open-mindedly expressed, will necessarily subjugate sexuality to categories, ideal types and stereotypes.

15 It is necessary to recall that any attempt to categorise phases of developments will willy-nilly suffer from simplification, rigidity and selectivity. The periodisation presented here is no exception to such a critique. However, when the purpose is to provide a general picture of the development from one phase, modernity, to another, late modernity, some level of generality and formalisation is required. I am well aware that the postulating three phases of the main drift in the history of sexology, as I have outlined here, produces an analytical distinction that does not do justice to everything written within this realm of social thought. Therefore, I urge the reader to bear with any unconscious omissions or conscious choices on my behalf. Any model, no matter how ingeniously constructed, must necessarily involve a reduction of the complexity of reality and simplification.

16 Any kind of typology, of course, rests on analytical distinctions and ideal typical features of occurrences in everyday life and is not a precise picture of the diversity and multifaceted complexity of positions people can take in the debate and discourse on sexuality. In this respect, my own typology also suffers from oversimplification.

17 Jeffrey Weeks (1995, 1998) has noted the two distinct sides of the same coin in the New Right movement: 'The paradox of the 1980s in countries like Britain and the USA was that an extreme economic individualism coincided with attempts at social authoritarianism: at restoring traditional values, the traditional family, tightening the barriers against radical change' (Weeks, 1998, p.44). Whereas the libertarian strand in the New Right offers a morality of choice, the Conservative variant is still heavily biased toward the morality of conformity. For an interesting presentation of the New Right ideology on amongst other issues sexuality in Britain, Anna Marie Smith's (1994) book offers exciting insights. For a more general discussion of the inherent instability of the New Right ideology see my *Utopia - A Critical Analysis of the New Right* (Jacobsen, 1994).

References

Albæk, E. (1999), *The Limits of Liberal Ethics: Homosexuals Between Moral Dilemmas and Political Considerations in the Danish Parliament*, Working paper, Department of Economics, Politics and Law, University of Aalborg.

Bauman, Z. (1991), *Modernity and Ambivalence*, Polity Press, Cambridge.

Bauman, Z. (1992), *Intimations of Postmodernity*, Routledge, London.

Bauman, Z. (1995), 'Searching for a Centre that Holds', in M. Featherstone, S. Lash and R. Robertson (eds.): *Global Modernities*, Sage Publications, London.

Bauman, Z. (1997), 'On The Postmodern Redeployment of Sex: Foucault's *History of Sexuality* Revisited', in Z. Bauman, *Postmodernity and Its Discontents*, Polity Press, Cambridge.

Bauman, Z. (1998a), 'What Prospects for Morality in Times of Uncertainty?', *Theory, Culture & Society*, vol. 15 no. 1, pp.11-22.

Bauman, Z. (1998b), 'On Postmodern Uses of Sex', *Theory, Culture & Society*, vol. 15 no. 3-4, pp.19-33.

Beck, U. and E. Beck-Gernsheim (1995), *The Normal Chaos of Love*, Polity Press, Cambridge.

Belsey, A. (1981), 'The 'Real' Meaning of Conservatism', *Radical Philosophy*, vol. 28, pp.1-5.

Benhabib, S. (1992), *Situating the Self*, Polity Press, Cambridge.

Bullough, V.L. (1994), *Science in the Bedroom: A History of Sex Research*, Basic Books, New York.

Connell, R.W. and G.W. Dowsett (eds.)(1992), *Rethinking Sex: Social Theory and Sexuality Research*, Temple University Press, Philadelphia.

Connell, R.W. and G.W. Dowsett (1999), 'The Unclean Motion of the Generative Parts: Frameworks in Western Thought on Sexuality', in R. Parker and P. Aggleton (eds.), *Culture, Society and Sexuality: A Reader*, University College of London Press, London.

Dahrendorf, R. (1968), *Homo Sociologicus*, Routledge and Kegan Paul, London.

DeLamater, J. (1981), 'The Social Control of Sexuality', *Annual Review of Sexuality*, vol. 7, pp.263-290.

Douglas, J.D. and F.C. Atwell (1988), *Love, Intimacy and Sex*, Sage Publications, Beverly Hills, CA.

Elias, N. (1994), *The Civilizing Process*, Blackwell, Oxford.

Eskapa, R. (1995), *Bizarre Sex*, Parallel Books, Bristol.

Foucault, M. (1978), *The History of Sexuality, Volume 1: An Introduction*, Penguin Books, Harmondsworth.

Foucault, M. (1983), 'Sexual Choice, Sexual Act: An Interview with Michel Foucault' (by James O'Higgins), *Salmagundi*, vol. 58-59, pp.10-24.

Foucault, M. (1985), *The History of Sexuality, Volume 2: The Use of Pleasure*, Penguin Books, Harmondsworth.

Foucault, M. (1986), *The History of Sexuality, Volume 3: The Care of the Self*, Penguin Books, Harmondsworth.

Freud, S. (1974), *The Pelican Freud Library, Volume 1: Introductory Lectures on Psychoanalysis*, Penguin Books, Harmondsworth.

Gagnon, J.H. (1975), 'Sex Research and Social Change', *Archives of Sexual Behavior*, vol. 4 no. 2, pp.111-141.

Gagnon, J.H. and W. Simon (1973), *Sexual Conduct: The Social Sources of Human Sexuality*, Aldine, Chicago.

Gibbs, L. (ed.) (1994), *Daring to Dissent: Lesbian Culture From Margin to Mainstream*, Cassell, London.

Giddens, A. (1976), *New Rules of Sociological Method*, Hutchinson, London.

Giddens, A. (1990), *The Consequences of Modernity*, Polity Press, Cambridge.

Giddens, A. (1991), *Modernity and Self-Identity: Self and Society in the Late Modern Age*, Polity Press, Cambridge.

Giddens, A. (1992), *The Transformation of Intimacy: Sexuality, Love and Eroticism in Modern Societies*, Stanford University Press, Stanford, CA.

Halley, J.E. (1993), 'The Construction of Heterosexuality', in M. Warner (ed.), *Fear of a Queer Planet: Queer Politics and Social Theory*, University of Minnesota Press, Minneapolis.

Hawkes, G. (1996), *A Sociology of Sex and Sexuality*, Open University Press, Buckingham.

Hawkes, G. (1998), 'Sexuality and Civilisation - Weber and Freud', in T. Carver and V. Mottier (eds.), *Politics of Sexuality - Identity, Gender, Citizenship*, Routledge, London.

Hunter, J.D. (1991), *Culture Wars: The Struggle to Define America*, Basic Books, Basic Books.

Jacobsen, M.H. (1994), *Utopia – en kritisk analyse af det ny højre*, Unpublished manuscript, University of Aalborg.

Jameson, F. (1991), *Postmodernism, or the Cultural Logic of Late Capitalism*, Verso, New York.

Kaplan, M.B. (1997), *Sexual Justice: Democratic Citizenship and the Politics of Desire*, Routledge, London.

Katz, J. N. (1990), 'The Invention of Heterosexuality', *Socialist Review* vol. 20 no. 1, pp.7-34.

Katzenelson, B. (1994), *Homo Socius*, Gyldendal, Copenhagen.

Kieslowski, K. & K. Piesiewicz (1990), *Dekalog*, Rosinante, Copenhagen.

Krafft-Ebing, R. von (1965 [1876]), *Psychopathia Sexualis: With Special Reference to Antiphatic Sexual Instincts - A Medico-Forensic Study*, G. P.Putnam, New York.

Luhmann, N. (1982), *Love as Passion - The Codification of Intimacy*, Stanford University Press, Stanford, CA.

MacInnes, J. (1998), *The End of Masculinity*, Open University Press, Buckingham.

Marcuse, H. (1956), *Eros and Civilization: A Philosophical Inquiry into Freud*, Routledge, London.

Mottier, V. (1998), 'Sexuality and Sexology - Michel Foucault', in T. Carver and V. Mottier (eds.), *Politics of Sexuality - Identity, Gender, Citizenship*, Routledge, London.

Parker, R.G. and J.H. Gagnon (1995), *Conceiving Sexuality: Approaches to Sex Research in the Postmodern World*, Routledge, New York.

Reich, W. (1974), *Listen, Little Man!*, Farrar, Straus, Giroux, New York.

Rival, L. et al. (1998), 'Sex and Sociality: Comparative Ethnographies of Sexual Objectification', *Theory, Culture & Society*, vol. 15 no. 3-4, pp.295-321.

Robinson, P.(1976), *The Modernization of Sex*, Cornell University Press, New York.

Ross, E. and R. Rapp (1983), 'Sex and Society: A Research Note from Social History and Anthropology', in A. Snitow et al., *Powers of Desire: The Politics of Sexuality*, Monthly Review Press, New York.

Sagarin, E. (1971), 'Sex Research and Sociology', in J. Henslin (ed.), *Studies in the Sociology of Sex*, Appleton-Century-Crofts, New York.
Schelsky, H. (1955): *Soziologie der Sexualität: Über die Beziehungen zwischen Geschlecht, Moral und Gesellschaft*. Hamburg: Rowohlt.
Seidman, S. (1991), *Romantic Longings: Love in America, 1830-1980*, Routledge, New York.
Seidman, S. (1992), *Embattled Eros*, Routledge, New York.
Sennett, R. (1998), *The Corrosion of Character: Personal Consequences of Work in the New Capitalism*, Norton, New York.
Simon, W. (1996), *Postmodern Sexualities*, Routledge, London.
Simon, W. (1998), *Postmodern Pulp: Gender as Skin*, Paper Prepared for the 18th Annual Meeting of Division 36 (Psychoanalysis) of the American Psychological Association.
Smith, A.M. (1994), *New Right Discourse on Race and Sexuality: Britain 1968-1990*, Cambridge University Press, Cambridge.
Smith, D. (1999), 'The Civilizing Process and The History of Sexuality: Comparing Norbert Elias and Michel Foucault', *Theory and Society*, vol. 28, pp.79-100.
Stein, A. (1989), 'Three Models of Sexuality: Drives, Identities and Practices', *Sociological Theory*, vol. 7 no. 1, pp.1-13.
Weeks, J. (1985), *Sexuality and Its Discontents: Meanings, Myths and Modern Sexualities*, Routledge, London.
Weeks, J. (1989), *Sex, Politics and Society: The Regulation of Sexuality Since 1800*, Longman, London.
Weeks, J. (1991), 'The Sphere of the Intimate', *Manchester Sociology Occasional Paper*, vol. 29, University of Manchester.
Weeks, J. (1995), *Invented Moralities: Sexual Values in an Age of Uncertainty*, Columbia University Press, New York.
Weeks, J. (1998), 'The Sexual Citizen', *Theory, Culture & Society*, vol. 15, pp.35-52.
Weber, M. (1948), 'Religious Rejections of the World and Their Directions', in H.H. Gerth and C. Wright Mills (eds.), *From Max Weber - Essays in Sociology*. Routledge, London.
Wrong, D. (1961), 'The Oversocialized Conception of Man in Modern Sociology', *American Sociological Review*, vol. 26 no. 2, pp.183-193.
Zeldin, T. (1994), *An Intimate History of Humanity*, Vintage, London.

8 'If People Believe Ideas are Real...': Women's Self-Perception as Active Individuals in Late Modernity

CATHARINA JUUL KRISTENSEN

Introduction

In a recent qualitative analysis of everyday life in late modernity, younger adult men and women present themselves as active individuals capable of influencing and planning their lives (Kristensen, 1998). Their self-perception resonates in the modern perception of the individual, while also challenging it.

Taken at face value, the phenomenon could lead to the two possible conclusions that younger adult men and women are equal, not only formally but also in reality, or that they have a wide range of real choices concerning their lives. Perhaps unsurprisingly, neither seems fully to be the case. We are, instead, dealing with a combination of the two.

In spite of the generally improved living conditions and formal rights of especially women and youth, and the partial individualisation (*Freizetzung*) of the individuals from the norms, values and life opportunities traditionally associated with gender, social class and generation experienced in post-War Denmark, statistics show continuous inequality between and within the two genders - also for the younger adults (Arbejdsmarkedsstyrelsen, 1995; Socialkommissionen, 1992).[1]

Similarly, Beck's convincing thesis of the 'institution-dependent control structure of individual situations' (*the standardisation*) (Beck, 1992, p.131), developing alongside the individualisation, challenges the self-perception. We are increasingly dependent upon the market and the welfare state, on fashions, education, social policy, economic cycles, etc.[2]

Inequality and standardisation thus limit the scope of action, again calling into question the prevalent self-perception of the interviewees.

The simultaneity of equality and inequality, individualisation and standardisation, that the interviewees' self-perception exposes, is characteristic of late modernity. It is a contradictory and changeable period within modernity. A period characterised by a complexity of modern and new phenomena. The dynamic character of modern society, however, is now radicalised (cf. Giddens, 1990; Ziehe, 1989), which explains the use of the prefix 'late'. The term 'late modernity' itself is borrowed from Giddens (1991). Yet my usage contains elements of what Giddens (1994) later identified as post-traditional society, Ziehe's (1989)[3] stress on individualisation and reflexivity, and elements of Beck's second modernity (most notably his inclusion of class and gender, and the complexity of change).[4]

In this chapter I focus on the self-perception as an active individual, capable of influencing one's life as *a strategy to handle everyday life* in late modernity. This strategy, I will argue, is developed as part of the interviewees' continuous negotiation, and thus also change, of available symbol positions in our culture. The modern notion of individuality is one such symbol positions. The development of the Danish welfare state and the socio-cultural environment set the frames[5] of such negotiations, while in turn being constructed by them.

My focus will be primarily on the paradoxes and prospects of *women* taking on the self-perception. While the use is prevalent both among the interviewed men and women, and thus also among the different social classes, I delimit the discussion to women adopting the self-perception. The discussion, however, is similar to that of class. The phenomenon, the women's self-perception, is analysed from the perspective of everyday life, i.e. individual people's lives and their relation to the re-creation and change of society.

The transformation of modern society, of course, is likewise addressed from the perspective of the individuals. As the phenomenon cuts across the issues raised in the Introduction to this volume, I restrict my initial comments to the concluding question. I argue here that contemporary society is characterised not by a lack of general social logic, but rather a combination. And it is exactly this complexity that blurs our view. The women's adoption of the modern notion of individuality points to a widening of the notion, which in turn may constitute a part of the transition, perhaps furthering the expansion of actual equality, (thus) giving way for yet unforeseeable social changes.

The Empirical Basis

The analysis is based on in-depth, qualitative interviews with a heterogeneous group of men and women born in the 1960s (nine men and nine women). The interviewees have thus grown up in late modernity. They are a part of a late modern generation. The interviewees all lived in the Greater Copenhagen area at the time of the interview (1995).[6]

Aside from the above common features the interviewees were all 'ordinarily well functioning' Danes.[7] They were people capable of handling the ups and downs of everyday life, who have the necessary resources and competencies to avoid chaos and dissolution. In other words the interviewees, were people who, to my knowledge, were without need of treatment or other forms of special assistance from society.[8]

During the analysis, I was struck – and intrigued - by the interviewees' frequent use of terms and phrases relating to the modern notion of the individual. This self-speech subsequently became a separate object of investigation.[9]

The outcome of this separate analysis is contradictory. The interviewees speak about their ability to plan and influence their own lives, about possibilities and limitations, and about coincidences. However, the phenomenon is so prevalent and rich in its form that it stands out as important.

From the perspective of everyday life theory, the self-perception can be seen as *a strategy to handle life in late modernity*, that is a strategy to handle the complexity and changeability of contemporary life. This is supported by the observation that the interviewees' self-perception is marked by an underlying or radical doubt. The interviewees thus act on the basis of a more or less conscious recognition that their actions are not the only ones possible, and that they may well be questioned or set aside. The self-perception is a symbolic construction that seems to have been adopted partly as it reflects concrete experience and partly out of necessity. But how are the concepts of self-perception and of everyday life strategies *initially* defined?

Self-Perception and Strategies

The concept of *self-perception*, or self-view, is closely related to individual world-view in that we always act within social contexts. I understand *self-*

and world-view to be our sense of who we are and where we belong, our feeling of the surrounding world and its composition, and our place in it.

Everyday life strategies are patterns of action directed at creating and re-creating a meaningful whole. They are a special part of the activities by which we handle the conditions of everyday life (Bak, 1997). The strategies can be more or less coherent, and they include both conscious and non-conscious action. A strategy is thus a metaphor for actions that can be identified as forming a larger set, directed more or less consciously at a general goal.

Everyday Life as Perspective

Everyday life is an *analytical perspective* on the relation between the individual's daily life and the re-creation of society. The perspective indicates

> a span of action between something common and something unique: something common in the sense that we all have an everyday life, and all these everyday lives make up the foundation for the re-creation of society; something unique in the sense that everybody has and creates their everyday life (Bloch, 1991, pp.15-16; my translation).

The points of departure for the analyses are taken in the daily life of individuals, as actualised in interaction with the close and more general social conditions. Everyday life, in other words, is produced through a constant handling of its conditions. And the conditions are in turn re-created and changed through this handling. In such an understanding of everyday life, individuals are (thus) seen as acting individuals.[10]

Everyday Life

Everyday life is the life we live every day, no matter who we are, where we are, or what we do. It includes all activities (actions, thoughts and feelings) and areas of life (e.g. one's family and work place), that we carry out ourselves - and are confronted with (Kristensen, 1999, pp.12-13).

Everyday life is produced through our continuous handling of its close and more general conditions now and throughout life. It is constantly re-created and changed through a mutual but asymmetrical process, a process where the conditions restrict and enable activity, and the activities influence the conditions - albeit more slowly and to a lesser extent.

In this chapter I focus on one element of the conditions of everyday life, *the symbolic order of taken-for-grantedness*. The symbolic order, Bech-Jørgensen argues, is the most fundamental condition for the handling of everyday life. It consists of a most often non-conscious knowledge of differences and possibilities, ethics and moral. It consists of normative differentiations (conceptions of e.g. good and bad, and right and wrong), differentiations of time and space, and a non-conscious knowledge of differences between people, e.g. gender and age differences (inter-subjective differentiations)(Bech-Jørgensen, 1994b).

The differentiations are structured as a symbolic order 'in that the activities are interpreted and attributed specific meanings, the origins of which are lost in the past, re-created and changed in the present, and reach into the future' (Horsgaard and Øland, 2000, p.50). The symbolic order is thus re-created, sustained and renewed by our activities.

The social structures or conditions (including the political, economic systems) thus delimit and are changed through our activities. Sometimes we make conscious attempts to challenge and change them, or consciously reflect upon these conditions. Most often, however, they are only part of the non-conscious stream of matters to be dealt with. They are not perceived of as structures (Mortensen, 1991).

The symbolic order of taken-for-grantedness is similar to Swidler's understanding of *culture,* where culture consists of 'available symbolic forms through which we can experience and express meaning' (Swidler, 1986, p.273).[11] The symbolic order of taken-for-grantedness, or culture, is com- mon, but is used in different ways by different people.

Handling I define as the activities by which we understand, manage and organise the conditions of everyday life. We thus seek to create order and a unified whole through our activities, a *meaningful whole*. This order is created through a conscious and non-conscious negotiation of our culture, the symbolic order of taken-for-grantedness.[12] Our self- and world-view is an integrated part of this meaningful whole. It makes up the mental part of what I have elsewhere identified as our *mental and concrete bases* (cf. Kristensen, 1998).

Our activities are thus both conscious and non-conscious. *Non-conscious activities* are those we take for granted, but can recognise and speak about when asked (Bech-Jørgensen, 1994a) or when they are otherwise questioned (e.g. through the confrontation with 'the other' and potentially unknown)(Kristensen, 1998). Our activities can furthermore be *symbolic*; i.e. attributed another meaning than the one they already have. Not a new meaning but a rephrasing or additional meaning (Gullestad, 1989). Finally, they can take the form of *strategies*.

Our daily activities are both great and small. We non-consciously re-create and change our meaningful whole, but we are also increasingly required to reflect upon our actions, plan, explain and defend (Giddens, 1991; Ziehe, 1989). Everyday life in late modernity is thus both taken-for-granted (Bech-Jørgensen, 1994a) and marked by radical doubt (Giddens, 1991). It is partly known and unquestioned, and partly open to questioning, revision and abandonment.

Below I discuss two possible explanations of why the self-perception as an active individual has been adopted as a strategy under the headings 'handling late modernity' and 'the ideology of sameness'. The former concerns late modernity as a real and felt condition of everyday life, and the latter the confusion of equality and sameness that seems to exist in countries such as contemporary Denmark. The explanations address both the paradoxes and prospects of the women's self-perception. They are, finally, seen as important, but not the only possible ones.

Before elaborating on what is meant by late modernity and the self-perception as a strategy, and presenting the two explanations, I will briefly outline my understanding of the modern notion of the individual.

The Modern Notion of the Individual

As has been argued by many feminist researchers, the modern notion of the individual is a social construction associated with *virtues* such as independence, activity, and purposefulness. It is a positively valued, exclusive, and excluding position.

The notion and privilege has traditionally been reserved for white, heterosexual men of the middle classes, thus excluding, among others, women. It is, in the terminology of Weedon, part and parcel of the liberal discourse of the individual, the 'free, rational, self-determining subject of modern political, legal, social and aesthetic discourses' (Weedon, 1987, pp.78-79).[13]

The notion is furthermore based on neutrality. Men and women alike are thus seen as absolute individuals who are formally equal, thus disregarding the fact that as concrete individuals they are 'faced with practices constituted on the basis of difference despite the 'sameness' rhetoric' (Gordon and Lahelma, 1995, pp.70-71). They are not socially, economically or politically equal. The neutrality of the individual has been accompanied, Gordon and Lahelma continue, by 'natural' attitudes towards, for example, gender. Women are thus seen as that which men are not (e.g. dependent), and which (therefore) have negative connotations (ibid.). Women are constructed as the 'other' - and as subordinate.

In their research Gordon (1994) and Yanay and Birns (1990) show that virtues traditionally ascribed to men (here predominantly independence and autonomy) are ever-present in the lives of women who more or less voluntarily challenge the dominant perceptions of how to be a woman.[14] The women, however, do not conform to the dominating images of women or mirror those of men, but develop alternatives,[15] thus both disputing and expanding them.

Returning to the issue of the abstract individual it might have been true that the individuals who were considered to be full citizens in the early days of liberal democracy (the white middle class men) were in fact equal. However, the expansion of civil, social and political rights has pluralised the group, bringing with it the potential for challenge and change. This is not to argue that the traditional notion of the individual is not biased or powerful. Instead, I seek to point out the immanent 'problem' of liberal democracy, the combination and contradiction of freedom and equality, accentuated by the inclusion of more groups as citizens - and by the development of the universal welfare state.

In Denmark, too, the modern notion of the individual has been continuously challenged. At the *formal level*, perhaps the most noticeable challenges were the introduction of universal suffrage in 1915, and the development of the welfare state.

The women of the late modern generations are thus less economically dependent on men (husbands/partners or fathers). It is common for these women to obtain an education, and to use it. The relatively comprehensive childcare provisions give parents (incl. lone parents) the opportunity to hold paid employment throughout adult life.[16] Thus 76 per cent of women are on the labour market, compared to 83 per cent of men (Arbejdsmarkedsstyrelsen, 1995).[17] However, the general cost of living also brings about a need for most parents to have paid employment. Being a housewife (or househusband), or opting for parental leave is thus only an economic option for the few.[18]

All adults are eligible to obtain either unemployment benefit or social benefits if unemployed or unable to work. And in contrast to many other West European countries social benefits and services are, generally speaking, based on the individual man or woman's situation - not his or her family's - in principle securing women's economic independence (Siim, 1997, pp.140-141).

Women's political representation has likewise increased in the post-war period. In the middle of the 1990s 34 per cent of the Danish MPs were women, as were 35 per cent of the government ministers posts. Women's political presence is highest in the elected boards in the kindergartens, schools and churches. Less surprisingly, perhaps, women make up the majority in the kindergarten boards (76 per cent) and 'break even' with men in the parochial church councils. In the schools boards women make up 44 percent of the elected members (Arbejdsmarkedsstyrelsen, 1995). Compared with most West European countries Danish women's formal political representation is relatively high at all political levels. Women in Denmark have thus gained, if not power, then at least presence.

It is my contention that although the formal rights and opportunities have improved significantly for women in post-War Denmark, the traditional notion of the individual and the privileges attached to it still penetrate our society, supporting structural differences and inequality. Although the formal political representation in Parliament, to mention just one issue, is high, women continue to comprise only one-third of the MPs, not half.

However, the self-perception among the female interviewees also points toward a (further) widening of the notion and a potential gain of power and influence - at least upon the course of their life. This development is confirmed by the statistically less visible, yet dominating socio-cultural tendencies, the increased individualisation and self-reflexivity (cf. the sections below).

As the title of this article indicates, we may be dealing with a *'Thomasian' phenomenon*, i.e. a phenomenon the women believe is true and therefore becomes true in its consequences.[19] Such perceptions can widen the individual person's scope of action.

Late Modernity

Contemporary Denmark is a *late modern welfare society* that alongside increased globalisation, technological development, consolidation of the welfare state and relatively high standard of living, has experienced an *increased individualisation* (Beck, 1992; Ziehe, 1989). Individuals have been set partially free from the dominating social forms of organisation, norms and values of industrial society, and experience a radicalised pluralisation of ways of life. The individualisation brings about the possibility and the demand for the individuals to form their lives and create meaning. The more fixed conditions of industrial society are dissolving. Globalisation and technological development bring about a situation where we are confronted with still more information about other ways of life, but also national changes play a part.

The individualisation is interrelated with *self-reflexivity*, our continuous reflection on our actions, motives, consequences, and alternatives. Self-reflexivity is an immanent part of all social action in modernity (Giddens, 1990) - and in late modernity a dominating cultural tendency (Ziehe, 1989). It involves knowledge about one's own and other's everyday life. It is both a possibility and a demand - and both seem to have become more prominent.

While individualisation demands, but also opens up, the opportunity to reflect upon oneself, self-reflexivity brings about further questioning of the modern, the predominant, and other taken-for-granted norms and values.

Contemporary Denmark is thus a society characterised by the simultaneity of modern and new types of gender, class and generational norms and values, by individualisation, standardisation and inequality. It is a society characterised by complexity and changeability. It is in interaction with this, that we have to handle everyday life.

The Self-Perception as a Strategy

Seen in light of everyday life theory, the self-perception as an active individual can, again, be understood as part of a larger everyday life strategy, the creation of a meaningful whole.[20] The strategies are all means of handling everyday life. They are developed in constant negotiation among the available symbol positions in our culture, the symbolic order of taken-for-grantedness. Particular choices make sense within such strategies. Just as particular, culturally shaped skills and habits are useful (Swidler, 1986, p.276). We are in other words reduced to using the known, while creating the new.

The meaningful whole we seek to create takes the form of a mental and concrete base (Kristensen, 1998). Such a base forms an often contradictory and changeable outset for activity. It is a fragile, yet necessary construction. The concrete part consists of different combinations and emphases of environments that we participate in (e.g. our work place and larger family) and the place we live. The mental part, closely intertwined with the concrete elements, includes in the case of the younger adults their perceptions of adulthood and their position in relation to this. Such perceptions are, in turn, developed via the continued negotiation among available cultural symbol positions. There are more or less dominant views on when and how to be adult, how to act as a man or woman at a given age in different settings, family tradition, etc.

The interviewees generally evaluated their present lives in relation to what I subsequently identified as 'symbols of adulthood': getting an education or having a job, having a permanent place to live, and having a partner or family of one's own (thus also being someone's partner, a father, etc.). Being adult meant being and having these things - or at least having the prospect of becoming and obtaining them in near future. They were criteria of success and individual peace (Kristensen, 1998).[21]

The modern notion of the individual is another of such symbol positions. But why have the women taken it on? And does the self-perception reflect reality? Statistics and the standardisation Beck writes about suggest that the real scope of action is limited. As does part of the women's experiences.

Let me now turn to the two selected explanations. Whereas 'handling late modernity' draws upon theory and empirical data alike, the 'ideology of sameness' is mainly theoretical.

Handling Late Modernity[22]

Late modern generations like the younger adults have to handle everyday life in the complex and changeable reality of late modernity. They are continuously confronted by a multitude of known and unknown phenomena, ways of life, and norms and values. As a consequence, large areas of life have now become objects of conscious reflexivity, and of demands and possibilities of choice, not only in theory but also empirically - it is a felt subjective condition.

Although the biographies of the late modern generations are often referred to as *choice biographies* because of the increased moral, legal and economical rein of action, my general analysis showed that the interviewees' choices were marked by their social backgrounds, their gender, the different social environments they have been part of throughout life (e.g. groups of friends, and work places), their experiences, the dominant norms and values that exist despite the pluralisation of ways of life,[23] and not least the standardisation that seems to be part and parcel of the individualisation (i.e. the individuals' increasing dependency upon the market and the welfare state) (Beck, 1992).[24] Thus, social structures and socialisation still divide and delimit the individuals' real scope of action. Social inequality and intolerance (Kristensen, 1999) exist side by side with individualisation and pluralisation, and leave some with more restricted options than others.[25]

The general analysis further showed that the interviewees were constantly confronted with demands of reflexivity and choice regarding issues that were taken for granted by the older generations. Formal education had become a realistic option, but it was also a perceived demand for the interviewees. The type of education to pursue, however, was not given for all. Along with culturally important issues such as how and where to live, marriage, having children and for some also work, it became an object of conscious reflexivity and the pressure of having to choose. The social mobility, the increased knowledge of other ways of life, the primary and lower secondary school's (*folkeskolen*) emphasis on the pupils' ability to take informed stands, and the dominating discourses about equal opportunities for all (social and gender equality), all seem to have contributed to intensifying the feeling but also the demand and possibility of choosing.

The interviewees spoke of experiences of having influenced their own or their family's life in a positive direction, of coincidence, and of limited options or difficulties in obtaining access to specific jobs on grounds of, for example, gender. This ambiguity and the more or less conscious recognition of the changeability and unpredictability of many of the more fundamental aspects of life (e.g. work, and personal relationships) brought about specific handling strategies. Self-perception as an active and independent individual is one such strategy.

The self-perception not only makes it possible to handle the different occurrences, and the more or less felt pressure of having to live up to the expectations of friends, family, the labour market and the educational system, but also to maintain a feeling of having a place and function in life, of being able, at least in part, to influence one's life in a positive way. Seen in this light, the self-perception as an active individual is a concrete part of the women's attempts to create meaning - and thus keep chaos at bay.

The Ideology of Sameness

Our heritage of liberal democracy assumes different disguises at different points in time. Notions such as equality and individuality and their meaning are both implicit and changing. At different points in history, different modern notions are brought to the foreground. The notions are all part of our more or less conscious self- and world-view, a part of the general way we look upon ourselves and the surrounding world. They are part of the symbol positions we negotiate between, each making different activities possible - or impossible.

Independence and responsibility are now on the public agenda again.[26] They are supporting and supported by the more privileged groups of society. The notions are part of the definition of normality, the socially constructed golden yardstick by which everybody is measured (cf. Horsgaard and Øland, 2000; Kristensen, 1999).

In countries like Denmark individuality is associated with self-reliance and being unique. This idea and ideal of the individual co-exists with strong notions of equality and sameness, thus creating a cultural tension. However, the tension not only exists between the idea of the unique, self-reliant individual on the one hand, and equality and sameness on the other. It has a third dimension: the cultural equation of equality and sameness (Gullestad, 1989).[27]

For Gullestad, these tensions bring about difficulties of handling difference and inequality (e.g. social and gender inequality) in many social situations. We thus generally value similarity, leaving difference and inequality in the background, and tend to form social relationships with people who are similar to us.

The notion of equality, Gullestad argues, is in consequence increasingly used within one and the same environment, not so much to exclude others but to as include 'people of our own kind' (ibid.). Whether or not this tendency is also increasing in Denmark can be questioned, but it is outspoken. The phenomenon of inclusion is similar to the conventional form of solidarity known from the labour movement and the co-operative movement. These have in turn penetrated and have been penetrated by Danish culture for more than a century.

The notion of equality, Gullestad continues, excludes neither hierarchy nor inequality. On the contrary, it has the function of hiding those very traits of society. We thus think equality, but in practice we organise inequality. Oppression and exploitation of all kinds are still less visible and often non-conscious (op.cit., p.119).

The self-perception as an active individual seems to disregard gender inequality - and perhaps also social inequality - and can thus be seen as part of this general cultural trend. While contributing, theoretically speaking, to the difficulties of addressing the issues politically or in close social relationships, the self-perception also allows the individual to act and thus change. The trend seems, again, to be contradictory.

From a slightly different perspective, Broch-Due and Ødegård (1991) argue that as a consequence of the post-war ideology of equality, it is a prevalent perception that we are all mainly human beings and only a little bit gender.[28] As a consequence of this ideology

> the dominance and power aspects of the gender relation have become illegitimate. Officially, we have put gender inequality behind us. To reintroduce the topic is threatening to both genders. 'Modern' men and 'modern' women *are* equal. An ideology of equality thus easily becomes an ideology of sameness (Broch-Due and Ødegård, 1991, p.77; my translation).

The phenomenon seems to have positive as well as negative aspects. It disguises inequality while also making action and change possible.

Conclusion

In this chapter I have addressed some of the paradoxes and prospects of especially younger adult *women's* self-perception as active individuals capable of influencing and planning their lives. They have thus taken on a self-perception similar to the modern notion of the individual, and its associated virtues of self-reliance, activity and purposefulness, a self-perception traditionally reserved for white middle class men.

This self-perception as an active individual is prevalent and rich in its form, but not exclusive. The contradictions of the interviewees' experiences - e.g. experiences of real choices and limitations, predictability and unpredictability, equality and inequality, radical doubt - and the observation of the likewise contradictory objective conditions, points to the conclusion that this self-perception is part of a strategy to handle everyday life in late modernity. It is a strategy to create a mental and concrete base from which to act, a meaningful whole, in a complex and changeable reality.

The self-perception is thus both a necessity to counter chaos and dissolution - or phrased differently, a necessity in order to continue being an ordinarily well functioning person in late modernity - and a reality based on experience.

Another possible, intertwined explanation is the cultural equation of equality and sameness, the ideology of sameness. As a combination of the political initiatives in post-War Denmark to further social mobility (and wealth) through equal access to education for all, and the cultural equation of such political initiatives and actual equality, women may have adopted the self-perception as an active individual.

The women's self-perception has both a negative and a positive side. On the positive side, it seems to have increased their realm of action. By believing something is real, it can, in other words, become real in its consequences. Adopting the modern notion of the individual can thus contribute to its widening - and perhaps also to the achievement of real equality. The 'other', in other words, is answering back - and gaining power. On the negative side, the self-perception may contribute to the disguising and neglect of gender inequality, making individual and wider political action and change difficult.

Seen from the perspective of everyday life, one of the characteristics of the transition of society is seemingly a widening of the notion of the individual to include women and their specific ways of negotiating the symbol positions associated with it. Women are becoming modern in their own way.

It is not possible to assess the consequences of the younger adult women's challenge and change of the modern, male bound notion of individuality, not even in the context of Denmark alone. Studies including social class/present social position and ethnicity are necessary in order to establish an adequate empirical basis for such assessments.

Nevertheless, the self-perception forms a part of the continuous challenge and change of this central notion in the Danish welfare democracy, adding to the promotion of the equally central but partly contradictory notion of equality. Women are again becoming modern, whilst simultaneously changing the core notions, making different or perhaps even new action possible.

Notes

1 The interviewees belong, broadly speaking, to the large cohorts that confronted high unemployment and strict admissions requirements in many branches of the educational system when young.
2 As will be elaborated below, Beck's thesis is echoed in my empirical findings.
3 As is known, there is a partial overlap between Beck's, Giddens' and Ziehe's theories concerning these issues.
4 It is not possible to specify exactly when different periods start or end. To my mind late modernity became apparent in Denmark after the 'economic boom' of the 1950s. Ziehe, from a German perspective, has described the radicalised modernisation that characterises late modernity as a 'cultural boom' succeeding the economic boom in a non-causal fashion. This also applies to Denmark. I thus roughly mark the beginning of late modernity as the 1960s. The active verb 'radicalised' is to be taken literally. The changes have continued since then.
5 As do the political and economic conditions. They will, however, be left in the background in this article.
6 A full account of my research method is too elaborate in this context. Hence I will only mention that my overall approach is phenomenological-hermeneutic, with an element of social-constructivism. I thus seek to identify, interpret and discuss socially constructed phenomena - not essence or truth. For an elaboration, see Kristensen, 1998.
7 In principle, the term 'Danes' includes the ethnic minorities. However, none of the interviewees come from these groups. The lack of presence is deliberate, in order to delimit the number of themes to deal with in the analysis.
8 The definition is an appropriation of Langsted and Sommer's definition of ordinarily well functioning children (cf. Langsted and Sommer, 1988).
9 The transcripts were re-coded, looking for explicit and implicit statements about e.g. 'choice', 'decisions', 'freedom', and 'independence', and compared with e.g. 'limitations' and 'coincidence', followed by overall interpretations of the interviewees' self- and world-views.
10 This approach, which is shared by Bech-Jørgensen, is similar to Giddens' theory of structuration (cf. Giddens, 1984). However, points of departure in Bech-Jørgensen and Bloch are, most prominently, taken in A. Schutz, A. Heller, and P.L. Berger and T. Luckmann (cf. Bech-Jørgensen, 1994a; Bloch, 1988, 1991).
11 Swidler elaborates this definition by writing that culture is a 'tool kit' consisting of 'such symbolic vehicles of meaning, including beliefs, ritual practices, art forms, and ceremonies, as well as informal cultural practices such as language, gossip, stories, and rituals of daily life' (Swidler, 1986, p.273). In contrast to Bech-Jørgensen, the largely non-conscious nature of our culture, and our handling of it, lies only implicit in Swidler.
12 By negotiation, I understand conscious and non-conscious exploration (cf. Drotner, 1993).
13 The notion is also closely related to that of the ideal-typical citizen, and, as Orloff (1993) shows, is reflected in mainstream literature on social rights, including Nordic research. The notion of citizenship has more recently been discussed in a feminist perspective by, among other, Lister (1997) and Siim (2000).
14 Respectively single women in an American, a Finnish, and a British city, and academic women in the USA (I am assuming. It is not explicitly stated).
15 That is, in the vocabulary of Gordon (1994), interdependence.

16 In Denmark the day-care provision is offered to children from the age of six months. However, the extent of the provision varies between the municipalities. In the municipality of Copenhagen public day care is not available before the child is 12-14 months old.

17 I have chosen to include statistics from the mid-1990s, the time of the interviews.

18 Some - most often the women - are forced to take parental leave (six months at 60 per cent of the unemployment benefit rate), due to lack of day care provision in their area.

19 I am, of course, paraphrasing the Thomas theorem: 'If men define situations as real, they are real in their consequences' (Thomas and Thomas in Ritzer, 1996, p.351). In the title, I have chosen to use the term people instead of men, as the latter can imply that men and males are one and the same.

20 The concept of strategy is used in a myriad of ways within sociology (cf. Crow, 1989). In its original meaning, a strategy is an art of planning operations in war, of course, with the aim of winning. It has, as Bak writes, been used as a metaphor within the social sciences, often with strong connotations of rational, calculating agents, who consciously maximise the outcome of their choices (Bak, 1997, p.68). The term can be successfully used as a part of analyses based on an understanding of society as a social construction, and thus also an understanding of individuals as active creators, or agents (cf. Crow, 1989; Swidler, 1986; Bak, 1997). However, as my own attempts illustrate (cf. Kristensen 1998, 1999), strategies are difficult to distinguish empirically from sets of activities, as both are more or less conscious and directed at some form of goal.

21 The example also illustrates the aforementioned mixture of the modern and the new in that the symbols of adulthood assemble the dominating norms of the earlier generations. At the same time, however, the actual 'nature' of e.g. relationships, and the combination of work and non-work/family life, differed from those for some.

22 The empirical findings referred to in this section are from Kristensen (1998), if nothing else is mentioned.

23 The interviewees' aforementioned evaluation of their present life in relation to the - on the surface - modern symbols of adulthood is an example of this.

24 The standardisation, for example, seems to set the frames of what I will term *new standard biographies*, especially during the youth period, biographies that are simultaneously marked by the educational system and the demand and feeling of continually having to reflect and choose (cf. Kristensen, 1998).

25 A smaller study of the everyday life of socially exposed lone mothers with more than two children shows, as an example, that the mothers feel they are stigmatised by the social authorities and other parents because of their situation, i.e. because they are either unemployed or have low-paid, low status jobs, because they do not have a husband/partner, and because they have comparatively many children (Kristensen, 1999).

26 I have in mind the immanent ideology of the 'active line' within social policy in Denmark (a Danish version of workfare implemented during the 1990s), stressing the individual's responsibilities towards the state - and perhaps unintentionally causing a partial individualisation of social problems.

27 Gullestad focuses on contemporary Norway. In my judgement, the cultural themes she identifies also apply to Denmark.

28 Broch-Due and Ødegård also write from a Norwegian perspective.

References

Arbejdsmarkedsstyrelsen et al. (1995), *Kvinder og Mænd*, Copenhagen.

Bak, M. (1997), Enemorfamilien, Forlaget Sociologi, Copenhagen.

Bech-Jørgensen, B. (1994a), *Når hver dag bliver til hverdag*, Akademisk Forlag, Copenhagen.

Bech-Jørgensen, B. (1994b), 'Hverdagsliv: Upåagtede aktiviteter og kønsmæssige forskelle', *Dansk Sociologi*, vol. 5 no. 1, pp.4-22.

Beck, U. (1992/1986), Risk Society. Towards a New Modernity, Sage, London.

Bloch, C. (1988), 'Om forskel mellem det kendte og det 'endnu-ikke-kendte' - om hverdagsliv og subjektivitet', in Bloch, B. et al., *Hverdagsliv og subjektivitet*, Akademisk Forlag, Copenhagen, pp.124-149.

Bloch, C. (1991), *'At nogen har brug for mig'. Om kvindearbejdsløshed, hverdagsliv og livsfaser*, Samfundslitteratur, Copenhagen.

Broch-Due, A. K. and Ødegård, T. (1991), 'Alt er menneskelig og kjønnet - samtidig og alltid: om forståelse av sosialt kjønn i samfunnsvitenskapene', *Sosiologi i dag*, no. 4, pp.76-99.

Crow, G. (1989), 'The Use of the Concept of 'Strategy' in Recent Sociological Literature', *Sociology*, vol. 23 no. 1, pp.1-24.

Drotner, K. (1993), 'Køn og kulturel ambivalens', in Drotner, K. and Rudberg, M. (eds.), *Dobbeltblikk på det moderne: Unge kvinners hverdagsliv og kultur i Norden*, Universitetsforlaget, Oslo. pp.170-194.

Giddens, A. (1984), *The Constitution of Society: Outline of the Theory of Structuration*, Polity Press, Cambridge.

Giddens, A. (1990), *The Consequences of Modernity*, Polity Press, Cambridge.

Giddens, A. (1991), *Modernity and Self-Identity: Self and Society in the Late Modern Age*, Polity Press, Cambridge.

Giddens, A. (1994), 'Living in a Post-Traditional Society', in Beck, U. et al.: *Reflexive Modernization: Politics, Traditions and Aesthetics in Modern Social Order*, Polity Press, Cambridge, pp.56-109.

Gordon, T. (1994), *Single Women: On the Margins?*, Macmillan, Houndsmill.

Gordon, T. and E. Lahelma (1995), 'Being, Having and Doing Gender in Schools', Centre for Women's Studies, University of Oslo, *The Working Paper Series*, no. 2, pp.69-80.

Gullestad, M. (1989), *Kultur og hverdagsliv: På sporet av det moderne Norge*, Universitetsforlaget, Oslo.

Horsgaard, M. and H. Øland (2000), *Empowermentorienteret socialt arbejde - en teoretisk forankring*, Final dissertation, Social Studies/Psychology, Roskilde University.

Kristensen, C. J. (1998), Senmoderne liv: Yngre voksne danskeres fortællinger om deres hverdagsliv, Ph.D. thesis. Department of Social Studies and Organisation, Aalborg University.

Kristensen, C. J. (1999), *Socialt udsatte enlige mødre med flere børn*, Dafolo, Frederikshavn.

Langsted, O. and D. Sommer (1988), Småbørns livsvilkår i Danmark, Hans Reitzels Forlag, Copenhagen.

Lister, R. (1997), *Citizenship: Feminist Perspectives*, Macmillan, Houndsmill.

Mortensen, N. (1991), 'Modsætninger og forsoninger mellem strukturer og aktører', *Politica*, vol. 23 no. 1, pp.42-59.

Orloff, A. S. (1993), 'Gender and the Social Rights of Citizenship: A Comparative Analysis of Gender Relations and Welfare States', *American Sociological Review*, vol. 58, June, pp.303-328.

Ritzer, G. (1996), *Sociological Theory*, 4th edition, McGraw-Hill Companies, New York.

Siim, B. (1997), 'Dilemmas of Citizenship in Denmark: Lone Mothers Between Work and Care', in Lewis, J. (ed.): *Lone Mothers in European Welfare Regimes: Shifting Policy, Logics*, Jessica Kingsley Publishers, London, pp.140-170.

Siim, B. (2000), *Gender and Citizenship - Politics and Agency in France, Britain and Denmark*, Cambridge University Press, Cambridge.

Socialkommissionen (1992), *De unge: Portræt af en generation i velfærdssamfundet*, Socialkommissionen, Copenhagen.

Swidler, A. (1986), 'Culture in Action: Symbols and Strategies', *American Sociological Review*, vol. 51 no. 2, pp.273-286.

Weedon, C. (1987), *Feminist Practice and Poststructuralist Theory*, Basil Blackwell, Cambridge.

Yanay, N. and B. Birns (1990), 'Autonomy as Emotion: The Phenomenology of Independence in Academic Women', *Women's Studies International Forum*, vol. 13 no. 3, pp.249-260.

Ziehe, T. (1989), *Ambivalenser og mangfoldighed. Tekster om: Ungdom, skole, æstetik, kultur*, Politisk Revy, Copenhagen.

9 Transformations of Identities in Rapidly Changing Societies

LARS DENCIK

1. Turbonomads in Postmodernity?

The processes of modernisation brought about Modernity. It is a social condition with which we are all too familiar. But modernisation will inevitably progress - continuous change is an endemic part of modernity as such. Most of us realise that we will have to leave behind the modern conditions we know, e.g. the well-functioning welfare states and advanced industrial societies of Scandinavia. There are those who claim they know what is going to replace it: economists, sociologists, theologians. And often they find an audience more than willing to listen to and believe them - it seems that the more complex the societal transformations gets, the stronger the desire for simplicity, order and predictability. Hence the flourishing market for false prophets (all prophets are false), regardless of whether they are traditional Marxist 'scientists', modern market analysts or mysterious new age metaphysists. But the future does not grow according to any plan planted in a soil of social conditions. Society, like knowledge, is an innovative system, not a closed mechanical system. The future is continuously shaped anew - and always arrives only day by day. But on the other hand, every day.

Today the processes of globalisation and the breakthrough of electronic information technology, by mutually reinforcing each other, are profoundly reshaping the conditions for social life and the predicaments of human existence in the developed world. Changes in turn generate further changes: when one condition within a system changes, the other parts that in one way or other are related to it will have to adapt to it, i.e. change their way of functioning. This in turn generates new requirements for change, and so on. As a consequence, the pace at which the social conditions of individuals change accelerates. Whatever used to be no longer prevails. The social lifetime of almost everything - technologies, production methods, communication systems, family patterns, sex roles, scientific 'truths,' political 'correctness', dress codes, eating habits and so on become shorter and shorter. Change becomes the natural order of things.

The world we live in changes, and changes continuously. And nobody can know what the future may bring. The only thing we can be sure of is that after modernisation comes *post*modernisation. This is how we will label the continuously ongoing development, or rather transformations, of modern societies such as the Scandinavian welfare states. It is a process of giving way for an as yet contourless society. It is not a description of a new condition - only in the rear mirror of History are there such things as crystallised social conditions - but a name for an ongoing process of social transformations.

To what degree modernity as we know it as a consequence will cease to prevail is not what concerns us here. Rather, the focus will be on the challenges for the individual facing these ongoing transformations, i.e. the fact that the social predicaments of individuals living in the modern world are undergoing continuous and rapid transformations. In what way will the outlooks, values, ideals, habits and competencies that people bring to the situation they are in 'fit' the new conditions they unavoidably will have to confront. In this process of uninterruptedly ongoing *post*modernization (Crook, Pakulski and Waters, 1992), individuals are doomed to lag behind the situation in which they each find themselves (cf. Arvidsson, Berntson and Dencik, 1994). How can individuals handle such *chronic uncontemporaneity* or time lag? You are what you are but you have to become what you are not: this seems to be one of the challenges that the process of postmodernisation poses to the individual and to nations. As the conditions of social life change, so do the conditions for individuals' identity formation in the highly developed part of the world. The identity of nations and states also changes. How? Does the fact that we live in rapidly changing societies imply that the identities of individuals living in these societies will also have to be open to continuous transformations? What would that imply? What kind of 'self' do individuals who must become 'turbonomads in postmodernity' have to develop? How will the transformations affect the self-image of established nation-states? Do mobile people need mobile identities? How could such identities be conceived? How are, identities constructed in a rapidly changing society? These are the questions we are going to address in this chapter.

2. Identities: Patterns in a Kaleidoscope

The philosophical, psychological and social condition for the concept of identity is the act of categorisation - to divide and sort phenomena into separate but internally homogeneous categories. In order to do so, meaningful distinctions must be made - similarities and differences must be identified, as well as differences among various similarities. Following Bourdieu, 'Differences define and confirm social identity' (1979, p.192).

For a person, *P*, to have a particular identity, *I*, means being identical with some other persons, *Ss*, with respect to some significant aspect, *A*, of their existence. Thus, identity denotes a relation of belonging. *P* and *Ss* belong to the same category of people, viz. to those who can be described by the characteristic *A*.

In the terminology of logic belonging is *in*clusion. However, every identity also marks a relation of *ex*clusion. To say that a person has a certain identity is also to say that this person is identifiable by belonging to a group distinct from all others. 'Invariably, such operation of inclusion/exclusion is an act of violence perpetrated upon the world, and requires the support of a certain amount of coercion', writes Zygmunt Bauman in his thought-provoking work *Modernity and Ambivalence* (Bauman, 1991, p.2).

The mathematical symbol '=', the sign for 'equals', expresses a relation of identity. What stands on one side of the sign is identical with what stands on the other side. Both have the same value. In theoretical terms: they belong to the same category.

The concept of 'identity' has its root in the Latin *idem*, which means 'the same'. This concept expresses a relationship of belonging. To have a certain identity means to be 'the same' as someone or some others. But you can be 'the same' in different ways! Philosophically, we can make a distinction between *numeric* identity and *qualitative* identity. In the first case, we refer to the same material entity, e.g. the morning star and the evening star. They appear at different times and in differing contexts but in reality it is one and the same star. The second case refers to two or more distinct objects sharing a particular characteristic, e.g. a number of automobiles, all of which are Volvos. Viewed from another perspective, however, the objects may also be categorised otherwise as, for example, limousines (regardless whether they are Volvos or not), station wagons, etc.

When it comes to human beings, we all are in one sense like the morning star and the evening star: we are and remain the same person throughout the life course. That is, we have a distinct numerical identity. In psychology, this is often referred to as one's 'personal' identity: this refers to what makes you 'identical with your self' - you are the person you are even if you have changed in some significant respect. Development and experience may lead to fundamental change, but the presence of personal identity means that a person still is the same. Identity in this sense is very banal yet extremely mystifying, as when Moses on Mount Horeb asked the Lord: Who are you? And the Lord replied, 'I am who I am' (Exod. 3.14). To have a personal identity is to be who one is. An individual's numeric identity over time is referred to as his or her *narrative* identity (Ricoeur, 1990).

In some respects, however, we are also like automobiles: we are equal to others in the sense that we belong to the same 'brand', as it were. The qualitative identity always expresses that persons possessing that particular quality belong to the same category, and as such, differ in some respects, from all other categories. We are 'Jews or Greeks', Swedes or Turks, men or women, etc. Important to note here is that an individual's qualitative identity may change depending on which category is in focus. In different situations, different qualities of the person are brought into focus. The person is viewed or reacted to as this or that, e.g. as a Swede, as a man, as a scientist, etc. He/she is then the same as some others in a *socially* significant way. The quality of the person that emerges as significant in a particular situation, i.e. the way the person is perceived by his/her environment in that situation, is his or her *social* identity (Tajfel, 1974; Tajfel and Turner, 1986; Turner, 1999; Abrams and Hogg, 1999; Brown, 2000; Capozza and Brown, 2000).

There are two important premises behind the social psychological concept of *social* identity: firstly, that the actual identity of any person is founded upon and shaped by social interaction, and secondly that there are many *latent* identit*ies* within every human being (cf. Hogg and Abrams, 1998).[1]

As individuals we are always and unavoidably involved in various kinds of social interaction. Since any social interaction takes place in a specific social situation, different situations in which interaction takes place bring various aspects of us to the surface. In one modern textbook of social psychology, author Hedy Brown claims that 'It is the situation in which people find themselves, rather than their predispositions which lead them to act the way they do' (Whetherell, 1996, p.23).

In any situation, the individual is faced with expectations and categorisations. She/he will always be seen not only as some*one* (being seen only as that is a characteristic of the rare relationships of unconditional love) but considered in her/his capacity of some*thing*. The particular capacity will socially determine the situation. You may be considered as a neighbour or as a Jew, as a southerner or a socialist, as daddy or as dangerous. One interesting description of the process of shifting social identities is Hazel Rosenstrauch's analysis of 'How Neighbours Became 'Jews' (Rosenstrauch, 1988) which Ulrich Beck has discussed in his essay 'Wie aus Nachbarn Juden werden: Zur politischen Konstruktion des Fremden in der reflexive Moderne'. One's social identity varies according to the situation: something has relevance in one context, something else in another. A social identity then, is not something you 'have' but rather something you 'do'. However, it is also common that (some) individuals are seen primarily in the capacity of something, for instance as immigrant, as Black, as Jewish or as female, irrespective of the contents of the interaction. That very aspect of the individual will then become his or her *generalised social identity.*

An orderly world is 'a world in which links between certain situations and the effectivity of certain actions remain by and large constant, so that one can rely on past successes as guides for future ones' (Bauman, 1991, p.2). Zygmunt Bauman states that in order to achieve such order modernity is obsessed by attempts at establishing stable categorisations. However, just as dust always crops up even in the most well-ordered room, so does modernisation allow *ambivalence* to always sneak in along the rifts of even the most established social categorisations. Social transformations always upset a given social order. Modernisation, and postmodernisation even more so, will thus continuously bring with them new ambivalences that will be counteracted by constant attempts at 'ordering'. With postmodernisation, a permanent battle is inaugurated: social transformation accompanied by constantly renewed ambivalences on one side and 'order as obsession' (Bauman, 1991, p.6) on the other side. Bauman cites the British historian Stephen Collins, who dates the birth of modernism to the 1700-century philosopher Thomas Hobbes: 'Hobbes understood that a world in flux is natural' (Collins, 1989, p.4). In other words that 'ordering', or more exactly the image of an order that is established, is always artificial. Uninterrupted transformations of the reality in which we live constantly break up the order established by our categorisations - 'the flux that order wished to contain, but in vain' (Bauman, 1991, p.9).

By the emanation of new phenomena and new living conditions it entails, social change thus becomes the breeding ground for new ambivalences that in turn instigate the extended and ever more precise classifications and categorisations in order to re-establish the threatened orderliness of the world. Successively more and sharper criteria are adopted to distinguish one category from the other - which in turn increases the ability to identify even more ambivalences. This, Bauman states, 'make modern times an era of particular bitter and relentless war against ambivalence' (Bauman, 1991, p.3).

Modernisation has forced people out of *Gemeinschaft* into a life of *Gesellschaft* (Tönnies, 1887). The processes of modernisation brought tremendous challenges to individuals understanding of themselves. The idea of a 'self' became a constitutive element in the making of a modern identity (cf. Taylor, 1989; Keupp and Höfer, 1997).[2] *Post*modernisation brings this further into a condition we may call *Networkschaft*.[3] Rather than being a 'state' in development, Networkschaft is a condition of continuously shifting conditions for people. One implication is that the individual will have to be more able to abandon former behavioural patterns, habits and familiar customs and develop ways of dealing with constantly novel conditions. However, he/she will also have to oscillate between an increasing number of roles, positions, and social arenas in daily life. Our understanding is that there are many 'identity potentials', i.e. 'latent identities', within every individual - and that with the current *post*modernisation of life, these tend manifest themselves even more. People will have to manage a pluralisation of social identities within their one and only numeric identity. What will be the psychological implications of this change? How will it challenge the individual's construction of his/her narrative identity?

As a prototypical example, let us examine the daily life of the modern child in the Scandinavian societies (cf. Dencik, 1995a, 1995b). For most young children, the daily life is divided in time, so that they share it between (at least) two different contexts or socio-ecological settings - we call them *sociotopes* - the family and the day-care institution, each with its particular set of expectations and behavioural challenges for the child. A *sociotope* we define as *a life-space that the individual lives in and has to cope with by adapting to its given social conditions*.

The notion of 'life-space' refers back to Kurt Lewin (1936, 1964) and has been defined as 'a momentary confluence of person qualities and properties of the psychological environment' (Altman and Rogoff, 1987, p.28).

A sociotope is limited by the material, social and cultural conditions which frame the person's world in that particular situation. In the case of the child, one of his/her sociotopes is the family. It may be depicted graphically as triangle like this:

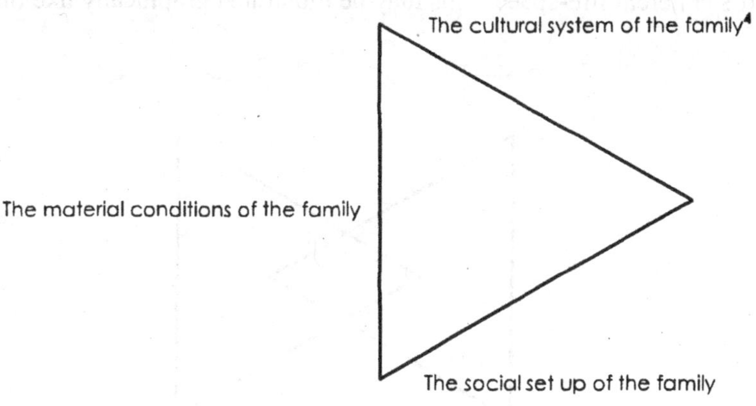

Accordingly the other sociotope to which the child also belongs, the day-care centre, may be depicted as a triangle like this:

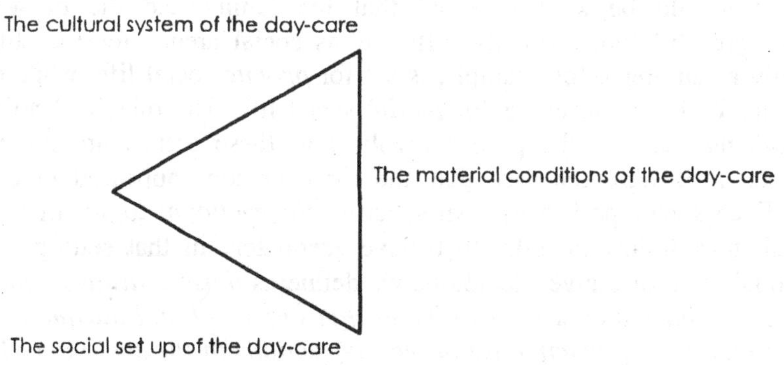

The child participates in both these settings, but to the child they are different social arenas, each with its own particular social scenography. The child has to cope with them by adapting to the particular social conditions of each one of them - and at the same time the child confronts the need to combine them, and yet be able to keep them apart. Even if the two arenas are very different as sociotopes, the child's very immersion in them leads to their combination so that the two sociotopes constitute the child's coherent life-space. This may be illustrated graphically like this:

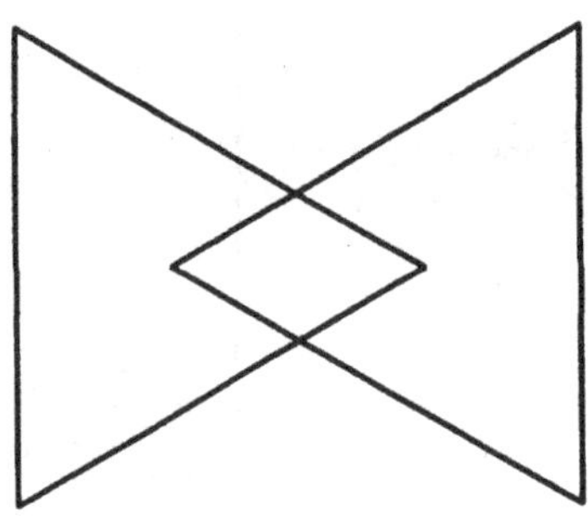

The model depicts a coherent system. The two 'wings' of the system create one another and the very interaction between them is a major force in the shaping of the child through a process of *dual-socialisation* (cf. Dencik, 1995a). It should be kept in mind that the family and the day-care institution are still fundamentally different as social arenas for the child. The family as an arena, for example, is set for *private* social life, while the day-care institution is an arena for *public* social life. The rules and norms for interacting between the parties involved in these arenas are not the same (even if it were the case that the same persons appeared in both arenas). Each sociotope has its own specific '*interactional logic*' that the individual must follow in order to behave adequately in that setting. The interactional logic of a given sociotope we define as *those attitudes, modes of behaviour and patterns of socialising that are valid and adequate for the individual when participating in the interactions in the sociotope.* The very constitution of the two different settings - the child's public day-care institution on the one hand and the private family on the other - carry different criteria for socially correct and adequate behaviour in each setting. Seen from the child's viewpoint, there are fundamental and significant differences between the day-care centre and the home (the family) as life-spaces.

From the onset of the early childhood years, living in two (or more) of these sociotopes with their respective interactional logics is a psychological challenge for modern children. On an everyday basis, the child is in fact a member of two *different social worlds*, or, viewed from a different perspective, needs to develop (at least) two different social identities.

Lewin describes the life-space 'as a dynamic field made up of continually changing person-environment regions and relationships [...] life-space exhibits continual activity and flow' (Altman and Rogoff, 1987, p.28). For many children in the modern world, this is certainly the case. It is not uncommon for a child to be confronted with frequent and often rather abrupt changes of his/her partners of social interaction during the course of a day (Dencik et al., 1988). The child's life-conditions consist of daily entry, accompanied by need for integration, and exits, demanding separation, from *both* of these institutions and social identities.[5] Thus, the child confronts the challenge to of having to mentally integrate these experiences as well as mentally and socially separate the two settings and identities from each other.

The way we conceive of this process is that human identity or 'personality,' if you will, becomes *kaleidoscopic* in character. It may be split into different facets, but still be integrated into a unified entity. Let us recall one of those pictures from psychological textbooks in which one can see either an old woman looking like a witch or a young elegant lady wearing a hat. Both are in the same picture, both are equally 'true' and both are created on the same empirical foundation. What you actually see depends on how you configure the empirical material, the lines, and how you distinguish the background from the figure. It is important to remember that we can only see one picture at a time and that we always see the individual in a particular way depending upon how we focus in the given situation. What determines how we view a person, in a certain situation, including ourselves? In order to answer this question, we must examine who or what may decide what is socially significant in any social interaction, particularly because that which is socially significant in acute situations will frequently be 'elevated' to a general description, i.e. become the generalised social identity of the individual. Schematically, we can follow this process along three polar distinctions:

a) First, the distinction of *who* is deciding how the identity of an individual should be perceived - whether the individual her-/him*self* or some *Alter*, who could be anything from some ruling convention within the social group, the law, or the institutional setting, to a kind of dictator with total control. By self-categorisations, singular individuals are transformed to group-members (Hogg and Abrams, 1998, p.21).

An interesting and frequent tension can be observed when the individual's own definition of himself does *not* coincide with that of the *Alter*. The new immigrants to Sweden and Denmark are a good example of this. By the administrative system they are called and treated as 'immigrants,' even as 'second or third generation immigrants', who in *this* capacity may be subject to certain administrative measures. In Sweden for example, one has established both an Immigrant Board and a Ministry of Immigration, the *raison d'être* of both being a categorisation of that kind.[6] However, immigrants tend to define themselves rather as Kurds, Chileans, Iranians, and so forth.

'The privilege of defining identity-criteria' has often been the privilege of those in power or of the majority of the social system. History gives us many examples of how men in power force their definition of identity upon certain people. A classic example is the anti-Semitic mayor Karl Lueger of Vienna, who in the beginning of the 20th century stated 'Wer Jude ist bestimme ich!' ('I decide who is a Jew!').

b) The second distinction is concerned with whether the criteria of categorisation are *objective* or *subjective*. To follow the thread from the example above: according to Jewish law, a child who has been born by a Jewish mother is a 'Jew'. This is an objective criterion and has nothing to do with how the individual sees this, whether she/he lives as a Jew or not. It is also possible to be a Jew because one *feels* Jewish, without having been born of a Jewish mother (but with a Jewish father, for instance). This subjective criterion may also be expressed by honouring Jewish traditions or identifying with the fate of the Jewish people.

Tensions arise when the objective and subjective definitions do not conform. This is very clear to those Kurds who wish to be Kurds but are not recognised as such by the Turkish state, or to assimilated German Jews (who thought they had abandoned their Jewish identity) when the Nazi racial laws were introduced.

c) Third, we make the distinction between an *absolute* categorical criterion of identity, according to which one is or is not something, and a *relative* one, according to which it is possible to be something to a greater or lesser degree.

It is possible, for instance, to be regarded or to regard oneself as more or less 'religious' according to objective or subjective criteria. However, a woman is pregnant or not pregnant - it is not possible to be 'a little pregnant'. When we look at national or cultural definitions from a similar perspective, we find ambiguities. It could be reasonable to say that to have a Danish identity is something you have or have not (e.g. Danish citizenship). But from another point of view it is equally reasonable to claim that one is, feels, more or less 'Danish' (considering appearance or lifestyle, for instance). The way in which the national, ethnic or cultural identity of an individual is decided within a certain social context is determined by whether the criterion in this respect is absolute or relative.

The ways, in which various identity criteria are used in order to determine the identity of a person, depend largely upon the power constellation in the actual situation. In rapidly changing societies, the power constellations are also transformed, which in turn affects the identity-formation of individuals.

3. 'I' Need a 'We' to Become Truly 'Me'

The problem of identity-making is not only or primarily an academic question. The concept of identity refers to the interaction between how an individual experiences the world subjectively and the cultural and historical framework, both of which influence this subjective experience. The development of an individual's identity is thus a social phenomenon. Each making of an identity has its particular (but frequently hidden) history: 'Identity can help us understand the fatal case 'we' that [...] comprises and excludes others,' notes the British sociologist Paul Gilroy, who adds that 'it is when one tries to figure out how one's belonging to one group or local community may be transformed into active solidarity that the language of identity becomes significant'. This means that 'the emergence of a unifying common identity is an important feature of the political process' (Gilroy, 1996, pp.20-21).[7] And it is even more so when we talk about identities associated with race or ethnicity: 'Ethnicity and race have played a prominent and often sensational role in human affairs in the 20th century', conclude the American sociologists Stephen Cornell and Douglas Hartman in their work about the meaning of identity in a changing world (Cornell and Hartman, 1998, p.233).

An identity is always particularistic: it points out the categories and their limits, according to which we manoeuvre in life and 'assists us in defining the limitations of our anachronistic local attempts to give Life meaning', according to Gilroy, because 'to *have* a certain identity expresses how the individual is most fundamentally attached: nationally, racially, ethnically, regionally or locally' (Gilroy, 1996, p.20).

This is the background against which we may understand a seeming paradox in contemporary society: the question of 'who you are' is of *less social* but at the same time of *greater psychological* importance for the individual. Such social affiliation - more or less inherited - that are traditionally ascribed to individuals as a definition of identity: race (Caucasian/Arian, Jew, Negro, and so on), gender, country or place of birth, family and social class, are now, due to the processes of postmodernisation, becoming less important, diluted and altered, in the most technologically and economically advanced countries. At the same time, there is a longing for, and attempts to find or establish new groups to which one experiences belonging and which can facilitate identity-making. An increasing feeling of insecurity about identity follows this process of postmodernisation which, in turn, seems to reinforce this endeavour.

Keeping in mind that the notion of 'identity' denotes 'the way in which the individual is most fundamentally connected', and thus concerns 'the meaning of life', as Gilroy (1996) puts it, we understand that the lack of (a feeling of) a rooted identity, in other words, a social belonging, may be experienced as an almost existential threat to the individual. The powerful social psychological forces producing this are encapsulated in the expression: 'I' need a 'we' to become truly 'me'.

In this social psychological perspective, the actions of men and women appear as a struggle to create and/or maintain social belonging - real as well as virtual. Individuals, as a matter of fact, seem to be prepared to walk through fire and water in order to be accepted in some social grouping and are also prepared to do a great deal in order to imagine belonging to some virtual group, an imagined membership in some 'reference group' of the individual.

We often see how this endeavour to belong and be counted - or rather the fear of *not* belonging - will adopt the character of an almost irresistible instinct on several levels. This *yearning for belonging*, as I call it, is illustrated by the following three examples:

Example 1: For many years I have studied children in day care centres and in their families (cf. Dencik, 1988, 1995a, 1995b, 1998). I have been interested in finding an answer to questions such as: what are the children 'actually' doing during the daily turbulence of the day-care day as well as in their interactions with family members? What is their underlying 'project'? In both of these arenas, I find that children most actively seek *belonging* - to be one of the group, to be counted as one of the members of the group. One indication of this desire is the fact that they spend much of their time being 'observational associative' (manifesting 'gazing behaviour'), that is staring intensely at the other children. When the children return home, they frequently seek body contact with their mother or father, not necessarily for any instrumental purpose, but 'only' in order to receive physical confirmation of their unconditional belonging.

We find this being part of the children's *active auto-socialisation* - a process not unlike the process of acquiring the language that will become one's mother tongue - expressed through an almost magnetic attraction to belonging to those groups that are at hand. In reality, this is a process with many overlapping phases. It may typically follow a pattern whereby the individual, the child in this case, watches and contemplates the actual social situation. After having formed some ideas about the behaviour and norms governing her current reference group, she will do the same – she imitates. When others in the group notice that she is doing the same as they, when she conforms, then she is also one *of* them. In other words: she has become *as* they are, she has socialised herself.

Example 2: For the individual, the crucial importance of this 'social instinct' is highlighted by situations in which this process does *not* lead to the sharing of a desired collective identity. This seems to have been clear to the author of the Bible. When God gave the laws separating the chosen people from their neighbours - and thus created a particular people - he said: 'After the doings of the land of Egypt, wherein ye dwelt, shalt ye not do: and after the doings of Canaan, whither I bring you, shall ye not do: neither shall ye walk in their ordinances' (Lev. 18:3). No, 'Ye shall do my judgements, and keep mine ordinances, to walk therein' (Lev. 18:4). What happens then to the person who does not conform? What is the cruellest punishment God might find for a 'non conformer'? - Expulsion; not being allowed to take part in the community: 'For whoever shall commit any of these abominations, even the souls that commit them shall be cut off from among their people' (Lev. 18:29). In the Nordic societies, we recognise this same phenomenon under another term. The punishment for not conforming is to be outcast, to be denied sharing any relationship, to be deprived of the right to a collective identity - to be 'outlawed' as it was called during the Nordic Viking age.

The same phenomenon of marginalisation in our times has surfaced in day-care centres, in schools and at work places. But the language is new: when individuals who seek to take part in, or to be members of various groups are denied membership, we call it 'ostracism' or teasing ('*mobbing*'); a phenomenon whose horrific efficiency lies in its existential injury to the affected, quite in line with being 'cut off from among their people' and with being 'outlawed'.

Example 3: Individuals who have been denied or lost their belonging often look desperately for a *new* belonging as a basis for a new identity-making. This frequently happens through defining, i.e. identifying, oneself in opposition to what one in a given situation at least does *not* consider oneself to be (cf. Barth, 1969). Lately, for example, we have witnessed how many of those who have lost their membership in a state system, such as the former citizens of the Soviet Union or Yugoslavia, almost at the same time have found a new foundation in some other ethnic identity - as Armenians, Azeris, Chechens or as Serbs, Croats, Bosniacs (Moslems) and so forth, which immediately provides a new framework and new conditions for their social lives.

In another context, I have developed the idea that it is 'the ways in which social interaction between groups is governed, such as during a conflict, that creates ethnic identities; social conflicts are not created by ethnic awareness amongst people'. Rather, ethnic awareness is heightened or even created by social conflicts (Dencik, 1993). Ethnicities may occur and fade away, depending on how the social interaction and the distinction between the conflicting groups are defined and maintained. Pierre Bourdieu has stated that the tastes that are characteristic of one group often contain distaste for the tastes of other groups. By pronouncing some difference, a group may acquire what might be called a *profit of distinction* - temporarily, or in some cases permanently (Bourdieu, 1979).

The use of this profit may vary, but frequently it is used in order to acquire additional advantages, for instance control over the territory of the group. When cultural identities are 'territorialised', the odour of *Blut und Boden*, a political expression of the idea that blood gives right to earth, begins to appear. A half century ago, this idea was the foundation of genocide and holocaust on the European continent. In our time we witness in the Caucasus, in former Yugoslavia, in the Middle East, and in other places how this idea leads to ethnic cleansing of people who are, or rather *are made*, ethnic deviants.

The concept of 'local identity' may be literally understood to mean an identity based on and belonging to a given geographical location. When different local identities clash, the fight for profit, distinction and territorial power begins. Modern history contains an abundance of examples of this phenomenon. Historically we also find many cases where various cultures have coexisted rather peacefully throughout the centuries. The town of Sarajevo could have been a symbol of this only a decade ago. Further back, during the Middle Ages, up to the Castilian-Christian assumption of power by the invasion of Queen Isabella and King Ferdinand and their expulsion of Jews and Moslems in 1492 in what is now Andalusia, people with varying cultural backgrounds coexisted and creatively flourished in *al-Andalus*. This is also partly valid for Vienna during the Austro-Hungarian Empire up to World War I. In the New York City today we find similar conditions.

What then have been the conditions supporting such coexistence? One condition appears to be that the legitimacy and authority of these societies has *not* been based upon any idea of the ruler as leader or representative of the interests of some particular ethnic group (or for that matter, majority). Rather, legitimacy of power is rooted in something *above* the people, above *all* peoples in the area. In al-Andalus, all power was seen as emanating 'from God'. In Austro-Hungary, the emperor ruled 'by the grace of God'. In the Soviet Union, the execution of power by the Party was legitimised by reference to its base in 'scientific socialism'. In former Yugoslavia, the sources of power rested in the heroic halo and charisma of one person - Marshal Tito. In the United States of America, the execution of power is founded on a secular, albeit sacred document - the Constitution.

What happens when a relation of belonging, founded on something over and above all particular groups, falls apart? Typically, power becomes managed by the representatives of the dominant group - which instead ostentatiously claims to be the representative of *the* people. And then, given that there are several local identities on site, the path is cleared for the exercise of power of one local identity over the others and, at the same time, the stage is set for ethnic cleansing.

4. Who are 'We'? The Case of Scandinavia[8]

As mentioned above, an identity is constructed by the relationship between how an individual subjectively experiences the world and the historic and cultural framework influencing this subjective experience. In a country like Sweden or Denmark, the shrinking importance of a local foundation for identity appears to be problematic. The question, then, is: Do Denmark and Sweden have any significant specific historical and cultural frameworks which affect the identity-making of individuals living in them?

Examining the historic picture of these two Scandinavian states, as socio-cultural frameworks for the making of individual identities, we find that up to the waves of immigration that started in latter part of the 20th century, very few countries can match Denmark and Sweden in terms of their ethnic homogeneity (exclusivity). Three criteria are usually used to measure the degree of ethnic homogeneity:

a) *Extension of language*: Denmark is one of the few countries with one language common to all of its inhabitants. The Danish language is exclusive to Denmark - it is not spoken in any other country. The same is on the whole true for Sweden and Swedish.[9] This is not the case with English, German or French, nor is this typical for countries such as the Netherlands, Belgium, and Switzerland; in those countries large parts of the population speak other languages. English, German and French are spoken by the inhabitants of countries other than England, Germany and France.

b) *Extension of religion*: In most countries there are relatively large groups of various denominations. Denmark and Sweden are among the relatively few countries that traditionally have a single religion common among all inhabitants. Until recently, the majority of those born in these countries automatically became members of the State church.[10]

c) *Length of national history*: Many of the countries existing today are relatively young nations, even within Europe. Germany and Italy became nations during the 19th century, Finland and Norway achieved their independence about a century ago, and so on. Few countries have national histories as long as that of Denmark and Sweden.

Cultural anthropologists estimate that there are a couple of thousand nationalities (ethnic entities) in the world; but there are only a couple of hundred nation states recognised according to international law. Just a handful of these meet all three criteria for ethnic homogeneity. And only very few ethnic/national entities can in fact *at the same time* muster linguistic particularity, religious homogeneity and a common history of many centuries. Denmark and Sweden belong to this sociologically very exclusive club of nations who, throughout history, have offered an extremely homogeneous cultural framework for the making of individual identity.

From the middle of the 19th century, the idea of the nation state gained momentum throughout Europe and then the striving for homogeneity entered a new and more active phase. Mandatory elementary schooling and universal military training were introduced in many of the European countries and in addition to their original purposes, they became the two greatest machines for ethnic homogenisation. The spelling primer and the raising of the flag have in fact been among the more powerful instruments in erasing local identities of a country. Yet, in contrast to such European countries as Russia, Germany, Italy and Spain, where the state was either periodically weak or at times turned its authority against the interests and endeavours of its own people (and therefore was met with suspicion and seen as malevolent), there is, in Denmark and Sweden, a unique experience of life under a centralised and involved, though 'benign' state.

This is one particular explanation for why state interventions have been seen as something rather positive and accepted as fairly reasonable in Denmark and Sweden. This positive view of the state has been a prerequisite for (and reinforced by) the construction of the modern welfare state between the early 1930s and the end of the 1980s. One of the premises for its success is that the people are one and homogeneous and that there is one clear and unchallenged 'we'; all are 'family members' in a common home, as it was expressed by the Swedish social democratic party leader and prime minister Per-Albin Hansson when he introduced the idea of harmonious unity upon which to construct a future *folkhem* ('home of the people') (Hansson, 1929).

'The people' in Denmark and Sweden have, for a long time, been one and homogeneous. There has been a clear and unchallenged understanding of who 'we' are. At this point we may recall the quotation cited above: 'Identity can help us understand the fatal case 'we' that [...] comprises and excludes others' (Gilroy, 1996, p.20).

What are the implications of the fact that Denmark and Sweden are among the oldest nation states in the world and that they have also been historically among the ethnically most homogeneous? How has the influx of immigrants and refugees over the last two centuries changed and challenged this? Who are 'we' now?

The two Scandinavian welfare states of Denmark and Sweden have differed in their response to the social challenges connected with the growing social pluralisation that is part and parcel of postmodernisation. In Sweden, the tradition of public administration dates back to the times of Greater Sweden in the 17th century, when the then almighty chancellor Axel Oxienstierna, introduced 'a uniform and efficient administrative system comprising a central, a regional and a local level [...] expressed in a statute that became part of the national constitution of 1634. This appears as unique in Europe of those days' (*The Swedish National Encyclopedia*, vol. 14, p.544). Out of this emerged a system of national administration according to which one bases the policies on recommendations by a commission of experts especially set up to investigate the issue and to find some general principles that can then be implemented as general social measures incorporating all citizens in the country. A prerequisite for this has been a tacit understanding that the people are one and homogeneous - the image that there is a clear and unchallenged 'we' for whom the policy is launched. This became even more accentuated by the building of the welfare state in the middle and last part of the 20th century. An unintended side effect of this long tradition of 'deductive' public administration in Sweden, based as it is on a postulated homogeneity and an ambition to achieve equality, has been a sharpened eye for and sensitivity towards social difference.

It is against this historic and sociological background that we should understand how the traditional Swedish self-image and administrative system is challenged by the emergence of new ethnic, religious and cultural groups within the country. What has occurred is a fundamental rupture with a long and deeply anchored administrative tradition - a transformation in self-understanding from a homogeneous Sweden to Swedes becoming a majority in a multiethnic state.

The readiness to master plurality and variation within the Scandinavian states, however, is not solely dependent on the systems and traditions of public administration. The *cultural* readiness, what is sometimes loosely referred to as the 'spirit of the people', is of no less importance. This is particularly evident in the case of Denmark. As in Sweden, what may be labelled micro-variations in human attitudes and behaviour - such as wrapping a piece of cloth around your hair or refraining from eating pork - are also in Denmark often attributed a macro-social significance. There is in Denmark one specific cultural factor related to that kind of reaction: the influence of the Danish 19th century writer, philosopher and priest Nicolai Frederik Severin Grundtvig.[11] Grundtvig's philosophy places strong emphasis on the significance of the *'folkefælleskab'* (the 'popular community') and on 'the national'. Grundtvig, in his works repeatedly emphasizes what he refers to as *'den danske folkestam'* ('the Danish people's tribe').[12] A positive expression of this emphasis on popular community is the stress placed on a rather special Danish social phenomenon and feeling - in Danish called *hygge* ('coziness'). *Hygge* denotes a kind of socialising aimed at having a pleasant and cosy time together by managing to avoid anything that is bothersome and conflict laden. The negative side of *hygge* is an uneasiness towards anything deviant that *per se* may disrupt this special feeling and therefore also disturb the sense of undemanding community that goes with the it.

Behind the conception of *folkefælleskab* ('popular community'), has been an unproblematised perception of congruence between two actually profoundly different meanings of the notion of 'people' - the people referring to the 'nation' or 'tribe', in Greek *ethnos,* and the people referring to 'citizens', in Greek *demos*. This conception of identity between *ethnos* and *demos* is well expressed in Thomas More's famous utterance *One race in one place*.

There are, however, no grounds to assume that people in Denmark are more 'racist' than the inhabitants in other European countries. Still, it is probably no accident that Danish expressions like *'den lille racisme'* ('petty racism') are used to describe the attitude manifested by many Danes in their daily interactions with *de fremmede* ('the strangers') - which is what Danes call the immigrants and refugees living in the country. This is an indication of the attitude that one, even if one actually has nothing against 'the others' as such, still - just because they are 'strangers' and thereby different - are not willing to welcome them into the social and everyday community. Ideally, as we have learned, this everyday community should be characterised by *hygge* - and any presence of 'strangeness' or 'otherness' would be automatically disruptive.[13]

Socially, this everyday community is manifested in the virtual exclusion of 'the strangers' from participation in work life. In the beginning of September 1999, the OECD published a statistical report on the relative unemployment levels amongst immigrants in the member states.[14] Denmark topped the list. A year later the director of the European Union Monitoring Centre on Racism and Xenophobia, reported that Denmark among the member states now is leading with respect to xenophobic attitudes.[15] There certainly is a lot of cosy togetherness (i.e.

'*hygge*') in Denmark, but many immigrants report that this cosy togetherness seems to be reserved for Danes only. The under side of this special kind of inclusive Danish '*Gemütlichkeit*' is the social exclusion of those who due to their national or cultural otherness remain outside the popular community ('*folke- fælleskabet*').

The two Scandinavian traditions, the Swedish 'Oxenstierna-tradition' of public administration and the Danish 'Grundtvig-tradition' of popular community, have become manifested in the recent transformations of these modern welfare states. An indication of this trend is demonstrated in the answer to the puzzling question: 'Why is the political discourse in Denmark dominated by issues relating to 'the strangers', even though they comprise only about 5 per cent of the population? Why is there virtually no open debate at all about these issues in Sweden, where approximately 15 per cent of the population now have non-Swedish ethnic background? Is there a fundamental difference with respect to how one identifies 'the people' in these two Scandinavian welfare states?

In the Swedish Oxenstierna-tradition of governing from above, 'the people' refer primarily to the citizens of the country, who are ideally entitled to uniform conditions and equal rights. In Sweden, there prevails a strong hegemony of 'political correctness', implying a social imperative to talk about and treat immigrants with 'equal rights' and decency. There is a public office called *Diskrimineringsombudsman* (Ombudsman to investigate complaints of ethnic discrimination). At present, no political party of any significance in Sweden has attempted to exploit xenophobia or voice hostile attitudes towards ethnic minorities for political purposes.

'The people' in the Danish 'Grundtvig-tradition' of perceiving community primarily refer to those sharing the same cultural and religious background and affiliations, in other words, the Danes. The influx of other ethnic groups into the country has challenged this identity, leading to a massive political mobilisation on the issue of *udlændingepolitik* ('policy towards the foreigners/strangers'). Populist political parties have successfully appealed to popular anxieties with respect to the social changes connected with postmodernisation.[16] Blatantly xenophobic statements by leading political personalities, and political proposals hostile towards immigrants and refugees seeking asylum in Denmark and aiming at restricting their equal rights have become ubiquitous. In their political agitation around the referendum in the autumn of 2000 on whether or not Denmark should join the European Monetary Union, even leading members of government and the governing Social Democratic Party, manifested a verbal brutality when speaking about, for example, 'the

Muslims', unheard of in other European countries, not to say social democracies.[17]

How can this be explained? An obvious answer is that the application of such a *political* rhetoric has enjoyed remarkable success in the sense that it attracts voters. But why? Because a xenophobic political rhetoric in Denmark - in opposition to Sweden - is met by a certain *cultural* resonance in broad segments of Danish society.[18]

Out of the two quite different Scandinavian traditions, the uniforming Swedish Oxenstierna tradition in public administration, and the Danish Grundtvigian understanding of popular unity, there emerge very similar social reaction patterns with respect to the perception of social differences. Both traditions, albeit in different ways, appear to have promoted an increased awareness of and sensitivity to social disparity. Hence, in Denmark and Sweden (probably more than anywhere else) minor variations in human relationships and behaviour seem to attain, or are ascribed, major social importance.

This tendency manifests itself so that what is *a little* different often tends to be regarded as *very* different; even *minor* deviations tend to be regarded as *huge* problems, and what is *different* is often perceived as *abnormal*. What is *not equal/same* comes to be regarded as a situation of *inequality* and therefore, according to the ideals of the modern Scandinavian welfare states, as *unjust*. This means that *measures* need to be taken by some relevant authority in order to uphold the identity of the State as a guarantor of equality.

5. From *Homo Sapiens* to *Homo Zappiens*

Can the identity of the State be upheld? Certainly not the *qualitative* identity - and this is what drives the whole debate today in a country like Denmark. In these days of integration of countries and nations, some participants in the debate fear that even the very *numeric* identity of the existing states in Europe will eventually also become dissolved. The Scandinavian welfare states will not remain what they are. What are the transformative forces behind this? There seem to be three processes of simultaneous influence in operation and at the same time reinforcing each other:

a) *The 'globalisation' of economic and cultural influences and information*: What happens economically and culturally in a local society like the Swedish or Danish is increasingly influenced by what happens elsewhere in the world. Developments in media and information technology have resulted in everything being 'here and now' - wherever you might be in the world. Time and Space dissolve. Everything is at once long- and short-lived, near and far away.

The consequences may seem paradoxical: globally a homogenisation is taking place. Everything is becoming more similar everywhere - airports and hotel lobbies in one part of the world look exactly like those in another part; commodities in our local store are the same as in the local store in Farfaraway. At the local level, however, pluralisation takes place - anything from anywhere in the world is at hand; we meet people from all corners of the world, and in our local stores we find items from all countries.

The time of local and national unified culture has passed. In its place we have what may be called '*globalised minority cultures*'. Everyone may retain their respective cultural practices, maintain their food habits, have access to their own culture - wherever the live. However, every culture needs a 'critical mass', a minimum level of population in order to stay alive. Today, those who constitute a small, perhaps particular, cultural minority may well be scattered all over the world. Being a member of this group is possible thanks to modern information and communication technology. Everywhere we may meet people from various '*digital diasporas*'. At the same time, others may wish to enclose themselves in the '*global ghettos*' of the Internet.

What once tied people together in a local or national unified culture, such as those in Scandinavia, was the geographical proximity to others in the same village, town or country. This is no longer true to the same extent. Today people may also stay in touch at a distance and feel close to others who do not live in their locality but with whom they share their views, lifestyle, and fate. People tend to become less 'citizens' (Fr. '*citoyens*') of the place ('*cité*') where they live and more '*netizens*' (Fr. '*netoyens*') of the social networks within which they live and between which they move.

b) *The 'individuation' of the conditions of life*: According to Anthony Giddens (1990), the 'disembeddedness' of individuals is one of the most notable consequences of the modernisation process. People become increasingly individuated in the sense that they tend to become more and more 'disembedded' from the social circumstances in which they were born. Being born Danish or 'Stranger', Jew or Greek, man or woman, nobility or working class, etc., has less and less determining social impact on the lives of the individuals in today's world. In this respect the process of modernisation has emancipated people from their inherited social ties and circumstances. Instead, they are more alone with this task and now have the responsibility to chose their course of life and to fulfil their potentials. Modernisation and in particular postmodernisation are increasingly compelling people to become 'project leaders over their own lives' (cf. Dencik, 1997).

c) *The 'pluralisation' of life styles*: One or two generations ago, almost all Swedes and Danes had grown up like all the others in village communities and company towns. All who worked on the farm or in the factory had gone to the same school, had their first communion with the same vicar, joined the same trade union and had peas and pork on Thursdays, etc. In comparison to this social *syn*onymity those who are neighbours in a modern suburb today are increasingly *a*nonymous. More varied ways of life as well as more possible life-styles are now present in the individual's human environment. Most obvious is the increasing number of people in the streets and neighbourhoods who come from and bring with them a different culture, religion and language.

Pluralisation also concerns family patterns. In addition to traditional nuclear families - who, by the way, no longer lead their lives so traditionally (cf. Dencik, 1997) - people in the Scandinavian welfare states are increasingly living in relationships as co-habs, 'sephabs' (separately living), collectives, sole providers, families of same sex, and probably also other family patterns. The same is valid for work relations. When industrialism peaked in the modern Scandinavian welfare states, there was not only mass production of commodities - people were also made collective union members *en masse*. Today people have more disparate and individual relations to the labour market. It is possible to be permanently employed, short term employed, employed on a project, working as a free-lancer, as a consultant, fully self-employed and in various combinations of the above. The presence of various cultural artefacts in the food stores, at restaurants and on our TV screens also bear witness to this ongoing pluralisation. People coexist across the boundaries of cultural background and more and more individuals have *several* and *dissimilar* social associations.

The dynamic interactions of these three transformative forces of modern societies, globalisation, individuation and pluralisation, yield several consequences of interest to us in this context:

- In pre-modern times the question of who one was or where one belonged was hardly raised at all. Modernisation of the Scandinavian welfare states, especially Sweden, at the end of the 19th and beginning of the 20th century consisted of a massive process of industrialisation and urbanisation. In the course of one generation, millions of people had to abandon their lives based on relatively isolated, traditional agrarian production forms. Instead, they joined new and large collectives: factories and unions, in hastily constructed apartment houses and consumer co-operatives etc. Modernisation of society confronted the individual with a new existential challenge. For the individual, the departure from traditional locally-based ways of life meant that the experience of who one was and where one belonged, was no longer so clear-cut. On the contrary, at once one's entire existence was fundamentally questioned. In other words: *identity became a problem.* Postmodernisation just accentuates this.

- The local culture within which people have been raised and shaped has until recently been a most efficient 'guide' for orientation in life. Postmodernisation, however, makes the anchoring in a culture of this kind, with its traditional manifestations, less and less adequate as guidance for the individual. In order for them to adequately cope with a new reality, people will increasingly have to liberate themselves from traditions. Such a *kulturelle Freisetzung* ('cultural release/freewheeling'), as the German professor of pedagogy Thomas Ziehe has called it (Ziehe and Stubenrauch, 1982) may be experienced as at the same time both liberating and confusing. The individual is increasingly unable to rely on given cultural traditions in handling their social life. Instead each of us will increasingly have to figure out by ourselves, alone and independently, how to handle the various situations confronting us in our daily lives. This means that the individual, to a greater extent than in the era we are now leaving behind, will experience some kind of *existential solitude* in that he/she will have to depend on his/her own ability for *reflection* in order to adequately relate to a continuously changing world.

- In the traditional *Gemeinschaft,* people living in their local communities had many different areas of concern in common. The emergence of *Gesellschaft* forced people to live with increasingly *partial areas of solidarity* in relation to others in their environment. Belonging was no longer what it had been. Locality progressively came to be of lesser importance as a foundation for identity. Solidarity among people and in society did not dissolve, but it became increasingly based upon other factors than residential proximity. Postmodernisation and the emerging *Networkschaft* make *geo*graphy lose even more of its power as the social glue keeping people together. Instead the *bio*graphy of the individuals, to a larger extent than in the era we now leave behind, tends to create the foundation for the formation of *increasingly criss-crossing solidarities* in society.

- Living in postmodernity means new conditions for social life and also a new predicament for the individual. People will increasingly have to share their everyday lives with those with whom they have no common experience, also in the Scandinavian countries. This situation demands that one will have to free oneself from the prison of one's own, local cultural parochialism. This in turn demands that individuals master a sufficiently 'elaborated language code' (Bernstein, 1977). This is not necessarily the same as several different languages, but implies that the individuals have the competence to master the language so that we can articulate ourselves in such a way that relative strangers may understand. But this competence also implies the ability to understand and to interpret the meanings of relatively unknown circumstances. Post- modernisation demands that individuals develop a sharpened '*social ear*', in the same sense that some individuals are gifted with a 'musical ear'. In this connection, experience of various cultural expressions will probably be an important resource for the individual to develop a *socially necessary capacity for empathy*.

- The population in historically homogeneous countries like Sweden and Denmark have until recently not had to face the idea that there may be different ways of being 'normal'. And the political and administrative institutions that make decisions, administer and influence people's lives are largely unaccustomed to the same fact. Postmodernisation, however, increasingly confronts them with evidence that there is no longer only one way of being 'normal'. Or for that matter a 'real Swede' or 'a real Dane'. State policies and public measures in these countries, directed, as they generally are, towards promoting social equality, will face the challenge of having to combine this ambition with becoming increasingly tolerant of

> social differences. Authorities will have to adapt their administrative routines to the unfamiliar idea that *one may be 'normal' in many different ways*.

Postmodernisation means that individuals will become 'immigrants in the future'. Like immigrants people will have to be at home in a new environment without feeling at home; they will experience a need to open up to the realities of the new world and at the same time to find ways of securing themselves in their cultural background. Accelerating change in all spheres of daily life require of contemporary man at the same time to charge belonging from the past and to abandon the habitual. How can this be achieved?

In the rapidly changing societies of today's world, almost all spheres of the individual's life become affected by the ongoing transformations. This, in turn, not only means problems of orientation but also opens up new opportunities for the individual. 'Through cultural freewheeling, identities may be tried, changed, conventionalised and withdrawn', says Thomas Ziehe. Postmodernisation deprives the individual of the possibility to 'experience identity as something one takes over and hence is determined for' (Ziehe, 1986; 1989). Identities are not stable, they do not disappear, but they are transformed. Incessantly. In reality, they emerge in the *meeting* of people with *different* relations of belonging. It is by relating to others that one becomes 'one self' (Mead, 1934) - as an individual and as culture. 'We must be others if we are to be ourselves', as George Herbert Mead expressed it (1932, p.194). Interaction with others assists individuals to transcend themselves, i.e. what is given by convention – and thus every one and every culture to become 'him-/her- it self'.

The old question of 'Jew *or* Greek', 'stranger'/immigrant *or* Dane/Swede', and so forth has been superseded by postmodern developments. More and more individuals are not either/or but *both/and* - and both to 100 per cent. It is as with the dualistic picture referred to earlier in this chapter: it may be perceived as a young elegant woman with a hat or as an old witch. Both pictures are equally 'true'. What you see depends on what you perceive in a given situation as background and actual shape, respectively. More and more people have several *simultaneous* frameworks of belonging to switch between. In one moment or situation one is a Jew, Moslem or Black; in the next moment, one is Danish or Swedish.

Identity should thus be understood as a dynamic property of a person. Any person contains a multitude of latent identities. Some of them, but far from all, become manifested in the course of social contexts in which the person finds him/herself. On the other hand, the process may be reversed. What has been manifested in a particular social condition, e.g. the Jewish identity of a bar-mitzvah boy, may fade away as the boy matures into adulthood, marries a non-Jewish woman, and becomes a respected citizen in a non-anti-semitic environment.

'How do you jew?' goes a modern Jewish joke. Actually it is more than a joke - it is a quite relevant question when investigating how, (Jewish) identities are shaped in the course of postmodernisation. Any identity, *I*, ethnic, national or religious is always based upon several elements, $e_{1\text{-}n}$: mythical beliefs, historical traumas and events, traditions and cultural habits, values, attitudes and outlooks, rites and rituals, etc. Not all elements are equally significant in defining someone as having the identity *I*. Nor does a particular element always have the same *Stellenwert* ('status') in the hierarchy of elements. In different epochs and in certain conditions, a particular *e* may surface as more salient than other *e*'s. What at a certain period in time, or in a particular social context, actually constituted the most decisive element in defining a person as having the identity *I* - for instance, the belief in one God and the participation in certain religious cults - may in a different era become less significant, whereas some other elements, a shared historic fate and the sense of belonging to a certain people - may instead become the salient elements in defining what constitutes the same identity *I*.

'A rose is a rose is a rose' - goes the famous line by the American poet Gertrud Stein. If this is true for roses, can the statement perhaps be true *mutatis mutandis* also for people's identity? A phrase such as 'a Jew is a Jew is a Jew', however, is obviously not valid in the course of human history: the ways in which people have defined themselves as Jews, have been defined as such by significant *Alters* have changed over time. Only within the last six decades of the 20th century have decisive new elements been added to the set of elements that make up the potential reference points for identifying oneself as a Jew, e.g. the Holocaust and the creation of the state of Israel. Meanwhile, some other previously important elements, such as having Yiddish or Ladino as one's mother tongue, have almost disappeared.

Jewishness, like other ethnic or national identities, is a *transformative phenomenon*. What constitutes 'Jewish identity' is furthermore partly optional. To some it may be religious observance, while for others it may be a particular historic consciousness. For instance of having been a potential victim for anti-semitic attacks. For others still it may be an identification with a particular political cause, such as the Zionist ideals (cf. Dencik and Marosi, 2000a).[19] Many people may oscillate between these elements, one being more significant at one moment and another element at another moment in the person's life history. The *relative* salience of the elements that may potentially be referred to in identifying oneself or someone else as, e.g. 'Jewish', change. It may thus be relevant to analyse the *dynamics of transformations* of a person's or a people's identity. However, social psychology has tried, without much success, to capture such a dynamics of identity. Among the promising conceptualisations aimed at capturing the flexibility in people's identities in the course of postmodernisation are *patchwork identities*, a term coined by David Elkind (1984), and '*multiple selves*' launched by Kenneth Gergen (1991).

In the perspective of postmodernisation, the diaspora Jewish experience may actually be quite prototypical for what many more individuals and peoples will experience. Therefore, I will elaborate a bit further on the case of diaspora Jewish identity in today's world. Briefly stated, contemporary diaspora Jewish identity can be framed within what somewhat heretically may be called a modern *Jewish trinity*. The cornerstones of this trinity are:

a) *Judaism as a religion:* Some Jews are 'religious', i.e. observant with respect to the rules and rituals prescribed by the religious system of Judaism. Others are not - but still they are 'Jewish'. Even to those Jews who are not 'religious', Judaism as a social and historical phenomenon is something they cannot avoid relating to in one way or the other.

b) *Jewishness as a prism through which one experiences the world*: All Jews belong to the Jewish people. Regardless of whether you live in, say, Copenhagen, Budapest, Buenos Aires, New York or Tel Aviv, a Jew is part of the same collective historic experience. From a sociological point of view, it does not really matter whether these are mythical reference points (for instance. about the Exodus from Egypt) or real events (such as. the Expulsion from Spain in 1492 or the Holocaust). Collective experiences of specific ethnic and historic bonds express themselves not only in cultural manifestations (food, folklore, music, and so on) but also at the individual level in certain more or less subtle idiosyncratic sensitivities, reaction-patterns and optics through which one experiences the world.

c) *The state of Israel as an existing reality*: Some Jews are Zionists - their Jewish identity corresponds largely with their engagement for the establishment and survival of the state of Israel. Other Jews are less involved in this, or even opposed to the Zionist idea. Many are a-Zionists, i.e. neither Zionists nor anti-Zionists. But regardless of how one is Jewish, it is virtually impossible to be a Jew today without relating somehow to the fact that Israel exists as a Jewish state. Like the *sociotopes* I mentioned earlier in this chapter, the *Jewish trinity* may be depicted graphically as a triangle like this:

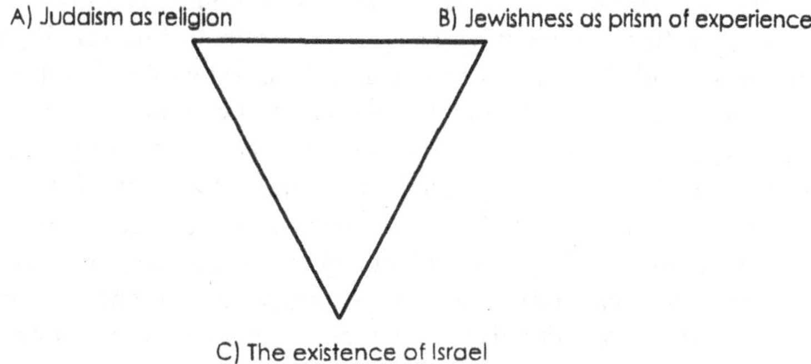

We may conceive of this triangle as the existential life-space of the Jewish identity. Individual Jews, of course, differ in their orientations and how they perceive of themselves as Jews: some are closer to one of the corners than others, who may be closer to another corner or perhaps far from all of them. Yet regardless of where a person stands as a Jew, the Jewish trinity constitutes the framework within which any modern Jewish identity exists.

Any Jew in the Diaspora is not only Jewish, however. Every Jew is also citizen in the country where he/she lives. As a Jew, one may be Danish, French, Hungarian, or Swedish. Being 'Swedish', for example, means that one is also 'inscribed' within some of the fundamental cornerstones of Swedish existence: As a Swede one live in a particular culture, is part of certain national history and is a citizen of a particular State. Like the Jewish identity, the Swedish identity can be framed within a triangle. The cornerstones of this *Swedish trinity* can be said to be:

a) *Citizenship in the Swedish state*: As a citizen in a state, you have certain rights and duties, such as the duty to defend your country or the right to participate in general elections. Some citizens have strong affiliations to their 'fatherland', others have more relaxed feelings, but regardless of whether one feels pride or shame, one is inevitably part of the country to which one legally belongs.

b) *'Secularised Lutheranism' as a cosmology*: Although Sweden is a Christian country, in which most of the citizens by tradition belong to the just recently abolished Lutheran *State* church (now 'the Swedish church, Christianity *as a religion* does not characterise the life of any larger segments of the inhabitants. Nevertheless people's everyday world view and daily life ethics in Sweden are profoundly coloured by certain Christian or rather Lutheran values: the Protestant ethic (cf. Weber, 1904) of hard work and diligence, combined with an outspokenly rational way of handling human affairs. In the formation of the modern Swedish welfare state this is amalgamated into a 'higher' cosmological unity that for want of a better label could be described as *secularised Lutheranism*. In such a cosmology virtually everything is measured according to its utility, nothing is really 'holy', and religiosity is a question of private inner beliefs. The very categories by which one organises and evaluates social affairs in Sweden are tinted by the tacit values and viewpoints of secular Lutheran cosmology.

c) *Swedishness as a prism through which one experienced the world*: By growing up in Sweden, by having Swedish as one's mother tongue and by having spent your formative years in a Swedish school you acquire a 'Swedish' way of perceiving the world. This may manifest itself in the way one perceives society and interprets social justice, but also in a rather special devotion to Nature as such. There is a way of appreciating wild forests, red cottages, empty landscapes, and beaming sunshine that is more or less 'typically Swedish'. The fact that the songs of the Swedish folklore and the special products of Swedish cuisine evoke positive associations and feelings among some Swedes is only because they are 'Swedish'. Like the *Jewish trinity* discussed above, a *Swedish trinity* may be depicted graphically as a triangle like this:

The identity of a modern Jew is always to be found within the existential triangle defined by the Jewish trinity. However, living in the Diaspora the Jew is at the same time inevitably also inscribed in another triangle, in this case the Swedish trinity. The two triangles are not mutually exclusive. One may be both Jewish and Swedish at the same time. And since both triangles form a fairly complete cultural frame of reference for the individual concerned, they are not complementary - it is not the case that the one contains what the other lacks. Nor is it the case that you are half this and half that. On the contrary, a person may have both identities, each of them 100 per cent, and simultaneously. The triangles thus overlap, but in a rather peculiar way: We may collapse the two trinities to describe the comprehensive socio-cultural framework of a Jewish individual in the contemporary Diaspora. The two triangles then form a well-known pattern:

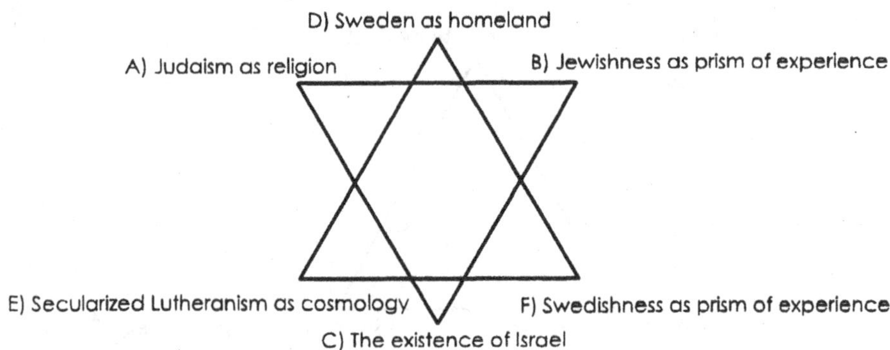

We may call this *The Star of David of the Diaspora*. As a model of a complex identity, it is certainly valid not only for Jews. Nor is the reasoning behind it restricted and relevant only to Sweden. *Mutatis mutandis,* the argument also holds for Muslims in Denmark, Turks in Germany, Iranians in France, and Palestinians, Bosnians and many others who have been forced to leave their local environments because of war, political reasons or economic hardship. An increasing number of peoples and individuals today are in some way or other *diasporic*. That is to say, they live somewhere else and with different life conditions than those where they had grown up. Those with whom they identify ('their people') and the life-style of which they consider themselves a part exist only in their imagination. The diasporic predicament implies that the person is at home in and commutes between (at least) two different sociotopes or frameworks of belonging. The diasporic individual, although always inscribed in the hexagon, does not necessarily have a fixed position within it. On the contrary without perceiving this as a loss of identity, individuals may frequently shift position within it according the social situation in which they find themselves.

Simmel once described the *stranger* as 'the man who comes today and stays tomorrow' (Simmel, 1908). 'Thus, the stranger remains the permanent 'slimy', always threatening to wash out the boundaries vital to native identity' (Bauman, 1991, p.67). Due to their built-in duality, by being neither a true outsider nor a true insider, but *both at the same time*, the diasporic individual is the archetypical example of man in postmodernity. Diasporics are the embodiment of incongruity and 'ineradicably *ambivalent'* (Bauman 1991, p.61).

The rapidly increasing number of individuals with multiple identities created by the processes of postmodernisation pose a growing and constant threat to those who 'have vested interests in maintaining the orderliness of the world' (Bauman, 1991, p. 2). The threat consists in the *ambivalence* that emerges when a person or new phenomenon may not unambiguously be classified and treated according to clear-cut and already established social categories. This is evidently the case when people do not fit any of the existing categories, or when they may be characterised according to several of them. Then certain acts of violence tend to be released: at first on the conceptual level. The German sociologist Joachim Matthes, in his review of Bauman's work on *Modernity and Ambivalence,* gives it a powerful expression: '*ein Gewaltakt, der an der Welt verübt wird*' (Matthes, 1994, p.293.) What is meant by this is that in attempting to impose old categories on an empirical reality that is in constant transformation - with postmodernisation and the rapid social changes it implies, the risk of doing so is magnified. An act of violence that hitherto has largely been overlooked takes place: a verbal rape of the world. And, one may add, when it then turns out that this 'rape' did not erase the ambiguity that caused it in the first place, the verbal violence is sometimes succeeded by raw and murderous physical violence - today euphemistically also called 'ethnic cleansing'.

A diasporic identity is always complex, but not necessarily a negative or burdensome condition, neither for society nor for the individual. Postmodernisation, on the contrary, may well imply that what formerly was seen as a disadvantage, a so-called 'double identity', may now become an asset in the new conditions of society and living, both for society at large and for the individual. In accordance with the phenomenon of dual-socialisation, mentioned earlier, I would rather call it a *dual-identity*. Such an identity provides the individual the possibility to *oscillate* between several perspectives and in that way see the world 'stereoscopically'. The increasing number and differing kinds of diasporic situations that people are drawn into under postmodernisation also provide the individuals a widened existential basis for developing enhanced abilities to critically understand their own existence and society. This in turn facilitates the continuous *self*-reflection which postmodern development of society will demand of the individual - for his/her own best. Now more than ever in history, we find ourselves with the demand of mobility - it is necessary to move between and 'perform' in several different social arenas. This requires continuous education of the individual, rethinking and new thinking. One has to develop new and adequate competencies related to ever-changing social circumstances. Not only geographical but also social and mental mobility is required from the individual to an extent never known before. The problem for many people is to be able to hold onto their *identity* in a changing world and to maintain their *integrity* while shifting between various latent social identities which more frequently have to be expressed.

In late modernity, individuals typically belong to several different social categories and thereby have access to a wide potential repertoire of latent identities. Each individual is unique with respect to which potential frameworks of belonging are combined to make up the person's narrative identity. The individual is at the same time identical with several others, and unique trough his or her unique combination of identifications with possible 'others' (cf. Hogg and Abrams, 1998, p.18).

In this connection, it is important to remember that identity-making is a dynamic process. 'Identity' as well as 'culture' is something that is being *created* in an ongoing process - in the encounter between people with *different* frameworks of belonging and in the individual's 'meeting' with various sides of him-/herself. Culture and identity develop through the intercourse of such meetings. In the process of postmodernisation, individuals as well as cultures, nations and states will be challenged to develop an openness and ability to *negotiate identity* towards various aspects of life. As a matter of course, they will attempt to hold onto their integrity by remaining 'themselves' while at the same time constantly having to confront the need to adapt to new conditions by becoming transformed in a continuous process of *creolisation* (cf. Hannerz, 1996).

Here again, one should realise that those images we may have of identity are always pictures, metaphors for something, and rather elusive. Sometimes metaphors help us capture something important in the precise way we wish to describe; but frequently, however, metaphors lead us astray and tie us to the understanding of something static.

Identity is sometimes depicted as 'having roots'. However, rather than looking for the roots of a person's identity in the local, as if a person were a tree growing out of the ground on which one was born, or even an element in the very soil of which it grows, the situation now demands more adequate metaphors to describe the identity-formation of individuals. 'What are roots good for if you can't bring them with you?' asked Gertrude Stein. Heinrich Heine, another exiled poet, also of Jewish heritage, referred to his German culture as a 'mobile fatherland'. Accordingly, we may conclude that mobile individuals require *mobile identities*.

A person's identit*ies* today should be understood in terms of actual social and cultural relationships rather than in terms of 'roots' in some local and more or less mythological *Heimat*. It is true that poets as well as politicians have traditionally worshipped their 'homelands'. And this tendency will certainly not decrease in the rapidly changing societies that characterise our world - the more dramatic the changes, the more intense the conservative resistance and tendencies of nostalgia. There are also reasons to believe that the entire relationship between being and feeling mentally, socially and geographically 'at home' and the process of postmodernisation will become increasingly complex (cf. Huber, 1999). Even if it is ever more crucial for people to develop the ability to feel 'at home in homelessness', those who 'have vested interests in maintaining the orderliness of the world', to quote Bauman (1991, p.2) again, will find new reasons to combat the ambivalence of human existence. New social polarisations are likely to occur: A nostalgia amounting to a kind of *social necrophilia* may become accompanied by attempts to defending and resurrect their lost and threatened 'homeland', on the one hand, with a cosmopolitan mentality open for social change and mental mobility on the other. A cosmopolite like the poet and Nobel Laureate Nelly Sachs, a refugee from Nazi Germany in Sweden, once expressed it this way: *Am Stelle von Heimat halte ich die Verwandlung der Welt* ('In place of homeland I place the change of the world').

From the perspective of the transformations implied by post-modernisation, our conventional understanding of Man will be challenged. A conventional image of a person's *personality* and *self* is that it contains or is built up around some kind of 'core' or 'nucleus'. Once it was perhaps an adequate image of what a person 'is', but today it is probably more misleading than directing our understanding in a relevant way. A conceivably better way to understand what a person 'is' in a turbulent world like ours is to conceptualise a person's personality and self more or less in the same way as we imagine, for instance, a whirlpool in the water or a wind. These phenomena do not exist 'as such'. They exist only as movements in a medium. In the same way a human being '*is*' the movement he or she produces in the social situations in which the individual lives and operates. In the age of postmodernisation, Man is not only a *Homo sapiens* but must also be a *Homo zappiens*.

Notes

1 One of the causes of the melancholia of ageing may be the growing insight that of all the many possibilities within every individual only some were given the chance to become realised.

2 One sign of this phenomenon is the recently formed *International Society for Self and Identity* (ISSI) that is also issuing a cross-disciplinary journal *Self and Identity* published in the UK by Psychology Press.

3 This notion resembles Castells' notion of 'network society' (Castells, 1996-1998). The second volume in this impressive three volume work deals especially with the problems of identity and the intensified tensions between the individual's ego and self-understanding and the networks he/she is woven into in the information age. Having analysed the collapse of centralised power systems, e.g. in the classic nation states, Castells senses other emerging nodes of identity 'It is in these back alleys of society, whether in alternative electronic networks or in grassrooted networks of communal resistance, that I have sensed the embryos of a new society, laboured in the fields of history by the power of identity' (Castells, 1996-1998, vol. II, p.362).

4 Including norms, values, ideals, habits, cultural practices, etc.

5 In this context, we should be reminded of David Elkind's cautious observations concerning the fact that children in modernity are confronted at an early age with increasing demands on mastering emotional independence. This might enhance many good qualities with the growing child. On the other hand, taking the child's emotional maturity too much for granted may increase the child's dependency in other fields (cf. Elkind, 1979).

6 This way of defining people turns something that is transitory into a quality: immigrant is not something you *are* - to move to another country is something you *do*. After that you live as a more or less accepted and equal citizen in the new country.

7 Danish, Swedish and German quotes are translated into English by the author.

8 Scandinavia comprises Denmark, Norway and Sweden. Having been commuting for a quarter of a century now between Sweden and Denmark, I know these societies quite well. I will therefore concentrate my presentation on these two countries and leave Norway out of the picture, although there are no *á priori* reasons to believe that Norway in fundamental ways differs from the general description I give of the other two Scandinavian states.

9 I here disregard some minor 'historic left-overs', e.g. the small Swedish speaking minority in Finland, now an independent republic, but for 500 years a part of the Kingdom of Sweden, and an even smaller Danish speaking minority in Slesvig, now a province in the northern part of the Federal Republic of Germany, but for many years before that a part of the Kingdom of Denmark.

10 The Lutheran branch of Christianity was technically abolished as the State Church in Sweden 1. January 2000, but still prevails as such in Denmark. This however should not be misinterpreted as a sign of widespread religiosity amongst the populations of these countries. The opposite is rather the case: in few countries is life more rationally contrived than in Denmark and Sweden.

11 See for example his *Nordens mytologi* published in 1808. Grundtvig is also known for having made the 'unmatchable discovery' ('mageløse opdagelse') of 'the gay Christianity' and for having inspired the 'idea of the church of the people' ('folkekirketanken') in Denmark and Norway.

12 On this point Grundtvig's ideas are similar - albeit both less elaborated and more outspoken - to those of the German 18th century philosopher Johann Gottfried von Herder.

13 According to this view, as expressed by a Danish publicist, 'it is all right that 'the foreigners' are different, only they should not be here - but if they absolutely have to be here, they should be and behave like us'.

14 OECD stands for The Organisation for Economic Cooperation and Development and is based in Paris.

15 The European Union Monitoring Centre on Racism and Xenophobia is lead by Dr. Beate Winkler and located in Vienna.

16 In 1972 the lawyer and self-proclaimed tax-evader Mogens Glistrup was succesful in forming a political party *Fremskridtspartiet* ('Progressive Party') that launched an openly populistic and increasingly xenophobic policy. In the 1990s, Fremskridtspartiet was succeeded by the *Dansk Folkeparti* ('Danish People's Party') lead by Pia Kærsgaard, a woman who, by adopting a violent political vocabulary, has had great success in putting the *udlændingepolitik* ('policy towards the foreigners') at the top of the Danish political agenda.

17 Such as the social democratic Minister of the Interior, Karen Jespersen.

18 The fact that this is so and that immigrants in Denmark tend to feel more excluded and marginalized than immigrants elsewhere seems to surprise the Danes themselves - having '*hygge*', socialising and seeking cosiness as they do among themselves.

19 In a recent survey of the Jewish communities in Sweden we found that all of these reasons were given, however to quite different degrees. Quite a few informants indicated that religious belief constitutes their basis for identifying themselves as Jewish, whereas the overwhelming majority stated that the feeling of belonging to a certain people is what make them identify themselves as Jewish (Dencik and Marosi, 2000b).

References

Abrams, D. and M. Hogg (1999) (eds), *Social Identity and Social Cognition*, Blackwell, Oxford.

Altman, I. and B. Rogoff (1987), 'World Views in Psychology: Trait, Interactional, Organismic, and Transactional Perspectives', in Stokols, D. and Altman, I. (eds.), *Handbook of Environmental Psychology*, John Wiley & Sons, New York.

Arvidsson, H.; L. Berntson and L. Dencik (1994), *Modernisering och välfärd - om stat, individ och civilt samhälle i Sverige* ('Modernisation and Welfare - on State, Individuals and Civil Society in Sweden'), City University Press, Stockholm.

Bauman, Z. (1991), *Modernity and Ambivalence*, Cornell University Press, Ithaca, New York.

Barth, F. (1969), *Ethnic Groups and Boundaries: The Social Organization of Cultural Difference*, Allen & Clawin, London.

Beck, U. (1996), 'Wie aus Nachbarn Juden werden: Zur politischen Konstruktion des Fremden in der reflexive Moderne', in Miller, M. and Soeffner, H.-G. (eds.), *Modernität und Barbarei: Soziologisches Zeitdiagnose am Ende des 20. Jahrhunderts*, Suhrkamp Verlag, Frankfurt am Main.

Bernstein, B. (1977), *Class, Codes and Control*, Routledge & Kegan Paul, London.

Bourdieu, P. (1979), *La distinction: Critique social du jugement*, Editions de Minuit, Paris.

Brown, H. (1966), 'Themes in Experimental Research on Groups from the 1930s to the 1990s' in Whetherell, M. (ed.), *Identities, Groups and Social Issues*, Sage Publications, London.

Brown, R. (2000), 'AGENDA 2000 - Social Identity Theory: Past Achievements, Current Problems and Future Challenges', *European Journal of Social Psychology*, vol. 30 no. 6, pp.745-778.

Capozza, D. and R. Brown (eds.) (2000), *Social Identity Processes: Trends in Theory and Research*, Sage Publications, London.

Castells, M. (1996-1998), *The Information Age: Economy, Society, and Culture*, vols. 1-3, Blackwell, London.

Collins, S. (1989), *From Divine Cosmos to Sovereign State: An Intellectual History of Consciousness and the Idea of Order in Renaissance England*, Oxford University Press, Oxford.

Cornell, S. and D. Hartman (1998), *Ethnicity and Race: Making Identities in a Changing World*, Pine Forge Press, Thousand Oaks, CA.

Crook, S.; J. Pakulski and M. Waters (1992), *Postmodernization: Change in Advanced Society*, Sage Publications, London.

Dencik, L. (1993a), 'Postmodernisation and Ethnification: Reflections on Xenophobia and Exile in Contemporary Modernity' in *Rescue-43. Xenophobia and Exile*, Copenhagen, Munksgaard.

Dencik, L. (1993b), 'Hemma i hemlösheten' ('To Be at Home in Homelessness'), in Jakubowski, J. (ed.), *Judisk identitet* (Jewish Identity), Natur och Kultur, Stockholm.

Dencik, L. (1995a), 'Modern Childhood in the Nordic Countries - 'Dual Socialisation' and its Implications', in Chisholm, L., Büchner, P., Krüger, H.-H. and M. du Bois-Reymond (eds.), *Growing Up in Europe*, de Gruyter, Berlin/New York.

Dencik, L. (1995b), 'Children in Day Care and Family Life - Observations from the BASUN project' in B. Arve-Parès (ed), *Building Family Welfare*, Swedish National Committee on the International Year of the Family, Socialdepartementet, Stockholm.

Dencik, L. (1997), 'The Position of Families in the Transformation of the Modern Scandinavian Welfare States' in Vaskovics, L. A. (ed.), *Familienleitbilder und Familienrealitäten*, Verlag Leske+Budrich, Leverkusen.

Dencik, L. (1998), 'Modernisation - A Challenge to Early Childhood Education: Scandinavian Experiences and Perspectives', *European Early Childhood Education Research Journal*, vol. 6 no. 2, pp.19-33.

Dencik, L. and K. Marosi (2000a), *Judiskt liv i Sverige: Levnadsvanor och attityder bland medlemmarna i de judiska församlingarna i Göteborg och Stockholm* ('Jewish Life in Sweden. Habits and Attitudes among Members of the Jewish Communities in Gothenburg and Stockholm'), Judiska Församlingen, Stockholm.

Dencik, L. and K. Marosi (2000b), 'Svenska judars judiska identitet' ('The Jewish Identities of Swedish Jews'), *Judisk Krönika*, no. 3, pp.29-32.

Dencik, L., C. Bäckström and E. Larsson (1988), *Barnets två världar* ('The Two Worlds of the Child'), Esselte/Studium, Stockholm.

Elkind, D. (1979), *The Child and Society*, Oxford University Press, New York.

Elkind, D. (1984), *All Grown Up & No Place to Go*, Addison-Wesley, Reading, MA.

Gergen, K. (1991), *The Saturated Self: Dilemmas of Identity in Contemporary Life*, Basic Books, New York.

Giddens, A. (1990), *The Consequences of Modernity*, Polity Press, Cambridge.

Gilroy, P. (1996), 'Diasporaen og identitetens omveje' ('Diaspora and the Digressions of Identity'), *Social Kritik*, no. 45-46, pp.20-21.

Hannerz, U. (1996), *Transnational Connections: Culture, People, Places*, Routledge, London.

Hansson, P-A. (1929), 'Folk och klass' ('People and Class'), *Tiden*. Stockholm.

Hogg, M. and D. Abrams (1998), *Social Identifications*, Routledge, London.

Huber, A. (1999), *Heimat in der Postmoderne*, Seismo Verlag, Zürich.

Keupp, H. and R. Höfer (eds) (1997), *Identitätsarbeit heute. Klassische und aktuelle Perspektiven der Identitätsforschung*, Suhrkamp, Frankfurt am Main.

Lewin, K. (1936), *Principles of Topological Psychology*, McGraw-Hill, New York.

Lewin, K. (1964), *Field Theory in Social Science*, Harper, New York.

Matthes, J. (1994), 'Mit Ambivalenz leben': Zygmunt Baumans halbherzige Kritik der 'Moderne', *Soziologische Revue*, vol. 17, pp. 292-297.

Mead, G.H. (1932), *The Philosophy of the Present*, A. E. Murphy, Chicago.

Mead, G. H. (1934), *Mind, Self and Society*, Ch. Morris, Chicago.

Miller, M. and H-G. Soeffner (eds) (1996), *Modernität und Barbarei: Soziologisches Zeitdiagnose am Ende des 20. Jahrhunderts*, Suhrkamp Verlag, Frankfurt am Main.

Ricoeur, P. (1990), *Soi-même comme un autre*, Le Seuil, Paris.

Rosenstrauch, H. (1988), *Aus Nachbarn wurden Juden*, Berlin.

Simmel, G. (1908), 'Exkurs über den Fremden', in *Soziologie. Untersuchungen über die Formen der Vergessellschaftigung*, Berlin, 1968.

Tajfel, H. (1974), 'Social Identity and Intergroup Behavior', *Social Science Information*, vol. 13, pp.65-93.

Tajfel, H. and J. C. Turner (1986), 'The Social Identity Theory of Intergroup Behavior' in Worchel, S. and W. Austin (eds.), *Psychology of Intergroup Relations*, Nelson Hall, Chicago.

Taylor, C. (1989), *Sources of the Self – The Making of the Modern Identity*, Cambridge University Press, Cambridge.

Tönnies, F. (1887), *Gemeinschaft und Gesellschaft: Abhandlung des Communismus und des Socialismus als empirischer Culturformen*, Leipzig.

Turner, J. C. (1999), 'Some Current Issues in Research on Social Identity and Self Categorisation Theories', in Ellemers, N., Spears, R. and Doosje, B. (eds.), *Social Identity*, Blackwell, Oxford.

Weber, M. (1904), *Die protestantische Ethik und der Geist des Kapitalismus*, in *Max Webers Gesammelte Aufsätze zur Religionssoziologie* vol. I, Tübingen, 1934.

Whetherell, M. (ed.) (1996), *Identities, Groups and Social Issues*, Sage Publications, London.

Ziehe, T. (1986), 'Inför avmystifieringen av världen: ungdom och kulturell modernisering' ('Facing the Demystification of the World: Youth and Cultural Modernisation'), in Löfgren, M. and A. Molander (eds.), *Postmoderna tider?* ('Postmodern Times?'), Norstedts, Stockholm.

Ziehe, T. (1989), *Kulturanalyser: ungdom, utbildning, modernitet.* ('Cultural Analysis: Youth, Education, Modernity'), Symposion, Stockholm.

Ziehe, T. and H. Stubenrauch (1982), *Plädoyer für ungewöhnliches Lernen*, Rohwohlt, Hamburg.

Part III

Globalisation, Knowledge and Democracy

10 Global Society as the Crisis of Democracy

HAUKE BRUNKHORST

The end of the epoch of the nation state could be dated, so Carl Schmitt believed, to the year 1963, the year he wrote a new foreword to a text originally published in 1932 entitled *Der Begriff des Politischen*, the 'Concept of the Political'. (Schmitt, 1963, p.10) His thesis goes back to ideas from the 1930s and 1940s on the imperialism and expansionism of 'transnational powers' (Schmitt, 1988, pp.255ff, 271ff, 295ff, 303ff).[1] At that time, political movements such as Fascism and Bolshevism, but also the American project of democracy, gave rise to a diagnosis of the times which - independently of Schmitt - was placed by Hannah Arendt at the very heart of her 1951 book on totalitarianism: the diagnosis of the *'Entstaatlichung der Politik'*, the de-statification of politics (Arendt, 1986).

The evolutionary achievement of the constitutional revolutions of the eighteenth century was to bridge the gap that already existed between the political system and the other functionally differentiated social systems (Luhmann, 1990, p.176). The republican constitution structurally binds the legal system to the political system by means of the co-institutionalisation of participatory rights of human beings as citizens and individual rights of citizens as human beings. By means of public self-legislation, citizens are supposed to control societal development and to coordinate the reciprocal freedom of their own actions. For Arendt, it was the very achievement of the nation-state to keep this societal development, which she characterises as the 'unnatural growth of the natural under control. The 'unnatural growth of the natural' distinguishes the development of modern industrial society from the old *oikos* based economy (Arendt, 1987, p.47). The new principle of society, what we would now call a functionally differentiated society, is what Arendt' calls 'expansion for expansion's sake' (Arendt, 1986, p.207ff). This expansion for expansion's sake can be the expansion of the economic system, but it can also be the expansion of a stateless political system that accumulates power for power's sake, and the latter is true for both imperialism and for totalitarianism. With the reflexive notion of 'expansion for expansion's sake' Arendt refers to the unlimited growth of capital and power which, in a historical and evolutionary perspective was made possible by the emergence of modern society and the principle of functional differentiation. The growth of capital and power in such a society no longer follows any human interests of self-preservation, neither national nor individual. The paradigmatic case is the development of the capitalist system. However, in 'Origins of 'Totalitarianism', Arendt demonstrates impressively that the imperialist and totalitarian growth of political power follows the same reflective mechanism as the growth of the system of capital and money. Power as well as capital develop all their productive and destructive forces for their own sake and not for the sake of human beings, nations, shareholders, owners of capital or those men or parties who are in power: 'Power [...] has been dissolved into a kind of dematerialized mechanism whose every move generates power' (Arendt, 1986, p.418).[2] The process of functional differentiation constitutes a social reality without normative integration, and the decentralized political system partly becomes the 'opponent' of the centered state power which is bound by the democratic constitution.

Many observations on the current global situation appear to confirm this trend. We have global politics, but no global state. Nation-states, indeed, are still the masters of international treaties and the representatives and appointees of these states, traversing the globe after each other from one conference to the next, continuing to sign pacts, casting votes in regional and global organisations, and pursuing military, political and economic crisis management. However, the sheer weight and movements of the global political system itself have become detached for so long from the power play of the segmentally organized inter-state world and become so independent that, today, they represent a social reality *sui generis*. Increasingly, individual states have turned from being drivers of the political system to being driven by the same system.

To the degree that state sovereignty becomes a juridical fiction without substantial validity, popular sovereignty becomes an ever more fictitious quantity. The democracy characterizing the state order of the West, so it appears, is developing from a fairly impressive reality back into an ever paler Utopia. In the wake of de-stratification, the independently developed might of executive political powers tears asunder the bonds linking it to the will of the democratic legislature. Viewing this globally networked social world, postmodern political scientists such as Guéhenno already speak of the 'end of democracy', but even classic scholars of modernity such as the theorist of democracy Robert Dahl take the end of *nation-state* democracy to be unavoidable (Guéhenno, 1994; Dahl, 1989). Naturally, Dahl would not wish to bid farewell to democracy along with the nation state; rather, he hopes for what he calls a 'third democratic transformation' (Dahl, 1989, p.311ff). This should bring not less but more democracy, as did the first democratic transformation from tribal rule to the city-state of antiquity, and the second from the medieval city-state or court-centered state to the modern nation-state in the constitutional revolutions of the 18th and 19th centuries, both of which represented clear democratic progress. The hope of a third democratic transformation, regarded from the historical perspective of the participant, is of course merely a utopia, as much endangered as full of promise, whose chances of realization are incalculable and unforeseeable. Things were not any different on the eve of the onset of the Greek *polis*, the Roman republic, or the French Revolution. We know these things better only later, in retrospect.

What has been recognizable so far is that the de-statification of politics, which in conjunction with the process of the global independence of remaining functional systems is leading to a massively one-sided societal progress, is clearly detrimental to democracy. The obverse side of this societal progress of globally functional systems (for politics, the economy, law, science, art, the sphere of intimacy, etc.) is the decline of democratic self-legislation, with the consequence that those problems of the social evolution of society formerly solved by the democratic state can no longer be solved and are actually growing daily. Scarcely has the Soviet system of the prophets of crisis fallen then the crisis reappears.

There are two problems which have from the very outset accompanied the transition of society from stratification to functional differentiation. Neither, apparently, can be solved by the functional systems themselves. Functionally specialised subsystems such as the deregulated market-economy cannot produce solidarity by means of their own autopoiesis (self-production). On the contrary, their systems integration of markets or autonomous state-power or institutionalized medical systems poses a new evolutionary stage of social-integration without solidarity or negative integration.[3] The process of functional differentiation from Marx to

Polanyi again and again has been described as a process of the destruction of all premodern types of hierarchical organic solidarity (Polanyi, 1997).

The first problem concerning the destruction of solidarity consists of the de-socialization of individuals. The evolution of functional systems presupposes the exclusion of individual consciousness from all access to social communication: a sharp distinction between the individual person and the societal community. The separation of the individual person from any fixed societal status, enforced and reflected by Protestantism and natural law theories, confronts this society with the problem of an unlimited and uncontrollable growth of individual consciousness and personal autonomy. From early modern times onwards, the ever more clearly apparent differentiation between psychic and social systems, between individual and society, has had the effect of an irreversible pluralization of world-views. Above all, the Protestant drive towards individualization makes religious confession dependent upon an external and pre-societal power: the purely individual conscience (Weber, 1978, p.17ff, p.536ff). This explodes the a priori perfect of a hitherto integrated collective consciousness, which from then on has to be recasted by contingent educational processes, and whose highly diverse results drive world-views into a collision course with each other, and finally into civil war.

No less critical is the second problem of capitalist accumulation and public education, which makes major differences out of minor ones and leads to the polarization of market-dependent income classes (Marx, 1969). Capitalist economy or public education produces by its own mechanisms of systems-integration what Niklas Luhmann has called a 'perverse selectivity': new social classes emerge which no longer depend on heritage but on the selective mechanisms of public education and free trade markets. In the 19th century, the growing working class becomes - as Marx has put it - a 'class of excluded people who are still included within society'. Capitalist economy needs the working people as living labour force, and as a force of production the workers are included in the system, but more or less excluded on the consumer's side. The consequence produced by the capitalist economy's own imperatives of reproduction threatens the system's self-preservation. Here too the a priori perfect of a hitherto hierarchically ordered society is dissolved, and the formation of classes becomes dependent upon contingent careers, whose consequences sharpen into the antagonistic class opposition of Capital and Labour.

Both these problems of the anarchically proliferating heterarchy of modern societies were impressively solved - in historical retrospect - by the democratic constitutional state established in the North Atlantic zone comprising Europe and North America. The rigid separation of law and morality and the linkage between positive law and (constitutionally positivized) subjective rights facilitated a legal institutionalization of world-view pluralism, while the inclusive principle of democratic self-legislation contributed to the participation of ever broader social strata and permitted the social state programming of society together with procedures of fair compromise formation.

Once the working class achieved unrestricted access to the political system, the realisation of democracy in terms of a social welfare state came to the top of the political agenda. In all North-Atlantic political regimes a new evolutionary stage of egalitarian organic solidarity has been institutionalized during the 20th century. In the long run, this was the main achievement of the constitutional revolutions of the 18th and 19th century. Whereas functional differentiation was the result of a blind process of social evolution, the constitutional control of political power, the introduction of human rights, and the democratic transformation of state sovereignty into popular sovereignty were effects of political revolutions. The success of these revolutions depended on the acceptance and acknowledgement of the people. Their intentions and self-understanding were involved, and these operated as a necessary condition of the revolutionary process. Modern revolutions gradually establish the unrestricted political inclusion of the whole population. The objects of law become the authors of legislation.

In the meantime, however, the limits of this solution have become recognizable. From the normative perspective of the human rights of all the participants in global social communication, the social injustice caused by a hugely unequal distribution of social wealth immediately strikes the eye, and it is no wonder that the 'Third World' as well as the 'Fourth World' have initially refused both democracy and the constitutional state and more or less openly fought against them. Furthermore, the factual evolution of a globally networked, functionally differentiated global society has marginalised democracy organized along state lines to the degree that democracy becomes ever more functionless. This is shown in particularly dramatic fashion in the originally innermost domain of modern democracy, in law itself.

Before I take up this last point, some remarks on terminology are in order. What is global society and why can it no longer be rationally integrated - or as Hegel put it, 'represented' - by the modern 'system of social ethics', the 'State'? Global society is society in the singular: there exists one, and only one, society. From the perspective of the participant, this was presumably so ever since the invention of language. We live, each of us, in one world and each new participant we encounter in communication always already appears within this world. For those acting within it, the social life world exists only in the singular. It first appears as a particular province only from the distanced perspective of the sociological observer. For the observer, life worlds and societies exist in the plural. And this also presents itself in modern society if - as in the tradition of social philosophy and sociology from Hegel to Marx, Durkheim and Weber - society is understood as a concrete totality: a culture or civilization, a human group, a historical construct, or national, regional or other collective subject. Yet, beyond this point, such an understanding has been inadequate to the highly abstract unity and global reality of modern society. An adequate understanding is reached only when 'society' is conceived along the lines of Niklas Luhmann and Jürgen Habermas as a communicative context (Habermas, 1981; Luhmann, 1984). From the perspective of the participant, the social life-world initially has to be minimally defined as a unity of communicative accessibility. This is something rather more abstract than a concrete totality. To my social life world belong all the communicative operations which appear within its horizon, whether they are familiar or strange, and belong to our respective regional culture or not. If communication comes about at all, the communicative unity of the social life-world is always already presupposed. So from the perspective of the observer, the same criterion of communicative accessibility holds for the identification of a society. With the aid of this criterion, we can then distinguish the singular global society from its predecessors in the plural. Societies in the plural existed as long as there were communicative contexts which were communicatively inaccessible to each other - in other words, until the threshold of modernity. Thereafter, there has existed only one society. It is important here not to confuse the singularization of society with its homogenization. Within this single society, many cultures are always communicatively accessible. Their members, however, cannot exit this society any longer, and it is therefore a global society which dictates to cultures and to substantial forms of life the conditions of their rise, development and transformation.

Modern society is thus global society from the very beginning, and the development of an ever more tightly-knit network, of ever more rapidly communicating media of dissemination and success-oriented media, has meanwhile led to the complete globalization of a society of functional systems which originally arose in Europe.[4] This society was once a European project, but it is so no longer. Extended to the dimensions of a global society, it has lost any European *'Sonderstellung'* or special status, as Max Weber phrased it, and it has been decentralized to the point where one can now say that Eurocentrism once did exist, but exists no longer. Each and everyone has to live in this society, and indeed - following the ongoing global destruction of household economies - each one lives within it as an individual, whether one wants it that way or not, whatever culture one comes from. It is the only society that there is, and everywhere within it is just as lacking in alternatives as its characterising individualism. Alternatives exist only within it, be they alternatives in terms of cultures and relations of production, class structures or ways of life, but these are not alternatives to functionally differentiated, individualized global society itself.

The process of globalization is in itself a deeply ambivalent phenomenon. On the one hand the process of globalization after World War II has in some respects made considerable progress in globalizing the former state-bound solidarity among strangers. This can be seen from:

1) The globalization of a *transnational network of legal relations*, private and public, from Lex Mercatoria to human rights, from maritime law to the United Nations Charter. Today a global legal system exists, that is no longer dependent on state power alone (Teubner, 1997).

2) *Legal personhood* has therefore attained a much broader meaning than *citizenship*. Even stateless persons today have a basic set of effective subjective rights, and human rights have some indirect influence even in countries like China (Cohen, 1996; Brunkhorst, 2000).

3) A rapidly evolving system of international and transnational contracts and institutions, supranational organisations and transnational courts are building a new level of *global governance* (Zürn, 1998; Oeter, 2000).

4) A *global human rights culture*, the global public of new media of dissemination, and non-governmental organisations are establishing an emerging global civil society (Cohen, 1996; Shute and Harley, 1993; Rosas, 1995; Thürer, 2000).

5) Civic virtues and human rights are given support by a growing minority in the global professional class of lawyers, physicians, scientists, bankers, and so on (Bertilsson, 2001).

But, on the other hand, the global public is only a *weak public*, and it is far from having the transnational power of binding decisions that is used to coping with the problem of the societal segregation of centre and periphery in modernity, nor is it able to transform the still existing global hierarchical organisation of solidarity, which is only weakly institutionalized, into strong egalitarian organic solidarity (Neves, 1992).

The globalization of markets, law, politics and education has now placed the two older problems of European modernity back on the agenda and with immediate impact, problems for which the democratic constitutional state had once found an impressive solution within its territorial borders: the problem of the pluralism of world-views, religions and cultures that clash with unmediated violence, and the problem of capitalism which has further developed into a global *'Räuber-kapitalismus'*, as Weber expressed it - a global robber capitalism (Wilke, 1998).

Where there is no democratic constitutional state with a clear separation between law and morality and no post-nation-state equivalent either, the interplay of societal individualism and cultural pluralism appears to end almost by necessity in fundamentalism. The return of religious civil war is the logical consequence. Fundamentalism is not something one is born into, as in a traditional society. Fundamentalism is not a matter of origins, estate, or caste. It is not a problem of millennial contradictions between 'civilizations'.[5] Fundamentalism arises only out of the mobilization of individuals. It arises from atomized, de-socialized individuals being drawn into a communal movement and it is therefore without preconditions. Fundamentalism acts in an almost postmodern way in its plundering of the semantic heritage, using it for its own rapidly changing goals. In this it resembles the older type of European nationalism. Fundamentalism is a consequence of the fact that the individual has been forced out across the world through functional differentiation.

As for the second problem, the dynamic of capitalist accumulation which follows a law of its own, and which today proceeds under the management of the global financial system, here only the democratic constitutional state has found a productive and, to some extent, egalitarian solution.

In the train of globalization - which I understand as the electronically accelerated intensification and networking of global communication - the problem of capitalism has shifted from inequality to exclusion from communication. One can of course travel the world today without, as previously, having to fear being treated as a foreigner without rights (Luhmann, 1993, p.573). Yet in order to enjoy this triumph, one needs money, a passport, a minimum level of education, etc. - in other words, you have to belong. And it is precisely this problem which global society cannot solve with its own means. In a globally networked world driven forward only by the mutually blind operations of its functional systems, problems pile up at the system's borders. This holds not only for the dangerous ecological conditions of the planet. The crisis expresses itself no less dramatically in the exclusion of millions of people from any social communication. For those who fall outside a functional system, be it in India, Brazil or Africa, or even as at present in many districts of New York or Paris, all others soon become inaccessible. Their voice will no longer be heard, often they are literally struck dumb.

The production of superfluous bodies, which are no longer required for work, is a direct consequence of globalization. And here the economic system has a negative primacy. It cannot steer society, but it can destroy it. If it collapses, almost everything else will collapse with it. This also holds true for all 'fixed and fast-frozen relations' between individuals set free (Marx and Engels, 1997, p.23). Those with no work have neither money, nor passport, nor opportunity to send their children to school and so on, and it can even become a serious issue of public debate - as in Brazil - whether their right to vote should be withdrawn. Describing the tragic situation of functionally superfluous people as class domination or exploitation (that is, as a social problem) is a massive, almost ideological downplaying of the problem, as Luhmann rightly emphasizes: 'While human beings count as persons within the sphere of inclusion, in the sphere of exclusion only their bodies appear to be important. Physical violence, sexuality and the elementary, compulsive satisfaction of needs are released and become immediately relevant, without being civilized through symbolic recursions' (Luhmann, 1997, p.632ff). The boundary line demarcating inclusion from exclusion is tangible in the baggage areas of passenger jets carrying the frozen-stiff bodies of those seeking asylum and work elsewhere, while those sitting with their counterfeit passports above in the passenger area have just managed to achieve inclusion.

It is these superfluous and unnecessary effects of heterarchically networked global society - unnecessary, that is, for the smooth functioning of the systems - which could be identified and corrected within the framework of the Western nation-state, and whose central steering medium has been and still remains law-enforcible, legally challengeable, democratically created and alterable through the procedurally informed will of the people (Maus, 1992; Habermas, 1992).

In the meantime, however, law has left the borders of the nation-state behind it and, closely entwined with the globalization of business and a de-statified politics, has turned into a self-reproducing, ever more tightly-knit fabric that encircles the planet as 'global law' (Luhmann, 1973, p.573ff). There is a global legal order beneath the level of the institutionalization of positive law. It is a legal order without a legally constituted state, and it extends from commercial law (Lex Mercatoria) across the internal legal codes of multinational firms, labor law, legislation pertaining to the professions, even laws governing sport, right through to positive international law and human rights (Teubner, 1997). In all these cases, nation-states are no longer the 'masters of international treaties', nor even the ultimate legislators. Global law functions without a state, in many areas as 'transnational private justice', but without being entrenched in the usual national or international systems of civil law (Teubner, 1996, p.236ff). Global society has a daily more tightly integrated legal order 'without central legislation or jurisdiction' (Luhmann, 1993, p.574). In its lack of transparency and lack of formal rationality and coherence, it resembles feudal law. It is here, in the system of global law, that the 're-feudalization' long feared by Ingeborg Maus seems to have become reality (Maus, 1986, 1992).

Globally networked 'polycontextural law' suits the uncontrolled evolution of fragmented global society. Here the dictum of Grotius is valid: *ubi societas ibi ius*, even when we are no longer dealing with a *societas civilis sive politica*. This is why no correction of the self-destructive dynamic of the global system is to be expected from a blindly proliferating global law; neither the civilizing of a pluralism hardened by fundamentalism nor the civilizing of capitalism and its dramatic exclusion effects.

The constitutional setting that works so well within the boarders of the Western nation-state fails within global polycontextural law and within the specific context of the state law of all the nations located on the periphery of the global society. Constitutions are - to pick up the typology developed by Karl Loewenstein - at best nominalist constitutions, that means constitutions without real normative impact (Loewenstein, 1959, p.151ff). The *overintegrated* minority regularily breaks the constitutional conventions while the *underintegrated* majority at best maintains the negative status of a passive object to the whole process of legal integration (Neves, 1992). Law can be built upon an autopoietic network *without* center and effective powers of legislation and jurisdiction, but - as Luhmann objects against Teubner - law that remains open for the direct access of 'opportunistic elites' and the particular interests of those groups in power (Luhmann, 1993, pp.58, 81). The consequence is that law loses its ability to draw borders that divide the spheres of freedom of all legal subjects equally.

These regressive traits appear particularly clearly where the most important evolutionary triumph of positive law is reclaimed: in the cancellation of the boundary separating law and morality. Not only, as Maus, Neves or Teubner show, are there to be found numerous examples in national constitutional law and transnational commercial law, but the most recent development of human rights, codified and positivized in quasi-constitutional fashion within the UN Charter, illustrates the same tendency.[6] As Martii Koskenniemi has stated in an important recent essay, the transfer of almost all competence for human rights from the General Assembly of the United Nations to the Security Council has precisely this consequence. The Security Council, rigged out with *carte blanche* powers and interpretative authority, uncontrolled by any public body or legal procedure, cordoned off from the General Assembly, freed from all limitations of power-sharing, engages in a random human rights interventionism (or, also, non-interventionism) that is only legitimized as yet by moral or putatively moral aims (Koskenniemi, 1998). Such a de-positivization and re-moralisation of human rights in the service of executive powers could hardly be a means to civilize the latent fundamentalist pluralism of individualized world-views and religions which have become dependent on moral-ethical decisions.

Furthermore, global law cannot be utilized in a court of law, and only in the rarest of cases can it be enforced. In a way comparable to old Roman civil law, the enforcement of international law is at the will of those who have the *power* to enforce it. The Security Council is in the same position as the old Roman *praetor*, who judged the cases but could not order the enforcement of his judgment. Nevertheless, the entire legal structure becomes dependent on the hegemonial powers whose clients all smaller powers have to become, if they want to get their right, in international affairs today as well as in civic affairs in ancient Roman times.

The existing world law is 'soft', not 'hard' law - law without sufficient material enforcement (Brunkhorst, 1996). 'Polycontextural law' is a caricature of the utopia of a multi-cultural society, a patchwork of minorities of the most diverse origin, split up into every conceivable type of normalizing power, as Michel Foucault mentioned, whether ethnic, religious, technological, professional, organizational, or whether exercised by the secret police, or by class specific, or whatever other critera (Teubner, 1996, p.245). It is law far removed from politics, without a constitutional form, without democracy, without hierarchy from below, without an unbroken chain of democratic legitimation.[7] This heterarchy is a rule without a ruler, but no mastery of law.[8] It blindly follows its own logic, uncoordinated, self-referential, chaotic, expansionist and imperialist (Teubner, 1996, p.252). The bond of constitutions that linked law and politics within the nation-state through 'hard' law, thus enabling the democratic legitimation of law, is torn asunder in global law. The question of the identity of the author of this law remains open, and thus unanswerable, just as the question of the future of democracy itself. But who if not the objects of this law themselves are to prevent continually changing coalitions of dictators, robber gangs and gangster syndicates from occupying the spaces left vacant, today here, tomorrow there, enveloping the world in violence and oppression?

The problems solved by the European nation-state have returned within global society. It may be that the second chance of modern democracy lies in the negative identity of the problems, even if the small-format solution of state segmentation hardly seems to have a future, and a different solution - on the way to the 'third democratic transformation' - cannot as yet be discerned.

Vague perspectives emerge at most at the regional level, for example in the European Union. Here it will be decided in the medium term whether a democracy is to exist which will force onto the independent systems of law and economy, at least in this region of the world, the 'power' which derives (in the phraseology of national constitutions) 'from the people', or whether any democracy will exist at all. Perhaps social evolution will reveal something better, but no proposals are to be expected from social evolution. While evolution will go this way or that, we still have to act; and to those acting there remains meanwhile only the hope that we will finally succeed in democratically shaping global society.

Notes

1 Cf. Carl Schmitt (1988, p.304): The 'load-bearing and formative quantities', as it goes in a text from 1939, 'are today no longer states, as in the 18th and 19th centuries, but empires'. The argument is an apologia, and is intended to relieve the war policy of the Nazi regime of any ties to existing international law between states (cf. Schmitt, 1985, pp.375).
2 For a more actual version of a similar theses about the new *raison d'etat*, see Klaus Dieter Wolf (2000).
3 On the consequences of hospitalisation, see Foucault (1978).
4 On the distinction between 'media of dissemination' and 'media of success', see Luhmann (1997, p.202ff).
5 This is the thesis of 'cultural idealism' (Huntington, 1993).
6 On constitutional and commercial law, see Maus (1996) and Teubner (1996).
7 On the democratic legitimation chain, see Böckenförde (1991, p.299).
8 On the paradox of 'mastery without a master', see Schütz (1997).

References

Arendt, H. (1986), *Elemente und Ursprünge totalitärer Herrschaft*, Piper, München.
Arendt, H. (1987), *Vita activa oder vom tätigen Leben*, Piper, München.
Bertilsson, M. (2001), 'Professions on the Road to Global Power: The Case of the Legal Profession', in this volume.
Böckenförde, E.-W. (1991), *Staat, Verfassung, Demokratie*, Suhrkamp, Frankfurt am Main.

Brunkhorst, H. (1996), 'Paradigmenwechsel im Völkerrecht?', in Lutz-Bachmann, M. and J. Boman (eds), *Frieden durch Recht*, Suhrkamp, Frankfurt am Main.

Brunkhorst, H. (2000), 'Right and the Sovereignty of the People in the Crisis of the Nation State', *Ratio Juris*, vol. 13 no. 1, pp.49-62.

Cohen, J. (1996), 'Rights and Citizenship in H. Arendt', *Constellations* no. 2, pp.164-189.

Dahl, R. (1989), *Democracy and its Critics*, Yale University Press, New Haven.

Foucault, M. (1978), *Wahnsinn und Gesellschaft*, Suhrkamp, Frankfurt am Main.

Guéhenno, J.-M. (1994), *Das Ende der Demokratie*, Beck, München.

Habermas, J. (1981), *Theorie des kommunikativen Handelns*, 2 vols., Suhrkamp, Frankfurt am Main.

Habermas, J. (1992), *Faktizität und Geltung*, Suhrkamp, Frankfurt am Main.

Huntington, S. P. (1993), 'The Clash of Civilizations', *Foreign Affairs: An American Quarterly Review*, Summer, pp.22-49.

Koskenniemi, M. (1998), 'Die Polizei im Tempel', in Brunkhorst, H. (ed.), *Einmischung erwünscht?: Weltbürgerrecht in einer Welt der Bürgerkriege*, Fischer, Frankfurt am Main.

Loewenstein, K. (1959), *Verfassungslehre*, Mohr, Tübingen.

Luhmann, N. (1984), *Soziale Systeme*, Suhrkamp, Frankfurt am Main.

Luhmann, N. (1990), 'Verfassung als evolutionäre Errungenschaft', *Rechtshistorisches Journal*, no. 9, p.176ff.

Luhmann, N. (1993), *Das Recht der Gesellschaft*, Suhrkamp, Frankfurt am Main.

Luhmann, N. (1997), *Die Gesellschaft der Gesellschaft*, Suhrkamp, Frankfurt am Main.

Marx, K. (1969), *Das Kapital*, 3 vols., Dietz, Berlin.

Marx, K. and F. Engels (1997), *Manifest der kommunistischen Partei*, Reclam, Stuttgart.

Maus, I. (1986), *Rechtstheorie und politische Theorie im Industriekapitalismus*, Fink, München.

Maus, I. (1992), *Zur Aufklärung der Demokratietheorie*, Suhrkamp, Frankfurt am Main.

Maus, I. (1996), 'Zum Verhältnis von Recht und Moral aus demokratietheoretischer Sicht', in Beyertz, Kurt (ed.), *Politik und Ethik*, Reclam, Stuttgart.

Neves, M. (1992), *Verfassung und positives Recht in der peripheren Moderne*, Duncker & Humblot, Berlin.

Oeter, S. (2000), *Internationale Organisation oder Weltföderation?*, in Brunkhorst, H. and Kettner, M. (eds.), *Globalisierung und Demokratie*, Suhrkamp, Frankfurt.

Polanyi, K. (1997), *The Great Transformation*, Suhrkamp, Frankfurt am Main.

Rosas, A. (1995), 'State Sovereignty and Human Rights: Towards a Global Constitutional Project', in *Political Studies* (Special Issue: Politics and Human Rights), vol. 18.

Schmitt, C. (1963), *Der Begriff des Politischen*, Duncker & Humblot, Berlin.

Schmitt, C. (1985), *Verfassungsrechtliche Aufsätze*, Duncker & Humblot, Berlin.

Schmitt, C. (1988), *Positionen und Begriffe*, Duncker & Humblot, Berlin.

Schütz, A. (1997), 'The Twilight of the Global Polis', Teubner, G. (ed.), *Global Law Without a State*, Aldershot, Dartmouth.

Shute, S. and S. Harley (eds.) (1993), *In Human Rights*, Basic Books, New York.

Teubner, G. (1996), 'Des Königs viele Leiber – Die Selbstdekonstruktion der Hierarchie des Rechts', *Soziale Systeme*, no. 2.

Teubner, G (ed) (1997), *Global Law Without a State*, Aldershot, Dartmouth.

Thürer, D. (2000), 'Citizenship und Demokratieprinzip: Föderative Ausgestaltung im innerstaatlichen, europäischen globalen Rechtskreis', in Brunkhorst, H. and M. Kettner (eds.), *Globalisierung und Demokratie*, Suhrkamp, Frankfurt am Main.

Weber, M. (1978), *Gesammelte Aufsätze zur Religionssoziologie, Vol. 1*, Mohr, Tübingen.

Willke, H. (1998), 'Komplexität und Demokratie', in Brunkhorst, H. (ed.), *Demokratischer Experimentalismus*, Suhrkamp, Frankfurt am Main.

Wolf, K. D. (2000), *Die neue Staatsräson – Zwischenstaatliche Kooperation als Demokratieproblem in der Weltgesellschaft*, Nomos, Baden-Baden.

Zürn, M. (1948), *Regieren jenseits des Nationalstaats*, Suhrkamp, Frankfurt am Main.

11 Professions on the Road to Global Power: The Case of the Legal Profession

MARGARETA BERTILSSON

In this chapter I shall address a straightforward question: What will be the role of the professions in the upcoming global society? Will they form a new transnational, de-territorialized upper class in pursuit of their own luxurious interests? Will they divide and serve interests other than their own? Or will they perhaps be subjected to other control mechanisms, which may weaken their own group interests?

Although these questions are straightforward, their answers are certainly complicated - and very speculative. They can be addressed only indirectly, by examining recent discussions concerning the legal profession in a global society. Professions differ in profile and outlook, and what may be true for the legal profession, may be less true for the medical profession, for architects, dentists, and so on. The aim of addressing just one profession is not to conclude the discussion, but rather to frame some questions that may be helpful in analysing the role of other professions in an increasingly global society. These questions will concern the following: will global professions accentuate the patterns of power and control that we already see occurring on the nation-state level - or will a different mode of conduct emerge?

Before exemplifying the question with the case of a global legal profession and its profile, I shall address the fate of the 'professional complex' as discussed in social theory of the last couple of decades. The purpose of such a presentation is to inquire whether globalisation processes intensify processes already in operation at the nation-state level, or whether there are other (emergent) processes at work on a more complex social level. Such questions help formulate profound social theory issues that deal with patterns of emergence: is the globalisation of society but an extension of already ongoing social processes at the nation-state level or a distinctively new societal development?

Pre-Modern Professions as Global Forces?

The gothic cathedrals one sees when travelling around Europe are emblems of the power of the craft once held by builders and architects. The legal profession prides itself on its ancient roots, and Roman Law, in its various forms of reception, is often assumed to be one of the constitutive pillars of Western civilisation (Berman, 1983). During the epoch of colonialism, Roman Law spread into the far corners of the globe; today it is hailed as one remote source of global legal discourse.

Organised as guilds in mediaeval society, lawyers, architects, builders, and scholars had an important role in spreading a material as well as intellectual culture across the European continent. In colonial times, their skills and practices spread to various corners of the world. Quite early on they developed the idea of the 'network society' in that they realised the power(s) that resided in social organisation (Castells, 1996-1998). As individual practitioners they were eventually in the hands of their masters, the emperors or kings, but as guilds they could unite and form a collective source of power. This is particular true of the scholars of the early universities in Southern Europe; they were but a mobile collective gathered around their masters, and as long as they stayed in the city of their choice, they became important financial assets. Emile Durkheim, in his study of the early European university guilds, tells the story of how these guilds could decide to break up from their sites if the burghers and/or local kings did not supply them with the requisite facilities (Durkheim, 1977). They travelled then to another city where their collective existence enriched local hostels and inns. Their mobile life-style came to an end, however, when scholars were given permanent shelters. When the scholar guilds were 'domesticated', their freedom of movement was considerably impeded, although their material conditions improved. The same conditions applied to the early Bologna lawyers: as commentators they could sell their services to local European rulers and kings, but as employees they could eventually expect a lordship for themselves.

Given this pre-history of professional 'roamers' in early Renaissance Europe, one could expect that with the global onslaught of today, there would be good reason for professional practitioners of various crafts to once again assume a free life-style and access to hitherto unseen and unrestricted universe of global work and travel.

With the rise of the nation-state, the professional guilds - whether university scholars or legal councils - became tied to their national masters/rulers. Providing expertise to their sovereign powers, they became strategic advisors spreading 'his master's voice' in different areas of life. Legal scholars were assigned a strategic role in bringing about modern state developments. They had a decisive function in gathering diverse sources of power into one central agent: the sovereign. The same is probably true of the early engineers, as their areas of competence were necessary in strengthening military power. Early on, the learned professions, lawyers, architects, painters, surgeons, and scholars of various kinds had access to science, and more importantly, they developed skills in applying science to local conditions. Renaissance science was no longer merely 'discourse'. It demanded increasingly sophisticated technological skills. Science became technical and evaluated for what it could achieve practically. Modern (natural) science is to a very great extent equivalent to technological exploitation. Modern professions are responsible for the technological exploitation and application of abstract science to practical concerns. In the language of Talcott Parsons, the modern professions are key actors in linking universalised knowledge and specific - contextualised - application (Parsons, 1966, 1967). The rise of modern mass-society, with its emphasis on mass education, health, and legal services, would not be possible in the absence of the modern professions of teaching, health and legal services. The 'professional complex' - as Talcott Parsons called it - is a key structural factor in the understanding of the rise of modern (Western) society (Parsons, 1977).

What is happening to this professional complex in the era of global development? As premodern forces, the guilds were an important factor in the rise of modern state society. They had the power to link tradition with scientific skills. There is no reason to believe that their historic mission would now be at an end; on the contrary, some professions seem to be especially enhanced by the rise of global power. This is due especially to their possession of linguistic and scientific skills, but also because modern science - be it medicine, dentistry, architecture, law or design - operates almost exclusively on the global level. Italian design or Danish architecture is culturally marked because of its global popularity. The natural and the technical sciences are today increasingly pooled as biotechnology now termed life science by EU and as such, marketed on a global scale.

Modern biomedicine no longer operates on the corporeal level (the individual) but on the 'dividual' level, where genes and gene pools are interesting to the extent to which they can be artificially produced and thus distributed on a mass-scale.[1] The case of biotechnology is especially in focus, as it is heavily value-laden: we resist gene-manipulated food on the domestic markets, but when confronted with the arguments that gene-manipulation may eventually solve the problem of starvation in the Third World, we are confronted with a serious ethical dilemma. These are the typical public issues now stirred up by the advance of bioscience technologies. For such technologies, bodies and nations are fairly uninteresting relicts of the past which professionals of various sorts will have to deal with. Certainly, modern science and modern technology generate new professions, but the old ones - law, medicine and dentistry - are not yet exhausted as historical actors. To translate abstract laboratory science into actual market potentials, to search for patent rights and distribute the services more equally are the future of that 'great arch' of professional action with which studies of professional power always have been concerned (Perkin, 1996). The notion of the great arch stands for the balanced demand that professions, also in the future, are concerned with both the market and the public (self-interest and public interest). If there is too much of a leaning to one side or the other, professions quickly lose trust and thus their 'honourable' social position in mediating collective interests.

Global markets rather than national states are likely to be the future masters of such professions. To the extent to which professional 'closures' arise as 'sources of power', with capacities to control and/or regulate both market and public, professions are potentially forming new globally operating ruling classes. The knowledge that they possess constitutes important elements of power, and will eventually be exploited as such. The question is whether such professional technical forms of power can operate free of context and form their own culture - or if such professional cultures are always part and parcel of a greater cultural web. Are professions as we have come to know them in the West potential global operators, or will their technical power be demarcated as merely

'Westernised' science and technology? Can the global discourse help shed light on the 'peculiarity' of Western theory and practice?

Discourses on Globalisation

Globalisation has emerged as the new topical issue in the social sciences in the last decade. It has the advantage, I would propose, that it carries a reference to 'out there': it is about something outside itself. It forces us to look at a reality, and is therefore refreshing in the social sciences, which for years have been enmeshed in their own narrative styles. The global world hangs together in one sense or another: its parts are interdependent, and the question is how and with what effects? Is the world around us turning more and more homogenous because of the spread of finance capital, consumption styles and de-localised artefacts such as Irish pubs and Bolivian folk music now found in all corners of the world? Or is the world turning more and more heterogeneous, as antithetical, polarised - if interrelated - discourses and surface phenomena keep emerging? Can the local be understood only by reference to the global, and can the global in turn only be understood by reference to its manifold and locally situated practices? On the whole, discussions on globalisation appear as various positions on a continuum, between the two nodes of homogeneity and heterogeneity, respectively (Featherstone et al., 1990).

Some observers have hailed the advent of globalisation as an instance of liberation and freedom, not least for financial capital, which can now easily move from region to region in search of cheap labour and ever-increasing market opportunities. The effect of global capital is that it unites the world into one common global work place, and spreading global consumption. Other voices in the globalisation arena express opposition not only against the term itself, but the social and cultural inequalities, which are said to lie in its wake. As an instrument of uncontrolled liberalism, globalisation has become a device to undermine the regulative efforts of the welfare state. Modes of resisting the global onslaught are regaled as flames of proud self-determination in a world choking the voice of local rules. From this point of view, such feudal efforts as those advanced by, for instance, Saddam Hussein, Slobodan Milosevic and today by the Palestinian freedom fighters can even be hailed, in the midst of their atrocities, as examples of resistance against US global military imperialism and Western hegemony.

Wherever we stand on that global continuum - the end poles of which are homogenisation and heterogenization - social science is recapturing its referential character; there is a world out there calling for our attention. Globalisation, in its many different usage, may thus have salutary effects on the social science community. It has the power to integrate widely separate discourses and to shape a common social scientific agenda. This requires, however, that we abandon the ideological overtones, which today seem to hamper serious inquiry and divide contemporary discourses into ideological blocks (Therborn, 1998, 2000).

In a recent discussion on globalisation, the Swedish scholar Göran Therborn distinguishes five 'topical discourses' (2000, pp.151-153): (1) *competition economics*, focusing on 'intensified world-wide competition and its implications for firms, workers and states'; (2) a *socio-critical* reaction against that very discourse; the problem of *state (im) potency* in the face of global economy; (3) the *cultural global discourse* focusing on such issues as the overwhelming 'Americanisation' of our material-symbolic world and the spread of 'McDonaldisation' to remote corners of the globe; (4) a concern with 'homogenisation processes although anthropologists eagerly promise that we are heading towards more and more 'hybridisation', 'creolisation' and the like; (5) *planetary ecology*, a concern with humankind in its interaction with an increasingly threatened nature. Therborn seemingly neglects the web of transport and communication, which allows these topical discourses to emerge as common, concerns of mankind in the first place. However different these five 'topical discourses' are on their surface, and however different the communities of knowledge that engage in critical exchange, the five discourses do share one feature in common: they are, with the possible exemption of the cultural discourse, quite specialised and, in the language of Luhmann, 'second-order' discourses (Luhmann, 1997). As a rule, a global discourse is a professionalized discourse, as it assumes a highly abstracted mode of human communication not governed by events in the here and now, but with events happening at any place.

The aim of this paper is to explore the sociological underpinnings of global discourse. By exploring the role of some major professions and the spread of professional knowledge in global development, it seems possible to illuminate what on the surface appear to be distinct ideological discourses and attitudes. For instance, how can one characterise the conduct of the legal profession in the globalisation process? Is it possible to detect the emergence of global legal culture breaking off from the previous tight link between law and the individual nation-state? The major professions were once central actors in the formation of the nation-state, and the question is whether they are equally central in global formation processes. Although I will limit my discussion to the legal profession, the purpose of the discussion is to try to shed light on the wider role of the professional complex in global society: do globalization tendencies heighten or weaken processes already in motion at a lower level, or do such tendencies produce new emergent phenomena?

Convergence Theory Revisited

At one time, convergence theory typically applied to the rise of 'industrial society', the technological power of which was seen as putting an end to the ideological efforts of the old 'class society' (Kerr et al., 1960). Today, convergence is again on the agenda - as globalisation. The old convergence thesis also embraced the rise of 'professional society', and it is my purpose here to re-address this complex, now on the global scene.

In sociological theory, the role of the professions and professional knowledge in social transformation is a well-debated and controversial issue. In the Golden Days of functionalist theories in sociology in the 1950s, the proclamation of a potential convergence between market capitalism and state socialism was at the heart of mainstream professional sociology. The theme of 'industrial society' and its functional requisites formed a common platform, on whose terms social development as increasing differentiation and specialisation was coached. From this point of view, societies could be graded along a modernisation scale. In sociology, these themes fused in 'the end of ideology' (Bell, 1960). At the time of the Cold War, professional sociology - and long before Anthony Giddens' recent invention - aimed at carving out a 'third way' for modern society, mediating Liberalism and Socialism. Central to these theories was the role assigned to the system of professional labour or the professional complex. A functional stratification system based on a complex division of labour was seen in the long run to absolve the old class antagonisms so characteristic of early industrial society (Davis and Moore, 1967).

A prerequisite for an advanced system of professional labour was a modernised higher education system based on merit and achievement among students. The old class lines that previously characterised academic circles were to be broken down, not least because they hampered the growth of specialised labour power. The reformation of the higher education system instituted significant policy reforms in many Western European societies after the Second World War and these reforms have been on the political agenda all through the second half of the 20th century. The lead in these reforms was - once again - found in the United States, where extensive educational state reforms were implemented in California, Michigan and New York State. I mention these policy reforms in the US higher education system as functional modernisation theories and modern 'professional' sociology to a significant extent stimulated them. Clark Kerr, perhaps the most well known advocate of 'industrial society', and a legendary President of the University of California, played a key role in bringing about educational reform in that state in the 1950s and 1960s. The investment in education reform and in scholarship activities supported by large American foundations after the Second World War (such as the Marshall, Carnegie, and Ford Foundations) had a huge impact in Western Europe. In a remarkably short time, a decade or so, European scholars and students turned their back on the old continental universities and hurried to the US in pursuit of doctorates and research fellowships. European higher education systems were never (and are still not) efficiently 'Americanised', but - and this is the important point - their yardstick for achievement was set for by the American system of higher education (Ben-David, 1977). The institutionalisation of modern empirical research in the social sciences was to a very large extent also a consequence of these higher education reforms in Western Europe (Wagner, 1990). Professional sociology education in many Western European countries was thus a functional requisite of the overriding cultural value system, which found its expression in the professional complex. It is necessary to keep in mind these auxiliary by-products of the professional division of labour in light of the profound critique that later targeted functional sociology, classic modernisation theories, and the convergence theory of social development.

The reactions against these classic theories of modernisation, structural-functionalism and convergence theory are well known among social scientists. Functionalist theories in general and their derivations in terms of social development were vehemently attacked on theoretical, methodological and ideological grounds. Often the two kinds of attacks merged, but it is analytically helpful to keep them separate. Theoretically and methodologically, sociological convergence theories were criticised on the following grounds:

1) Failure to bring history (or the actor) back in.
2) Ignorance of world-system dynamics: centres and peripheries.
3) Neglect of discourse theory - professional micro-power.

1) Failure to Bring History (or the Actor) Back In

Despite their liberal-social concerns, theories of convergence based on functionalist reasoning came under heavy attack, amongst other things, for reading history from a 'modernist' point of view. Although these theories had been constructed so as to counteract the Hegelian-Marxist position in classic social theory, they could nevertheless be criticised for harbouring the same analytical principles of a *causa finalis* as their predecessors. Modern neo-Weberian conflict theories in sociology began as a critique of functionalist reasoning and its overarching tendencies to focus on consensus, contractual agreement and systemic balances rather than on power, interests, domination, conflicts and compromises within concrete historical settings (Collins, 1975). The understanding of social development from within a unilinear - evolutionary - logic, realising itself in history as increasing differentiation and specialisation, with modernisation, capitalism and democracy as its end results, was now criticised for its historical and political one-sidedness. The United States of America, the primary location of functionalist sociology, was not necessarily the endpoint of history but one form of capitalist development and of social domination.

With regard to 'the professional project', the new orientations in social theory had considerable consequences for studies of various professions. As Dietrich Ruschemeyer pointed out in his comparative studies of the legal professions in Germany and in the United States, the social basis of professional power was very differently based in the case of Continental Europe as compared to the Anglo-Saxon world (1973, 1986). In Continental Europe the law professions were intimately tied to state power, and the expansion of the state led to a concomitant expansion of legal services and of the legal profession. The predominant market orientation of the key professions in the US, those of doctors and lawyers, was deeply entrenched in the particular history of US society. The understanding of various professional modes of conduct required deep-seated historical understanding of the diverse power-contexts in which professions were embedded. State and market societies, respectively, provided the leading professions with different sets of power-nexus with regard to authority, collective interests, and client contacts. There was no immediate reason to believe that these deep-seated historical variations were to diminish or to converge in the foreseeable future. On the contrary, these societies could very well pursue different lines of social development, and thus types of professional domination. Thus, modernisation could no longer be viewed as a one-dimensional process where the professions gradually played a key role. Analysis of the professions in any particular society demanded analysis of their structural power settings and relations to other key social actors: the state, the polity, dominant classes and market situations (Torstendahl and Burrage, 1990).

Another epoch-making study criticising the professional project of modernisation theories was Magali Sarfatti-Larson's *The Rise of Professionalism: A Sociological Analysis* (1977). Her Marxist-inspired analysis of lawyers, doctors and engineers in the United States in the 20th century revealed the transformation of the US class system pivoting the key professions as merging with, or else, replacing the old capitalist class. The new professional service society was evolving into a powerful system of giant, opaque organisations based on monopoly capital. Instead of breaking up the capitalist class system, the major professions had in fact strengthened their source of power. As part of monopoly capitalism the professional service system had evolved as a self-reproducing source of money transferral in terms of which clients were constantly and unknowingly exploited. From this point of view 'professionalism' was but the ideological self-deceit of advanced capitalism and its peculiar form of class-domination. Sarfatti Larson's study of a new form of social exploitation in the name of professional services efficiently undermined the naive 'altruist ethos' upon which earlier theories were based.

Sarfatti-Larsen's study has been characterised as a 'collective mobility project' in terms of which professional practitioners - as a collective and because of their privileged closures sanctioned by state power - move up the social ladder. Such a collective mobility project is seen as a radical critique of the functionalist belief in 'individual mobility' in industrial society. A group of practitioners - such as lawyers - collectively close off either the supply or the demand side of professional services in order to save their own privileged status position and high incomes. The supply side is closed off by not letting other related professions enter their privileged territory, and the demand side is closed off by *numerus clausus* with regard to student training. In a society in which entries into the elite are based upon 'credentials' rather than on privileged birth, the higher education system is in the centre of attention (Collins, 1979).

In the spirit of the 'collective mobility project' staged by Sarfatti-Larsen, several other critical studies of professional power appeared, mostly in the United States. American lawyers were typically seen as 'ambulance chasers' in that they saw a profit in any insurance claim, no matter its origin. Indeed, the critique of US law and US lawyers as a threat to social development (rather than its central bearer) accelerated in the 1970s and 1980s. Litigation claims hampered all segments of US society, and the American lawyers threatened their fellow professionals in surgery, engineering, academia and so forth (Crozier, 1984). The threat of 'being taken to court' and forced to pay a huge claim could efficiently bury any initiative with uncertain outcomes (as is typically the case when professional services are offered).

The critique of functionalism from a conflict-theoretical position often assumed - especially in the case of studies of major professions - an ideological form. It was basically a theoretical critique directed against functionalist premises. Instead of unity, systemic balances, uneven development, power and interests (subjective or collective) were now seen as the base of social life, hence also a crucial component in the study of professions. Historical differences, actors' positions within localised systems of power, and strategic games were now assuming a comprehensive theoretical interest. The 'professional project' was by no means refuted by the critical (conflict) position, but our understanding of it was radically altered. The professional project was now interpreted as the rise of new powerful actors to legitimacy - and money. The class system in advanced capitalism must take into account the new historic actors - the professional practitioners. Also Marxist class theory was clearly affected by the professional complex, since professional actors often occupied 'contradictory class positions' (Wright, 1978).

In the wake of the critical spirit in studying the thrust of modern professions into class-power, one branch of studies launched a new progressive reading based on 'intellectuals' in the Marxist and Gramscian tradition (Gouldner, 1979; Konrád and Szelényi, 1979). The 'new class project' offered an understanding of the radical potentials of professional (mass) power. Due to the explosion in mass education, the enlargement of the modern state (the New Deal, the welfare state) and the consequent burgeoning of both supply and demand of professional services in advanced capitalist countries (as in more advanced socialism), segments of the professionally educated from within different specialities would be inclined, so it was posited, to join more progressive and leftist forces in society, thus curbing monopoly power from within. Such speculations were not solely idealistic, but were also based on employment statistics: the mass of practitioners now finding themselves in a tight market for services would perhaps gain by enlarging their services to groups which previously had little or no access to professional advice. Radical lawyers, doctors, academics, and radical clergy now joined leftist projects both in their home countries and abroad. The radicalisation of segments of professional practice was characteristic of the late 1960s - as it had been before in the 1930s, though on a smaller scale. Mass education helped in 'curbing the passions and the interests' in that there was a surplus of professional labour and services, especially in the welfare society.

As I am about to study in greater detail the global profile of the legal profession, it is worthwhile here mentioning how radicalisation affected the 'most conservative professionals' of them all, the jurists and the lawyers. Indications of such radicalisation were their increasing interest in and proclivity to enter government welfare programmes, legal aid services, or general reform movements - not least in the Third World. One standing criticism directed against the legal profession is its intimate link to powerful actors, from the emperors and kings in previous times, to powerful government and market agents in modern times. The radicalisation of the late 1960s brought about, among other things the 'legal aid' movement, under whose auspices less privileged groups obtained access to legal council. Lawyers joined various consumer and citizens groups, thus strengthening segments of 'civil society' against the market and the state. It is difficult to assess the long term social effects of such radicalisation measures, but they have certainly made an impact upon modern cultures in advanced societies, both in the United States and in Western Europe. Collective 'mobilisation' (rather than Sarfatti Larson's 'collective mobility') with regard to issues such as localisation of sites for nuclear waste, chemical disposal, and establishment of the EU project among citizens is more often than not spearheaded by leading jurists.

Segments of radical lawyers and jurists have entered the criminal justice system, offering services to those prisoners who are at the bottom of the social ladder and often permanently excluded from participation in social life. In the case of Scandinavia, radical lawyers have often assumed a high profile in that they have had immediate access to governmental circles. This is particularly true of Norway but can be found in other Scandinavian countries as well.

However, in a later US discussion surveying how the 'new class project' has affected the legal profession, using hindsight, i.e. after the radical waves of the sixties, Szelényi and Martin (1989, pp.256-288) advanced the view that the radicalisation of US lawyers appears less pronounced. They say that this group has re-entered the 'collective mobility project' (rather than the collective mobilisation project of radical lawyers), and that this turn is probably due to the rise of 'corporate law' and large law firms where lawyers can earn a fortune. Further on in the discussion, I shall turn to this phenomenon of 'mega-law' because of its immediate relevance for studying global legal processes.

2) Ignorance of World-System Dynamics: Centres and Peripheries

While the critical interpretation and reformulation of the professional complex in terms of a more advanced class system flourished within highly developed countries such as the US and in Western Europe, its international pendant was formulated along the lines of world-system theory (Wallerstein, 1974, 1980, 1989; Frank, 1969). Such theories certainly did not address the professional complex explicitly, but rather as a component of world capitalism. The role of lawyers, economists and political consultants in furthering Western (or US) domination was a topic of concern, not the least in Latin American countries, where endogenous revolutionary movements were violently crushed. The Peace Corps, which sent young students and trainees abroad, was now attacked as a link in Western domination and control.

Economic at the bottom, world-system theory addressed the relation of the centre(s) and the peripheries, and the theme of exploitation on a global scale. While the centre(s) grew immensely rich, the peripheries grew proportionately poorer, and this asymmetry was seen to be a consequence of imposed development programmes, which in the name of modernisation, were spread around the world.

But parallel to the 'new class project' in the West, a radicalised stratum of indigenous intellectuals emerged to world fame in the wake of the critique of modernist development theories. These were the 'native intellectuals' of Latin America, Africa, and Asia. Fidel Castro, Frantz Fanon and Mao Tse Tung are names that made a lasting impression on 'world consciousness' at the time. In the peripheries new revolutionary movements arose demanding 'new' intellectuals who could inflame poor farmers, labourers, and indigenous population groups. These revolutionary intellectuals were to raise the consciousness of 'oppressed people' from the debasement they had experienced for centuries in the hands of Western colonisation and oppression. The tone of Frantz Fanon in *the Wretched of the Earth* (1968 (1963)) was mighty in convincing Western oppressors of the colonising tendencies of their own neutral-scientific technological language:

> I am ready to concede that on the plane of factual being the past existence of an Aztec civilisation does not change anything very much in the diet of the Mexican peasant of today. I admit that all the proofs of a wonderful Songhai civilisation will not change the fact that today the Songhais are underfed and illiterate, thrown between sky and water with empty heads and empty eyes. But it has been remarked several times that this passionate search for a national culture which existed before the colonial era finds its legitimate reason in the anxiety shared by native intellectuals to shrink away from that Western culture in which they all risk being swamped. Because they realise they are in danger of losing their lives and thus becoming lost to their people, these men, hot-headed and with anger in their hearts, relentlessly determine to renew contact once more with the oldest and most pre-colonial springs of life of their people [...] Perhaps this passionate research and this anger are kept up or at least directed by the secret hope of discovering beyond the misery of today, beyond self-contempt, resignation, and abjuration, some very beautiful and splendid era whose existence rehabilitates us both in regard to ourselves and in regard to others (pp.209-210).

The theme of colonisation was transferred from the peripheries to the centre as it entered into the midst of Western (professional) discourse. The dependency relations and the theme of domination at the heart of the criticism by 'native intellectuals' against Western language and practices infected - ironically (!) - the grammar of Western professional power. Professional practices in law, medicine, social work, and in academia generally were now criticised for their 'colonising' of everyday syntax/diction and understanding. As a consequence, the logic of science was severely criticised for harbouring hegemonic power. Western feminism, in particular, gained from the colonising discourse, since women were seen as oppressed victims of impersonal powers and understanding. New social movements, such as the Green movement, inspired by the colonisation theme and fuelled by the message that we need to emancipate ourselves from the technical-scientific elite, arose across nations and continents.

3) Neglect of Discourse Theory - Professional Micro-Power

The discovery of dependency relations in 'professional discourse' and clients' concern led to yet another 'critical turn' in the study of professions. Most well known in this genre is probably the range of studies inspired by Michel Foucault. At the heart of this critical turn is the study of the immanent power which resides in professional talk and the practices that it generates. Professional practices, of whatever sort, are seen as the emergence, consolidation and reproduction of invisible power structures in terms of which the life practices of common actors are stripped of spontaneous engagement and human vitality. In the nature of categorisation, of applying labels and epithets, lies an immediate interest in controlling and thus subsuming 'the other'. Critical discourse studies aimed at re-discovering the original, the 'native' discourse and practices that had been suppressed in the name of progressive science and technology.

In the case of law, Jürgen Habermas also seized upon the colonising theme and introduced in the midst of a liberal theory of law and justice, law's double bind: law as 'system' and as 'understanding', or *Lebenswelt* (Habermas, 1981, 1992). On the system level, law had developed as a technical administrative science threatening law as life-world understanding, as mediator of claims to rights and justice. The acknowledgement of a 'double bind' in legal discourse, and for that matter in most professional discourses having once been anchored in the day-to-day understanding of mutual exchange, led to a critical turn in the study of the professions: how and to what extent did professional (discourse) practices reproduce symbolic power? In what way were these practices the non-reflected agent of oppression - despite claims to the contrary? In the case of legal discourse, contemporary juridification processes came to be viewed from within this double perspective: on the one hand, the increase in legal right-claims in modern society expanded the socio-legal horizons of broad citizen-strata. On the other, the formalisation, and thus abstraction from everyday understanding that such right-claims entailed, also meant that individual as citizens not only became more and more dependent on experts, but more seriously, were increasingly 'individualised' and thus separated from their human collectivity. At the base of Habermas' critique of legal rights is the power of discourse to alienate men from one another.

Moral rights claims are firmly anchored in the classic symmetry between rights and duties: moral rights of the ego must be balanced against the duties of the other. This symmetry is broken when rights are formalised legally: legal rights are enforced whatever their costs for the community as a whole. By the same token, the expansion of right claims by means of law, characteristic of advanced capitalist societies, may also reproduce subjective interests, the results of which may endanger the sense of community - and thus law itself.

Other such critical legal studies re-introduced into the Western legal hemisphere the need for 'legal pluralism'. Typical for Western legal language has been the suppression of community justice in the favour of 'formal law' (de Sousa Santos, 1992, 1995). One of the achievements of recent legal pluralism and critical legal studies has been to supplement formal law with its required anchoring in 'communal justice'. In the case of non-western law, and in the absence of a liberal state and parliamentary democracy, 'communal justice' has recently emerged as a very popular topic of legal anthropological studies.

The discovery that 'professionalisation' (in this case illustrated by the predominant juridification processes in modern society) was a double-bind process with unforeseen consequences has had enormous consequences in the study of the professions and of professionalisation generally. Not only has it led to a range of studies in which the subtle micro-power of professional practices in law, medicine, psychiatry, social work, academia and so on has been made the subject of critical discourse studies. It has also led to cleavages in the self-understanding of some major professions in terms of which the previous taken-for-granted form of professional understanding is questioned from within (Beck, 1986). Self-help programs within the area of health, legal support schemes, and community activation programmes are devices by which clients are requested to participate in the formulation of needs and in the solution of their own problems.[2]

Whatever our stance with regard to professional power, whether we welcome it or not, it is a non-questioned assumption that modern (global) society remains profoundly embedded in an ever increasing spectrum of professional practices and expertise. As has been noted, for instance by Ulrich Beck in his popular book on 'risk society', modern dangers such as environmental pollution are not visible to the ordinary eye, but require for their registration sophisticated measurement devices (1986). In this regard, critical discourse studies can supply no functional remedies, as ordinary understanding is at a loss in registering specifically modern types of risks and dangers; those which cannot be seen, heard or smelled but nevertheless potentially exist as dangerous scenarios in modern global society. Such putative existence, as in the case of ecological dangers, has recently been disputed. It is being said that collective (expert) interests in raising funds for their own (research) activities help to re-enforce such dangers, and thus profit from the colonisation of discourse! But what if these dangers are real ones, and we refuse to take action now?

The proliferation of uncertainties, risks and dangers in an endless stream produces an ever-increasing need of professional - specialised - services in modern society. The rise of global society is broadening and deepening the spectrum of uncertainties and thus also possibilities. It is in this context of a 'world-opening' that we should regard the menace of a global professional class. Professional communities of knowledge, because of technical and audio-visual facilities, can now operate - and do operate - on a worldwide scale, thus producing common knowledge communities. But the question is if such convergence processes at the level of advanced knowledge necessarily pose a threat to local knowledge, or if the uncertainty embedded in such universal understanding might presuppose and even advance 'local knowledge'. It is from within this dialectic of 'global-local' that I will conclude by looking into the contours of a recent discussion regarding a 'global legal profession'.

Globalisation and the Legal Profession

A debate has recently emerged with regard to the menace of a global legal culture, or world legal practices, which under the auspices of *lex mercatorum* seem to spread all around the world.[3] The legal phenomena of 'mega-law' and 'mega-lawyering' have been of increasing concern for legal and social scholars. Such large-scale law practices, not circumscribed by any territory and thus free of governmental control, seem to be spreading their operations from Shanghai to Chicago, from London to Buenos Aires. Some scholars fear that such a phenomenon will finally erase the deep-seated cultural and national differences that have characterised the legal profession for centuries.

Despite an alleged common core stemming from the world-wide influence of Justinianus' *Corpus Juris Civilis* from the sixth century, there have evolved national legal cultures, some resembling each other more than others, as rather closed symbolic circuits handling the operation of state power. Surely, dominant legal cultures have exerted power on less powerful ones, and planted foreign legal schemes on local justice. By means of imitation, some legal codes (such as Code Napoleon) have reached far beyond their countries of origin. Common law countries, primarily in the Anglo-Saxon world, have generated a different legal culture than in the civil law world (of continental Europe). Typically, the law profession has been far more powerful in common law countries than civil law countries. With the rise of independent nation-states, however, national cultures have as a rule taken pride in relating state legal power with societal legitimacy. Major efforts at codification have often engendered nationalist mobilisation and sentiments, thus seeing in legal sovereignty the ultimate victory of a nationalist culture. While many other key professions, like medicine and technology, have assumed more similar characteristics across national cultures over the years due to the internationalisation of science and technology, the legal profession has remained staunchly 'national' in its dependence on state law.

However, the notion of convergence has in recent decades regained its currency in studies of current trends concerning the inner transformation of the legal profession on a worldwide basis (Dezalay, 1990; Dezalay and Garth, 1996). In focus is the rapid emergence of 'mega-law' and 'mega-lawyering' (Galanter, 1983). In its initial formulation, mega-law related to the rise of large law-firms, especially in the United States. In this sense, mega-law was above business law and became a corollary to the rise of large corporate firms such as IBM, General Motors and Apple Computers. Such big law firms were seen as the responsible agents of the enormous litigation claims characteristic of US business life. Relations between big firms - and for that matter between big firms and the US Government - assumed belligerent features, and were for that matter also seen as a possible impediment to the normal operation of market capitalism. With the fall of socialism and the rapid capitalisation of the world market, Americanised mega-law has assumed a global profile: big law-firms today operate globally, with offices in all major cities where banking and corporate finance has their domicile.

The question, however, is whether mega-law today is limited to business and corporate finance, to the realm which already in Roman Law was referred to as *lex mercatorum*? There are some indications that such mega-law also operates in the field of public law. Some years ago, lawyers for not allowing The Church of Scientology to operate in Germany sued Bundesstat. Amnesty International harvested a victory when the former General Augusto Pinochet, during a stay in England, was accused of crimes against humanity. Later, The High Court of the House of Lords declared that Pinochet had no diplomatic immunity and could be taken to court. However, because of frailty and old age, the British government let the former general return to Chile in the hope that he could stand trial in his native country. International law has long been considered a weak version of state law because it had no sovereign power behind and possessed no real sanctions apart from moral ones. The climate has rapidly shifted, and 'human rights' are assuming, even for lawyers themselves, a conspicuous role in today's global agenda. The 'global culture of rights' is spreading fast, and it is an open empirical question whether this alacrity has something to do with the phenomenon of mega-law, now operating also outside the realm of *lex mercatorum*. Indeed, it seems reasonable to ask whether or not mega-law itself has become a generic feature of global capitalism and global society.

As stated earlier, the phenomenon of mega-law and its corollary on the level of legal conduct, mega-lawyering started as an American innovation. Marc Galanter has noted the deep cleavage that exists in US legal life between its 'upper state', elite lawyers with their corporate clients, and its 'lower state', of less privileged lawyers who primarily took on individual clients and who operated in a restricted area of rural towns (1983). This deep cleavage in the US legal profession was not a new discovery but had for decades informed many other studies (Auerbach, 1976). What Galanter claimed, however, was that it had become much more accentuated and was likely to be a permanent feature, with great ramifications for the structure of law and for the legal profession in the future. Mega-lawyering, Galanter said, was in fact to be considered a 'great innovation' of lawyering in this century, and marked a structural shift similar to that from general medical practice in medicine to hospital medicine. As a consequence, law was becoming much more technical and scientific, and as a consequence much more effective. The 'gentleman lawyer' had given place to the technical legal administrator and consultant.

What makes mega-law firms so effective in their operation is their extension in space and their fund of informants and network contacts that enable them to efficiently monitor their fields of operation. Lawyers employed in such firms are highly specialised, and they typically work as a team whereby they exploit each other's specialities and attain a very high level of sophistication in a relatively short time. Their (corporate) clients, likewise, also possess a level of sophistication very seldom present in 'ordinary law'.

A typical feature of American law has always been its 'uncertain face': lacking clear authority structures (more pronounced in continental law), legal outcomes are like games. Such features provide local legal professionals with a great latitude of interpretation; the unanticipated consequences have led to 'an immense proliferation of law and at the same time an increasing awareness of its indeterminacy and problematic character' (1983, p.161). The effects of mega-law may, in the view of Galanter, possibly lead to a transformation of the typical American 'litigating-bargaining' complex:

> Investment of massive amounts of time, relentless investigation, exhaustive research and lavish deployment of expensive experts imposes on the other side corresponding expenditures, endless delays, and costly disruptions of their normal operations. If not everything is an open question, sufficient investment can make almost any matter sufficiently problematic that it takes considerable money and time to lay it at rest. Pursued in multiple forums, with brazen insistence on extracting the last measure of formal entitlement, and offering little hope of respite – such litigation raises the bluster and stratagem of ordinary litigation to lethal proportions. Litigation in the mega-law mode is distinctive in the way that mobile high technology warfare between superpowers differs from the set piece battles of an earlier day (Galanter, 1983, p.163).

Formerly, war was something that occurred between sovereign political states. To the extent to which modern political culture has domesticated war by means of international treatises, it has moved into the market place; mega-law firms are replacing erstwhile war offices. Galanter's point is that, mega-law today, with its origins in corporate law, is by no means limited to business life. On the contrary, public law, he suggests, is assuming some of the same features, although it lacks the ample funding of its commercial variety. Yet, contrary to the latter, public law, as a general rule, has the investment of much greater authority. Backed by social movements, by concerned citizens, and by the general 'moral climate', public law suits (and the threat that they introduce) can drastically change 'normal business'.

In this context, stressing the point that mega-law is no longer limited to corporate law, Galanter relates the case of a 'successful antitrust lawyer with a big Chicago law firm' who offered his services to help various citizens groups opposing nuclear plant licenses:

> First, he demanded mountains of technical documents from the plant's builders and then used them to challenge the adequacy of the construction; one group of witnesses was kept on the stand nearly three months defending the plan's design [...] Finally, Consumer Power capitulated, it agreed to install $28 million worth of added environmental safeguards at the Lake Michigan facility in return for an agreement by Mr. Cherry's clients to withdraw their opposition. 'We had a $130 million plant standing idle and needed to get it running', says Mr. Selby, the utility's president (Galanter, 1983, p.168).

Today, mega-law is no longer only a US phenomenon. After many years of ongoing debates between the Danish and the Swedish governments as to the location of the Barsebäck nuclear plant in southern Sweden, situated only 20 km away from the capital of Copenhagen, the Swedish government decided in 1998 to gradually close down its operation. However, as the nuclear plant was a joint private/public company, private investors in Germany (Preussen Electra) as well as in Norway (its state energy agency, also recently privatised) filed a suit in the European Court against the Swedish Government for unduly expropriating private property. The Swedish government kept to its decision and a settlement was eventually reached between Sweden and the multi-national owners of the nuclear plant. Ironically, the nuclear plant of Barsebäck might in any case have had to close off its operation for pure profit reasons, as nuclear energy has difficulties in disposing of its waste: citizen groups keep resisting, having their areas designated as 'waste lands'. It is not yet as common in Scandinavia that citizen groups are exploiting mega-law, but there is no reason why this should not occur more frequently in the future. Social protests by means of law appear today to have assumed more and more of global features.

Mega-Law and World Capitalism: Convergence/Divergence

In the wake of recent discussions on mega-law and world-system theory, a debate has ensued as to whether mega-law as such is a corollary of world capitalism, or rather a feature of a special form of (Western) capitalism. As this issue is of importance more generally for global professions in their rise to world power, it is worthwhile relating this debate in some more detail.

The French lawyer and sociologist Yves Dezalay, in a series of publications, has explored 'The internationalisation and restructuration of the legal field' (Dezalay 1990; Dezalay and Garth, 1996). He sees the field of mega-law as firmly entrenched in market capitalism, and is seemingly unwilling to explore its influence on public law. The 'legal big bang', he says, 'followed straight after the *financial big bang*' that occurred in Europe after the events of 1989, with the fall of the socialist countries, and was strengthened by the European Maastricht Treaty of 1992. The market for legal services then underwent 'an unprecedented expansion' (1990, p.280). Dezalay contends that the 'renewal of the law' has had a detrimental impact upon the idea of 'social law' previously furthered by the European welfare states. *Lex mercatorum* breeds a new type of lawyer who 'develops the mechanisms which can structure and regulate international finance' (ibid.). These lawyers now leave the old nation-states and reproduce the bifurcation system of American law in Europe: an upper-level strata of well-educated international lawyers 'infatuated with Brussels' and a lower-level strata of primarily female lawyers and low-paid legal professionals performing the less prestigious work at the local national base. The feminisation of the legal profession is today a pronounced feature all over Europe, especially in Scandinavia (Bertilsson, 1995).

Dezalay sees the globalisation of the market in legal services as a straightforward 'Americanisation'. It is the American mega-law firm that provides the model for the current tendencies of a global legal convergence:

> The Wall Street law firm, invented over a century ago in response to the demands of American finance and industry, has become a model for similar developments everywhere, as the local lawyers, in a struggle for survival, feel that they also must adopt the model of the *corporate law firm* (Dezalay, 1990, p.281).

Transnational economic relations demand 'an array of basic rules' in order to ensure stability and predictability. The expansion of the international economic arena has made the need for such basic rules even stronger. National bureaucracies were long important devices for ensuring such stability and order. In today's arena of 'global capitalism', however, we are faced with the 'de-localisation of capital markets and the spread of international exchange relations which are outside state regulation, especially as regards taxation and the surveillance of work conditions' (ibid., p.283).

Behind these massive transformation processes stands an army of 'grey-suited experts: international lawyers, corporate tax accountants, financial advisors, and management consultants' (ibid.). These new global functionaries, says Dezalay, are profiting from a lack of involvement on behalf of politicians, and they do in fact introduce an elementary sense of order in that chaotic global field: they have no other legitimacy than that of technical expertise and no other motives than that of profit (their consultancy fees). These new global experts make up the new transnational 'ruling elite', and their 'proliferation [...] is the best indicator of the importance of the process of homogenisation of global economic space' (ibid., p.284). Their increasingly global presence, with law firms in big capital cities throughout the world, secures an American-style culture of 'litigociation' (Galanter, 1983): a multi-layered process of simultaneous involvement of the judicial process and private negotiation can exploit the threat of law's 'uncertain face' while offering an abundance of compromises. Taking place in the grey zone between formal and informal regulations, this system of global 'litigociation' means that several other 'economic mediating agents' appear on the scene, and threaten international lawyers' privileged access to law: 'the law and its practitioners no longer have the monopoly over the formal regulation of social relations' (ibid., p.289). Whether this mixture of high-level professional expertise on the global financial scene under the reign of *lex mercatorum* leads to the 'the end of law', or to its further technical proliferation (as Weber had already predicted) is at this time uncertain.

Dezalay concludes that the victory of *lex mercatorum* on the world scene is an 'irreversible' fact, pushing back earlier concern for social justice. Dezalay's concern, however, is unwarranted. It rests on the firm judgement that mega-law and corporate law-firms are identical phenomena, and that they cannot be distinguished from each other. But as Galanter has indicated, and as previously discussed, mega-law also becomes increasingly conspicuous in public and international law, thus keeping the flame of social justice burning in the midst of global exchange and production. Not being backed by commercial capital, public interest law has a considerable advantage; people back it.

The question, then, is whether the thesis of legal convergence, as argued by Dezalay and others, is really all that convincing in the midst of global capital exchange. Richard Appelbaum, an American sociologist, has recently argued for an opposite thesis based on world-system theory and its corollary of a much greater cultural diversity, also with ramifications for legal culture (Appelbaum, 1998). In examining the 'East Asian challenge' to US and European business hegemony in the world of capitalism, he posits that 'informal relations' of *guanxi*-type (based on close mutual obligations between actors) have a vast advantage in the Diaspora cultures influenced by Chinese forms of capitalism as seen in China, Hong Kong and Taiwan, in Vietnam, Singapore, Malaysia, Indonesia (1998, p.172). This is, he says, the 'most rapidly growing part of the global economy', a claim that must wait further assessment given recent financial crises in this part of the world. Drawing upon world-system theory, Appelbaum proposes that the world capitalist system is 'entering a new, polycentric phase in which economic power (although not necessarily political power) is shifting across the Pacific' (ibid., p.173). 'Legal pluralism' rather than 'legal convergence' accompany this polycentric phase. The thesis of legal pluralism in the global arena, strongly advocated by de Sousa Santos (1992, p.1995), emphasises the 'co-existence within the nation-state of international and national legal orders articulated in different ways with the nation-state legality' (de Sousa Santos, 1992, p.133).

The transnationalisation of the legal field, therefore, does not necessarily result in a convergence thesis whereby American business firms hold the upper hand, but in the diversification of legal forms generally. Also at stake in the legal pluralism debate, advanced by Appelbaum and drawing upon de Sousa Santos, is the final blow to the hegemony of liberal law theory, centred in the Western nation-state with its predominant valuation of formal relations of justice and its corresponding devaluation of 'popular justice'. The dominance of a special class of lawyers - and the class of professionals more generally - ultimately relies on these Western forms of legal agencies, the sovereignty of the nation-state and that of the American law-firm.

Appelbaum takes special issue with the recent study of Dezalay and Garth (1996) where Chinese, and more specifically Hong Kong, legal culture is studied as a field in transition by which Western legal practices are increasingly being adopted. According to Dezalay and Garth, the 'key agencies of legal transformation' in East Asia have been the American law firms. The law firms have entered Chinese culture in two waves, first in the late 1970s with economic liberation, and secondly, after the Tiananmen Square uprising in 1989. According to these authors, there has been a virtual explosion of Chinese lawyers, and this sudden rise should be seen in light of the suspicion of an older ideology, expressed as follows: 'chain the lawyers to the tree outside the courthouse' (cited in Appelbaum, 1998, p.177). Dezalay and Garth expect that Chinese business culture will move towards formal law and 'in particular the US variant' (1996, p.273), which will reinforce their larger thesis of legal convergence on a world level.

In his critique of the convergence thesis, Appelbaum is of the opinion that the Dezalay/Garth argument rests on a flawed assumption: 'that American and European transnational corporation (and their associated legal practices) will continue to dominate global trade' (Appelbaum, 1998, p.177). The 'long twentieth century' (Arrighi, 1994) associated with American economic hegemony may come to an end, as East Asia with its 'business Diaspora and other transterritorial capitalist organisations' now rises to economic power (ibid.). Appelbaum refers to what Hopkins and Wallerstein have termed 'global commodity chains' (1986, p.159), 'nodes' or operations that comprise pivotal points in the production process' (Appelbaum, 1998, p.182). He further distinguishes between 'producer-driven' and 'buyer-driven' commodity chains. In the former type, large industrial enterprises play the central role in controlling the production process, while in the former 'large retailers, brand-named marketers, and trading companies play the pivotal role in setting up decentralised production networks in a wide range of [low-wage] exporting countries' (Appelbaum, 1998, p.183). In these latter types of commodity chains, commercial rather than industrial capital typically hold the greatest power (ibid.). It is Appelbaum's further contention, drawing upon the work of Gary Hamilton (1990), that these 'buyer-driven commodity chains' are becoming increasingly important in shaping global export relations. Accompanying such buyer-driven commercial agencies is a different form of much more personal trust relations between bargaining partners, best illustrated by *guanxi*-relations. These mutual trust-relations based on personal contacts and wide web-relations at the ground level among a network of customers really form the 'East Asian challenge' to the dominance of a Western political class of technical lawyers.

Conclusions: On Global Professional Powers

At the outset of this discussion, I mentioned the possibility of studying globalisation as emergent forms of social processes whose tendencies will either strengthen or weaken forms already found at an earlier stage of societal development. In the centre of attention has been the rise of a professional complex, such as that which we have seen emerging in all advanced industrial societies, whether of market or state type. I have surveyed different arguments in the understanding of the structural implications of such a professional complex. The functionalist argument was that the long-lasting consequences of professionalization would result in a weakening of the old class structure and the formation of new forms of social stratification. The counter-arguments typically claimed that the rise of the professional complex augmented and reinforced the class structures in advanced capitalism. What will happen when professional power(s) assume global forms? Will global professions evolve and form new hegemonic powers of governing beyond the reach of politically elected actors?

By examining the recent discussion of the rise of a global legal profession, seen as a consequence of the transnational spread of *lex mercatorum* and of corporate law, we have seen that various social forms of such legal power(s) may in fact be evolving. It has been assumed that the rise of mega-law - of transnational global law firms - occurs solely in the corporate realm of business transactions, and as a consequence, that a new global class of business lawyers will rise to power. These are, as Yves

Dezalay claims, the grey-suited law experts whose massive corporate interests and financial assets at hand will pulverise more traditional legal concerns with social justice. The question I wanted to raise in this context was whether or not the emergence of mega-law - 'an irreversible fact' as Dezalay says - will also have consequences for public law and, thus, for social justice.

For how do we really account for the sudden rise of a 'global rights culture'? Human rights claims today possess power to intervene in traditional state law that has for centuries been sanctioned by the principles of sovereignty. Is it an effect of mega-law now taking hold of public law as well? Why should not law's 'uncertain face' also be exploited in the realm of public action and public interests? Why should mega-law be bound to corporate law-firms? Why should it not enter the world of public and civic organisations as well? An efficient exploitation of legal services in order to advance the interests of a collective organisation, a local settlement group or a state agency may very well achieve well-deserved results, and will in any event lead to a rapid proliferation of law generally.

Social justice claims on a global level seemingly assume different forms than in the more limited case of the national-state. In the case of the latter, justice claims have been redressed to a very significant degree, finding a balance in the distribution of individual rights with regard to education, pension rights, vacations, sick leave, etc. Although these rights may be achieved collectively, they are implemented on the individual level. In the global case, however, liberal rights theory is typically challenged by 'collective rights': the rights of indigenous peoples, rights of a diffuse nature, rights of Black people, the rights of French-Canadians to speak their own language, the rights of women, the securing of a National World Heritage, etc. The collectivisation of rights is a typical achievement of an increasingly global society, as traditional 'body-states' could recognise only individual rights. Hence the new legal forms have had decisive impact on the emergence of a global world-society.

Under the auspices of mega-law, new public concerns can arise in the form of legal action. For as is valid in mega-law more generally, the client-relation is shifting from that of an individual to that of a collective: an organisation of actors, a social collectivity. It is not that mega-law, as an instance of global law, cuts through national law, but rather, that it affects national law from within (Sassen, 2000). Typically, the legal pursuits of modern states have changed in order to harbour the new public concerns stemming from environmental issues, consumers interests, human rights, endogenous peoples rights, women's rights etc. In all these and similar instances, the sources of law are no longer stemming from a nationally circumscribed culture, but global issues are penetrating the jurisdiction of the nation-state and, thus, surfacing as national law. Global law is not something wholly separate from national law, as it is only the latter that commands a valid jurisdiction: global law, in order to be a valid legal source, must be ratified by national law and enter the court-room from the inside. It is from this perspective that one can re-address the issue of legal convergence: are different legal cultures, under the impact of globalisation, converging or diverging?

There is no easy answer to the question of legal convergence/-divergence. Neither is there an easy answer to the related question: will a global class of jurists emerge as a dominant class? As I have argued, the proclamation of a global class of lawyers seems at this stage unwarranted for several reasons: there may be different forms of world-capitalism, a producer-driven and a consumer-driven, and the legal experts of these two types differ accordingly. Whereas Western capitalism and culture more generally assume specialisation and differentiation with regard to their knowledge cultures, other non-western forms of capitalism (like that in East Asia) are apparently much less driven by such needs. It cannot be ruled out that in the long run these different types will intermingle with regard to their social forms, producing a new nexus of the professional complex, perhaps weakening the high degree of cognitive specialisation prominent in the West.

And if legal pluralism rather than legal convergence can be claimed in the midst of capital exchange and the world-market of goods, why should such legal pluralism not also be found in public and civil life more generally? Could it not be that the recent upsurge of human rights would gradually assume more attenuated social forms, harmonising the claims of individuals against the collectivity? As social life unfolds and assumes new and complex forms, new rights claims may emerge, hopefully with an ability to avoid the excesses of the two previous types of rights: individual liberal rights and sovereign state tyranny. Human rights must be implemented in local cultures, and the process of such implementation may affect the essence of such right-claims profoundly. From this point of view, social and legal theory have much to learn from globalisation processes as we now move in a symbolic environment with much greater complexity, and with many more situating factors which we must account for.

Yet what about the global 'class' of lawyers? If plural rather than convergent forms of legal life are emerging in the world-system, the postulate that there exists a 'class' of professional actors with distinct (profit) interests seem equally misplaced. The existence of a class of actors with definite interests on a world-level seems much less credible than in the case of the nation-state. A plurality of interests, perhaps even antagonistic, may come into play on the world-level of legal discourse, as 'the class of lawyers' must link and situate their interests with those of other cultural actors. Such global legal evolution is also in line with the early insights of Emile Durkheim as to the (modern) predominance of restitutive rather than repressive law (Lukes and Scull, 1983). Restitutive law requires its practitioners to have a much more intimate contact with 'the matter of the case', and its unforeseen consequences may thus enforce *localisation* in the midst of globalisation. Under such conditions the hegemonic powers of law and of lawyers risk imploding from within: more law may at the same time mean less law!

The professional complex as we knew it from classical social theory, here illustrated by the fate of the legal profession, will most likely assume new and complex forms when transposed to the world level. I have by no means exhausted the topic here, but have only tried open up a new field of inquiry. To study globalisation from the point of view of emergence theory with regard to social forms and social processes does not seem to be a wholly futile undertaking.

Notes

1 A recent incident concerning the establishment of an Icelandic gene-pool is an illustrative case in point. As a relatively isolated island population for centuries, Icelanders have developed a remarkable immune system and thus a resistance to many diseases. An Icelandic biochemist, in addition to being a Harvard professor, recently applied for patent rights in establishing an Icelandic gene-bank as a possible global commercial enterprise. When known to the public, these activities caused uproar among Icelanders, who consider their bodies and genes to be their own personal/national/cultural possessions. The same kind of population experiments can probably be found among endogenous populations today all over the world, calling into question the old distinctions between nature and culture. Whether it is agreeable to us or not, such health-exploitive schemes are likely to be even more frequent in the future.

2 We frequently read in the daily press of such new groupings, now on a global scale, as doctors and lawyers 'without borders': such rescue teams individuals or groups of professional practitioners intervene in time of crises in order to give immediate support. A case in point is the presence of medical aid in today's Kosova, where the 'Doctors without borders' assumes the same neutral stance as does The Red Cross. Such massive

human crises call for immediate action, and in such settings the 'colonising' charge seems highly misplaced.

3 *Lex mercatorum* is already in Roman Law nation-less, as it originates among merchants belonging to different territories sharing no common jurisdictions. In the early Middle Ages *lex mercatorum* splits itself off from the 'laws of the city' and develops *in casu* (from individual cases) at big market places, where an overriding interest lay in making the legal process as short as possible in order not to unduly disturb trading (Anners, 1974I, p.149).

References

Anners, E. (1974), Den Europeiske Rättens Historia, vol 1, Almquist & Wicksell Förlag, Stockholm.

Appelbaum, R. (1998), 'The Future of Law in a Global Society', *Social and Legal Studies*, vol.7 no.2, pp.171-192.

Arrighi, G. (1994), *The Long Twentieth Century*, Verso Press, London.

Beck, U. (1986), *Risiko Gesellschaft*, Suhrkamp, Frankfurt am Main (Engl. Translation, 1992, *Risk Society*, Polity, Cambridge).

Bell, D. (1960), *The End of Ideology*, Free Press, Glencoe. Ill.

Ben-David, J. (1977), *Centers of Learning: Britain, France, Germany, United States*, McGraw Hill, New York.

Berman, H. (1983), *Law and Revolution: The Formation of the Western Legal Tradition*, Harvard University Press, Cambridge, Mass.

Bertilsson, M. (ed.) (1995), *Rätten i Förvandling, Jurister mellan stat och marknad*, Nerenius & Santerus, Stockholm.

Castells, M. (1996-1998), *The Information Age: Economy, Societey, and Culture*, 3 vols., Blackwell, Oxford.

Collins, R. (1975), *Conflict Sociology: Toward and Explanatory Science*, Academic Press, New York.

Collins, R. (1979), *The Credential Society: An Historical Sociology of Education and Stratification*, Academic Press, New York.

Crozier, M. (1984), *Trouble with America*, University of California Press, Berkeley.

Davis, K. & W. E. Moore (1967), 'Some Principles of Stratification', in Bendix, R. and Lipset, S. (eds.), *Class, Status and Power*, Routledge and Kegan Paul, London.

de Sousa Santos, B. (1992), 'State, Law, and Community in the World System: An Introduction', *Social and Legal Studies*, vol.1, pp.131-142.

de Sousa Santos, B. (1995), *Toward a New Common Sense: Law, Science, and Politics in its Paradigmatic Transition*, Routledge, New York & London.

Dezalay, Y. (1990), 'The Big Bang and the Law: the Internationalization and Restructuration of the Legal Field', *Theory, Culture and Society*, vol.7, pp.279-293.

Dezalay, Y. & B. Garth (1996), *Dealing in Virtue: International Commercial Arbitration and the Transaction of a Transnational Legal Order*, Chicago University Press, Chicago.

Durkheim, E. (1977), *The Evolution of Educational Thought,* Routledge and Kegan Paul, London.

Fanon, F. (1968 [1963]), *The Wretched of the Earth,* Grove Press, New York.

Featherstone, M. (1990), 'Global Culture: An Introduction', *Theory, Culture and Society*, vol.7 nos.2-3, Special Issue on Global Culture.

Frank, A. G. (1969), *Sociology of Development and the Underdevelopment of Sociology*, Zenit, Reprint no. 1, Lund.

Galanter, M. (1983), 'Mega-Law and Mega-Lawyering in the Contemporary US', in Dingwall, R. and Lewis, P. (eds.), *The Sociology of the Professions*, Macmillan, London.

Gouldner, A. (1979), *The Future of Intellectuals and the Rise of the New Class*, Seabury, New York.

Habermas, J. (1981), *Theorie des Kommunikativen Handelns,* Vol II, Suhrkamp, Frankfurt am Main.

Habermas, J. (1992), *Faktizität und Geltung*, Suhrkamp, Frankfurt am Main.

Hamilton, G. & Cheng-Shu Kau (1990), 'The Institutional Foundation of Chinese Business: The Family Firm in Taiwan', *Comparative Social Research*, vol.12, pp.95-112.

Hopkins, T. and I. Wallerstein (1986), 'Commodity Chains in the World Economy Prior to 1800', *Review*, vol.10 no.1, pp.157-170.

Kerr, C. et al. (1960), *Industrialism and Industrial Man*, Heinemann, London.

Konrád, G. & I. Szelényi (1979), *The Intellectuals on The Road to Class Power*, Harcourt Brace & Jovanovich, New York.

Luhmann, N. (1997), *Die Gesellschaft der Gesellschaft*, 2 vols. Suhrkamp, Frankfurt am Main.

Lukes, S. and A. Scull (1983), *Durkheim and the Law,* Martin Robertson, Oxford.

Parsons, T. (1966), *Societies: Evolutionary and Comparative Perspectives*, Prentice Hall, New York.

Parsons, T. (1967), *Social Theory and Modern Society*, Free Press, New York.

Parsons, T. (1977), *The Evolution of Societies* (ed. Jack Tiby), Prentice Hall, New Jersey.

Perkin, H. (1996), *The Third Revolution: Professional Elites in the Modern World*, Routledge, London/New York.

Ruschemeyer, D. (1973), *Lawyers and Their Society: A Comparative Study of the Legal Profession in Germany and in the United States*, Harvard University Press, Cambridge, Mass.

Ruschemeyer, D. (1986), *Power and the Division of Labour*, Polity Press, Cambridge.

Sarfatti-Larsen, M. (1977), *The Rise of Professionalism: A Sociological Analysis*, University of California Press, Berkeley/Los Angeles.

Sassen, S. (2000), 'Territory and Territoriality in the Global Economy', *International Sociology*, vol.15, no.2, pp.372-394.

Szelényi, I. and B. Martin (1989), 'The Legal Profession and the Rise and Fall of the New Class', in R. Abel and Ph. S.C. Lewis, (eds.), *Lawyers in Society. Comparative Perspectives*, University of California Press, Berkeley/Los Angeles.

Therborn, G. (1998), 'Challenges and Issues of Globalizations', *Presentation at FRNs International Conference on Globalizations*, Stockholm 22-24 October.

Therborn, G. (2000), 'Globalizations: Dimensions, Historical Waves, Regional Effects, Normative Governance', *International Sociology*, vol.15 no.2, pp.151-180.

Torstendahl, R. & M. Burrage (1990), *The Formation of Professions. Knowledge, State and Strategy* (eds.), Sage, London.

Wagner, P. (1990), *Sozialwissenschaften und Staat: Frankreich, Italien, Deutschland 1870-1980,* Campus Verlag, Frankfurt am Main/New York.

Wallerstein, I. (1974, 1980, 1989), *The Modern World System*, 3 vols., Academic Press, New York.

Wright, E. O. (1978), *Class, Crises and the State*, New Left Books, London.

12 Modern Reflexive Leadership

ØJVIND LARSEN

1. Reflexive Modernity

Modern society is currently undergoing tremendous change. This also has a decisive impact on how society's institutions are to be led. Regardless of which institutions one looks at, one discovers a concern with finding new forms of leadership. All public institutions are in a period of great transformation. It is no longer self-evident how a school or a hospital should be led. Even in an institution as rich in tradition as the church, doubt about leadership practices has arisen. The same could be said about many civil society institutions such as the Red Cross, Amnesty International, Save the Children, etc. In the world of business there is also a great transformation going on with regard to leadership. In addition, there are an ever-increasing number of new institutions which have an entirely different dynamic and flexibility than previous institutions, and are oriented towards creating new knowledge in new fields. Institutional innovation in the so-called 'new economy' should also be mentioned in this context.

Many sociologists argue that we are moving from one form of modernity to an entirely new form of modernity. They speak of a transition from early to late modernity, from modernity to post-modernity, from the first to the second modernity, from simple to reflexive modernity, etc. (Bauman, 1997, 2000; Beck, 1997, 2000; Giddens, 1990; Kumar, 1995; Lash, 1999; Wagner, 1994). In the following I will focus on *the reflexive dimension* in the transformation of modernity, and what consequence this has on the formulation of new understandings of leadership, which one could call *modern reflexive leadership*. By extension, in the following, this new form of modernity will be defined as a *reflexive form of modernity*. This special situation should be seen in connection with the broader discussions of the transformation of modern society which are presented in the other articles collected in this volume.

The profound transformation of modern society is driven by an escalation in communication. Today, there are practically no impediments to communication between people all over the world. One could speak of a communicative 'release' of modern society, a process that has been underway since the late Middle Ages. The great changes in production and the expansion of commerce throughout the world laid the foundations for global communication, which increased exponentially in the 18th and 19th centuries due to the discovery or creation of new technologies for production, trade and transportation. European colonialism and expansion throughout the world promoted these forces at the global level. However, the great revolutions in European history, such as the Renaissance, the Reformation and the French Revolution, have also paved the way for moving communication to the center of European society. In the 20th century, the telegraph and telephone made it possible for almost anyone to communicate throughout the whole world. Informational media, such as newspapers, radio and especially television, have contributed to tying the world together. In the past decade, the Internet has brought about great changes that in principle give people the chance to be *virtual* participants in global society. One could speak of a revolution which has just begun. Despite the fact that many of these transformations are only in their nascent stages, we can already see the tremendous consequences they have on many of the institutions of modern society.

So long as they have been oriented towards democratic forms of governance, political institutions have always been subject to a demand for public insight or transparency. Though such demands have historically been associated with democratic governance, further new communicative demands are being made on political institutions. Communication is now so widespread that individual political institutions appear to the public as illegitimate historical relics if they attempt to protect themselves from open communication. An example of this is the Danish government's attempt to hide its nuclear weapons policy on Greenland in the 1950s. Researchers could travel to other countries and obtain documentation and information which the Danish government would not divulge. In practice, it is no longer possible to constrain communication through power. Political institutions can only persist if they communicate in a credible manner.

The institutions of civil society have also become inextricably linked to communication. Greenpeace is a good example of an institution that has invested greatly in public communication. A most notable example of this is the Brent Spar campaign, in which Shell sought to dispose of an oil platform in the sea (Grolin, 1999, pp.264-292). However, Greenpeace also suffered a credibility loss when it was shown that some of the information that they publicly circulated about the oil platform was not completely accurate.

The administration of public institutions is also in a state of great change. The old rule-oriented, legally based bureaucracy that Max Weber so elegantly described at the beginning of this century has lost its youthful radiance. Modern administration must be based on communication and be capable of entering into dialogue with its citizenry on all issues. This process is promoted by the new communication possibilities and technologies. Within only a few more years, all citizens should be able to be served via the Internet.

This communicative transformation of institutions also impacts the business world. No longer can business solely be about increasing capital. Companies must be able to communicate with their environments. One can again take up Shell as an example. After the Brent Spar incident, Shell went to great lengths to go into a public dialogue with civil society institutions about the values upon which the company is based. In this effort, Shell has held a series of roundtable meetings throughout Europe with representatives of civil society institutions in order to reach generally acceptable corporate norms. These norms are now publicly listed on Shell's homepage: *www.shell.com.* On the whole, it has become quite common for companies to publish a statement of the values which guide the firm, and also engage in so-called 'ethical accounting' along with their financial accounting.

It is no longer sufficient to merely act strategically to attain a given goal. The examples given above show that purely strategic leadership can create great difficulties for an institution as soon as one has to account for the norms that provide the foundation for decisions. The Brent Spar example again serves well here. From a strategic perspective, Shell had a well-devised plan for how they would dispose of their oil platform. What the ensuing affair showed, however, was that it was also necessary to account for the norms upon which the company is based, as well as going into dialogue with other interested parties about these norms. In purely strategic action, the normative dimension is suppressed or is forced to defer to the goal to be obtained.

It is not just external relations between institutions that are characterized by increased communication. It is also relations internal to institutions. There are sociological theories within the systems theory tradition that understand institutions as in fact constituted through communication. Communication is also attaining an increasing significance within action theory perspectives. The individual actor or participant in an institution must personally be able to reflexively examine his actions.

It is precisely the modern leader who is confronted with this change within institutions in his daily activities. He is continuously confronted by the problem of how he should lead, and thereby the question of *which criteria* lay the foundation for his leadership. Thus, it is the basic orientation in leadership which is up for discussion, and thereby ultimately how we should understand leadership. This is basically a philosophical issue, as it inquires as to the criteria for leadership. Modern leadership therefore raises what I call the matter of philosophy of leadership.

2. Philosophy, Leadership and Reflexive Modernity

Philosophy deals with the question of criteria and their validity. Therefore, within philosophy one can make a distinction between good and bad criteria. Philosophy is thus not bound to what exists. It attempts, rather, to take a stand. This is the essence of philosophy. It is this position taking which makes leadership philosophy so relevant in modern society, and also has led to the establishment of the philosophy of leadership as a separate sub-field of philosophy. The continuous creation of new fields occurs in philosophy, just as in all other academic disciplines. It should be noted that the philosophy of leadership falls under the domain of practical philosophy. Thus, it is clear that there is a great tradition throughout the history of philosophy that deals with leadership. One can even read the whole of practical philosophy's history as a philosophy of leadership tradition, in as much as the whole of the practical philosophical tradition deals with political leadership and the criteria which lay the foundation for political leadership, which is ultimately articulated in ethics. In Plato one finds an inner connection between ethics and politics and an identification between the good political leader and the good city-state. Aristotle creates a distinction between ethics and politics, but at the same time retains the idea that an inner connection exists between the two. Aristotle's ethics and politics are inextricably connected and have an inner unity. This unity is maintained throughout the history of philosophy in the stoics, Augustine, and Thomas Aquinas. In what is called the modern breakthrough in the history of philosophy, that is to say, the period of the Renaissance and the Protestant Reformation, this inner connection between politics and philosophy is broken. Politics is made independent, as a goal in itself, which is no longer accountable to ethics, for the first time in history by Machiavelli. Luther also separates out politics as an independent domain from a theological perspective, breaking any necessary inner connection to religion and ethics by differentiating between the divine and temporal regimes. On the one hand, this can be interpreted as a *liberation* of the political as a temporal matter which need not observe a superior ethical or religious dimension. On the other hand this can also be understood as an instrumentalization of the political, which is *no longer able* to refer to a superior religious or ethical dimension. From the latter perspective, one can speak of the *fall* of politics in as much as it loses the criteria which would hold it in grace and obligate it to the good. To use Aristotle's terms, one could speak of politics' transition from a *praxis*, an ethical action, to a *poieisis*, a doing. This simultaneously opens up for a transition from political *leadership* and thereby politics as *leadership* to a new understanding of politics as what can be called *management*. Management means steering. The principal point in all management is that by manipulation of institutions one can get people to act in a particular way. Using the Greek word *technae*, one could speak of a technique or manipulation of people. It is this latter understanding which from the 1700s slowly began to spread to all of society's institutions via the forces of technological innovation and the capitalist economy, forces which continue to transform society to our day. Leadership has ever increasingly become management, regardless of whether one speaks of political leadership or leadership of economic and technologically oriented institutions and companies. In recent years, *management thinking* has also begun to make inroads into the institutions which are central to reproduction of personal life, such as educational, rehabilitation, health and social care institutions. Instrumental rational (*Zweckrational*) planning and economic parameters have become ever more decisive in such institutional contexts.

Marx and Weber, each in their own particular way have, insightfully expounded upon the increased importance of management thinking. Marx demonstrated how the capitalist economy and technology overturn the entirety of modern society and transform social relations into technical, instrumental relations that are subject to the authority of abstract, content-less values. Weber extends these ideas by highlighting the fact that we not only see a technical-instrumental transformation of material social relations. Our means of understanding and comprehending are also subject to this imperative such that we become bound to forms of understanding which make it difficult for us to at all see other dimensions than the dimensions which are mediated through the instrumental rationalization of all social relations. Thus, according to Weber, management thinking becomes the 'natural' way for us to think and relate to each other within the institutions of modern society, as this becomes the only adequate way of relating within the institutions of modern society. All other ways of relating and understanding, according to Weber, represent regression, which cannot measure up to means-end rationality. Weber was highly ambivalent about the means-end rationalization of modern society, as he on the one hand saw this as the rationalization of social relations, and on the other as a form of domination which implied a loss of meaning and freedom. According to Weber, modern social relations ultimately become meaningless forms of domination which suppress every human freedom that could not be included in this form of rationality. Weber claims that all we have left is a memory, a *mimesis*, that it could have been otherwise in the respect that in his comprehensive historical studies, he could see that it had been otherwise, that there were other historical possibilities. Meaning and freedom for Weber were ultimately associated with the metaphysical and the religious, while at the same time he could not deny that the forms of social understanding, technologies and sciences available to modern individuals have led to a rationalization and differentiation of life forms which indeed in this respect represent a loss, but at the same time bind us in such a way that we could not stop this rationalization and differentiation without falling back to life forms that in Weber's estimation would be an historical regression. In Western rationality, Weber thus saw the preeminence of the modern, which was crowned to conquer the whole world. For Weber there was no historical alternative to Enlightenment thought such as it has been historically manifested in the ever increasing domination of instrumental rational action in all aspects of life with technology and the economy as the historical avant-garde. Weber lived just long enough to see the first great collapse of this Western instrumental rationality in the mass slaughter on the battlefields of World War I.

It was Horkheimer and Adorno, who in the face of the totalitarian regimes of the 20th century - Nazism and Stalinism, the increased power of destruction unleashed by modern technological advances in World War II, the Nazis' mass murder in Auschwitz and the atom bomb over Hiroshima, gave the dominant Western instrumental rationality its theoretical death-blow in their book *Dialectics of Enlightenment*. In this work they placed this form of rationality in a global historical perspective and posited that with rationalization itself a fall has occurred which can be traced back to the first exchange, which brought abstraction into the world (Horkheimer, 1988). Enlightenment, according to Horkheimer and Adorno, had its dialectic that would necessarily lead to total conquest and destruction. Only in philosophy and art could the historical possibilities which were missed be remembered as a *mimesis* (Adorno, 1973, p.15ff). According to Horkheimer and Adorno it is at this historical ground-zero that all modern philosophy of leadership must take its point of departure if it is to be credible. The ever-dominating management thinking is, according to Horkheimer and Adorno, the great challenge that all philosophy of leadership must take as its point of departure and be its object of critique.

In the Critical Theory tradition there is a squelching pessimism which, like a complete bottomless depression, extinguishes every hope of improvement. However, Horkheimer and Adorno have exposed some of the decisive, central tendencies in modern society. It is therefore important to retain the critique, while at the same time attempting to reach a new communicatively oriented understanding of modern society.

It is in this connection that Habermas's theory of communicative rationality is important. Through this theory, Habermas critiques both Weber's, and Horkheimer' and Adorno's interpretations of Western society, in that he shows that communication has a decisive importance in the new form of modernity (Habermas, 1981). This new form of modernity can be called, as Habermas does in his theory, a reflexive form of modernity.

The communicative transformation of modernity has led to the need to articulate *a new understanding of leadership* which stands in opposition to the predominant management thought. My thesis is that the modern global and reflexive communication society beckons for a new form of leadership which can be termed communicative or *reflexive leadership*.

What is meant by this is leadership which first builds upon a radically free communication where there is no hindrance in access to information, and subsequently is built upon each relationship being mediated through communication which ultimately must always afford the possibility of *a reflection over reflection* in communication. Such reflexive leadership opens the possibility to relate to the normative issues inherent in modern society.

3. Leadership – A Sociological Definition

In the following we will examine more closely a sociological definition of leadership. Weber differentiates between the exercise of power on the one hand and *Herrschaft* or (legitimate) domination on the other (Weber, 1972, p.542ff). Power consists of one person attaining his or her will over the will of another. Domination consists of someone attaining their will over another by the power of the authority which the former has over the latter, leading the latter to obey a command by the former due to a perceived obligation to obey. By extension, leadership is understood as the exercise of authority on the basis of voluntary obedience.

This understanding of leadership points out domination's decisive importance for every context in which leadership is involved. It is also realistic in that it is not conceivable that institutions can normally be led by the exercise of power. The exercise of power is the exception in all social contexts. In a given social context it is usually domination that is decisive in determining the actions of agents in institutions. Thus it is important to define the various forms of authority that influence the lives of individuals in institutions.

In extending this analysis, Weber examines how domination can be established in an institution. Weber writes that all domination comes to expression and functions through administration. Here he takes direct democratic administration as his point of departure. This is defined as a state where domination is reduced to a minimum, and where everyone in principle has the same qualifications to exercise authority. From a sociological perspective, this is a form of administration which ideal typically is without a relationship of domination. Weber sees democratic administration as a typological borderline-case which is not socially sustainable, and thus stands no chance of surviving in modern mass society. Weber gives three reasons for this. The first is that a power struggle will develop between groups in society. The second reason is that a qualitative and quantitative growth in administrative tasks will occur, tasks that cannot be dealt with through direct democracy. The third reason is that the administration of mass society leads to the establishment of a professional administration with structures that can be collegial and monocratic, that is to say all functionaries work under a single unity-creating executive leadership (Weber, 1972, p.548).

When the many cannot govern themselves, according to Weber, a circle of individuals inevitably establishes for itself a relationship of dominance over the many. The advantage of the few governing over the many, according to Weber, is that the ruling minority has the possibility to quickly reach agreement and create and lead rational planned action with the aim of maintaining their position of dominance (Weber, 1972, p.548). Thus, according to Weber, a minority can easily suppress a mass action or social discourse which threatens them so long as the challengers have not themselves created an equally effective contract to carry out a rational planned action with the goal of conquering dominance. A further advantage of dominance residing among the few is that they can keep their intentions, resolutions and knowledge secret. Dominance by the few, according to Weber always has an air of secrecy around it. Weber identifies especially formal rational dominance with the tendency for a single or few leaders to assemble a group of individuals who are used to following orders around them, individuals for whom their part of the spoils of ruling lies in the system's survival. Thus, a regime of command and force is established to secure the persistence of domination. This is what Weber calls an 'organization' (Weber, 1972, p.549). The 'master' is what Weber calls the leader or leaders who have not received their authority to lead from those they rule over. Those persons who put themselves at the disposal of leaders of the above-mentioned type are called the 'apparatus' of the leaders by Weber. The social structure of legitimate domination, according to Weber, is primarily associated with the type of relationship that exists on the one hand between the master and the apparatus, and on the other, all those under the sway of legitimate domination. Here the principles of the organization play a role, that is to say, the distribution of order-giving authority.

The central problem in legitimate domination for Weber is thus how authority is founded or legitimated (Weber, 1972, p.549). The official should know why he should obey his superior, and those who are under a system of legitimate domination should know why they should obey officials and the master. The question of the legitimization of domination, according to Weber, is not merely the result of theoretical or philosophical thought but, rather, is rooted in the real structural differences between empirically existing forms of authority. The reason is that all power, indeed even every life chance, needs to be grounded and legitimated. This is no less the case for all social authority. According to Weber there are only three possible means of legitimating authority: charismatic, traditional, and legal legitimacy (Weber, 1988, p.475). Each of these forms of legitimization has a characteristic staff and means of administration, and their own distinct social structures, and are ideal-typically dominant in different forms of institutions and societies.

Traditional authority, Weber's first form of legitimate authority builds, as the name indicates, upon tradition (Weber, 1988, p.478). The word tradition comes from Latin and means 'to pass along'. Traditional authority is based on the belief that the social order and the power of the master has existed from time immemorial and that these orders are holy. The purest type here is patriarchal authority, where the relationship of authority is characterized by mutual interconnection. Here it is the family father, the lineage's patriarch, the father of the country, who rules. The patriarch or master gives orders, the administrative staff serves the master, and the subordinates obey the master. The administration comprises of individuals who are personally dependent upon the master, or in the case of a lineage or friendship group, of people who have professed loyalty to him. The legitimacy of the patriarchal administrative staff is entirely dependent upon what the master finds desirable in each individual instance. The exercise of power follows more or less the contours of what the administrative staff can get away with without subordinates ceasing to obey. When the master is obeyed, it is based on tradition, which in the final instance is holy. This implies as well that the master can only rule within the parameters of tradition. New laws cannot be made. New laws can only be decreed if they are 'discovered' to have existed in the past. Such is the case, for example, with Solon's law which was decreed in Athens in 592-591 BC, and Josiah's reform law which was promulgated after being found in the temple in Jerusalem around the year 620 BC. Outside the reach of traditional norms, the will of the master is only bound by the boundaries of what the master feels to be reasonable in a given case or what his passions drive him to command. Traditional authority is thus a mixture of traditional norms, subject in the given moment to the contingent passions of the master. The administrative staff can also have an estate structure (Weber, 1988, p.479). Here the servants are not the personal servants of the master, but independent, socially prominent notables due to their own autonomous situation. They have either been granted an office or have inherited it in a legal manner through purchase, pawn or lease. This is estate-authority. The competition among office or estate holders for authority and income delimit administrative areas from each other. Ruling power here is shared between the master and his staff, which has either acquired its administrative role itself, or has had it bestowed as a privilege. This division of power makes estate-based administration relatively particularistic.

The second form of legitimate authority which Weber takes up is *charismatic* authority. Charismatic authority is founded upon an affective personal dedication to the master and his gifts of grace, his charisma, which can be particular magical skills, revelations, heroic deeds, or spiritual or rhetorical powers (Weber, 1988, p.481ff). Dedication to the charismatic master is perennially as new as the first flush of love and devotion. According to Weber, the purest type is the authority of the prophets, war heroes, and demagogues. The authority of the charismatic master creates discipleship or a will to follow characterized by personal affiliation. The master is a leader and his followers are disciples. The master is personally obeyed solely because of his personal qualities and not because of his legally or traditionally sanctioned position. The administrative staff is chosen purely on the basis of charisma and personal devotion. The professional competence of the officer plays no role, nor does his connection to a given estate. It is only the master's commands and charismatic characteristics that determine the extent of the tasks which the master's staff and servants can legitimately carry out.

Magic is the charismatic master's spiritual area. The basis for charismatic authority is thus belief in the prophet or the acknowledgement of the powers that were bestowed upon the charismatic master. Therefore, he is only obeyed so long as he possesses these characteristics. When his god leaves him, when he is robbed of his heroic powers, or the masses lose confidence in his leadership qualities, his authority disappears. In any case, his authority cannot, according to Weber, be seen as derived from the acknowledgement of those under his domination. It is, on the contrary, based on an obligation to acknowledge and believe in the master; an obligation which the master demands for himself and failure to submit will be harshly punished by him. The charismatic master becomes in this way one of history's great revolutionary powers - most of the great transformations in history have been led by charismatic masters. However, according to Weber this form of leadership in its pure form is entirely of an authoritarian nature (Weber, 1988, p.483).

Legal authority, Weber's third type of legitimate authority, is authority based on ratified law. Legal authority is based on the conception that any law can be created or rescinded through formally correct legislation (Weber, 1988, p.475). The purest form of legal authority is bureaucratic authority (Jespersen, 1996).

According to Weber, it is not only the modern state and municipality that is organized along the typology of legal authority. We see this same pattern of authority in modern capitalist companies, and in every sort of modern organization that has a defined goal and disposes over a functionally based, hierarchically organized administrative staff. The administrative staff is comprised of officials selected by the leader, and those who obey are members of the community - be they citizens of a political community, members of a political party or organization, employees of an organization, or colleagues in an academic institution.

It is not the *person* who is obeyed because of his personal rights, according to Weber, but rather, the legally ordained rule which determines who should be obeyed and the extent to which he should be obeyed. Those who command also follow the rules - be they laws, proclamations, regulations or abstract norms, which apply within a domain demarcated through objective considerations. The typical official is, according to Weber, a professionally trained official whose employment is contractually regulated with a given wage based on his placement in a hierarchy and not on the volume of his work, a predictable career advancement ladder, and a secure pension. Bureaucratic administration is professional work carried out based upon a functionally delimited official duty. Ideal administration, according to Weber, is based upon making decisions in a rigid, formal manner based on rational rules, and in the eventuality that these rules fail to provide secure guidance, then based on an objective view of what is prudent. Personal motives are to play no role at all, and decisions are to be taken in a calculated manner based on the rules, without personal views. The duty to obey is arranged in a hierarchy of posts, where the lower are subordinate to the higher and where there is an established procedure to appeal decisions. What is central here is that there is discipline within the organization.

According to Weber, bureaucracy is technically the purest form of legal authority (Weber, 1988, p.93). However, Weber believes that no authority can be exclusively of a bureaucratic character, that is to say be led entirely by officials employed under contract. The highest leaders in politics must be either monarchs - that is persons with inherited charisma, or popularly elected presidents - persons with popular charisma, or elected by a parliament where it is members of parliament who decide. Leaders in organizations and companies must in the same manner be more or less of a charismatic type.

Weber develops his theory of three types of authority in a society in which technical-instrumental rationalization becomes increasingly predominant and elevated to an ideal to be striven for, and where the legally based bureaucracy comes to stand for the highest form of rationalization of society's institutions. Thus, bureaucracy appears to be a pure form of management. The question remains, however, what type of authority is adequate when modernity radically transforms itself in such a way that communication takes on decisive importance in social relations, as is the case in reflexive modernity?

Weber's three ideal types of authority are not wholly unproblematic; their deficiencies appear especially in a modern communicative society. Traditional authority is problematic in that it relates explicitly to tradition. It is precisely tradition which is vanquished in modern communicative society through escalating reflexivity. Traditional authority cannot therefore be adequate as a basis for legitimate authority in modern reflexive society. Charismatic authority is problematic in that it is a conditional authority that is based on the individual master's passions, which are beyond discussion. Such authority is of a totalitarian character and is irreconcilable with the demand for communication within the institutions of reflexive modernity. Legal authority is the only one of Weber's three ideal types that is relevant in reflexive modernity. Legal authority is a thoroughly rationalized authority based on instrumental rational action. It is here that this form of authority's managerial nature lies. It is also here that the limits for this form of authority in the reflexive modern world lie. Legal authority is a *purely formal authority* that *does not immediately* lead to *the mutual understanding on the basis of the good argument* that is required in the institutions of reflexive modernity. The basic rationality of this form of authority is instrumental rationality. Legal authority will, in practice, continue to be important in reflexive modernity. It is, however, necessary to extend Weber's types of legitimate authority by adding a *fourth type of legitimate authority* which is directly related to the communicative rationality which is now central to reflexive modernity, where mutual understanding based on the good argument thereby also attains an immediate importance. Such a new type of authority could be called communicative authority or *reflexive authority*, and the exercise of such authority could be called communicative or *reflexive leadership*. In the following I will examine a philosophical definition of this type of leadership.

4. Leadership – A Philosophical Definition

Leadership is found in all societies. There is no known society where leadership has not played a central role in the reproduction of social life. Therefore, discussing leadership is nothing new; leadership has been a central topic throughout history. A reflective contemplation on leadership, in which the criteria that form the basis for leadership, first surfaces in recorded history in Greek philosophy. Philosophical considerations on the issue of modern leadership would thus be well served by reviewing how Plato and Aristotle viewed the issue of leadership. Both have contributed interesting observations on this topic.

Plato's *Republic* can be read as a treatise on leadership philosophy, reflecting over what form of leadership is desirable in the city-state, and what types of leadership are detrimental to good leadership. Plato emphasizes that it is philosophers who should be the true leaders of the city-state, as they act in accordance with their insight about the idea of the good. To Plato, it is thus *insight about the good* and *rational argumentation based on this* that is decisive for leadership. Thus, as far back as Plato, leadership has been conceived in terms of *reflection*. One can discuss whether Plato seriously meant that philosophers really should lead the city-state, or whether this proposal was meant to create a yardstick for being able to critique other forms of governance which he viewed as sub-optimal or detrimental. Both readings can be seen as important in the context of the philosophy of leadership. On the one hand, it can be seen as an attempt to define good leadership as consisting of acting in accord with the idea of the good for the city-state. On the other hand, one creates the ability to *critique* forms of leadership that do not live up to the idea of the good, and thus must be seen as detrimental in contrast to this idea. The primary opposition which Plato treats is that between reason and desire. Leadership which is in accord with reasoned insight about the good stands in contrast to leadership carried out in accord with desire.

At the beginning of the *Nicomachean Ethics* Aristotle criticizes Plato, arguing that is it *not practically possible* to attain sufficient insight into the idea of the good (Aristotle, 1982, I p.4ff). In the *Politics*, Aristotle therefore recommends a pragmatic leadership, where with the help of reason one can attempt *in practice to find the best possible leadership* without believing that a form of leadership exists that is built upon the idea of the good (Aristotle, 1977, IV p.7ff). In this connection, Aristotle retains the opposition between reason and desire. It is desire that brings leadership into decline. Subsequently, Aristotle points out that there are many different forms of leadership, and what is decisive in selection between these different forms is what type of institution is to be led. One can say that Aristotle *differentiates the concept of leadership* in terms of the specific institutions that are to be led.

Plato correctly points out that all questions about leadership must be posed in relation to considerations based on reason. Next, he presents a concept of decline that serves as a fruitful way of looking at institutions. In modern society it can be difficult to follow Plato's thinking about good leadership. However, if one follows Aristotle's critique of Plato, one can see from a pragmatic standpoint what type of leadership is desirable in relationship to society's varying institutions.

In his prelude to his *Philosophy of Right*, Hegel draws our attention to the fact that the understanding of politics and institutions in ancient Greece was too narrow, being based on a conception of general customs to which the individual was subjected (Hegel, 1955, p.13ff). According to Hegel, this conception breaks down in modern society because of what he terms 'incessant self-reflection' (Hegel, 1955, §124-126). What is meant here is that the social order can no longer be taken to be given. The whole of the social order is an object of reflection inasmuch as the individual practically carries out this reflection. One can conclude that social relations can only be understood as reflected relationships in modern society. The individual, according to Hegel, can only be bound to the common in an external sense, and thus must therefore ultimately stand free to reflect on the common social order. In this critique, Hegel in a truncated form takes up a basic issue which separates the antique from the modern world. This also has great importance for the philosophy of leadership.

If the good, which provides the basis for leadership in Plato, cannot be determined, we must then ask *what principle* can comprise the basis for leadership. In modern times it is Kant who is central to the formulation of this principle. One can say that Kant is modernity's greatest philosopher as he placed autonomy and reflexivity at the center of his moral philosophy. In his *Critique of Practical Reason*, Kant argues that individuals should live in accord with the principles that they elaborate through the use of reason (Kant, 1974, §8). Autonomy means making one's own laws with the help of reason. Reflexivity thereby consists of relating to the laws that reason has dictated. *Reflexivity thus consists of reason's relationship to itself*. Herein we find *the basic principle for all modern leadership*. In modernity, no one can promulgate anything other than law. On the other hand, any law can be contested. Therefore, there is a universalism in modernity. It is always possible to question the validity of a law.

The great problem thus is how reflexivity and autonomy can be institutionalized. Hegel raises this question in his critique of Kant. According to Hegel, it is simply not sufficient to establish autonomy and reflexivity as principles, one also has to explain how it is possible to institutionalize these principles. Hegel attempts to solve this problem in his *Philosophy of Right*. But in the end, neither can Hegel find the path from the autonomy and self-reflection of the individual to the common reasoned order of institutions. To Hegel this is because people live in the clutches of desire and therefore act to attain their own good. Plato's problem thus recurs. In his *Philosophy of Right*, Hegel reaches the conclusion that ultimately it is only the prince who can ordain common norms for society. This is why many deem Hegel to be a totalitarian philosopher. One must however be aware that Hegel attempts to solve a problem already raised by Plato. One must also be aware that this matter is not so clear cut as Hegel also stated that within individual guilds norms can be formulated which are common for each guild. There is thus, according to Hegel, a possibility for a mutuality in bourgeois society's individual institutions, but this mutuality in individual institutions does not necessarily lead to a common or general mutuality, and thereby to a common moral order.

This is the same issue that Habermas takes up in his theory of communicative action. Habermas wants to find out *what* mutuality means in modern society and *how* it can come to expression in institutions. What is new in Habermas' theory of communicative action in relation to Kant and Hegel is that he makes *the reflexive into a mutual relationship between individual members of the linguistic community*. This means that the whole conception of autonomy and reflexivity which for Kant and Hegel is bound to the individual subject's reflection is for Habermas a *linguistic relation* between subjects. According to Habermas, mutuality lies in the essence of language, and the telos or aim of language is to achieve mutual understanding (Habermas, 1981, p.387). Here we initially see a new formulation of Kant's ideas about autonomy and reflection, as was described above. But on further inspection we see that Habermas is confronted by the same problem as Hegel in relation to Kant, namely *how* the linguistic community takes form in institutions. Habermas has spent a great deal of his recent work trying to solve this problem, but he has also treated it in his very earliest work (Habermas, 1962). Throughout his writings, Habermas has indicated that the linguistic community is mediated through public spheres in institutions and in political life in general. Therefore, for Habermas it is of paramount importance to create public spheres or spaces within institutions in which the members of institutions can freely express themselves. Thus, Habermas' theory ultimately ordains democracy as the form of governance that can secure the free dialogue, as democracy is rooted in the public dialogue.

In his theory of communicative action, Habermas is however aware that society cannot be reproduced solely through communication in linguistic communities. There are numerous areas where the systemic reproduction of society can reduce the need for negotiation and dialogue. In this connection Habermas builds upon Luhmann's systems theory.

Modernization, according to Luhmann, means increased differentiation in the establishment of systems, such that a series of specialized systems are established which each on their own reproduce themselves through self-referential and closed internal communication (Luhmann, 1985, pp.30). In this context, where systems 'create themselves,' Luhmann speaks of autopoetic systems (Luhmann, 1985, p.43). The point here is that there is not just communication within an individual system, but also communication between systems. It is this mutual friction both within and between systems which creates space for reflexivity. In this regard Luhmann sees modern society as extremely reflexive. Intense communication is carried out both within an individual system and between individual systems. Communication is however bound to the media of the individual systems, such as money, power, influence, etc, and *inner* communication between the different systems *cannot* take place. The individual systems are thus limited in their relations to each other. The great advantage with autopoetic systems is that the complexity within each system is reduced to expression in a simple medium. Here money is the model for all other media, in that money has the capacity to reduce the complexity in the global market to a simple expression.

All interaction between different systems can also be called autopoetic in the sense that there is no overarching rationality from which it is possible to evaluate the individual systems or the relationship between systems. Blind-spots can exist within individual systems that can only be seen through mutual observation between different systems. These observations are, however, bound to the individual system from which they are undertaken. There is thus no observation that can claim preeminence over other systems or stand above them.

The strength of autopoetic systems lies in their making social life manageable through differentiation and complexity reduction. Reflexivity comes about through mutual observation. Reflexivity, however, lies also within systems, as it comes to expression in inner reflection in relation to the media that mediate the system. In this connection Luhmann speaks of a 'differentiation of reflexive mechanisms' (Luhmann, 1985, p.612ff). From this point one cannot however connect to what from a hermeneutic perspective could be called a totalizing interpretation which is achieved through mutual understanding in a dialogue as in Habermas' theory of communicative action. Such an interpretation is impossible within systems theory (Luhmann, 1985, p.622). Consequentially, Habermas' theory of communicative action holds greater prospects for a more comprehensive understanding of leadership than Luhmann's systems theory because Habermas' theory both affords the opportunity for leadership through dialogue in public spheres in institutions and through system oriented expansion within institutions. In other words, one could say that the modern leader should be able to lead through differentiated forms of communication in institutions.

5. Modern Reflexive Leadership

Thus, reflexivity is decisive for modern leadership inasmuch as reflexivity entails a relationship to communication. One can therefore say that the modern leader is confronted by modernity in the sense that he must act in direct relation to modernity's communicative spirit, and his enterprise can only succeed under the condition that he succeeds in relating reflectively to communication. This can only be accomplished in communication with others.

The most fundamental point in modern reflexive leadership is that there is no longer anything given. This does not mean that nothing in the social should appear as given. Things do appear as given. The world and institutions appear as given. We always find ourselves in a particular situation and a particular tradition. But what is radically new is, as reflexivity means, each and every situation is open to interpretation and thereby also for action. The reflexive thus transcends the situation by insisting that nothing is beyond reflection. One can say that reflection opens a situation from the inside and lays it open for consideration.

The modern leader is confronted with numerous different demands that must be dealt with in a single decision. These demands can emanate from different institutions, interests, and rationalities, and they rarely cohere. It is therefore the task of the leader to deal with the various demands through a decision that is borne by communication. It is only the decision that can condense and summarize the reflexive in a single expression that can become an action. What is decisive here is how decisions are made. The Danish philosopher Ole Fogh Kirkeby believes that a leader is entirely left unto himself when he is to make a decision (Kirkeby, 1998, p.249ff). This understanding is insufficient in modern society. There is no direct path from consideration to decision. Here one would always talk about a leap. What is interesting, however, is that this leap can be overtaken by consideration, such that a decision can be considered, and the actions to take place subsequent to a decision can be considered. The reflexive is found both at the beginning of a situation and at the consummation of the action that was decided upon. The reflexive can thus be said to be in place continuously in modern institutions.

It is therefore of paramount importance that the reflexive can come to expression. Another Danish philosopher, Ole Thyssen, who is deeply influenced by Luhmann's systems theory, believes that the reflexive comes to expression when differing values and morals clash, such that it becomes imperative to consider which values are valid. Thyssen speaks in this context of ethics as a second order morality (Thyssen, 1997, p.237). By this he means that ethics is created through common dialogue on varying values and moral positions. It is characteristic, however, that Thyssen also fails to state how this dialogue should be institutionalized.

It is in this context that Habermas' idea about the public sphere or publicity becomes so important, as it is the public sphere that affords the possibility for many diverging interests, rationalities, and systems to meet in the same institutional place, and thereby come into contact with each other. One can therefore claim that modern reflexive leadership prefers that public spaces be created within the institutions of modern society. It is first when such public space is created that these institutions can really meet the demand for communication that is leveled at and demanded from within modern reflexive institutions. This demand on modern institutions is posed from all sides. External demands for communication are made, demands that are on par with the demands citizens in a reflexive society make for a full and open form of communication. As stated above, modern society has taken on such a radically communicative character that refusing to communicate is chastised. All institutions have to go into dialogue with their surroundings.

However, there are also demands from within organizations, that all members be given the opportunity to come forth in a dialogue about all circumstances in the institutions. That there exist particular topics and circumstances that cannot be discussed breeches the basic communicative principle of modernity. The leader also has an interest in publicity within an institution. This publicity may initially appear to be a threat to his authority, in that communication itself represents a relativization of authority. All the while the modern leader is pressured to communicate, meaning that he cannot avoid communication if he is to maintain his authority on the conditions of modern society. All authority that is not communicatively grounded appears as unambiguously illegitimate in modern society. Thus, it is actually modernity which poses the communicative demand and conditions on the modern leader in such a way that he cannot avoid them, and thus must ensure that institutions are constructed in such a manner that he can actually act communicatively. There is thus an inner relationship between leadership and the institution such that modern reflexive leadership can only develop in a reflexive institution. The modern leader can therefore easily find himself in an institution that fails to live up to the demands for publicity that are leveled at modern institutions. In such a case it is up to the modern leader to contribute to creating public space within the institution. He should aim to create publicity within the institution as it is through this publicity that he as a leader can live up to the communicative principles of reflexive modernity. Leaders surely have an opportunity to make decisions within the confines of an individual system, as in Luhmann's theory (Luhmann, 1985, p.399ff; Thyssen, 1997, p.72ff). Nevertheless, an institution cannot be led exclusively in this manner in reflexive modernity. There will always be decisions that arouse irritation and resistance, or simply need to be discussed through. Such problems can only be satisfactorily solved when they are openly discussed in the public sphere, where various perspectives can confront each other. Reflexive leadership, therefore, always ultimately builds upon an acknowledgement of the good argument among interested parties in the linguistic community.

6. Ethics and Leadership

Modern reflexive leadership is normatively bound insofar as it is possible to express norms in language. It is here that modern reflexive leadership shows its preeminence over other understandings of leadership. To an increasing extent it is necessary to explain the norms and principles that comprise the basis for a decision within an institution. This is not just the case for public administration institutions and civil society, where norms are already very important. To an increasing extent it is also important for private sector companies to adeptly communicate with actors in their environment.

The great importance of being able to take up ethical issues emanates from communication itself in modern society. All communication in itself is value-filled inasmuch as all statements directly or indirectly contain values which bear the statement. When different statements collide, ethical issues necessarily arise which call for an independent discussion. Therefore, modern leadership also has a value dimension which results in much discussion about 'value-based leadership'. It is important to note, however, that the expression 'value-based leadership' can have two meanings. The expression conjures up the idea that there exist certain given values that are basic to leadership. Such an understanding of value-based leadership goes against the basic trajectory of reflexive modernity as sketched above. In the new modernity, all values are the object of reflection, and this makes it more correct to speak of reflexive leadership rather than value-based leadership. It is precisely through reflection that values are formulated in accord with modernity. Reflexive leadership is therefore basically a form of value-based leadership to the extent that reflexive leadership contemplates values.

This relationship is the same for individual actors who carry out their professional roles within an institution. Here one can speak of a *professional ethic*, inasmuch as each profession usually contains a long tradition of what is right and wrong. Such a tradition will always be challenged in modern society by the processes already mentioned above; it is only when professional ethics have been the object of reflected debate that one can speak of a valid ethic for the individual. An ethic cannot merely be assumed or overtaken; it must always be the object of reflection by the individual professional actor. All professional ethics must therefore also ultimately be of a reflexive character and thereby demand public discussion. This can either take the form of an open and public discussion within the given institution, or within a given occupation's professional organization. In the latter case, a tension is already created between the institution in which the professional works and the professional organization in which the dialogue proceeds, which can even lead to ethical conflicts between these two institutional contexts.

One can also speak of particular ethical dilemmas becoming *personal ethical dilemmas* for a member of an institution. This is usually the case where the individual cannot reflexively subscribe to the way ethical issues are framed within an institution. It is precisely in such situations that it is important that a public space exists within an institution where individuals within the institution can air their ethical dilemmas.

Ultimately it is an issue of recognition - individuals in modern society demand to be able to reflect over their actions in an institution. One can no longer demand unconditional obedience, one can no longer even demand obedience which does not even recognize the one who obeys. The recognition that is discussed here can only be carried on in public within an institution.

Now we arrive at the central question of how it is possible to construct or rearrange the institutions of modern society in such a way that they come to rest on a foundation that is reflected, and thereby affords mutual recognition of all interested parties within and between institutions. It is in this context that so-called 'ethical accounting' by institutions becomes important (Zadek, 1997). Ethical accounting can be seen as an attempt to create what could be called general customs or norms within institutions that are to apply to the given institution. Of interest here is that such norms can only be formulated by involving all interested parties in an open dialogue about what norms should govern within the institution. No leader or leadership can formulate norms without taking into consideration the interested parties within an institution. Therefore, it is important that ethical accounts are compiled in accord with the procedures that meet general approval. It is only then that an ethical account can be accepted.

This brings us to the connection between modern reflexive leadership and democracy. Modern reflexive leadership can only develop within the context of a democratic society because it is only democratic societies that allow the possibility to create public spaces within institutions. It is these public spaces that are the hub of reflexive leadership.

Democratic society doee not just allow for the creation of public spaces within *individual institutions*. It also allows institutions to engage in mutual criticism of each other. Contained in the former is the *utopian dimension* of modern society - that through *internal* changes, all interested parties in a given institution can speak to each other on an equal basis. Contained in the latter is the *realistic dimension* of modern society - that *mutual criticism* between institutions can contribute to developing *internal* communication within institutions.

This latter dimension is in reality the most important, in that it is not reasonable to expect an institution on its own to morally sustain itself. It is necessary for different institutions to relate to one another and thereby engage in *critique*. This keeps institutions morally alive.

Weber would be of the opinion, as noted above, that democratic administration is a typological borderline case that is not socially sustainable in modern society. By extension, he would see it as neither possible nor advisable to create public spaces within institutions. The existence of public spheres is not compatible with Weber's ideal-typical conception of the hierarchical, legally-based bureaucratic institution.

In his theory, Habermas points toward a different form of modernity in which both the utopian and realistic dimensions noted above are brought in. Habermas, however, believes that economics and administration comprise separate, independent systems, which all things considered should be mediated by the systemic media of money and power. This being said, the stature of the legal system has increased its presence in

Habermas' recent works, decreasing the pure systemic perspective on the economic and administrative spheres (Larsen, 2000, p.110). Habermas' theory is more ambivalent than Weber's with regard to the possibility of creating public spaces in institutions because Habermas incorporates both the communicative action perspective and the autopoetic system perspective. One can say that Habermas radicalizes Weber's theory in two opposing directions. On the one hand, Habermas' theory contains the communicative and normative action orientation discussed above, which Weber would have deemed naive. On the other hand, Habermas incorporates a Luhmannian oriented autopoetic system perspective which sees the whole of Weber's theory of action as naive.

Even if one maintains Weber's and Habermas' skepticism towards the possibility of creating public spaces within single institutions on their own initiative (though Habermas and Weber give different reasons for this position), there is an essential point in *not* discarding the creation of public spaces within institutions as an unrealistic, utopian vision. What is important to note is that all institutions in reflexive modernity are exposed to communicative demands they cannot avoid. Throughout the world, a new agenda has been set for institutions, such that this change can even be *empirically* detected in how institutions communicate internally and with their surroundings. Once again let us return to the Shell example. When a huge corporation like Shell is compelled to go into active dialogue with actors who surround it, not least through the Internet, it is evident that leadership in the corporation deems it *necessary* to run the company in the reflexive manner that modernity demands. Thus my thesis is that such pressure on institutions to communicate with their external environment will *necessarily* lead to a change in *inner* communication in the individual institution for the simple reason that the discussion taking place on the company's home page cannot be kept from spilling over to internal matters and actors. This can be exemplified rather simply. When a Shell employee in Pakistan writes on Shell's homepage that Shell in Pakistan is fraught with nepotism in its hiring practices, and this can be read all over the world, over time this must lead to changes in the hiring practices of Shell in Pakistan and thereby to increased public space within the institution. Shell cannot live long with an image of nepotism. What is discussed here is a general ethical challenge to all companies, and it is here that the realistic in the ethical challenge lies. No company can avoid this challenge for long without losing competitive advantage.

Theoretically, it is impossible to say *how much* reflexivity will permeate individual institutions, but it is theoretically possible to say something about *how* modernity is changing in a reflexive direction and *why* reflexivity is becoming a *basic norm* for all institutions of modern society.

There is thus an inner connection between modern reflexive leadership and democracy. One can say that democracy will dictate a norm for the form individual institutions should take. In a dynamic democratic society it is no longer viable for individual institutions to shield themselves from reflexivity. Public discussion implies that all institutional circumstances can be brought up to discussion. Reflexive leadership ends up ultimately where it belongs, namely in a form of political leadership. One can unabashedly see reflexive leadership as a further extension of modern society in the sense that it is reflexive leadership within individual institutions that creates the possibility for ethics and norms to develop in a reflected manner. Reflexive leadership can therefore be seen as an attempt to answer the question that Plato and Aristotle posed: How is it possible to create common norms in the city-state? Kant and Hegel subsequently reformulated the very same question in terms of how it is possible to create common norms in society based on mutual recognition. None of the above mentioned philosophers have solved the problems they posed. Habermas has indicated that the answer must include the creation of public spheres wherein normative contradictions can meet. Reflexive leadership can thus be seen as an attempt to create space for such a meeting, and in this manner contribute to the realization of modernity in the form of an open society comprising reflexive attitudes towards social relations in the institutions of modern society.

References

Adorno, T. (1973), *Negative Dialektik*, Suhrkamp, Frankfurt am Main.

Aristotle (1977), *Politics, XXI*, in: *Aristotle in Twenty-Three Volumes*, The Loeb Classical Library, Harvard University Press, Cambridge, Mass., and William Heinemann Ltd., London.

Aristotle (1982), *The Nicomachean Ethics, XIX*, in: *Aristotle in Twenty-Three Volumes*, The Loeb Classical Library, Harvard University Press, Cambridge, Mass., and William Heinemann Ltd., London.

Bauman, Z. (1997), *Postmodernity and its Discontents*, Polity Press, Oxford.

Bauman, Z. (2000), *Liquid Modernity*, Polity Press, Oxford.

Beck, U. (1986), *Risikogesellschaft. Auf dem Weg in eine andere Moderne*, Suhrkamp, Frankfurt am Main.

Beck, U. (1997), *Was ist Globaliserung*, Suhrkamp, Frankfurt am Main.

Giddens, A. (1990), *The Consequences of Modernity*, Polity Press, Cambridge.

Grolin, J. (1999), 'Industrien i risikosamfundet - egimitet, subpolitik og dialog i Brent Spar sagen', in Nielsen, K. Aa., Greve, A., Hansson, F. and Rasborg, K. (eds.), *Risiko, politik og miljø i det senmoderne samfund*, Forlaget Sociologi, Copenhagen.

Habermas, J. (1962), *Strukturwandel der Öffentlichkeit. Untersuchungen zur einer Kategorie der bürgerlichen Gesellschaft*, Herman Luchterlan Verlag, Neuwied.

Habermas, J. (1981), *Theorie des kommunikativen Handelns*, vol. I-II, Suhrkamp, Frankfurt am Main.

Hegel, G.W.F. (1955), *Grundlinien der Philosophie des Rechts*, Philosophische Bibliothek Band 124a, Felix Meiner, Hamburg.

Horkheimer, M. and Th. Adorno (1988), *Dialektik der Aufklärung*, Fischer Taschenbuch, Frankfurt am Main.

Jespersen, P.K. (1996), *Bureaukratiet - agt og effektivitet*, Jurist- og Økonomforbundets forlag, Copenhagen.

Kant, I. (1974), *Kritik der praktischen Vernuft*, Philosophische Bibliothek Band 38, Felix Meiner Verlag, Hamburg.

Kirkeby, O.F. (1998), *Ledelsesfilosofi*, Samfundslitteratur, Copenhagen.

Kumar, K. (1995), *From Post-industrial to Post-Modern Society*, Blackwell, Oxford.

Larsen, Ø. (1990), *Ethik und Demokratie*, Argument-Verlag, Hamburg.

Larsen, Ø. (2000), *Administration, Ethics and Democracy*, Ashgate, Aldershot.

Lash, S. (1999), *Another Modernity - A Different Rationality*, Blackwell Publishers, Oxford.

Luhmann, N. (1985), *Soziale Systeme: Grundriss einer allgemeinen Theorie*, Zweite Auflage, Suhrkamp, Frankfurt am Main.

Plato (1987), *The Republic*, Penguin, Hammondsworth.

Thyssen, O. (1997), *Værdiledelse*, Gyldendal, Copenhagen.

Wagner, P. (1994), *A Sociology of Modernity*, Routledge, London.

Weber, M. (1972), *Wirtschaft und Gesellschaft*, Fünfte, Revidierte Auflage, Besorgt von Johannes Winckelmann, J.C.B. Mohr (Paul Siebeck), Tübingen.

Weber, M. (1988), 'Die drei reinen Typen der legitimen Herrschaft', in *Gesammelte Aufsätze zur Wissenschaftlehre*, Herausgegeben von Johannes Winckelmann, 7. Auflage, J.C.B. Mohr (Paul Siebeck), Tübingen.

Zadek, S., P. Pruzan, and R. Evans (1997), *Building Corporate Accountability*, Earthscan Publications Ltd., London.

List of Contributors

Margareta Bertilsson (born 1944), Professor of Sociology at the University of Copenhagen, Denmark since 1994. She is presently a member of the Executive Committee of the European Sociological Association and an associate editor of the *European Journal of Social Theory*. Her interests are in the field of general social theory, and more specifically the relation between social theory, law, morality and sociology of knowledge. Some recent publications are *Det goda livet: Om renässansen för en borttappad disciplin* (The Good Life: On the Renaissance of a Lost Discipline) (joint ed.) (1996), Stockholm and Lund; *Socialkonstruktivisme: Bidrag til en kritisk diskussion* (Social Constructivism: Critical Views) (joint ed.) (1988), Hans Reitzel, Copenhagen; *From a Doll's House to the Welfare State: Reflections on Nordic Sociology* (joint ed.) (1998), ISA-Publication: Social Knowledge, Heritage, Challenges, Perspectives, Madrid/Montreal; 'The Balkan Tradegy: A Universal or a Particular Issue', in *European Societies, Fusion or Fission* (eds. Thomas Boje et al.) (1999), Blackwell, Oxford.

Hauke Brunkhorst (born 1945), Professor of Sociology at the University of Flensburg, Germany. Major publications include *Der Intellektuelle im Land der Mandarine* (1987), Suhrkamp, Frankfurt; *Herbert Marcuse - Zur Einführung* (1987), Junius, Hamburg, with G. Koch, *Theodor Adorno - Dialektik der Moderne* (1990), Piper, Munich; *Der Entzauberte Intellektuelle* (1990), Junius, Hamburg; *Gemeinschaft und Gerechtigkeit* (joint ed.) (1994), Fischer, Frankfurt; *Solidarität unter Fremden* (1997), Fischer, Frankfurt; *Demokratischer Experimentalismus* (1998), Suhrkamp, Frankfurt; *Adorno and Critical Theory* (1999), University of Wales Press, Cardiff; *Hannah Arendt* (1999), Munich, Beck; *Das Recht der Republik* (joint ed.) (1999), Suhrkamp, Frankfurt; *Globalisierung und Demokratie* (1999), Suhrkamp, Frankfurt; and *Einführung in die geschichte politischer Ideen* (2000), Fink, München.

Mikael Carleheden (born 1958), Associate Professor of Sociology at the Department of Social Science, Örebro University, Sweden. His latest publications include *Det andra modern: Om Jürgen Habermas och den samhällsvetenskapliga diskursen om det moderna* (Second Modernity: On Jürgen Habermas and the Social Theoretical Discourse of

Modernity) (1996), Daidalos, Göteborg; 'An Interview with Jürgen Habermas'; *Theory, Culture and Society* vol. 13 no. 3, 1996. (with René Gabriels); 'An Interview with Michael Walzer', *Theory, Culture and Society* vol. 14 no. 1, 1997 (with René Gabriels); 'Another Sociology - The Future of Sociology from a Critical Theoretical Perspective', *Dansk Sociologi,* special issue vol. 9 September, 1998; 'Reconstructing Epistemology: Toward a Post-Positivist Conception of Social Science', *Sociologisk Arbejdspapir*, Aalborg Universitet, vol. 1 no. 3, 1999; 'The Emancipation from Gender: A Critique of the Utopias of Postmodern Gender Theory', in *Moulding Masculinities* vol. 1. (eds. S. Ervø/T. Johansson), Ashgate, forthcoming.

Lars Dencik (born 1941), Professor of Social Psychology at the University of Roskilde, Denmark. His latest publication is *Children and Family in the Postmodern Society* (joint ed.) (1999), Hans Reitzel, Copenhagen, but he has also for several years written extensively on children and family life.

Gorm Harste (born 1955), Associate Professor in Sociology at the Department of Political Science, Aarhus University, Denmark. Author of a number of books and articles concerning social and political theory as well as historical sociology, particularly on critical theory, systems theory, the writings of Kant, Durkheim, and Luhmann, the risk society, modernity and European state building.

Bo Isenberg (born 1964), PhD Candidate at Lund University, Sweden and Lecturer at the University of Kalmar, Sweden. His PhD thesis on the images of modernity of Max Weber, Hans Blumenberg and Robert Musil will be completed in 2001. His latest publications include 'Answering the Question: What is Culture?', in Yamamoto, Andrew and Rabinow (eds.) (1998), *Philosophical Designs for a Socio-Cultural Transformation*, Tokyo, EHESC, Rowman & Littlefield; (ed.) (1998), *Sociology and Social Transformation: Essays by Michael Mann, Chantal Mouffe, Göran Therborn and Bryan S. Turner*, Lund University, Lund, Department of Sociology, Research Report no. 1; and 'To Bide One's Time: Robert Musil and Modernity', *Res Publica* no. 38, 1998.

Michael Hviid Jacobsen (born 1971), PhD Candidate and teaches sociology at the University of Aalborg, Denmark. His latest publications centre around the themes of death and modernity in *The Myth of Homo Immortalis* (1997), the reign of positivism in *The Search for Sociological Truth* (1999), and ethics and fieldwork in *How Dangerous is Dangerous Fieldwork*? (1999), both published in the series *Sociologisk Arbejdspapir*. He is currently writing his PhD-thesis on the social construction and maintenance of rituals in childbirth and funeral ceremonies and is also working on introductory texts to the maverick sociologies of respectively Erving Goffman, C. Wright Mills and Zygmunt Bauman.

Nikolas Kompridis, Lecturer in Philosophy at the University of Dundee, Scotland. He has written extensively on issues dealing with philosophy and critical theory and is the author of the following books: *In Times of Need: Habermas, Heidegger and the Future of Critical Theory* (forthcoming), Northwestern University Press, Evanston; *Crisis and Transformation: The Aesthetic Critique of Modernity from Hegel to Habermas* (forthcoming), University of California Press, Berkeley; and *Philosophical Romanticism* (forthcoming), Routledge, London.

Catharina Juul Kristensen (born 1963), Assistant Professor at the University of Roskilde, Denmark. Her latest publications include *The Meeting of the Waters: Individuality, Community and Solidarity* (1997), Scandinavian University Press, Oslo; *Socially Exposed Mothers with Many Children* (1999), Dafolo, Frederikshavn; and '*Skilled Workers in Unskilled Jobs*' (2000) (with Søren Voxted), in *Worlds of Employment* (eds. J. Lind and D. Mortimer), LEO-group, Aalborg.

Øjvind Larsen (born 1946), Associate Professor, PhD, at Copenhagen Business School, Denmark where he teaches philosophy and sociology. Latest publications include *Modstandens etik* (The Ethics of Resistance)(1988), Tiderne Skifter, Copenhagen; 'Imaginary Democracy', in *Danish Yearbook of Philosophy* (1998), Museum Tuscalanum Press, Copenhagen; and *Admini- stration, Ethics and Democracy* (forthcoming), Ashgate, London.

Klaus Rasborg (born 1957), Associate Professor, PhD, at Roskilde University, Denmark and Danish translator of Ulrich Beck's *Risikogesellschaft* (1986). His latest publications include *Sociology and Modernity* (joint ed.) (1998), Columbus Press, Copenhagen; *Risk, Politics and Environment in Modern Society* (joint ed.) (1999), Danish Sociology

Press, Copenhagen; and 'The Transformation of the Welfare State and Civil Society in the Risk Society' (2000), Roskilde University Press, Roskilde.

Steven Seidman (born 1948), Professor of Sociology at the University of New York at Albany, USA. His latest publications include *Romantic Longings: Love in America 1830-1980* (1991), Routledge, New York; *Embattled Eros: Sexual Politics and Ethics in Contemporary America* (1992), Routledge, New York; *Contested Knowledge: Social Theory in the Postmodern Era* (1994), Blackwell, Oxford; *The Postmodern Turn: New Perspectives on Social Theory* (ed.) (1994), Cambridge University Press, Cambridge; *Social Postmodernism: Beyond Identity Politics* (joint ed.) (1995), Cambridge University Press, Cambridge; *Queer Theory/-Sociology* (ed.), (1996) Blackwell, Cambridge, Mass.; and *Difference Troubles: Queering Theory and Sexual Politics* (1997), University Press, Cambridge.

Index